This Realm of New Zealand is an excellent, historically based account of the roles and responsibilities of the Queen in Right of New Zealand and her Governors-General in our present day constitutional monarchy. The authors also put forward carefully formulated proposals that give full weight to the essentially democratic nature of New Zealand's constitution, the balance between law and convention, and the virtues of flexibility to enable future development. *— SIR KENNETH KEITH

New Zealand is a democratic constitutional monarchy, one of Queen Elizabeth II's sixteen realms. This book provides a comprehensive account of how the Queen, the Governor-General and the Crown interact with our democratically elected leaders under New Zealand's unwritten constitution.

The authors explain how these islands in the South Pacific were first brought within Queen Victoria's dominions, the arrangements then made for their future government, and how those arrangements developed over time with the pressure for democracy and responsible government to become New Zealand's current constitution. They discuss the responsibilities of, and interactions between, the key office-holders: the Sovereign herself; her representative, the Governor-General; the impersonal and perpetual Crown; and the Prime Minister, other Ministers and Members of Parliament. All of them affect in some way the government which runs the country day-to-day. In an afterword, the authors examine some of the key issues to be considered should New Zealand become a republic.

The parliamentary democracy that we take for granted can conceal New Zealand's ultimate constitutional underpinnings in the monarchy. But, as the authors make clear, the Sovereign still delegates the authority to govern to the people's elected representatives. And understanding the roles of the Queen, the Governor-General and the Crown will be critical as we look forward to debates about the possibility of a republic in New Zealand.

DAME ALISON QUENTIN-BAXTER is a distinguished public and international lawyer. She began her career as a member, and later the head, of the Legal Division of what was then the Department of External Affairs, and was a New Zealand representative at a number of conferences on the making or application of international law. Later she was a lecturer in law at Victoria University of Wellington where she taught constitutional history and law. From 1987–94 she was the director of the New Zealand Law Commission. Dame Alison has acted as a constitutional advisor in New Zealand and other jurisdictions including Niue, Fiji, the Republic of the Marshall Islands, and Saint Helena. She is the author of a report leading to the Sovereign's issue of the 1983 Letters Patent Constituting the Office of Governor-General of New Zealand, *Review of the Letters Patent 1917 Constituting the Office of Governor-General of New Zealand* (Cabinet Office, 1980), editor of *Recognising the Rights of Indigenous Peoples* (Institute of Policy Studies, 1998) and she has contributed a number of chapters and articles in books and journals. Dame Alison was appointed a Dame Companion of the New Zealand Order of Merit for services to the law, and is a Companion of the Queen's Service Order.

PROFESSOR JANET McLEAN is a professor of law at the University of Auckland where she teaches constitutional and administrative law. A graduate of Victoria University of Wellington and the University of Michigan, she previously held the position as director of the New Zealand Institute of Public Law at Victoria University of Wellington, and the chair in Law and Governance at the University of Dundee, Scotland. She is the editor of *Property and the Constitution* (Hart, 1999) and author of *Searching for the State in British Legal Thought* (Cambridge University Press, 2012) and has contributed numerous articles and chapters in leading books and journals.

This Realm of New Zealand

The Sovereign
The Governor-General
The Crown

Alison Quentin-Baxter and Janet McLean

AUCKLAND
UNIVERSITY
PRESS

First published 2017
Auckland University Press
University of Auckland
Private Bag 92019
Auckland 1142
New Zealand
www.press.auckland.ac.nz

ISBN 978 1 86940 875 6

Published with the assistance of the New Zealand Law Foundation

A catalogue record for this book is available from the National Library of New Zealand

Cover design by Spencer Levine

MIX
Paper from responsible sources
FSC® C016973

Printed in China by 1010 Printing International Ltd

In memory of Robert Quentin Quentin-Baxter
1922–1984

Husband of Alison and a teacher of us both

CONTENTS

ACKNOWLEDGEMENTS

During the long gestation of this project we have incurred a number of debts. We have been greatly assisted throughout the project by the Office of the Prime Minister and Cabinet. Rebecca Kitteridge and Michael Webster, Clerks of the Executive Council, have both provided practical assistance by way of access to files held by the Cabinet Office, as well as friendship and support. The team at the Cabinet Office read parts of the book in draft. We are grateful for permission now to draw freely on the material in the 1980 Report reviewing the Letters Patent 1917, and do so without further acknowledgement, except when quoting its words, or citing it as the source on a particular point. We have also received general guidance from the royal household.

Anna Fleming provided invaluable research of the archival and primary materials. Some of her perceptions are reflected in the book. Sonali Perera's research assistance improved Chapters 3 and 11. Without Claire McGeorge's careful cite-checking and other research assistance and support we would never have made it across the line. We are grateful to Rt Hon Sir Kenneth Keith, Justice Matthew Palmer, Paul Rishworth QC and other anonymous readers. Dr Dean Knight read the entire manuscript and his generous and detailed comments were of great assistance. Needless to say, none of the readers agreed with everything we have to say. The Law Foundation gave financial support and Lynda Hagen, its director, invaluable moral support. Finally, our heartfelt thanks go to Sam Elworthy and his team at Auckland University Press.

CHAPTER 1

The Purpose of this Book

This royal throne of kings, this scepter'd isle, . . .
This precious stone set in the silver sea, . . .
This blessed plot, this earth, this realm, . . .[1]

That is how Shakespeare described the realm of England in the reign of King Richard II.[2] A "realm" is a kingdom. From the 15th century to halfway through the 20th, his successors remained the Kings or Queens of a single realm, although it had spread around the globe. Eventually the idea of a single indivisible realm became untenable. When Queen Elizabeth II came to the throne in 1952, she was recognised as having become the Sovereign of seven separate realms. One of them was New Zealand.[3] Their equal and independent status gives the Sovereign a direct and personal connection with each of what are now her 16 realms. The United Kingdom remains a realm, but its government no longer has any constitutional role in any of the others.

In this book we tell the New Zealand story: how these islands in the South Pacific were brought within Queen Victoria's dominions, the arrangements then made for their future government, and how those arrangements developed to become New Zealand's constitution today. We discuss the responsibilities of, and interactions between, the key office-holders: the Sovereign herself; her representative, the Governor-General; the impersonal and perpetual Crown; and the Prime Minister, the other Ministers and all the Members of Parliament. There are others, too, with on-stage roles.

The time is overdue for telling, or retelling, the story of how New Zealand's present-day constitution was shaped. There is an urgent need to broaden

1 William Shakespeare *King Richard II* at II.i.40, 46, 50.
2 1367–1400.
3 Chapter 6 The Letters Patent, the Governor-General and the Realm of New Zealand.

the understanding of the people who live under it, and to make them better informed about the implications of any proposals for constitutional change. An increasing proportion of New Zealand citizens were born elsewhere: a common British heritage or knowledge of the Treaty of Waitangi cannot be taken for granted. Popular culture tends to confer on members of the royal family a kind of celebrity status. The monarchy's place in the workings of the political and constitutional system is largely invisible. Many young people, including those studying law at New Zealand universities, are more familiar with the United States Constitution than their own. The aim of this book is to make the workings of the New Zealand constitutional monarchy more accessible, and to correct some common misunderstandings about how it works.

In this book we explore the ways in which the Sovereign became interwoven in the history and fabric of the New Zealand constitution: how Queen Victoria came to reign over its three main islands, and also others, further offshore, and later Sovereigns eventually became recognised as the King or Queen in right of New Zealand; how monarchy became constitutional monarchy in response to the demands for democracy; and how New Zealand gradually acquired full self-government, free of the United Kingdom Government's control. We also trace developments in the institution of the monarchy itself — including the recent changes to the laws of succession to the throne.[4] In doing so, we examine the personal roles of the Queen in right of New Zealand and of her representative, the Governor-General, at the present day. We also identify important functions of the impersonal Crown.

A main feature of the New Zealand constitution is that the powers of government are often vested in the Sovereign, or the Governor-General, instead of in those who make the decisions about when and how to use them. It therefore conceals the democratic revolution it achieved — the recognition that the Sovereign or her representative must act on the advice of Ministers who are elected Members of Parliament. That revolution left the location of executive powers with the Sovereign but put their exercise into the hands of the people's elected representatives who, collectively, have the confidence of Parliament. Some of the ancient forms and language have lingered on, including in relation to land tenure,[5] but they have had to be adapted to modern New Zealand circumstances and expectations.

The Sovereign issues a legal instrument known as the Letters Patent constituting the office of Governor-General of New Zealand. In that instrument, she delegates to the Governor-General, and, through the Governor-General,

4 Chapter 4 The Sovereign in Right of New Zealand: The Institutional Role.
5 Discussed in Chapter 3 Constitutional Monarchy: Key Concepts.

to Ministers and officials, her executive authority and powers of government. Because that instrument is the basis of New Zealand's executive government, we describe it at some length.[6] As in the making of the Letters Patent themselves, almost all of the powers now exercised personally by the Sovereign or the Governor-General are required to be exercised on the advice of responsible Ministers. In discussing the extent of the Governor-General's duty to act on that advice, we identify the relevant "unwritten" rules of practice, known as constitutional conventions. The conventions enable the powers still legally vested in the Sovereign or the Governor-General to function acceptably in a modern democracy.

The main exception to the duty to act on ministerial advice concerns the powers exercised in the process of forming or changing a government otherwise than after a general election at the end of Parliament's three-year term. In that area the Governor-General has important powers, but it is not easy to determine how far, within the governing principles, he or she still has a limited element of personal discretion. We have tried not merely to describe the relevant practices in New Zealand and elsewhere, but also to identify gaps in the constitutional conventions as currently formulated, and sometimes to suggest reforms. In doing so we seek to dispel the widely held impression that, as in colonial times, the Governor-General still acts as a constitutional backstop or "guardian of the constitution", and accordingly may exercise the powers to appoint or dismiss a Prime Minister, grant or refuse a dissolution, or act or refuse to act without, or against, the advice of a Prime Minister whose government retains the constitutional right to govern.[7] Instead we recommend ways in which the recognised duty to keep the Governor-General informed could be made more meaningful and emphasise the fact that not only the Governor-General but also the Prime Minister and all the other constitutional actors share the responsibility of making the constitution work as it should.[8]

On the same note, we discuss the role of the Sovereign or her representative in assenting to Bills in order to give them the force of law. We consider whether it would ever be proper to refuse such assent. Certainly, there is no longer a recognised discretion to refuse assent, but the fact remains that a Bill does not become law until it has received the royal assent. Again we emphasise the associated constitutional duties which fall on other actors such as the Clerk of the House and the Attorney-General.[9] The Governor-General's position as

6 Chapter 6 The Letters Patent, the Governor-General and the Realm of New Zealand, Chapter 7 The Office of Governor-General and Commander-in-Chief, Chapter 8 The Governor-General in the Executive Branch.

7 Chapter 10 Guardian of the Constitution?.

8 Chapter 9 Finding and Changing a Prime Minister.

9 Chapter 11 The Governor-General in Parliament.

Commander-in-Chief has also been regarded as a source of unspecified powers in respect of the Defence Force. We explore the historical origins of that office and its relevance today.[10]

From very early times and to the present day, many Māori have aspired to and developed a special relationship with the reigning Sovereign.[11] Some aspects of that relationship have no doubt been mythologised, or have remained primarily aspirational, but others have served important political, symbolic and constitutional purposes. We consider the character of those relationships and their implications for the future of the constitution. The Sovereign and the Governor-General are also a part of New Zealand's constitutional life in ways that are even less well known. In the first quarter of the 20th century the Cook Islands, Niue, Tokelau and the Ross Dependency were brought within the boundaries of New Zealand or put under its administration. Along with New Zealand itself, and with the agreement of their governments, those countries and territories together comprise the Realm of New Zealand. We consider New Zealand's relationships with the other parts of the Realm, although the main focus is on New Zealand itself. In discussing the constitution as a whole, we draw both parallels and contrasts with the Sovereign's larger realms, the United Kingdom, Canada and Australia.[12]

Meanwhile, the Governor-General's role has been quietly modernising and continues to evolve. We trace the development of the Governor-General's exercise of the Head of State role in representing New Zealand in the sphere of international relations.[13] We also look at the ways in which successive Governors-General have been innovative in building relationships and interacting with other New Zealanders in a wide range of settings.[14]

That brings us to a special objective in writing this book. In April 2010 the New Zealand Parliament debated a private member's Bill aimed at bringing about — or at least raising the possibility of — a major constitutional change. The Head of State Referenda Bill proposed a nationwide referendum, or perhaps two referendums, giving New Zealanders the choice of keeping the Sovereign as their Head of State or substituting a Head of State elected either by at least 75 per cent of the members of the House of Representatives or directly elected by the people.

As it turned out, there was not then a majority in Parliament willing to give the Bill even a first reading so that it could be referred to a select committee.

10 Chapter 6 The Letters Patent, the Governor-General and the Realm of New Zealand.
11 Chapter 13 The Crown as a Party to the Treaty of Waitangi.
12 Chapter 4 The Sovereign in Right of New Zealand: The Institutional Role.
13 Chapter 14 Exercising the Head of State Role.
14 Chapter 14 Exercising the Head of State Role.

It therefore lapsed. Those who spoke against it considered that there were other, more urgent, constitutional issues requiring Parliament's attention. There was no real discussion of the substance. The House divided on party lines. There was not much comment in the news media. It therefore appeared that the idea of moving away from New Zealand's monarchical constitution was not then a live issue. From our point of view, the most interesting feature of the Bill was the assumption that replacing the Governor-General with a New Zealand citizen as the country's Head of State was all that would be required. We explain that making a republican constitution would be a larger task, although it could of course be done.

In an Afterword to the book we consider the possibility that at some time in the future the people of New Zealand may wish seriously to consider giving themselves a republican constitution. Our goal is not to take sides in that debate. We regard ourselves as interested but impartial constitutional lawyers and commentators. We do not advocate change to a republic, but nor do we oppose it. We give some thought to what becoming a republic would involve, and identify some of the main issues that would need to be considered.

The Sovereign, the Governor-General and the Crown are deeply embedded in the New Zealand constitution and other law. They can be removed easily enough, but, with their removal, other aspects of the constitution and the law would also disappear, including the whole of the executive branch of government. That aspect of the constitution would therefore need to be reconstituted. The people of New Zealand would need to make choices about the form the republican constitution should take. That said, it would not be necessary to open up an unlimited range of possibilities about the nature of the constitution itself. New Zealand has a parliamentary system of government. The executive branch is drawn from among the elected Members of Parliament, the legislative branch. In our view, the parliamentary system serves New Zealand well and should be retained. On that basis, a republican constitution could be made to work in practice much as the constitutional monarchy works now.

In the book as a whole we have tried to establish a benchmark by exploring the dynamics of the present constitutional monarchy. Where there are gaps or uncertainties, we have made proposals for clarification. With a better understanding of the way the constitution works now or could be made to work, New Zealanders will be better equipped to meet the challenges of the future, whatever form they may take. We aim to provide a comprehensive account of New Zealand's monarchical constitution as it operated in December 2016. In doing so, we have drawn on the wealth of published material that bears on the continuing significance of the monarchy. Some areas, however, have remained largely outside the range of the commentators. One is the nature and purpose of the Letters Patent constituting the office of Governor-General. The current instrument (amended in minor ways since it was issued by the Queen in 1983) was largely based on a 1980 report for the Prime Minister's Department by one of the authors, Alison Quentin-Baxter. This book incorporates and builds on those parts of her 1980 Report that still remain relevant.

We hope that the book will help people to understand the New Zealand constitution as it is now and to make it work well. For those who hold constitutional office or have the responsibility for giving constitutional advice, or are affected by what governments do or do not do, we believe it will fill some gaps in the existing sources. It may also be of professional interest in some of the other realms. But we do not think of it as a book that is just for the professionals. Although it is written within the discipline of constitutional law and must be footnoted accordingly, we have tried hard to make it a book that readers who are not lawyers can enjoy. We see potential readers and users as including people working in other fields or with other interests, including, we hope, members of the general reading public. The constitution belongs to all New Zealanders. Whether or not they are consciously "interested" in the constitution as such, all have an interest in how it works for them, and for their country.

CHAPTER 2

Building the Modern Constitution

1
SETTING THE SCENE

The beginning

Captain William Hobson, an officer in the Royal Navy, sailed for New Zealand at the end of August 1839. His Instructions required him:[1]

> to treat with the Aborigines of New Zealand for the recognition of Her Majesty's Sovereign authority over the whole or any part of those islands which they may be willing to place under Her Majesty's dominion.

"Treating" with the Māori inhabitants of New Zealand meant entering into a treaty.

Hobson's Instructions also set out a plan for the immediate and longer-term government of the new British colony. Some British subjects had already settled there, and more were planning to follow. In the expectation that New Zealand would become a British colony, Queen Victoria had already exercised her power to make provision for its future government. When Hobson landed in the Bay of Islands to carry out his mission, he carried with him a Commission from Queen Victoria appointing him as Lieutenant Governor "in and over that part of Our territory which is or may be acquired in sovereignty in New Zealand".

1 Instructions from Lord Normanby, Secretary of State for Colonial Affairs, to Captain Hobson (14 August 1839). These Instructions were supplemented by further Instructions from Lord Normanby to Captain Hobson dated 15 August 1839. Both sets of Instructions were published in GBPP 1840/283 and are reproduced in WD McIntyre and WJ Gardner (eds) *Speeches and Documents on New Zealand History* (Oxford University Press, Oxford, 1971) at 10 and 17.

In this chapter we trace the development of New Zealand's present-day constitutional arrangements from their British colonial origins so far as they affect the main players in our story: the Sovereign, the Governor-General and the Crown. We begin with the Queen's acquisition of sovereignty. That, without more, would not have provided the new colony with a government, or established any rules or principles about the kind of government it should have. Between 1840 and 1870, the three branches of government assumed their present form, and the modern relationship between a Governor and his responsible advisers was put in place. The working relationships developed during that period colour the functioning of the constitution today.

In the 1920s and 1930s, New Zealand, already one of the self-governing British Dominions, became an independent state, entirely separate from the United Kingdom, except in continuing to recognise the reigning monarch as the Sovereign in right of New Zealand. In that period the Crown became divisible. That divisibility gave New Zealand a voice of its own as a member of the international community, and led also to its full constitutional autonomy. But it was not until after World War II that New Zealand's constitutional law was brought fully into line with what had already become the practice.

In 1986 the New Zealand Parliament removed the last, long-unused remnant of the United Kingdom Parliament's former power to make laws for New Zealand and took the symbolic step of making the Queen in right of New Zealand, rather than the Governor-General (who continues to represent her), formally a part of the New Zealand Parliament.

The story as a whole identifies the process by which New Zealand has become a democratic and independent state. It also shows how, in the course of that process, the main features of the modern constitutional monarchy assumed their present shape.

Queen Victoria's acquisition of sovereignty

In obedience to his Instructions, Hobson negotiated with the Māori chiefs assembled at the Bay of Islands and a treaty was drawn up. It was first signed at Waitangi on 6 February 1840. The parties were described in the preamble as "Her Majesty Victoria, Queen of the United Kingdom and Ireland", and "the confederated and independent Chiefs of New Zealand".[2] Copies of the Treaty

2 Preamble to the Treaty of Waitangi as reproduced in the English language in the Treaty of Waitangi Act 1975, sch 1.

were later signed in other places around New Zealand by other iwi and hapū, although by no means all.

Some British officials thought that the Queen had already acquired sovereignty over some parts of New Zealand under English law through their settlement by British subjects. In English law that was a recognised way of acquiring sovereignty, and English settlers were regarded as having brought English law with them. In 1839, however, the Colonial Office wanted the Queen's sovereignty to be extended to all parts of the three main islands, but only with the agreement of the Māori inhabitants. To that end, the English version of the Treaty of Waitangi provided that the chiefs who signed the Treaty were ceding their own sovereignty to the Queen of the United Kingdom. In English law, on the cession of sovereignty over foreign territory by a foreign Sovereign to the King or Queen of the United Kingdom, the ceded territory became a British colony.

Copies of the Treaty for signature by other tribes were taken around the country. But some iwi and hapū, in both the North Island and the South Island, never signed. Meanwhile, the first organised boatload of British settlers had arrived in Wellington and the settlers had given themselves their own form of government,[3] an initiative which alarmed the Governor, as did the news that the Nanto-Bordelaise Company was implementing plans to establish a French settlement in New Zealand, at Akaroa.[4]

Largely for those reasons, Hobson, on 21 May 1840, made two Proclamations in the name of Queen Victoria. The first recited the making of the Treaty under which "all rights and powers of sovereignty" over the North Island had been ceded to Her Majesty, and proclaimed that, from the date of the Treaty, 6 February 1840, "the full sovereignty of the Northern Island of New Zealand vests in Her Majesty Queen Victoria, her heirs and successors, for ever". The second Proclamation contained an operative provision in similar terms, but without reference to the Treaty. The Proclamations were instruments of annexation. Any doubt, at least as a matter of English and international law, about her acquisition of sovereignty over the whole of New Zealand had been laid to rest.

We are conscious that this is a very bald and incomplete account of the events and one told entirely from a colonial and British law perspective. From the perspective of English law in respect of the colonies it was simply assumed that there was not already a constitution or government operating

3 Kenneth Roberts-Wray *Commonwealth and Colonial Law* (Stevens & Sons, London, 1966) at 155–156.

4 Thomas Lindsay Buick *The French at Akaroa: An Adventure in Colonisation* (New Zealand Book Depot, Wellington, 1928) at 67–68.

in Aotearoa/New Zealand.[5] Sovereignty, as the word is used in the colonial context, is now seen as very much a loaded term. What is clear is that from the beginning the settlers had expectations that they would be enabled to govern and Māori had expectations that they would continue to govern themselves. Indeed, recent scholarship[6] suggests that the framers of the English text of the Treaty intended to establish government over British settlers, for the protection of Māori. Māori tribal government and custom were to be maintained. British sovereignty was not necessarily seen as inconsistent with plurality in government and law.

As we now explain, the drive to obtain self-government, free of United Kingdom interference, took many years, and Māori self-government became subsumed in that process.

2
BECOMING A SELF-GOVERNING COLONY

New Zealand's early institutions of government

In the exercise of her prerogative power as the Sovereign of any territory she might acquire, the Queen had already enlarged the boundaries of New South Wales so as to include ". . . any Territory which is or may be acquired in sovereignty by Us, our Heirs or Successors within that Group of Islands in the Pacific Ocean, commonly called New Zealand . . .".[7] The lawyers had advised that, as some parts of New Zealand were seen as having already become a settled colony, the Queen could give it only an elected legislature, a step that was seen as premature.

By August 1840, however, the United Kingdom Parliament had authorised the Queen to make New Zealand a separate colony with a non-representative government.[8] Under that authority, Hobson was appointed as Governor by Letters Patent, known as The New Zealand Charter,[9] which established a standard form of Crown colony government. But by mid-1845 the Secretary of State for the Colonies was warning the Governor that, before long,

5 Compare Mamari Stephens "To Work Out Their Own Salvation: Māori Constitutionalism and the Quest for Welfare" (2015) 46 VUWLR 907 at 924ff.
6 Ned Fletcher "A Praiseworthy Device for Amusing and Pacifying Savages? What the Framers Meant by the English Text of the Treaty of Waitangi" (PhD Thesis, University of Auckland, 2014).
7 Letters Patent dated 15 June 1839 issued by Queen Victoria.
8 New South Wales Continuance Act 1840 (UK) 3 & 4 Vict c 62.
9 Reproduced in *Speeches and Documents on New Zealand History*, above n 1, at 54–56.

demands would be made for "the extension of representative government to New Zealand". That, he explained, would require the members of the body with the power to make laws for the colony to be elected by popular vote.

The drive for representative government

A year later, in 1846, the United Kingdom Parliament enacted an elaborate scheme for representative institutions in New Zealand at the local, provincial and national levels.[10] Sir George Grey, by then the Governor, protested vigorously that Her Majesty would not be giving her subjects the advantages of self-government as intended:[11]

> Instead, she will give to a small fraction of her subjects of one race the power of governing the large majority of her subjects of a different race. . . . [T]he race which is in the majority is much the most powerful of the two; the people belonging to it are well-armed, proud, and independent, and there is no reason . . . to think that they would be satisfied with, and submit to, the rule of the minority.

On 7 March 1848, the United Kingdom Parliament suspended the introduction of countrywide representative institutions for a period of five years. The settlers, especially those in Wellington, were outraged by the delay.[12] In the next few years, however, as settlers continued to pour in and their number in relation to the size of the Māori population increased, Grey's assessment of the situation changed. In 1851, Grey received the news that the Secretary of State was intending to bring in a Constitution Bill for New Zealand. He immediately put forward his ideas, particularly the need for effective law-making at the provincial as well as a central level.[13] They were duly reflected in the "Act to grant a Representative Constitution to the Colony of New Zealand" that received the Royal Assent on 30 June 1852.

10 New Zealand Constitution Act 1846 (UK) 9 & 10 Vict c 103.

11 Despatch from Sir George Grey to Earl Grey, Secretary of State for the Colonies (3 May 1847) GBPP 1847/892 at 42–45, reproduced in *Speeches and Documents on New Zealand History*, above n 1, at 63–64.

12 See, for example, Letter from Mr T Dorset to Earl Grey (27 August 1849) GBPP 1850/1136 at 45.

13 Despatch from Sir George Grey to Earl Grey (30 August 1851) GBPP 1842/1475. See also Alex Frame "Lawyers and the Making of Constitutions: Making Constitutions in the South Pacific: Architects and Excavators" in D Carter and M Palmer (eds) *Roles and Perspectives in the Law: Essays in Honour of Sir Ivor Richardson* (Victoria University Press, Wellington, 2002) 277 at 279–281.

The New Zealand Constitution Act 1852 (UK)

The new Constitution Act[14] was brought into force by Proclamation on 17 January 1853. It established a central legislature for New Zealand, called the General Assembly. On the model of the United Kingdom Parliament, the General Assembly consisted of the Governor, an appointed Legislative Council and an elected House of Representatives. Section 71 provided for self-governing Māori districts — though it was never implemented.

The first meeting of the General Assembly

When the General Assembly met for the first time, in 1854, the minds of the elected members were focused on an issue that the New Zealand Constitution Act 1852 had not addressed. The Act made no provision at all for the executive branch of government. That was a matter not customarily dealt with by legislation, in Britain or in the colonies. The responsibility for executive government remained with the Governor, acting in accordance with his Instructions from the United Kingdom Government and with the advice — so far as he was obliged to accept it — of an Executive Council consisting only of the senior officials under his authority. He had a discretion to act contrary to their advice as long as he explained to the Colonial Office his reasons for doing so.

But, in 1854, the leading settlers in New Zealand, including those elected to the House of Representatives, were well aware of the significant developments that had occurred in Canada. These had been set in train in 1839. In that year, Lord Durham had presented to the United Kingdom Parliament his memorable "Report on the Affairs of British North America". It has since been described as "one of the greatest State papers in the English language".[15]

Lord Durham's Report

Lord Durham had been appointed as Governor-General and Lord High Commissioner of the British North American colonies, some of which were then in a state of near rebellion. On his return to England, he wrote a report on

14 The Constitution Act 1852 (UK) 15 & 16 Vict c 72. To avoid confusion, the Act is referred to in this book as the New Zealand Constitution Act 1852 (UK), the name by which it was generally known.

15 *The Encyclopaedia Britannica: Volume VIII* (11th ed, Cambridge University Press, Cambridge, 1910) at 706. Lord Durham, whose family name was Lambton, had been assisted in Canada by Charles Buller and Edward Gibbon Wakefield, in whose emigration schemes he became interested, serving as Chairman of the New Zealand Company until his death in July 1840.

the reasons for the unrest, and also the remedy. The unrest, he said, stemmed from the continuing clashes between the elected legislatures and the Governors and their officials. Such clashes had occurred especially in Lower Canada (Quebec), where there was a contest between the French and English races. But, he pointed out, there had been similar clashes among the homogeneous populations of Upper Canada (Ontario), Prince Edward Island, New Brunswick, Nova Scotia and Newfoundland. His conclusions were as follows:

> . . . In all of them the administration of public affairs is habitually confided to those who do not co-operate harmoniously with the popular branch of the legislature; and the Government is constantly proposing measures which the majority of the Assembly reject, and refusing its assent to bills which that body has passed. A state of things, so different from the working of any successful experiment of representative government, appears to indicate a deviation from sound constitutional principles or practice.[16]
>
> . . .
>
> The wisdom of adopting the true principle of representative government and facilitating the management of public affairs, by entrusting it to the persons who have the confidence of the representative body, has never been recognised by the government of the North American Colonies. . . . This entire separation of the legislative and executive power of a State, is the natural error of governments desirous of being free from the check of representative institutions. Since the revolution of 1688, the stability of the English constitution has been secured by that wise principle of our Government which has vested the direction of the national policy . . . in the leaders of the Parliamentary majority.[17]

Lord Durham noted that there seemed to be an idea that, in colonies, the relationship with Britain required the character of representative institutions to be modified by retaining the right of the Crown to nominate the officers of the executive government, without any reference to the wishes of the community they served. But, said Lord Durham, there was no way of making such an arrangement palatable to the representative body concerned. Harmony could only be restored by strengthening the people's influence over their government — on the principles that had been found perfectly efficacious in Great Britain itself. He then continued:[18]

16 GM Craig (ed) *An Abridgement of Report on the Affairs of British North America by Lord Durham* (McGill-Queen's University Press, Quebec, 2007) at 46.

17 At 49–50.

18 At 138.

> I would not impair a single prerogative of the Crown; on the contrary, I believe that the interests of the people of those Colonies require the protection of prerogatives, which have not hitherto been exercised. But the Crown must, on the other hand, submit to the necessary consequences of representative institutions; and . . . carry on the Government . . . by means of those in whom that representative body has confidence. In England, this principle has been so long considered an indisputable and essential part of our constitution that it has really hardly ever been necessary to inquire into the means by which its observance is enforced. When a ministry ceases to command a majority in Parliament on great questions of policy, its doom is immediately sealed.
>
> . . . If Colonial Legislatures have frequently stopped the supplies, if they have harassed public servants by unjust or harsh impeachments, it was because the removal of an unpopular administration could not be effected in the Colonies by those milder indications of a want of confidence, which have always sufficed to attain the end in the mother country.

Lord Durham then explained that the introduction into the colonies of what has come to be called "responsible government" would be very simple. The colonial Governor should be instructed to ensure the cooperation of the Assembly in his policy by:[19]

> entrusting its administration to such men as command a majority; and if he were given to understand that he need count on no aid from home in any difference with the Assembly, that [difference] should not directly involve the relations between the mother country and the colony. This change might be effected by a single despatch containing such instructions; or if any legal enactment were requisite, it would only be one that would render it necessary that the official acts of the Governor should be countersigned by some public functionary. This would induce responsibility for every act of the Government.

This system, Lord Durham admitted, would place the internal government of the country in the hands of the colonists themselves. But the matters that concerned the "mother" country were very few. The United Kingdom Government accepted Lord Durham's Report as the basis of its future policy in the Canadian colonies. Responsible government was introduced there in the manner he had proposed.

19 At 139.

The introduction of responsible government in New Zealand

At the first session of the new General Assembly, in June 1854, the House of Representatives presented a respectful address to the acting Governor. It requested him to give serious and early consideration to a resolution of the House recording that, amongst the objects that the House desired to see accomplished without delay, "the most important is the establishment of ministerial responsibility in the conduct of legislative and executive proceedings by the Governor".[20]

The British Government's response to this address was as follows:[21]

> . . . Her Majesty's Government have no objection whatever to offer to the establishment of the system known as responsible government in New Zealand. They have no reason to doubt that it will prove the best adapted for developing the interests as well as satisfying the wishes of the community.

The Secretary of State pointed out that, contrary to what appeared to be the impression in New Zealand, legislative enactment by the General Assembly was not required to bring about this change. In the United Kingdom itself:

> . . . the recognised plan of Parliamentary Government, by which Ministers are responsible to Parliament, and their continuance in office practically depends on the votes of the two Houses, rests on no written law but on usage only. . . . Unless, therefore, there are local laws in existence which would be repugnant to the new system, legislation seems uncalled for . . . ; and if uncalled for, such legislation is objectionable, because the laws so enacted would probably stand in the way of the various partial changes which it might be necessary to adopt in the details of a system in its nature liable to much modification. . . .

On the receipt of the authorisation from London, the acting Governor dissolved the General Assembly so that a new general election could be held. After two short-lived attempts to form a government from among the newly elected members of the House of Representatives, a stable Ministry took office in mid-1856. New Zealand's system of representative and responsible government was in place, in the form it retains today.

20 Extract from the Minutes of the Proceedings of the House of Representatives (6 June 1854).
21 Despatch from Earl Grey Secretary of State for the Colonies, to RH Wynyard, Officer Administering the Government (8 December 1854) GBPP 1834–5 HC 160 at 39–40.

Removing the constraints

There was still, however, a long distance to travel before a New Zealand Government and Parliament would be able to make policy decisions and enact legislation free of the constraints that the United Kingdom Government and Parliament could then still impose. Those constraints were a direct reflection of the "Imperial interests" referred to by Lord Durham in his 1839 Report. The progressive removal of the constraints over the period beginning in the early 1860s, and extending to 1947 and beyond, reflects New Zealand's constitutional journey, first from colony to self-governing Dominion (a title formally conferred in 1907), and then from self-governing Dominion to independent state.

3
JOURNEY TO INDEPENDENCE

The nature of Imperial interests

Colonisation, as a phenomenon, has been known since the time of the Phoenicians. It involved the settlement of a state's subjects in lands beyond its borders on the basis of continuing constitutional links with the mother country and an exchange of benefits, usually in the mother country's favour. In British colonies, the sovereignty of the reigning monarch provided the constitutional link. Britain afforded its colonies physical protection against internal or external attack. In return, the mother country received the benefits of access to raw materials or produce, outlets for any surplus in its own population and opportunities for profitable investment, leading in turn to increased trade internationally and a better standard of living at home. Not surprisingly, colonial constitutions were designed to protect and maximise the economic benefits of colonisation and keep to a minimum the need for any financial outlay by Britain itself.

Lord Durham's Report had identified the aspects of government that, in his view, needed to be excluded from the powers of colonial legislatures and executives, in order to protect Imperial interests. These were the control of the constitution of the form of government; the regulation of foreign relations and of trade with the mother country, the other British Colonies, and foreign nations; and the disposal of public lands. By the time New Zealand had acquired representative and responsible government, those constraints had taken a more or less standardised form.

Constitutional controls

The United Kingdom Government made regular use of two techniques in order to control the actions of a colonial legislature and its responsible government. The first was to limit the law-making powers of the legislature. The General Assembly was authorised to make laws for the "peace, order and good government" of New Zealand. In itself, that formula granted an unfettered power to make laws. There was, however, a simple proviso: no such laws were to be repugnant to the law of England.[22] The meaning of that proviso in the law of all British colonies would need clarification by the Westminster Parliament,[23] but, in the case of New Zealand, "the law of England" would continue to include the main provisions of the New Zealand Constitution Act itself. Any question about law-making competence, including the issue of repugnancy, was one of law, for determination by the courts. It may surprise some that, from 1852 to 1947, New Zealanders lived under a constitution that was supreme law. The courts could and did determine the validity of legislation, and did so without any untoward consequences for the separation of powers.

The exercise of the General Assembly's law-making powers was also controlled by the discretion expressly conferred on the Governor, acting in accordance with his Royal Instructions, to assent to a Bill passed by both Houses, or to refuse assent, or to reserve a Bill for the signification of Her Majesty's pleasure. He could also return such a Bill to either House, with suggested amendments.[24] In addition, Her Majesty, acting in accordance with the advice of her Privy Council, had the power to disallow a Bill assented to by the Governor,[25] and to assent, or refuse assent, to a Bill that had been reserved for the signification of her pleasure.[26] These powers are discussed in more detail in Chapter 11.

In the executive sphere the Governor had a second source of controlling authority. Some matters were required to be reserved for the decision of United Kingdom Ministers. In other cases the Governor might need to be advised by the Executive Council rather than by a single Minister, or by some other person or body. The ultimate source of controlling authority was a broad discretion to act in the exercise of a personal discretion, subject, however, to the duty to report to London on his reasons for doing so.

22 New Zealand Constitution Act 1852, above n 14, s 53. See further BV Harris "The Law-Making Power of the New Zealand General Assembly: Time to Think About Change" (1984) 5 Otago Law Review 565.
23 Colonial Laws Validity Act 1865 (UK) 28 & 29 Vict c 63.
24 Section 56.
25 Section 58.
26 Section 59.

The Royal Instructions

From the beginning, a Governor exercising the powers conferred on the holder of that office was required by his Commission of appointment — and later by standing Letters Patent constituting the Office of Governor or Governor-General — to act in accordance with the Royal Instructions given to him by the Sovereign, acting through or on the advice of United Kingdom Ministers. In their day, the directions contained in a colonial Governor's Royal Instructions ranged from the minute to the profound.

The Royal Instructions often had the force of subordinate legislation. Any exercise of prerogative or statutory powers contrary to the Royal Instructions was technically ultra vires — outside the Governor's powers. But, in some cases, developing constitutional conventions made the Royal Instructions obsolete long before they were formally amended or repealed. The tacit recognition of that fact meant that there were few, if any, appeals to the letter of the law rather than its spirit.

The Governor's role after 1856

We shall now look at some examples of the ways in which a New Zealand Governor, and later a Governor-General, gradually became free of any duty to act in accordance with Instructions from the United Kingdom Government. Occasionally, a change in the constitutional conventions was reflected by a change in the Instructions, but, more often, convention simply overtook the Instructions or even the constitutional power itself. In some cases the exercise of the power concerned was recognised as having become a matter solely for the decision of the New Zealand Government of the day. In others the powers themselves became unusable.

In the process, the Governor or Governor-General eventually ceased to be the servant of the United Kingdom Government and became solely the New Zealand representative of the distant Sovereign. The difficult question, and one that we follow up in later chapters, is whether a residue of the once substantial administrative authority of a colonial governor still lives on, as a function of the office of Governor-General today.

Responsibility for Māori affairs and land

Colonel Thomas Gore Browne's Commission as Governor had provided that, in executing his powers and duties, he was to act with the advice of the

Executive Council, in accordance with his Instructions.[27] These had required him in all cases to consult with the Executive Council,[28] but had given him a general discretion to act in opposition to its advice as long as he reported to London as quickly as possible his reasons for doing so.[29]

By 12 March 1856 Gore Browne was writing to the Colonial Secretary as follows:[30]

> 2. [. . .] On matters affecting the Queen's prerogative and imperial interest generally, I should receive advice [from Ministers]; but when I differ from them in opinion, I should, if they desire it, submit their views for your consideration, but adhere to my own until your answer is received.
>
> 3. Among imperial subjects, I include all dealings with the native tribes, more especially in the negotiation of the purchases of land. My responsible advisers would probably fix the amount to be expended in any one year in the purchase of land; but at that point their interference should cease.
>
> 4. The Governor alone is responsible to Her Majesty's Government for the tranquillity of the colony, which would be endangered even by the ordinary and inevitable change of opinion consequent on a change of my advisers. . . . [Then followed further reasons why the advice he would receive was likely, if acted on, to plunge the country into war or inextricable difficulties.]
>
> 5. If my views are correct, it is evident that the Chief Land Commissioner and his subordinates must take their orders from me alone.

On its way to the Secretary of State, Herman Merivale, by then Permanent Under-Secretary at the Colonial Office, annotated this despatch as follows:[31]

> I do not, for my own part, agree with the Governor. I do not think it possible, with advantage, to withhold native affairs from the cognizance of the responsible advisers, the matter being so closely connected with other points of domestic administration.

27 "Commission of Colonel Thomas Gore Browne CB as Governor of New Zealand" [1856] I AJHR B5 at 2–3.

28 "Instructions to Colonel Thomas Gore Browne, CB, Governor of New Zealand" [1856] I AJHR B5 at 6, cl 19.

29 Clause 21.

30 Despatch from Governor Gore Browne to Rt Hon Sir G Grey (12 March 1856) GBPP 1860/2719 at 193, reproduced in *Speeches and Documents on New Zealand History*, above n 1, at 121.

31 Minute of Herman Merivale CO 209/135: PRO.

During the whole of his term, Gore Browne acted on his own responsibility in all his dealings with the Māori tribes and their leaders on issues that included the King movement and the Waitara dispute. War seemed imminent. Alan Ward concluded that:[32]

> [t]he settlers generally hoped for a decisive subjugation of the Maori while the English Government and troops were already so heavily implicated. But . . . [t]he Colonial Office was not fully persuaded that the King movement was incompatible with British rule and felt that Browne was unduly excited by the term "King". Accordingly Browne was recalled and Sir George Grey reappointed, at his own suggestion.

On his return to New Zealand, Grey was ready to work with his Ministers, and there was broad agreement about the general direction of policy on Māori issues, but the continuing existence of his separate adviser, the Native Secretary, who had remained free of ministerial control and took instructions only from the Governor, was a running sore. In late 1861 Grey agreed to consult his responsible Ministers in relation to "native affairs" and all other native matters in the same manner as upon all other subjects.[33] The Colonial Secretary, the Duke of Newcastle, sanctioned that step because "the endeavour to keep the management of the natives under the control of the Home Government has failed".[34]

That, however, was not the end of the matter. By that time a major argument was brewing between the New Zealand and British governments about how long substantial British forces would need to remain in New Zealand and which government should bear the substantial cost involved. Both the House of Representatives and the Legislative Council had adopted addresses to the Queen repudiating any ministerial responsibility for native affairs. In response, the Duke of Newcastle rejected, in considerable detail, the claim of the two Houses that the British Government had been the author of the war in Taranaki.

In his long despatch to Governor Grey,[35] the Duke referred to the colonists' consistent claim that the Home Government should cease to manage native affairs. He insisted that the Home Government did not require the consent of

32 Alan Ward *A Show of Justice: Racial "Amalgamation" in Nineteenth Century New Zealand* (Auckland University Press, Auckland, 1973) at 124.

33 Despatch from Governor Sir George Grey to the Duke of Newcastle (30 November 1861) GBPP 1862/5363, at 27–28, reproduced in *Speeches and Documents on New Zealand History*, above n 1, at 108.

34 Despatch from the Duke of Newcastle to Governor Sir George Grey (26 May 1862) GBPP 1862/5363, at 79–81.

35 Above n 34.

the colonists for the relinquishment of responsibility for native affairs. On that matter, as on other colonial affairs, the Governor would generally be bound to give effect to the policies which his Ministry recommended and for which they would be responsible. The Duke then continued:

> I say, generally, because there remain several contingencies in which it would be your duty to act upon your own judgment in opposition to theirs.
>
> You would be bound to exercise the negative powers which you possess, by preventing any step which invaded Imperial rights, or was at variance with the pledges [on] the faith of which Her Majesty's Government acquired the sovereignty of New Zealand, or [was] in any other way marked by evident injustice towards Her Majesty's subjects of the native race.
>
> In the interests of the colonists themselves you might find yourself bound, under conceivable circumstances, to appeal from your Government to the General Assembly, and from the General Assembly to the constituencies, in case the policy recommended for your acceptance appeared to you clearly disastrous.

That passage has been reproduced because it was the first articulation, in relation to New Zealand, of a Governor's only alternative — other than his own resignation — to accepting the advice of his responsible Ministers. The Colonial Secretary was referring obliquely to a Governor's power to dismiss the leader of a government — and, with him, the other Ministers — and to appoint in his place another member of the legislature who was prepared to advise a dissolution. On the basis of that advice the Governor would then be able to dissolve the General Assembly so that a new general election could be held.

The possible need for such a step might arise in two different circumstances. The first was a situation in which interests of the utmost importance to the United Kingdom Government were at stake. Secondly, the Duke of Newcastle, in his 1862 despatch, also saw the Governor as having a duty to dismiss a government and, if necessary, dissolve Parliament "in the interests of the colonists themselves . . . in case the policy recommended for your acceptance appeared to you clearly disastrous".

Newcastle went on to state that the Governor still had a personal responsibility for decisions about the deployment in New Zealand of Her Majesty's forces. He was at liberty to consult his Ministers, but the responsibility would rest with the Governor and the Officer in Command. Finally, the Duke made the point that the safety of the colonists depended for the time being on Imperial troops, maintained at the expense of Great Britain. That gave Britain the right to insist that the colonists' native policy, on which peace or war depended, should be just, prudent and liberal. On that depended Great Britain's willingness to continue that assistance.

Even then, the drama was not over. The arrangement under which the Governor and his responsible advisers had competing responsibilities often led to clashes. Gavin McLean describes the various confrontations that put Grey on a collision course not only with some of his Ministers but also with many Māori, with the successive commanders of the Imperial forces, and, "finally and most fatally", with the Colonial Office itself.[36] In 1867, Grey received a summary notification of his recall.[37] His successor, Sir George Bowen, had a better sense of his constitutional position, but, even so, got caught up in an attempt, at the request of the Legislative Council, later backed by the House of Representatives, to delay the departure of the last Imperial regiment. After many delays, the 18th Imperial regiment sailed from New Zealand in February 1870, but not before Bowen had been reprimanded by Earl Granville, by then the Colonial Secretary, for supporting the government's efforts to delay their departure when outbreaks of guerrilla warfare were at their height.[38] Māori affairs and internal defence then came fully under local ministerial control.[39]

We have described in such detail the responsibility for Māori affairs and land acquisition in the period between 1856 and 1870 because it helps to explain momentous events in the relationship between Māori and settler governments at large and because the interactions of the Governor, his Ministers and the Colonial Office throw considerable light on the nature of a duty to act on the advice of the responsible Ministers. It was practically impossible for the Governor to exercise responsibility in a way that would satisfy the conflicting interests involved.

Responsibility for foreign relations and trade

"The regulation of foreign relations and of trade with the mother country, the other British Colonies, and foreign nations" was the second of the three Imperial interests that Lord Durham identified in his 1839 Report. Those interests were protected in two main ways. First, the New Zealand Constitution Act 1852 (UK) contained a simple prohibition on the enactment of legislation

36 Gavin McLean *The Governors: New Zealand's Governors and Governors-General* (Otago University Press, Dunedin, 2006) at 64–69.

37 Despatch from the Right Hon Duke of Buckingham to Sir George Grey dated 18 June 1867 [1867] I AJHR A1 at 46.

38 Gavin McLean, above n 36, at 77.

39 CC Aikman and JL Robson "Introduction" in John Lochiel Robson (ed) *New Zealand: The Development of its Laws and Constitution* (2nd ed, Stevens & Sons, London, 1967) 1 at 11.

imposing any duty on articles imported for the supply of Imperial forces, or imposing any dues or levies on imports or exports, or on shipping, contrary to or at variance with any treaty.[40] That section remained in force until the repeal of the 1852 Act by the Constitution Act 1986, but, after 25 November 1947,[41] any conflicting Act of the New Zealand Parliament would have been seen as having impliedly repealed that constraint.

From the time of the introduction of responsible government until 1907, a Governor's Royal Instructions contained provisions requiring him not to propose or assent to Bills affecting Great Britain's trading interests, or to reserve such Bills for the signification of Her Majesty's pleasure.[42] A little later, the Instructions imposed a similar duty in respect of any Bill imposing differential duties, or appearing inconsistent with obligations imposed on Her Majesty by any treaty,[43] or appearing to prejudice the trade and shipping of the United Kingdom and its dependencies.[44] As we later show, however, the constraints in terms of foreign relations and trade were later swept away by changes in the status of the former self-governing colonies themselves.

The constitution of the form of government

Lord Durham did not spell out his reasons for including "the constitution of the form of government" among the United Kingdom's Imperial interests in respect of a colony. Clearly, however, colonial constitutions had to be controlled, because they were the main means of protecting the United Kingdom's more material interests of an Imperial kind. Lord Durham's concept of responsible government would gradually undermine the continuing viability of constitutional controls. The reality was that, in the areas where a colonial Governor was required to act on the advice of his Ministers in the colony, Her Majesty was already being separately advised. There was no natural point at which that process of transferring responsibility from the United Kingdom Government to the government of a colony would have to come to a halt. Once responsible government had been firmly bedded in, the only real constraints on a colonial government's freedom of action were those imposed by the colony's practical

40 New Zealand Constitution Act 1852, above n 14, s 61.
41 On that date the Statute of Westminster took effect as part of New Zealand law.
42 Instructions to Governor Gore Browne, above n 28, cl 15.
43 Most, if not all, of the relevant bilateral treaties have either been expressly terminated, or been superseded by later multilateral treaties. For the purposes of the Royal Instructions, a "treaty" did not include the Treaty of Waitangi.
44 "Commission of His Excellency Sir G Grey KCB, Together with the Royal Instructions Accompanying the Same" [1862] I AJHR A1 at 5, cl 6.

dependence on continuing British protection (a motivating force foreseen by Durham), and any others which, for its own reasons, the colonial, or later the Dominion, government chose to impose on itself.

The recognition of the former self-governing colonies as "Dominions" (with a capital "D") was a milestone on their road to a more equal constitutional relationship with Britain. The word "dominion" had long been used to describe a country or territory over which the Sovereign had "dominion", or, to use another word, sovereignty. Such countries and territories were often referred to as part of the Sovereign's "dominions", until the word later went out of fashion. That usage was reflected in the 1867 Act of the United Kingdom Parliament which brought about the federation of the British colonies north of the 49th parallel. It provided that Canada would be "one Dominion".[45] After that, Canada itself soon became known as "the Dominion of Canada".

Dominion status

Over the next 40 years, "Dominion" became a generic description. In 1907, the Colonial Conference of that year decided that all the colonies within the sovereignty of the British Crown which had, by then, become self-governing would be described as "self-governing Dominions". In the same year, at the request of the New Zealand Parliament, King Edward VII conferred on what had up to then been the Colony of New Zealand the official title, "Dominion of New Zealand".[46] We take up later in this chapter the story of the eventual abandonment of "Dominion", both as a generic term, and as part of New Zealand's official name. For the time being, however, Dominion status was a welcome step forward. With it came the relaxation in the extent to which Governors or Governors-General were expected to withhold assent to a Bill passed by the Parliament of the Dominion concerned. Other aspects of that status as it was then seen were, however, of more concern.[47] At the 1911 Imperial Conference, the New Zealand Prime Minister, Sir Joseph Ward, had reiterated the request of earlier New Zealand statesmen for a voice in the making of the British

45 British North America Act 1867 (UK) 30 & 31 Vict c 3, Preamble and s 3.

46 "Despatch from the Secretary of State for the Colonies, Enclosing Copy of Order in Council and Proclamation by His Majesty the King Declaring that the Colony of New Zealand Shall be Called and Known by the Title of the 'Dominion of New Zealand'" [1907] I AJHR A2a at 2–3.

47 See, in the case of New Zealand, Letters Patent Constituting the Office of the Governor and Commander-in-Chief of the Dominion of New Zealand and accompanying Royal Instructions [1908] I AJHR A2 at 14.

foreign policy on which New Zealand's security depended. Herbert Asquith, the British Prime Minister, rejected the proposal on the ground that:[48]

> [i]t would impair if not altogether destroy the authority of the . . . United Kingdom in . . . all those relations with Foreign Powers, necessarily of the most delicate character, which are now in the hands of the Imperial Government, subject to its responsibility to the Imperial Parliament. That authority cannot be shared.

If that was the case, there could be only one other way of accommodating the different interests of Britain and the various Dominions. Their governmental authority would need to be exercised separately. That was made apparent in a way that would see the Dominions become separate members of the international community.

On 6 August 1914, the British Prime Minister, Asquith, explained to the House of Commons the reasons why Britain, in defence of Belgium, had entered the war against Germany. He pledged that the struggle would be conducted with all the resources "not only of this United Kingdom, but of the vast Empire of which it is the centre".[49] That statement reflected the fact that, as the status of the Dominions then stood in both constitutional and international law, not only Britain itself, but also New Zealand and the other Dominions were at war with Germany.[50]

The part they took in the fighting came to be recognised as entitling them also to a part in making peace. Canada, Australia, New Zealand and South Africa (as well as India) were separate signatories to the Treaty of Versailles, and, as a consequence, separate members of the League of Nations constituted by the treaty. The British Foreign Secretary of the day recognised that, in Paris in 1919, "the status of the Dominions and India was settled once and for all".[51] They had become separate states in international law. For a long time, however, they still looked to the Sovereign as their Head of State to act on their behalf in formal relations with other states. In Chapter 14 we show that the Governor-General, as the Sovereign's representative, now exercises all aspects of the Head of State role in international law.

Within a decade, the implications of statehood in international law led the United Kingdom Government to dismantle all of the legal devices and

48 "Report of the 1911 Colonial Conference" (Cmd 5745, 1911) at 71.

49 Quoted in J Spender and C Asquith *Life of Herbert Henry Asquith: Volume 2* (Hutchinson, London, 1932) at 114–115.

50 Robson, above n 39, at 15.

51 Telegram of 27 October 1922 from Colonial Secretary, London, to Governor-General, Ottawa, reproduced in *Documents on Canadian External Relations: Volume 3: 1919–1925* (Department of External Affairs, Ottawa, 1970) at 85.

constitutional conventions which had been put in place in its former colonies for the purpose of protecting the "Imperial interests" of the mother country.

The discussions about the future relationship linking the Dominions to Britain and to one another are recorded in the reports of a series of conferences among their Prime Ministers and other representatives in the period between 1917 and 1930.[52] Reading the proceedings today, it is striking how far the United Kingdom Government had been able to move since 1911.

In 1926, the Canadian Prime Minister, Mackenzie King, pressed the United Kingdom Government to come up with a restatement of the Governor-General's role at the forthcoming Imperial Conference, later that year. The then British Prime Minister, Lord Balfour, chaired a committee which recognised that the constitutional position had evolved to an ultimate, sustainable stage. His name is forever associated with the following declaration:[53]

> They [Great Britain and the Dominions] are autonomous communities within the British Empire, equal in status, in no way subordinate to one another in any aspect of their domestic or external affairs, though united by a common allegiance to the Crown, and freely associated as Members of the British Commonwealth of Nations.

It later became clear that there was still some distance to travel before the last of the old constraints was removed, but, already, the relationship was changing too fast and too far for New Zealand's comfort. By 1931, most of the legal steps consequent on the Balfour Declaration had been put in place, but it was 1947 before New Zealand was ready to accept them. By that time New Zealanders had fought alongside Britain and the other members of the Commonwealth in another world war. A greater sense of identity and self-confidence had replaced the mixture of loyalty and dependence that had prompted the country's earlier reluctance to change the formal legal position. Finally, the National Party's desire to abolish the Upper House of Parliament — a step still needing to be authorised by the United Kingdom Parliament — persuaded it to join with a Labour Government in giving the New Zealand Parliament full power to make laws, a step achieved in the manner described below.

52 "Report of the Imperial War Conference 1917" (Cmd 8566, 1917); "Report of the Inter-Imperial Relations Committee of the Imperial Conference of 1926" (Cmd 2768, 1926); "Report of the Conference on the Operation of Dominion Legislation and Merchant Shipping legislation 1929" (Cmd 3479, 1929); "Report of the Imperial Conference 1930" (Cmd 3717, 1930).

53 "Report of the Inter-Imperial Relations Committee of the Imperial Conference of 1926" (Cmd 2768, 1926) at 2.

The equality of status recognised in 1926 had affected four main institutions or areas relevant to this book. The Sovereign was still regarded as the symbol of the free association of the members of the Commonwealth. They were seen as united by their common allegiance to the reigning Sovereign.[54] That concept foundered when India became a republic in 1947, but wished to remain a member of the Commonwealth. In 1948, allegiance itself ceased to have its former significance as the basis of a common British nationality. From then on, each member of the Commonwealth would provide for its own separate citizenship.

In 1930, it had also been assumed that all the Commonwealth countries would be able to agree on a single form of the royal style and titles by which their Sovereign would be known, and would make the necessary provision in their law.[55] That assumption, too, had to be abandoned in 1952, when it proved impossible to agree on the titles of Queen Elizabeth II.[56] The members of the Commonwealth continued to recognise the Crown as the symbol of their free association, and the Sovereign as the Head of the Commonwealth. The governing principle is that Her Majesty acts exclusively on the advice of the responsible Ministers in what have become each of her realms.[57] That principle was first enunciated in the context of the appointment of a Governor-General, but was seen as having general application.

Another enduring principle is that the Governor-General of a realm is:[58]

> the representative of the Crown, holding in all essential respects the same position in relation to the administration of public affairs . . . as is held by His Majesty the King in Great Britain, and that he is not the representative or agent of His Majesty's Government in Great Britain or of any department of that Government.

It followed that the Governor-General should no longer be the official channel of communication between the United Kingdom Government and the government of a realm. The Governor-General should, however, be supplied with copies of all documents of importance and in general should be kept as fully informed of Cabinet business and public affairs as is the King in Great Britain. The Governor-General would be appointed by His Majesty on the advice of the responsible Ministers in the Dominion concerned, tendered after informal consultation with His Majesty through any agreed channel of communication.[59]

54 The Statute of Westminster 1931 (UK) 22 Geo 5 c 4, Preamble.
55 The Statute of Westminster, above n 54, Preamble.
56 See Chapter 4 The Sovereign in Right of New Zealand: The Institutional Role, around fn 72, at 63.
57 See 1930 Imperial Conference Report, above n 52.
58 1926 Imperial Conference Report, above n 52.
59 1930 Imperial Conference Report, above n 52.

All of these matters, too, are further discussed in the chapters dealing with the office of Governor-General and his or her role.[60]

The Report of the Inter-Imperial Relations Committee of the 1926 Imperial Conference discussed at length the relations of the various parts of the then British Empire with foreign countries. It also considered how far the Dominions should follow analogous procedures in their future relations with one another.[61] Increasingly, however, the diplomatic relations between members of the Commonwealth are being assimilated to those between foreign states.

The Statute of Westminster

The final product of the work of the 1926, 1929 and 1930 Imperial Conferences took the form of recommendations for the enlargement of the legislative powers of the Parliaments of the Dominions, and restrictions on the reach of the future laws of the Parliament at Westminster. Effect was given to those changes in the Act of the United Kingdom Parliament known as the Statute of Westminster 1931 (UK). That Act made law for Great Britain itself and for all the members of what it called "the British Commonwealth of Nations". Significantly, that term had replaced "British Empire" as a collective description of Great Britain and the Dominions.

The Statute of Westminster came fully into force for Canada, South Africa and the Irish Free State on the date on which it received the royal assent.[62] For Australia, New Zealand and Newfoundland, the main operative provisions in sections 2, 3, 4, 5 and 6 of the Act were not to come into force until adopted by their respective Parliaments.[63] Even then, the Statute of Westminster was not to confer any power to alter the constitutional legislation of Canada,[64] Australia,[65] or New Zealand,[66] except to the extent that the relevant Parliament already had that power. After 1931, however, United Kingdom Governments generally acted in accordance with what the preamble to the Statute of Westminster had already recognised as a constitutional convention. They sought and obtained the prior consent of New Zealand to any Act of the United Kingdom Parliament or comparable prerogative instrument extending to New Zealand as part of its law.[67]

60 See Chapters 6 to 10.
61 1926 Imperial Conference Report, above n 52.
62 11 December 1931.
63 Section 10.
64 Section 7.
65 Sections 8 and 9.
66 Section 8.
67 See, for example, His Majesty's Declaration of Abdication Act 1936 (UK) 1 Edw 8 & 1 Geo 6 c 3,

In 1947, the New Zealand Parliament, in a complex process, adopted sections 2 to 6 of the Statute of Westminster. The adopting Act came into force on 25 November 1947.[68] It provided that any future request to the United Kingdom Parliament to make laws for New Zealand would have to be made by Act.[69] At the same time, Parliament passed another Act requesting the United Kingdom Parliament to amend the New Zealand Constitution Act 1852 (UK) so as to authorise the Parliament of New Zealand to alter, suspend or repeal all or any of its provisions.[70] As requested, the United Kingdom Parliament then made provision to that effect. The New Zealand Constitution (Amendment) Act 1947 (UK)[71] came into force on 10 December 1947. On that date, New Zealand acquired the legal power to amend its own constitution.

At that point, the United Kingdom Government and Parliament had done everything they needed to do to release New Zealand from such of the former constraints as had still remained on its own ability to control what, a hundred years earlier, Lord Durham had referred to as "the constitution of the form of government". In both constitutional law and international law, New Zealand had become an independent state. There were some loose ends still to be tidied up, but nothing that was done later added anything material to what had already been achieved.

Title "Dominion" no longer seen as appropriate

Earlier in this chapter, we referred to the use of the word "dominions" to describe all the geographical areas that, at one time or another, had been brought within the sovereignty of the Crown. We explained that the self-governing colonies came to be known as Dominions within the British Commonwealth of Nations, and that Canada and New Zealand had each adopted the word "Dominion" as part of the country's official name. In the years following the adoption of the Statute of Westminster, marked by the participation of the Dominions in another world war, the continuing use of the term "dominion", with or without a capital "D", fell into disfavour. For one thing, the "Dominions" did not include the United Kingdom, although it and the Dominions were said to be of equal status. For another, the non-self-governing territories administered by the United Kingdom, Australia or New Zealand

Preamble. But compare Prize Act 1939 (UK) 2 & 3 Geo 6 c 65, s 4(1)(b).

68 The Statute of Westminster Adoption Act 1947 (Cth), s 2.

69 Section 3.

70 The New Zealand Constitution Amendment (Request and Consent) Act 1947.

71 10 & 11 Geo 6 c 46.

that had been brought within the sovereignty of the Crown were also part of the Sovereign's "dominions".

From about 1946 on, Canada and New Zealand quietly dropped the use of the word "Dominion" as part of the country's name. In Canada, that reflected its original adoption as a matter of usage. Although, in New Zealand, the name was conferred by King Edward VII's 1907 Proclamation, and it has never been thought necessary expressly to revoke it, the Proclamation must now be regarded as spent. The former Dominions began to describe themselves simply as "members of the Commonwealth", without the adjective "British". Soon, they were joined by the "new" Commonwealth members that came to independence in the post-war years. The first was India, followed by the other countries formerly administered by the United Kingdom, New Zealand or Australia that, after independence, wished to retain their connection with the Commonwealth.[72] Some of them had never been within the Sovereign's dominions. Others, which had formerly been part of the Sovereign's dominions, became republics on independence. The Sovereign's relationship with all the present members of the Commonwealth is further discussed in Chapter 4.

The Letters Patent constituting the office of Governor-General of New Zealand now use the expression "Realm of New Zealand" as a collective term to describe all the countries and territories within the sovereignty of the Queen in right of New Zealand.[73] The word "Realm", however, is not part of New Zealand's name. In some contexts, as a matter of usage, that name is informally coupled with its Māori-language counterpart and the country is referred to as "Aotearoa/New Zealand".[74]

A new Constitution Act

In 1986, the New Zealand Parliament enacted a new Constitution Act.[75] The Act brought together some of the most important constitutional provisions in the existing statute law.[76] It replaced the few remaining provisions

72 Ireland is treated "as if" it was a Commonwealth member.

73 The constitutional status of the countries and territories concerned, other than New Zealand, is further described in Chapter 6 The Letters Patent, the Governor-General and the Realm of New Zealand, under the subheading The territorial reach of the Letters Patent, at 104–106.

74 In the English language, "Aotearoa" is usually rendered as "Land of the Long White Cloud". The name was supposedly given by those in the voyaging waka who first sighted the distant view of the high mountains, usually covered by cloud.

75 Constitution Act 1986.

76 For a commentary on the reasons for the Act and on its provisions see *Constitutional Reform: First and Second Reports released by the Minister of Justice, the Hon. Geoffrey Palmer* (Department of Justice, Wellington, 1986).

of the New Zealand Constitution Act 1852 (UK), so far as they were then in force and still remained relevant. Because it was designed to replace the entire fabric of the 1852 Constitution Act as modified by the Statute of Westminster 1931 (UK), it revoked or repealed most of New Zealand's earlier legislation in the constitutional field.[77] That step, however, did not affect the continuing force of any earlier grant of constitutional powers.[78] The Constitution Act 1986 was but a further step in a process begun after 1947 of replacing almost all of the United Kingdom Acts that had been part of New Zealand law, many of them enacted in the 19th century or earlier, with up-to-date enactments in more modern language.

In substance, the Constitution Act 1986 did not greatly change the content of the earlier law, but in terms of the country's constitutional history it was an important step in the "patriation" of the law constituting the legislative branch of government and providing for the structure of the executive branch, so far as that is governed by statute. In those fields, New Zealand no longer relies on laws made by the Parliament at Westminster. The Constitution Act 1986 therefore has a symbolic significance. As will be seen, however, it did not involve any break in legal continuity or purport to confer any powers that Parliament did not already have.

Parliament's law-making powers

Section 15(1) of the Constitution Act 1986 simply provides:

> The Parliament of New Zealand continues to have full power to make laws.

Although, in form, the provision is self-contained, the operative words "continues to have" require its effect to be gauged by looking back at what had gone before. That is all the more necessary because, in New Zealand, a question had arisen about the extent of Parliament's powers to make laws having extraterritorial effect. By that we mean laws affecting persons or things outside New Zealand, such as ships on the high seas or New Zealand troops stationed in other countries.

The New Zealand Parliament's "full power to make laws" includes the power to enact legislation, even though it is "repugnant to the law of England". That

77 Constitution Act 1986, ss 26 and 28. See also *Constitutional Reform*, above n 76.
78 Interpretation Act 1999, s 17.

was established by the Statute of Westminster.[79] The Statute also empowered the Parliament of a Dominion to repeal or amend a United Kingdom Act that was part of its law.[80]

United Kingdom Parliament no longer able to make laws for New Zealand

Section 15(2) of the Constitution Act 1986 made another change in New Zealand's constitutional law that had virtually no practical consequences but considerable symbolic significance. It provided as follows:[81]

> No Act of the Parliament of the United Kingdom passed after the commencement of this Act shall extend to New Zealand as part of its law.

The provision brought to an end the Westminster Parliament's power to make laws for New Zealand. In United Kingdom law, the enactment of such a law was simply an exercise of the plenary law-making power of Parliament recognised by the common law. After New Zealand adopted the Statute of Westminster, the advice and consent of the New Zealand Parliament was required (a procedure which was used only once, to give New Zealand the power to amend its own constitution).[82] The corresponding power had already been removed in respect of Canada, though admittedly, that step had been taken by the Parliament at Westminster.[83] In the case of New Zealand, the Officials Committee, which in 1986 considered changes to the 1852 Act, was of the view that the enactment of legislation by the New Zealand Parliament alone would be just as effective in achieving the desired result, particularly if the Statute of Westminster were also revoked in its application to New Zealand. On that basis, the Constitution Act 1986 declared that no future Act of the United Kingdom Parliament would extend to New Zealand as part of its law.[84] The extent to which any earlier United Kingdom legislation continues to have effect in New Zealand law is now set out in the Imperial Laws Application Act 1988 — an Act passed by the New Zealand Parliament.

79 The Statute provided that the Colonial Laws Validity Act 1865 (UK) 28 & 29 Vict c 63 would not apply to any law made after its commencement by the Parliament of a Dominion: s 2(1).

80 Section 2(2).

81 The 1986 Act came into force on 1 January 1987: s 1(2).

82 New Zealand Constitution (Amendment) Act 1947 (UK) 11 Geo VI c 4.

83 Canada Act 1982 (UK) 30 Eliz II c 11, s 2.

84 Constitution Act 1986, s 15(2); Department of Justice *Constitutional Reform: Reports of an Officials Committee* (Wellington, New Zealand, 1986) at 2.6–2.8.

The Constitution Act also took the symbolic step of making the Queen in right of New Zealand, rather than the Governor-General (who continues to represent her), formally a part of the New Zealand Parliament.

The nature of the New Zealand constitution

At this point it is possible to draw some conclusions about the nature of New Zealand's present-day constitution. Since 1 January 1987, when the Constitution Act 1986 entered into force, the constitution can be seen as having become patriated, in the sense that its statutory provisions are now set out in various Acts of the New Zealand Parliament, or in United Kingdom statutes recognised by the New Zealand Parliament as part of New Zealand law. Although the legislative authority of the New Zealand Parliament was originally conferred by the United Kingdom Parliament, that does not in any way detract from the reality or completeness of the constitutional independence from the United Kingdom that New Zealanders enjoy.

The history of how New Zealand developed a system of self-government informs the present-day functioning of the constitution. As we shall see in Chapter 13, the promises of self-government to Māori were never delivered, despite numerous petitions to successive Sovereigns and Governors and attempts to create forums for Māori representation. The early struggles between Governors and settler governments may suggest reasons why Governors and Governors-General have been and continue to be kept at arm's length from the policy-making process.

The gradual acquisition of constitutional autonomy depended on two important concepts making constitutional change possible: the divisibility of the Crown (creating the Queen in right of New Zealand); and constitutional convention. We turn now to consider in more detail those concepts.

CHAPTER 3

Constitutional Monarchy: Key Concepts

1
THE MAIN FEATURES

How New Zealand became a monarchy is explained in Chapter 2, but just how New Zealand came to be a *constitutional* monarchy in which political power resides in the people's elected representatives requires some further elaboration. New Zealand's constitution is monarchical, parliamentary and democratic. The monarch still has significant legal powers, but those powers must be exercised by or through the elected Members of Parliament who form the executive branch of government. The real decisions are made by the Prime Minister and the other Ministers who make up the executive branch of government. In the "parliamentary" system, also known as the "Westminster" system, the executive government is formed from among the elected members of the legislature. The political party or parties which together command the political support of a majority of the Members of Parliament are entitled to form the government. It is the government which makes the policy decisions, directs government administration, and controls the collection and expenditure of money. In the words of the Cabinet Office Manual, "[t]he Queen reigns but the government rules".[1] The parliamentary system of government may be contrasted with constitutions, such as that of the United States of America, where there is a strict separation of powers, and the head of the executive branch, the President, is separately elected and exercises power independently of the legislature.

1 Kenneth Keith "On the Constitution of New Zealand: An Introduction to the Foundations of the Current Form of Government" in Cabinet Office *Cabinet Manual 2008* (Department of the Prime Minister and Cabinet, Wellington, New Zealand, April 2008) at 3, citing Walter Nash in the Parliamentary Debates on the Royal Titles Act.

In this chapter we explain some of the underlying concepts and principles of the British constitutional system which New Zealand has inherited. They have been essential to the development and operation of the constitutional monarchy and will be discussed more fully in the later chapters — particularly Chapters 8 to 11. We also explain that some of the ideas historically associated with the monarchy of an earlier age never came to apply in New Zealand. That is true, as we will show, in respect of the Queen's role in the tenure of land.

2
FROM MONARCHY TO CONSTITUTIONAL MONARCHY

Any explanation of how a monarchical system developed into a constitutional monarchy begins in England — and long before the United Kingdom Government sent its representatives to Aotearoa/New Zealand.

When George III, acting without or contrary to ministerial advice, tried to collect taxes from the North American colonies, they rebelled and declared themselves to be a republic. After winning the revolutionary war, the "Founding Fathers" drafted a constitution for the newly independent state. The Sovereign was replaced by what was, in effect, an elected King called the President who headed the executive branch of government. Influenced by Montesquieu's arguments for the separation of the executive, legislative and judicial powers, the constitution provided for the separate election of the members of a bicameral legislature. It was essential to the framers of the US Constitution that there should be rivalry and contest between the executive and legislative branches of government. This was intended to create limits on government action.

British political leaders reacted in their own way to George III's attempts to act independently of his Ministers. He was the last British monarch to have such success in imposing his will. The Kings and Queens who followed sometimes had strong opinions which they made known to their Ministers, but, generally speaking, they observed what had come to be seen as their duty to act on the advice of their responsible advisers. Democracy was not achieved by a revolution or a completely new constitutional beginning but by a process of constitutional evolution.

The "bloodless revolution" of 1688 had already established that the law courts would give effect to the laws made by Parliament when they conflicted with the powers or rights claimed by the Sovereign. That was one of the central conditions, set out in the Bill of Rights 1689, on which Parliament offered

William and Mary the throne.[2] Parliament was from then on to prevail over the King's putative powers to tax, to spend and to make laws.

The effective exercise of the Sovereign's executive, as opposed to legislative, powers by the Prime Minister and Cabinet was more gradual and less clear cut. Before the 18th century "kings were their own prime ministers".[3] Yet even in the late 17th century, the Sovereign's advisers, known first as Privy Counsellors and later as Ministers, had often been Members of Parliament. That became the rule. Sir Robert Walpole's Whig Ministry (1721–42) "laid the foundations" for the transfer of power to a Prime Minister.[4] The emergence of distinct political parties began to affect the formation of governments. During this time, it came to be accepted that a government could not be appointed to, or remain in, office unless it had and retained the support of a majority in the House of Commons. The King's favour, while still necessary, was no longer sufficient. Eventually, even the King's favour was no longer necessary and the right and power to govern came to depend on the support of the House of Commons. Kings ceased to attend Cabinet in person[5] and were content to act on the advice of their Ministers.

Collectively the Sovereign's advisers became known as "the Cabinet" and the leader of the government as the Prime Minister. By the 1780s, members of Cabinet would be expected to resign from that office when the Prime Minister lost the confidence of the House. The concept of Cabinet collective responsibility to Parliament originates in the recognition that its members stand or fall together. The government could change between elections if the government led by the Prime Minister lost the confidence of Parliament. That remains a distinctive aspect of a parliamentary, as opposed to a presidential, system of government. The concept that the executive government must have and retain majority support in Parliament is known as the system of "responsible government".

Despite these quite radical changes in the location of political power, there was no change to the formal site of constitutional authority. Executive authority, including the prerogative powers and privileges recognised by the courts, and therefore having the force of law, remains vested in the Sovereign, but is exercised by the Sovereign on the advice of Ministers or directly by Ministers and officials themselves.

2 1 Will & Mar Sess 2 c 2.

3 GW Jones "The Office of Prime Minister" in Herbert Van Thal (ed) *The Prime Ministers (Vol 1): Sir Robert Walpole to Sir Robert Peel* (Allen & Unwin, London, 1974) 11 at 15.

4 Elizabeth Wicks *The Evolution of a Constitution: Eight Key Moments in British Constitutional History* (Hart Publishing, Oxford, 2006) at 53.

5 In 1781: see Peter Hennessy *The Prime Minister: The Office and its Holders Since 1945* (Allen Lane, London, 2000) at 45.

The constitutional monarchy was in place in the United Kingdom at the time when New Zealand became a British colony. From its inception, and for some time afterwards, the actions performed in the Sovereign's name in respect of New Zealand were taken by successive Governors acting on their Royal Instructions. In reality the Instructions were planned by the Colonial Office, a Ministry responsible to the Secretary of State for the Colonies, a member of the government in power at the time and therefore responsible to the United Kingdom Parliament. As we explained in Chapter 2, through the operation of political forces in the United Kingdom and in New Zealand and changes in both policy and practice, executive power was gradually transferred to New Zealand elected governments led by Premiers and later by Prime Ministers. Yet, as a matter of constitutional law, the executive authority of New Zealand remains vested in the Sovereign in right of New Zealand. The offices of Prime Minister and other Ministers and the institution known as the Cabinet are not even mentioned in the New Zealand Constitution Act 1986.

So if formal legal power and real political power reside in different office-holders, how is government able to function in practice? New Zealand's firmly established parliamentary democracy relies on three important concepts. The first is the formal delegation of authority by the Sovereign to the Governor-General, in the Letters Patent constituting that office, to constitute and appoint various other offices and delegate his or her authority (explained and discussed in Chapters 7 and 8). Formal delegation, however, is not the whole mechanism: it is supplemented by the concept of constitutional conventions and the further concept of the Crown as a corporation. We discuss these concepts in turn.

3
CORE CONCEPTS

Constitutional conventions

Constitutional conventions are generally accepted rules of practice regulating the conduct of the constitutional actors, especially the Sovereign, the Governor-General, Ministers and officials. Conventions emerge out of practices and authoritative statements of Imperial Conferences, Cabinet Manuals and the like and often out of a combination of practice and distilled statements of principle derived from practice. They do not have the force of law and cannot be directly enforced by the courts. Nevertheless, they are just as important, and are obeyed more faithfully than many laws.[6] Often, constitutional conventions have the effect of controlling the exercise of a decision-making power and even of transferring its exercise from those in whom the power is vested to those who have been elected to govern.

In a constitutional monarchy, constitutional conventions are indispensable. They work to control and transfer the exercise of the legal powers vested in the Sovereign: the Sovereign may exercise the executive authority vested in her only in accordance with the established constitutional conventions. The most important of these is that the Sovereign and the Governor-General act in accordance with the advice of responsible Ministers. This is the case in all but a few instances which we shall go on to identify in later chapters. Like other constitutional conventions, that convention reflects the democratic values which underpin the parliamentary system of government. That fact is signified by the time-honoured practice that a document signed by the Sovereign or the Governor-General is countersigned by the Prime Minister or other Minister who tendered the advice.[7]

Writing in 1959, Geoffrey Marshall and Graham C Moodie seem to capture the essence of the purpose that constitutional conventions serve, not just in the British constitution and others based on that model, but in other types of constitution as well. In their view, in determining whether a particular custom or practice is a constitutional convention, "a crucial question must always be whether or not a particular class of action is likely to destroy respect for the established distribution of authority".[8] They argued that "a breach of convention is likely to induce a change in the law, or even in the whole constitutional structure".[9] In their view, that characteristic was particularly true of the conventions limiting the powers of the monarch. A breach of the conventions would endanger the status or even the existence of the monarchy.

In later chapters, there are many references to the relevant constitutional conventions, especially those governing the relationship between the Queen or the Governor-General and their New Zealand Ministers. In looking at whether a particular convention exists, and, if so, at its significance, we will ask ourselves two questions. Would the constitution still work if there were no convention of the kind postulated? If the answer to that question is "no", we will think about what would be likely to happen if such a convention

6 Geoffrey Marshall and Graeme C Moodie *Some Problems of the Constitution* (Hutchison, London, 1959) at 27.

7 For example, the Prime Minister countersigns the Commission appointing a New Zealand Governor-General — see Chapter 7 The Office of Governor-General and Commander-in-Chief, under the subheading Appointments are made by the Sovereign, at 118.

8 *Some Problems of the Constitution*, above n 6, at 41.

9 At 41.

were broken. The remedies may often be drastic. They may include the Governor-General's dismissal of the Prime Minister; the Queen's dismissal of the Governor-General on the Prime Minister's advice; and, in an extreme case, the office of Governor-General and of the Sovereign herself might be put at risk.

The Crown

The second concept that serves to reconcile ancient notions of personal rule with modern democratic government and bureaucracy is the idea of "the Crown".

Numerous powers and rules associated with government are attributed to the Sovereign by law. These special powers and privileges are commonly associated with governmental authority, whatever form a constitutional government takes. (In the United States, for example, on the birth of the republic, many of the powers of the former Sovereign were simply relocated in the elected President.) The Sovereign's prerogative took the form of powers, privileges and immunities. Prerogative powers included powers to act in an emergency and to maintain public order, powers associated with the conduct of war, the power to take property for public use, and the power to pardon convicted prisoners. The Sovereign also enjoys special privileges, including protection from being sued, and in litigation more generally. A statute does not bind the Sovereign, for example, unless the statute explicitly says so.[10] The exact definition and enumeration of these various powers and privileges need not detain us here. The extent of such powers and privileges has, over time, come to be defined and limited by statute and the courts. Consistent with the Bill of Rights 1689, which is also part of the law of New Zealand,[11] Parliament has the power to define, constrain and limit[12] the Sovereign's prerogative powers. The courts are also able to both define the scope of prerogatives and to supervise the manner of their exercise.

In the United Kingdom, New Zealand, and elsewhere in the Commonwealth, the practical exercise of such powers by Ministers and officials rather than the Sovereign personally is made possible, not only by formal delegation, but also by the notion of the Crown. The concept of the Crown which underlies references to Her Majesty, the Sovereign, or the Governor-General represents the

10 This presumption is given statutory expression in New Zealand in the Interpretation Act 1999, s 27.
11 Imperial Laws Application Act 1989.
12 The associated consent procedure is discussed in Chapter 11 The Governor-General in Parliament, under the subheading Consent to Bills, at 244–246.

state as an abstract, perpetual legal person in whom the assets and liabilities of the state vest and the powers, prerogatives and immunities of the state inhere.

The Queen and Crown as a corporation

The legal personality of the New Zealand state derives from the natural person of the Sovereign. The Sovereign acting in her political, as distinct from her personal, capacity is considered to be a special kind of common law corporation — usually (though not always or necessarily) referred to as "the Crown". This concept serves a number of important practical purposes. The Crown signifies a legal person and office which endures over time and outlives particular Sovereigns and governments. It also represents a legal actor who can own land and other assets, borrow money, enter into contracts, sue and be sued, and exercise prerogative and other powers on behalf of the whole of government. Importantly, for present purposes, the Crown, considered as a corporation, is one of the means by which actions of Ministers and civil servants can be treated in law as the actions of the New Zealand state. Through this framework, Ministers and civil servants are, under certain conditions, able to share in the Sovereign's privileges and immunities.[13] Most fundamental of all, the natural person of the Queen constitutes a number of distinct common law corporations which represent her different realms. After the Balfour Declaration, discussed in Chapter 2, the Crown became "divisible" not just politically but legally. The Crown was able to enjoy separate legal personality in respect of each of her realms.[14] If we did not have the Queen in right of New Zealand and the Crown to supply the corporate legal personality of New Zealand, we would need something else.

It is because the idea of the Crown as a corporation has had to do such a lot of work, including adapting rules originally designed for a time of personal rule to modern parliamentary and bureaucratic government, that the exact nature of the Crown as a corporation remains somewhat obscure. The common law is not settled about the precise characteristics of this special corporation and the case law is sparse, confusing and mainly English in origin. Ministers and public servants are sometimes considered to be the means by which the Crown acts but not as constituting the Crown itself. Sometimes Ministers have been treated as the Crown's "alter ego". Another view is that the Sovereign, Ministers and public servants together *constitute* the Crown as a corporation aggregate.

13 There is a controversy about whether the Crown also supplies the legal personality to exercise ordinary person powers such as to enter into contracts, publish materials and so on.

14 This has been recognised by the courts in, for example, *R v Secretary of State for Foreign and Commonwealth Affairs* [1982] QB 892.

Not only is the case law confusing, current New Zealand legislative usage also appears to be inconsistent.[15]

A functional analysis may help to explain the different approaches. A narrow view of the Crown (as referring to the Sovereign alone) may be an appropriate way of understanding the function of the state as property owner and the bearer of liabilities. So, to take an example, the Land Act 1948 vests land in Her Majesty and describes grants of fee simple title as issuing from Her Majesty. This wording clearly treats the Crown as a "corporation sole" (to use a technical legal term). The monarch does not "own" the land for her personal use; it vests in her in her political capacity as the legal representative of the New Zealand state as a whole. Her Majesty is the legal person in whom the real property of the state and underlying title vests. She acts in her political capacity and by means of her New Zealand servants (as the common law has traditionally viewed her officials). However odd this legal fiction may seem, it would be even more odd to suggest that Ministers and civil servants too are part of the Crown or the state for the purpose of property ownership. We return to the discussion of this particular legal fiction shortly.

There has been a different legal controversy about who constitutes the Crown for the purpose of suing public officials for legal wrongdoing. It arises from the common law precept that the "King can do no wrong". Under the common law, Crown servants (comprising public servants and Ministers), but not the Crown itself, could be held personally liable in tort for intentional or negligent wrongdoing. That was held to be so even if the Crown servant were acting under superior orders. The 19th-century English case *Viscount Canterbury v Attorney-General*[16] has been understood as holding that the Crown cannot be held vicariously liable for the acts and omissions of its servants.

Even though in practice the government regularly indemnified its liable servants, judges and academics have long criticised these ideas as ill-fitting modern government bureaucracy.[17] Various suggestions for reform have since been mooted: the Crown could be seen as including Ministers and public servants for liability purposes with the effect that either public servants could *share* in the Crown's immunity; or that the Crown could be

15 The Public Finance Act 1989, for example, defines the Crown or Sovereign as meaning: "the Sovereign in right of New Zealand; and including Ministers and all Departments" but an amendment to the Act by the Public Finance (Mixed Ownership Model) Amendment Act 2012 defines the Crown as the Queen in right of New Zealand but does not include Ministers explicitly within that definition.

16 (1843) 41 ER 648.

17 See, for example, *Adams v Naylor* [1946] AC 543 (HL); Martin Loughlin "The State, the Crown and the Law" in Maurice Sunkin and Sebastian Payne (eds) *The Nature of the Crown: A Legal and Political Analysis* (Oxford University Press, New York, 1999) 33 at 33.

held directly liable for the wrongful actions of its officials; or the Crown could simply be made vicariously liable for the actions of its servants (assuming financial liability but not moral blame for the wrongful actions). The latter approach was adopted in New Zealand through the enactment of the Crown Proceedings Act 1950. It makes provision for the Crown to be held vicariously liable for tortious actions committed by its servants (reversing the rule in *Viscount Canterbury*).

What has remained unclear as a matter of New Zealand law, however, is whether the Crown Proceedings Act 1950 allows for the common law development of an action against the Crown *directly* for a collective or systemic failure involving multiple wrongdoers or agencies. A recent Law Commission report recommended that such an action should be possible. Although the government rejected this particular recommendation, the Law Commission report led to the amendment of section 6 of the Crown Proceedings Act 1950 to allow the Crown itself to be sued in tort in situations in which its employees are immune under section 86 of the State Sector Act 1988. Whatever was originally intended by the amendment, the implication is that the Crown can now be held directly liable in tort for the actions of Crown employees, acting in good faith in the performance of their duties, functions or powers, while enjoying a legislative grant of immunity under the State Sector Act.[18] The full implications of these changes are still to be tested in the courts. For present purposes, this example shows that who or what constitutes the Crown is affected by legislation, the common law and the nature of the legal issue at stake. Context is everything.

To give another example of how the Crown is differently conceived in different contexts, the Treaty of Waitangi Act 1975 not only treats the Crown as capable of wrongdoing (in breaching the Treaty of Waitangi) but it defines the Crown in the very broadest terms (though notably it largely leaves matters of redress to political rather than legal judgement).[19]

The broader lesson which we can take from the modern New Zealand practice is that the Crown is defined differently according to the policy implications of a particular area of law. How the Crown is conceived of as a legal person depends on the function which the Crown is performing, and how the particular area of law — contract, tort, property, administrative law — constructs the Crown. For example, the common law rules which attach to the Crown ensure that Crown agents cannot be held liable for the contracts

18 Ministers of the Crown (who are not employees) are only entitled to indemnification rather than immunity: see Law Commission *The Crown in Court: A Review of the Crown Proceedings Act and National Security Information in Proceedings* (NZLC R135, 2015).

19 For a discussion see Chapter 13 The Crown as a Party to the Treaty of Waitangi.

made by them on behalf of the Crown. In this respect the common law rules of agency treat Crown servants differently from other agents. Contextualised legal and policy analyses need to be undertaken into who constitutes the Crown rather than some general theoretical inquiry. The answer Parliament chooses, however, will have consequences for whether the Crown is understood to be a corporation aggregate or sole for the particular purpose.

Modern managerial and legislative practice has tended to give legal status to the Chief Executives of government departments. They, and not the Crown, employ public servants. They administer departmental funds that are separate from the consolidated fund. They are a repository of immunities under section 86 of the State Sector Act. They are often granted powers by statute. One could well argue that in contemporary public administration and the work-a-day world of government, Chief Executives provide the legal personality or quasi-personality for government departments.

The legal concept of the Crown serves a purpose even here, however, in providing the background or default rules which allow the bureaucracy to operate notwithstanding changes in organisational and managerial fashion. There have periodically been pleas for a more "whole of government approach". The idea of the Crown represents that more holistic sense of the government enterprise working to a single purpose. The legal personality of the Crown can help to repair defects in conferrals of power, to maintain continuity during periods of departmental restructuring, and to contribute to policy coherence despite departmental silo cultures. In seeking to modernise understandings of the Crown, there is a need to ensure that the new concepts will outlast changes in bureaucratic and managerial fashion. The functional usefulness of the underlying concept of the Crown helps to explain its longevity.

References to the Queen and Crown in New Zealand law are pervasive, inconsistent with one another and conceptually difficult. If anything, New Zealand's legal and political practice refers much more often to the Crown than its Canadian, Australian and even UK counterparts. The proliferation of the "Crown" terminology in legislation such as the Crown Entities Act 2004 and the different understandings of the Crown in the Treaty of Waitangi context have not clarified matters.

Even so, many of the ideas associated with constitutional monarchy were beginning to develop long before Aotearoa/New Zealand became a colony. Constitutional conventions and the flexible concept of the Crown have together continued to aid in the modernisation and democratisation of the New Zealand constitution, notwithstanding the fact that the legal powers and immunities once associated with monarchy but still useful for present-day governments still reside in the Queen. In the next section we discuss one aspect of the British understanding of constitutional monarchy which did not survive its transplantation to Aotearoa/New Zealand intact and had to be adjusted to local circumstances. According to English law, British subjects bring the common law with them to a settled colony so far as it is applicable to the circumstances of the colony. Sometimes the imported law has to be adjusted to local circumstances. We noted earlier that the monarch supplies the legal personality for the ownership of state assets and property, including real property. She is also considered to hold the "underlying title" to land. We return now to the legal fiction that the Queen holds title to all land and discuss its implications in the New Zealand context.

The Queen as the repository of land and underlying title

There are two different kinds of Crown interests in land according to English law and international practice. These are *imperium* (referring to the territorial interest or underlying title) and *dominium* (referring to the property or ownership interest). It is the former territorial interest or underlying title which is associated with the monarch's right of jurisdiction and sovereignty. The distinction between *imperium* and *dominium* is sometimes hard to grasp. This is due to feudal aspects attaching to the common law notion of tenure and the difficulties in applying laws developed in England to the unique circumstances of New Zealand.

In the system of feudal landholding established in England after the Norman Conquest, *imperium* and *dominium* tended to be merged: "all England was not merely the territory but also the property of the Crown".[20] According to the Norman theory of tenure, all land was held of some lord and ultimately of the Crown. At the time of conquest, King William parcelled up the country and granted it to his followers. The King's grant gave rights over land and created services due in relation to land within an elaborate social hierarchy with the King at its apex. Land was said to be "held of the Crown" rather than "owned" by it in a modern sense. Landholding connoted public and reciprocal duties.

Some of the lands taken at the time of the conquest still make up the "Crown Estate" in England and Scotland. The Crown Estate also includes what is left of the church land taken during the Reformation, land taken by the Crown on the abolition of the Scottish episcopacy, land taken through enclosure and forfeiture, land that has reverted to the Crown because of the property owner's death without heirs (escheat) and land which has been purchased (such as Regent Street). In other words, the Crown Estate is made up of some land

20 John William Salmond *Jurisprudence* (6th ed, Stevens & Haynes, London, 1920) at 495.

which has its origins in feudal tenure and which once vested in the monarch at a time of personal rule (ancient possessions), land which has reverted to or been taken by the Crown in the exercise of its special powers, and land which has been acquired by ordinary purchase.[21]

These lands were voluntarily surrendered to Parliament and the Treasury by George III in 1760 and have been surrendered at the beginning of each subsequent reign. Since that time the Crown Estate has been administered and controlled by independent trustees. In return, the monarch receives out of the surplus revenues a sum to pay for the official expenses of her office. This was called the Civil List. The Sovereign Grant Act 2011 set the individual agreements between incoming monarchs and incumbent governments on a firmer footing. The Civil List has been abolished. The Queen now receives a percentage of the surplus revenues of the Crown Estate.[22] These revenues pay for maintaining the royal household and the royal palaces and residences, and for travel to royal engagements on behalf of the UK Government. The Queen, as Duke of Lancaster, holds the Duchy of Lancaster as well as other estates, and her heir holds the Duchy of Cornwall.

In addition to establishing that the New Zealand taxpayer does not pay for the Queen or her office (except for royal visits to New Zealand), the important point arising from the discussion so far is that the Crown Estate in the United Kingdom has historical origins different from those which apply to New Zealand Crown lands and to the notion of the Crown grant in New Zealand. New Zealand lands were never personal to the monarch and the applicable legal concepts do not represent the remnants of a time of personal rule.

As we have mentioned, the law of England at the time of the acquisition of the colony was carried with them by the English settlers and became part of the law of New Zealand in 1840 but only "so far as applicable to the circumstances of the Colony of New Zealand".[23] How much of the English law of tenure applied in New Zealand? In the earliest New England colonies the Crown had exacted quit rents from its lands, as one of the burdens of feudal tenure.[24] That practice changed after 1660 when, according to English law,

21 See the text and appendix to Ralph B Pugh *The Crown Estate: An Historical Essay* (HM Stationery Office, London, 1960).

22 The Queen has voluntarily paid tax since 1993.

23 English Laws Act 1858 (UK), s 1.

24 G Edward White *Law in American History, Volume 1: From the Colonial Years Through the Civil War* (Oxford University Press, New York, 2012) at 90. Tenures were abolished in Virginia in 1779. The Constitution of the State of New York, s 11 states: "The people of this State, in their right of Sovereignty, are deemed to possess the original and ultimate property in and to all lands within the jurisdiction of the State; and all lands the title to which shall fail from a defect of heirs, shall revert or escheat to the people."

new grants of lands came to be held in "free and common socage" (or free of any pledge of exchange). New Zealand lands, therefore, were never understood as being subject to feudal obligations. But other residual concepts relating to feudal tenure have lingered and there have been conflicting understandings of the *extent* to which they do and should apply in New Zealand.

The common law, as well as international law, understands the Crown to hold underlying title — sometimes referred to as radical title. Underlying title refers to the Crown's sovereign and jurisdictional interest in territory. The common law has also considered the Crown to be the *source* of all title and the owner of "unoccupied" lands.

The circumstances in the colonies were very different from those in England where existing estates were well known and established in the law, the law of primogeniture restricted the ability to alienate lands, and unoccupied land was relatively scarce. A potential claim by the Sovereign to unoccupied land for which no subject could show a title was potentially much more significant in its application to a new colony. In New Zealand, the Land Claims Ordinance 1841 gave effect to this doctrine. It declared as vested in the Queen or Crown, dominion or proprietary rights over all unappropriated lands in the colony. By this Ordinance, unappropriated or waste lands became the "Crown or Domain lands of her Majesty, her heirs and successors" but the Crown's property interest was explicitly made "subject to the rightful and necessary occupation and use thereby of the aboriginal inhabitants of the said colony". The same Ordinance affirmed that part of Article II of the Treaty of Waitangi giving Her Majesty sole right of pre-emption — that is, the exclusive right to purchase lands from Māori.

The Imperial Waste Lands Act 1842 and successive Lands Acts of the New Zealand Parliament required land to be freed from Māori interests before the Crown could dispose of it by grant to settlers. The Crown acquired land under that Act by means of purchase and extinguishment of Māori customary land and by the acquisition of waste lands. Such land vested in Her Majesty, and certificates of title to such land are still in her name.

Existing Māori property rights became recognised as one set of "relevant circumstances" that affected the application of English law in New Zealand. By 1840, both international and the applicable common law recognised existing native property rights to land and other possessions even upon cession of their sovereignty. (New Zealand, unlike Australia, was never viewed as *terra nullius* or unoccupied). The recognition of existing native title is also evident in the terms of Article II of the Treaty of Waitangi itself. An example of how the English common law was considered subject to local circumstances and existing property rights can be found in the judgment of Stout CJ in *Baldick v Jackson*.[25] The Chief Justice held that the statute of Edward II concerning the King's revenue and treating whales as a royal fish:[26]

> has no applicability to New Zealand, and though the right to whales is expressly claimed in the statute of 17 Ed II, c 2, as part of the Royal prerogative, it is one not only that has never been claimed, but one that it would have been impossible to claim without claiming it against the Maoris, for they were accustomed to engage in whaling; and the Treaty of Waitangi assumed that their fishing was not to be interfered with — they were to be left in undisturbed possession of their lands, estates, forests, fisheries, etc.

The question of the extent to which Crown radical title to land was and remains informed by feudal notions and how far it has been limited or otherwise affected by existing Māori interests has been the cause of numerous political and legal disputes — including, most recently, those over rights to the foreshore and seabed.

Even though feudal structures never applied in New Zealand, some remnants of a feudal *narrative* have lingered. According to feudal doctrine in English law, the Crown is the overlord of all land, and subjects hold land as mere tenants under grants emanating from the Crown. New Zealand legislation treats the Queen as the fount of all title to land (except Māori customary title). This entails not only artifice and fictions, but also presents difficulties of logic. As the Law Commission pointed out in its 1992 Preliminary Paper *Tenure and Estates in Land*,[27] "where the Crown owns land by acquisition or purchase, it may hold the land in fee simple from itself".[28] In making a case for reform, the Law Commission concluded that "no one creating a new property system today would contemplate introducing the concept of tenure".[29]

Given New Zealand's circumstances, the Sovereign's legal relationship to territory in New Zealand differs significantly in important respects from the English position.

What are the alternatives then, to the English legal notions that derive from feudal doctrines? A simple substitution of the Governor-General for Her Majesty as the deemed holder of underlying title and of title to the different kinds of public lands would not only maintain the current legal fictions, it would potentially compound them.

25 (1910) 30 NZLR 343 (HC).
26 At 344–345.
27 Law Commission *Tenure and Estates in Land* (PP20, 1992).
28 At 18.
29 At 18.

Some other, creative and New Zealand-specific, alternatives have been mooted: the idea of a feudal superior could be replaced by the idea of the Treaty of Waitangi as the source of all land title.[30] Title would be derived from the constitution (conceived of as stemming from the "people of the land" or tangata whenua) rather than from an individual "person". Different kinds of public or Crown land could vest in different sets of trustees on behalf of the people of New Zealand. This would provide an opportunity to delineate and systematise Crown land which is currently subject to a diverse range of regulatory regimes — for example, Land Act land, National Park and Reserve land and Conservation Act land.

In addition it would be possible to institute a system of allodial title by which land is held in the possession of the owner without being subject to any feudal superior. Allodial title would remove a number of anomalies in New Zealand's tenure system. The Crown would no longer be the grantor of fee simple title — either to itself or to anyone else. There are numerous models of systems of autonomous landholding subject to "public rights" operating in parts of Europe, Scotland and the US. Recognition that land is held in trust for future generations can be built into such a framework.

A novel New Zealand approach to these issues has already been taken in the Marine and Coastal Area (Takutai Moana) Act 2011. It identified different kinds of rights and duties relating to the foreshore and seabed, such as the Crown's radical or underlying title (sovereignty at domestic and international law, an ability to regulate), the public's rights (of navigation and access), duties to maintain structures, and so on. But rather than declaring any one the owner (questions of ownership being the very point of political contention), the Marine and Coastal Area (Takutai Moana) Act 2011 declared that no one owns or is capable of owning the foreshore and seabed. The effect of the statute is to delineate the different kinds of interests in such areas.

The Sovereign currently serves as the legal person in whom public land and underlying title vests. She, in her corporate and political capacity, is also conceived of as the person who grants fee simple and lesser forms of title. Going forward, there are a number of ways to conceptualise land title without recourse to feudal or colonial narratives, whatever form the New Zealand constitution as a whole may take.

30 The idea apparently originated in Professor Alex Frame's legal advice to the government in relation to Treaty of Waitangi settlements.

4
CONCLUSION

In this chapter we have explained the crucial part that constitutional conventions and the concept of the Crown play in democratising and modernising the monarchical constitution. We shall come back to constitutional conventions again in the context of choosing Prime Ministers, dissolving Parliaments, calling elections and assenting to legislation. We have introduced too the idea of the Crown as supplying the New Zealand state with the legal personality to hold assets, spend money, to sue and be sued. As we shall see in more detail in Chapter 13, in its many and nuanced forms, it is also a fundamental part of the Treaty of Waitangi relationship today.

Many of these notions were inherited from Britain more or less intact. Other aspects of constitutional monarchy, in particular feudal notions of land tenure and sovereign grant of land, have had to be adapted to the unique circumstances of New Zealand.

Having explained some of the history of colonisation, and some of the core concepts which will inform the remaining chapters, we now consider recent developments in the institution of the monarchy itself as it operates in respect of New Zealand — including changes to the law of succession.

CHAPTER 4

The Sovereign in Right of New Zealand: The Institutional Role

1 THE CONSTITUTIONAL HERITAGE

Queen Elizabeth II accedes to the throne

"*The King is dead. Long live the Queen.*" Those are the stark words that traditionally announce the death of an English monarch and the accession to the throne of his or her successor. King George VI died in his sleep early on the morning of 6 February 1952.[1] Reflecting the maxim "the King never dies", and in accordance with the law governing succession, his elder daughter, Princess Elizabeth, immediately acceded to the throne. No formalities were required in order to bring this about, but some consequential procedures followed.

Meetings of the Accession Council

As soon as practicable, the Accession Council met in London to proclaim the successor. The Accession Council comprised all the members of the Sovereign's Privy Council and certain other leading citizens. In United Kingdom law, the Accession Proclamation overcomes what is thought to be a common law rule that all things done by or in respect of a reigning Sovereign lapse on his or her demise. The Accession Proclamation continues in existence any

1 "The London Gazette Extraordinary of Wednesday, 6 February 1952" (6 February 1952) 39457 *The London Gazette* 755 at 755.

Parliament then in being. But if Parliament is then adjourned or prorogued, it is required to meet. When it does so, members of both Houses must take a fresh oath of allegiance to the new Sovereign. The Accession Proclamation also continues the use of the Great Seal and other seals, and the holding of all offices under the Crown.

The Accession Proclamation proclaimed that:[2]

> . . . the High and Mighty Princess Elizabeth Alexandra Mary is now, by the Death of our late Sovereign of Happy Memory, become Queen Elizabeth the Second, by the Grace of God Queen of this Realm and of all Her other Realms and Territories, Head of the Commonwealth, Defender of the Faith.

When the Accession Council met again on 8 February, the Queen made her Accession Declaration. She declared that she would work to uphold constitutional government and to advance the happiness and prosperity of her peoples, spread as they were the world over:[3]

> . . . I shall be inspired by the loyalty and affection of those whose Queen I have been called to be, and by the counsel of their elected Parliaments.

Among the "representatives of the other members of the Commonwealth"[4] who attended one or both meetings of the Accession Council were the New Zealand High Commissioner in London, and, as members of the Privy Council,[5] the Prime Minister of New Zealand, the Rt Hon Sidney Holland, and the Leader of the Opposition, the Rt Hon Walter Nash, both of whom happened to be in London at the time.

Proclamations in New Zealand

The news of the King's death reached New Zealand late in the evening of Wednesday 6 February 1952. The Governor-General received formal notice from the King's Private Secretary at 1.10 am on 7 February. By then, the Cabinet had already arranged to meet.[6] The first official response was the

2 "Supplement to the London Gazette Extraordinary of Wednesday, 6th February, 1952" (7 February 1952) 39458 *The London Gazette* 757 at 757 [Accession Proclamation].

3 "Second Supplement to The London Gazette Extraordinary of Wednesday, 6th February, 1952" (8 February 1952) 39463 *The London Gazette* 837 at 837.

4 Accession Proclamation, above n 2.

5 The appointment of New Zealand holders of high political office as members of the Privy Council was an honour granted by the Sovereign on the advice of the United Kingdom Prime Minister, acting at the request of the Prime Minister of New Zealand.

6 As already noted above, the Prime Minister, the Rt Hon Sidney Holland, was then in Europe.

Acting Prime Minister's formal, black-bordered notice of the King's death, published the next morning.[7]

Later in the morning, the Governor-General made an Order in Council containing recommendations about the public observance of mourning for the late King, and directing that the New Zealand ensign be flown at half-mast on public buildings until sunset on the day of the King's funeral. Made in the exercise of the prerogative, the Order carefully distinguished between the things that the Governor-General, acting on the advice of his Ministers, had the power to order, and those trenching on the rights of the people — the holding of solemn services of public worship and mourning, and the display by all ships in port of their ensigns at half-mast. In respect of those things, the Governor-General in Council[8] could issue only an "invitation".[9]

Later that day, the Governor-General, again acting on advice, made a Proclamation for the purposes of the Demise of the Crown Act 1908,[10] formally notifying the death of the King.[11] "Demise" is a technical term referring to the transfer or devolution of property or powers, especially on a person's death. "Demise" thus came to refer to the death itself, especially of the Sovereign.[12] As in the United Kingdom, the 1908 Act preserved the effect of things done in New Zealand by the former Sovereign. The existing Parliament remained in office, and, if not in session, it was not required to meet until the time already set. Then, however, the Members of Parliament were required to take a fresh oath of allegiance to the new Sovereign. The sole purpose of the proclamation was to preserve the force of things done in the former Sovereign's name after the demise of the Crown and before the publication in the Gazette of a Proclamation notifying the demise.[13] That provision reflected the fact that it had once taken a long time for news of the Sovereign's demise to reach New Zealand.[14]

7 *New Zealand Gazette Extraordinary* No 8 (7 February 1952) 159.

8 In an enactment, "Governor-General in Council" or a similar expression means "the Governor-General acting on the advice and with the consent of the Executive Council": Interpretation Act 1999, s 29.

9 "Death of His Majesty — Public Observance of Mourning" *New Zealand Gazette Extraordinary* No 8 (7 February 1952) 159.

10 The 1908 Act had consolidated earlier New Zealand legislation which, in turn, had replaced the inherited United Kingdom statutes that had originally established the consequences of the demise of the Crown.

11 "Proclamation notifying the Demise of the Crown" *New Zealand Gazette Extraordinary* No 9 (7 February 1952) 161.

12 See William Little *The Shorter Oxford Dictionary on Historical Principles* (3rd ed, Clarendon Press, 1944). See also *Constitutional Reform: First and Second Reports released by the Minister of Justice, the Hon. Geoffrey Palmer* (Department of Justice, Wellington, 1986) at 33.

13 Demise of the Crown Act 1908, s 4.

14 The Demise of the Crown Act 1908 has now been replaced by a provision in the Constitution Act that, on the death of the Sovereign, all things done during his or her reign retain their full effect: see Constitution Act 1986, s 5.

On Monday 11 February a Proclamation of Accession[15] heralding the new Queen was publicly read out on the steps of Parliament. It was signed by the Governor-General, the Acting Prime Minister, the other members of the Cabinet, the Chief Justice, the Acting Leader of the Opposition, and the senior Member of Parliament for a Māori electoral district, as a representative of the Māori people. All flags on public buildings were mast-headed from the time of the proclamation until sunset that day, before again being flown at half-mast until after the funeral of the late King.

As in London, the Proclamation of Accession publicly read in Wellington was not required by any law. It can, however, be seen as signifying the will of the people of New Zealand that the new Sovereign should reign over them. In announcing the Queen's accession to the throne, the Proclamation included the royal style and titles by which she would initially be known in New Zealand.[16] The wording followed exactly that of the Accession Proclamation made in the United Kingdom. But, in the New Zealand proclamation, "this realm" was New Zealand, not the United Kingdom. The royal style and titles of the new Sovereign had yet to receive the assent of the Parliaments of all the Commonwealth realms,[17] but the formulation that the United Kingdom — and New Zealand — had used in their Accession Proclamations foreshadowed the eventual outcome, a matter discussed below.

One Sovereign, many realms

"Equal in status, in no way subordinate to one another"[18]

We chose to begin this chapter on the Sovereign as Queen of New Zealand with the accession to the throne of Queen Elizabeth II because, for the first time on the death of the monarch, the formal accession processes in the United Kingdom were carefully designed to take full and explicit account of all the new Sovereign's constitutional roles.[19] The Queen's accession to the throne

15 "Proclamation of Accession of Her Majesty Queen Elizabeth II" *New Zealand Gazette Extraordinary* No 12 (11 February 1952) 197. The form of the Proclamation had been approved by Order in Council on 8 February.

16 In contrast to the position in the United Kingdom, the Proclamation was not required by law. A separate Proclamation for the purposes of the Demise of the Crown Act 1908, then in force, and requiring only the announcement of the King's death, had already been made.

17 Statute of Westminster 1931 (UK) 22 & 23 Geo V c 4, Preamble. See Chapter 2 Building the Modern Constitution, after fn 61 at 28–29.

18 See the discussion of the Balfour Declaration in Chapter 2 Building the Modern Constitution, after fn 51, at 25–26.

19 For the procedures followed at the time of the accession of King George VI, after the abdication of King Edward VIII, see below, this chapter, around fn 45, at 57–58.

of the United Kingdom also made her the Queen of what were then her six other realms.[20]

In parts 2 to 4 of the chapter we discuss three aspects of the Sovereign's status and attributes in respect of her role as Queen of New Zealand. The first is the law governing the succession to the Crown. That law has recently been modernised so that, in future, the female and the male members of the royal family will become heirs to the throne in the order of their birth, without regard to their gender. The second is the royal style and titles of Queen Elizabeth II as the Queen of New Zealand. While still including an element common to all her realms, they now take a form approved by the New Zealand Parliament. The third is the Queen's coronation, a religious ceremony performed in Westminster Abbey but designed to be meaningful for New Zealand and her other realms. Although the Sovereign is the Head of the Church of England, the Sovereign has never been the Head of what is now the Anglican Church in Aotearoa, New Zealand and Polynesia. The coronation ceremony is now in a form which recognises the diversity of the Sovereign's subjects. In her Realm of New Zealand she has a purely secular role.[21] In New Zealand itself, all citizens and foreigners within her protection owe allegiance to the Queen in right of New Zealand.[22]

With that introduction, we now pick up the story we had begun. By what right did the Princess Elizabeth Alexandra Mary become, on the death of her father in 1952, Queen of the United Kingdom and of her other realms, including New Zealand?

2
THE LAW OF SUCCESSION

The development of the law of succession

The Constitution Act 1986 now expressly recognises that, on the death of the Sovereign, all the functions, duties, powers, authorities, rights, privileges and dignities belonging to the Crown pass to the Sovereign's successor,

20 Canada, Australia, New Zealand, South Africa, Pakistan and Ceylon. Since then, South Africa, Pakistan and what is now Sri Lanka have become republics, and a number of other Commonwealth countries became independent as monarchies. Others have retained their monarchical constitutions. The Queen now reigns over 16 realms: the United Kingdom, Canada, Australia, New Zealand, Jamaica, Barbados, the Bahamas, Grenada, Papua New Guinea, the Solomon Islands, Tuvalu, Saint Lucia, Saint Vincent and the Grenadines, Belize, Antigua and Barbuda, St Kitts and Nevis.

21 See below, this chapter, around fn 89 ff, at 66–69.

22 See below, this chapter, around fn 115 ff, at 70–71.

as determined in accordance with the Act of Settlement 1700 (UK)[23] and the other law of New Zealand.[24] The provision applies to all the prerogative and statutory powers and other attributes of the Crown.[25]

A hereditary right to the throne had always been important, although the Anglo-Saxon Kings were elected by the Witan or Great Council, from among members of the royal family — a practice still reflected in the coronation ceremony of the present day.[26] After the Norman Conquest the notion of a hereditary right to the throne grew stronger as it became associated with the feudal law governing the descent of land. Even so, kingship based on parliamentary endorsement was always important.

The Reformation brought bitter division between the supporters of Kings and Queens who had adopted the Protestant religion and of those who wanted a monarch adhering to the Church of Rome. James II who had converted to Catholicism was seen by his opponents as having abused the rights and liberties of his subjects. The Bill of Rights[27] declared that James II had abdicated, that the throne had become vacant, and that William and Mary, Prince and Princess of Orange, had jointly become the King and Queen of England. It also made provision for the future succession,[28] debarring any person who was a Roman Catholic, or married to a Roman Catholic, from succeeding to or remaining on the throne. All persons acceding to the throne were required to take an oath of adherence to the Protestant religion.

In 1700, a further parliamentary settlement became necessary, to avoid a failure in the line of succession. The Act of Settlement 1700 settled the Crown on a granddaughter of James I, Princess Sophia, widow of the Elector of Hanover, and the heirs of her body being Protestants. The Act repeated the disqualification of any person who was a Roman Catholic or married

23 12 & 13 Will III c 2. The relevant provisions of the Act of Settlement, ss 1, 2 (as amended by the Succession Declaration Act 1910 (UK) 10 Edw VII & 1 Geo V c 29) and s 3 (omitting all the words after the words "the Church of England as by law established") continue to be part of the law of New Zealand: Imperial Laws Application Act 1988, s 3 and sch 1. The Accession Declaration Act 1910 (UK) has force in New Zealand law: Imperial Laws Application Act 1988, s 3(3).

24 Constitution Act 1986, s 5(1). That subsection refers to the Act of Settlement "and any other law relating to the succession to the throne", but, in the context, that can mean only "other law which has effect in New Zealand". The subsection then provides that otherwise, the death of the Sovereign is to have no effect in law for any purpose. That provision replaced the Demise of the Crown Act 1908.

25 Unless the context otherwise requires, the same rule applies to every reference to the Sovereign in any other document or instrument in force after 1 January 1987: Constitution Act 1986, s 5(2). The provision appears to refer to documents or instruments made or entered into by private persons or corporations. Compare the Demise of the Crown Act 1908, s 7.

26 *Halsbury's Laws of England* (4th ed, reissue, 1998) vol 8(2) Introduction: Basic Principles of the Constitution of the United Kingdom at [35].

27 Bill of Rights 1689 (UK) 1 Will & Mar Sess 2 c 2.

28 The declaration referred not only to "England" but also to "France and Ireland and the dominions thereunto belonging".

to a Roman Catholic, and also the requirement that all persons acceding to the Crown must "join in communion with the Church of England as by law established". Both the Bill of Rights 1689 and the Act of Settlement 1700 are part of the law of New Zealand.[29]

The effect of the law of succession

In establishing the line of succession to the throne, both the Bill of Rights and the Act of Settlement stipulate that, on the death of the ruling monarch, the "heirs of the body" of the deceased monarch succeeded to the Crown. The effect was to apply the common law rules of inheritance, which recognise the right of male primogeniture, as they applied to entailed interests in real property in England before 1926.[30] Accordingly, the Sovereign's eldest male child succeeded to the throne. A female child succeeded only if she had no living brothers. If there were two or more female heirs who were sisters, there was an exception to the law of primogeniture as it applied to land. The eldest sister succeeded to the throne.[31] Thus when King George VI died leaving no sons and two daughters, the elder daughter succeeded to the throne as Elizabeth II.[32]

Accordingly, the law concerning the succession gave preference to male heirs over females. It also disqualified heirs to the throne who were Roman Catholics, married to a Roman Catholic, or not in communion with the Church of England.

As the old religious schisms gave way to greater religious tolerance, the discriminatory nature of the law of succession would be questioned. But there were significant barriers to making any changes to the law. These obstacles were the product of statute and Commonwealth constitutional conventions, as we shall now explain.

29 Imperial Laws Application Act 1988, s 3 and sch 1.

30 *Halsbury's Laws of England* (4th ed, reissue, 1998) vol 12(1) Crown and Royal Family at [10]. An "entailed" interest was one that passed land on within a family, usually to one heir in each generation. In that way estates were kept intact and their economic viability was maintained. The common law rules of inheritance of land were abolished in the law of England by legislation in 1925, but that did not affect the law of succession to the throne.

31 At [10]. The sisters do not share the throne as coparceners; "coparcener" is a medieval legal term meaning someone who has a share or part in something with another or others.

32 At [10].

The Commonwealth conventions

The Statute of Westminster principles

The preamble to the Statute of Westminster 1931 (UK) recorded that:[33]

> . . . the Crown is the symbol of the free association of the members of the British Commonwealth of Nations, and as they are united by a common allegiance to the Crown, it would be in accord with the established constitutional position of all the members of the Commonwealth in relation to one another that any alteration in the law touching the succession to the throne or the royal style and titles shall hereafter require the assent as well of the Parliaments of all the Dominions as of the Parliament of the United Kingdom.

Even before adopting the Statute of Westminster,[34] New Zealand was bound by the conventions recorded in the preamble.[35] Although the Statute of Westminster is no longer part of the law of New Zealand,[36] the conventions recorded in the preamble remain binding, except so far as they have themselves undergone change.[37]

An early change to the law of succession

Surprisingly soon after the enactment of the Statute of Westminster 1931, Great Britain and the Dominions found it necessary to alter the law of succession to the throne in serious circumstances. They excluded from the line of succession a King who had been forced to renounce the throne because he was seen as making himself unfit to retain it.

On the death of King George V on 20 January 1936, his eldest son, Edward, the Prince of Wales, came to the throne as King Edward VIII. Later that year, the King's determination to marry Mrs Wallis Simpson, a twice-divorced American woman, met with the implacable opposition of the British Prime Minister, Stanley Baldwin, and his Cabinet. Although no formal advice on that matter was ever tendered to the King, Baldwin made it clear to him that the marriage would be unacceptable.[38] Both in Britain and the Dominions, there

33 Above n 17.
34 See Chapter 2 Building the Modern Constitution, after fn 61, at 29.
35 See Statute of Westminster, above n 17, s 10.
36 See Chapter 2 Building the Modern Constitution, fn 77, at 31.
37 Constitution Act 1986, s 26. For a recent analysis of the present-day situation see Anne Twomey "Changing the Rules of Succession to the Throne" (Sydney Law School, Legal Studies Research Paper No 11/71, October 2011) <http://ssrn.com/abstract=1943287>.
38 Vernon Bogdanor *The Monarchy and the Constitution* (Oxford University Press, Oxford, 1997) at 138.

was public support for Baldwin's stance. Marriage to a divorced woman would have been inconsistent with the King's role as Supreme Governor of the Church of England.[39] More fundamentally, divorce was still frowned upon, morally and socially. Many were concerned that the marriage might be so divisive as to threaten the stability of the monarchy itself.[40] Only the Government of the Irish Free State was prepared to acquiesce, disavowing any interest in the British Crown.[41]

In the face of that opposition, the King, on 10 December 1936, declared his irrevocable determination to renounce the throne for himself and his descendants.[42] Effect was given to the declaration in an Act of the United Kingdom Parliament passed the following day.[43] His Majesty's Declaration of Abdication Act 1936 recited that the Dominion of Canada, pursuant to section 4 of the Statute of Westminster 1931 (UK), had requested and consented to the enactment of the Act, and that the Commonwealth of Australia, the Dominion of New Zealand and the Union of South Africa had assented to it.[44] The Act took effect immediately on the giving of the royal assent by King Edward VIII, on 10 December 1936.

At the time, neither Australia nor New Zealand had adopted section 4 of the Statute of Westminster.[45] The assent of each to the enactment of the United Kingdom Act was given by their Parliaments, but by means of a resolution, rather than an Act. The South African assent to the United Kingdom Act was given only by the executive branch of government. Both Australia and South Africa chose to enact their own laws altering the law of succession, as did the Irish Free State. How the assent was to be indicated once the different realms had achieved further independence was to be tested by the 2011 proposals for change in the law of succession.

Modern change

An agreement in principle

With the October 2011 Commonwealth Heads of Government Meeting (CHOGM) about to begin in Perth, Western Australia, the United Kingdom Prime Minister, the Rt Hon David Cameron, publicly urged the Prime Ministers

39 See below, this chapter, after fn 92, at 66.
40 Bogdanor, above n 38, at 139.
41 At 141.
42 His Majesty's Declaration of Abdication Act 1936 (UK) 1 Edw VIII and 1 Geo VI c 3, Schedule.
43 Preamble.
44 Accordingly, it was not continued in force as part of New Zealand law by the Imperial Laws Application Act 1988.
45 See Chapter 2 Building the Modern Constitution, after fn 61, at 29.

of the 15 other realms of which the Queen is the Head of State to consider some important changes to the law of succession. On 28 October, Cameron announced that the Prime Ministers of the 16 Commonwealth nations concerned had taken the opportunity to meet together in Perth, and had reached unanimous agreement on the following points:[46]

> Firstly, we will end the male primogeniture rule, so that in future the order of succession should be determined simply by order of birth, and we have agreed to introduce this for all descendants of the Prince of Wales.
>
> Put simply, if [as their first child] the Duke and Duchess of Cambridge have a little girl, that girl will one day be our queen.[47]
>
> Second, we have agreed to scrap the rule which says that no one who marries a Roman Catholic can become monarch.
>
> Let me be clear, the monarch must be in communion with the Church of England because he or she is the head of that church.
>
> But it is simply wrong that they should be denied the chance to marry a Catholic if they wish to do so. After all, they are already quite free to marry someone of any other faith.
>
> We agreed today that this has to change.

The Prime Ministers undertook to work together towards a common approach, with a view to unanimously advising the Queen of their views and seeking her agreement.[48]

In her speech opening the 2011 Commonwealth Heads of Government Meeting in Perth, the Queen, speaking as the Head of the Commonwealth, referred to the theme of the year, "Women as Agents for Change":[49]

> It reminds us of the potential in our societies that is yet to be fully unlocked, and it encourages us to find ways to allow girls and women to play their full part. We must continue to strive in our own countries and across the Commonwealth together to promote that theme in a lasting way beyond this year.

46 Prime Minister's Office "Prime Minister unveils changes to Royal Succession" (28 October 2011) <www.number10.gov.uk/news/prime-Minister-unveils-changes-to-royal-succession/>.

47 In fact the first child was a boy, Prince George.

48 Commonwealth Secretariat Press Release "CHOGM 2011 Communiqué" (30 October 2011) <http://archive.kubatana.net/docs/demgg/chogm_communique_2011_111030.pdf>. Before signifying agreement in respect of the Realm of New Zealand, the New Zealand Prime Minister consulted the Prime Minister of the self-governing state of the Cook Islands, the Premier of the self-governing state of Niue and the Ulu of Tokelau. See further Chapter 6 The Letters Patent, the Governor-General and the Realm of New Zealand, after fn 15, at 110–112.

49 "The Queen at the CHOGM Opening Ceremony" (28 October 2011) The Commonwealth <http://thecommonwealth.org/media/news/queen-chogm-opening-ceremony>.

The speech was widely regarded as signalling the Queen's own approval of an important initiative affecting the future role of women within the royal family.

Commentators had earlier suggested that some of the other Commonwealth realms might regard the introduction of legislation affecting the monarchy as politically problematic,[50] so the unanimous agreement in principle was a pleasant surprise. New Zealand was asked, and agreed, to chair a working group that would seek to facilitate the implementation of the agreement in principle.[51] Coordination was necessary because any change in the succession to the Crown was a matter not just for the United Kingdom, but also the Sovereign's other realms, as we now explain.

The implementation of the 2011 agreement

The 1931 convention that any change in the law of succession to the Crown requires the consent of all the Commonwealth realms was expressed in a form which contemplated the passing of an Act by the United Kingdom Parliament, at the request and with the consent of the Parliaments of all the other realms, given by an Act of their own Parliaments, and taking effect as part of the law. Anne Twomey has shown that, even in 1936, not all the other realms were able or willing to get their Parliaments to enact authorising legislation in advance of the enactment of the legislation in the United Kingdom, rushed through so precipitously.[52]

By 2012, no other realm still gave the United Kingdom Parliament the power to make laws for it, even with its consent.[53] Acting alone, it would therefore need to take the first step in giving effect to the agreed changes to the law of succession, but the change could not be brought into force until the other Commonwealth realms had signified their consent in an appropriate way. The nearest they could come to the 1931 convention in its literal form was by enacting legislation themselves.[54] The Succession to the Crown Act 2013 (UK) received the royal assent on 25 April 2013, but it was not to come into force until a date and time set by Order in Council. In New Zealand, where the Act of Settlement 1700 and other relevant Imperial enactments had expressly

50 Rodney Brazier "Legislating about the Monarchy" (2007) 66(1) CLJ 86 at 102.
51 See Commonwealth Secretariat Press Release, above n 48.
52 Twomey, above n 37.
53 In respect of New Zealand see the Constitution Act 1986, s 15.
54 That was a course favoured by Anne Twomey "Two approaches to the application of succession to the throne in the realms" (unpublished paper, 2012).

been declared to be part of the law,[55] the Royal Succession Act 2013[56] closely followed the form of the United Kingdom Act,[57] as did the Australian Act.[58] The Canadian legislation attracted controversy and took the form of assent to the UK legislation.[59] Three other realms enacted legislation.[60]

The other nine realms took a different course.[61] The realms concerned took the view that legislation was unnecessary. They saw their constitutions as establishing that any reference to "the Sovereign" was a reference to the reigning King or Queen of the United Kingdom and her other realms. Constitutions in that form reflect the fact that, although the Crown is divisible in a legal sense, the same person is the King or Queen of each of the realms.[62]

The convention restated

On the basis of that recent experience, the convention governing changes to the law of succession can be restated. The need for the agreement of all the Sovereign's realms is still the governing principle. Any agreed change will need to be implemented in the law of the United Kingdom. Each of the other realms will need to decide what changes, if any, need to be made in its own constitution or other law. There will, however, be a need to ensure that, at all times, the same person is or will be the Sovereign in all of the Commonwealth realms.[63]

55 See above, this chapter, fn 23 and accompanying text at 54–55.

56 The Act received the Governor-General's consent on 17 December 2012, but the main operative provisions, pts 1 and 2, were to come into force at a time, and on a date, to be appointed by Order in Council.

57 The United Kingdom Act, the Succession to the Crown Act 2013 (UK), had amended the Royal Marriages Act 1772 which had also been declared to be part of the law of New Zealand. The New Zealand Act, however, declared that the Royal Marriages Act had ceased to be part of the law of New Zealand, while continuing to exclude from the succession close heirs to the throne who marry without the Queen's consent, but validating the marriages of those not close in the line of succession who had married without that consent: see Royal Succession Act 2013, ss 7, 8, 9 and 12.

58 Succession to the Crown Act 2015 (Cth).

59 Succession to the Throne Act C 2013 c 20. This was subject to unsuccessful challenge in *Tesky v Attorney-General* 2014 ONCA 612.

60 Barbados, St Kitts and Nevis and St Vincent and the Grenadines: see Bob Morris "The Succession to the Crown Act 2013 has landed" (13 April 2015) The Constitution Unit <https://constitution-unit.com/2015/04/13/the-succession-to-the-crown-act-2013-has-landed/>.

61 Antigua and Barbuda, the Bahamas, Belize, Grenada, Jamaica, Papua New Guinea, St Lucia, the Solomon Islands, Tuvalu: see Bob Morris, above, n 60.

62 Letter from Alison Quentin-Baxter to Rebecca Kitteridge (Clerk of the New Zealand Executive Council) (16 April 2012).

63 In New Zealand, the Royal Succession Act 2013 came into force at 1 pm on 26 March 2015 (New Zealand daylight time) per Royal Succession Act Commencement Order 2015, cl 2.

3
THE ROYAL STYLE AND TITLES

Their significance

Since William II came to the throne of England in 1087, the Kings and Queens of what is now the United Kingdom of Great Britain and Northern Ireland have adopted a particular style — or name — and titles — or descriptions — on coming to the throne.[64] Monarchs of the same name are distinguished by an ordinal number, retrospectively if necessary. Most, if not all, elements of the royal style and titles have a political or symbolic significance. The United Kingdom Parliament became the arbiter of what should be included and what should be left out.

By the Act of Union 1707 (UK),[65] Parliament gave effect to the Treaty of Union of the separate Kingdoms of Scotland and England. From then on, all formal changes made to the royal style and titles were authorised by the United Kingdom Parliament, generally or specifically. The preamble to the Statute of Westminster 1931 recognised that, in future, all the Commonwealth countries, sharing a common allegiance to the Sovereign, would need to consent to any further changes in the royal style and titles to be made by the United Kingdom Parliament.[66]

The first such change was made in the course of recognising the independence of India and its new republican constitution. The United Kingdom Parliament assented to the omission of the title "Emperor of India", in a provision of the Indian Independence Act 1947 (UK).[67] On 25 August 1947, the New Zealand Parliament assented to the omission, and to its implementation in a Royal Proclamation made under the Great Seal of the United Kingdom.[68] It was the last time that the Great Seal would be used on a royal document taking effect in the law of New Zealand. The subsequent decision of a Commonwealth conference that India would be admitted to membership of the Commonwealth even though it was a republic suggested the likelihood of further change.

64 "Royal Styles and Titles in England and Great Britain" <www.heraldica.org/topics/britain/royalstyle_uk.htm>.
65 6 Ann c 7. See also Union with Scotland (Amendment) Act (UK) 1707 6 Ann c 40.
66 See above, this chapter, fn 33 and accompanying text at 57.
67 10 & 11 Geo VI c 30, s 7(2).
68 Royal Titles Act 1947, s 2. The "Realm" there referred to was "Great Britain" which by then excluded "Ireland", although Ireland was still separately referred to in the royal style and titles of King George VI.

The royal style and titles of the Queen of New Zealand

In December 1952, the Commonwealth Prime Ministers met again to discuss the royal style and titles of Queen Elizabeth II, but, by then, it had become clear that it would be hard to reach agreement on a single version that would be acceptable to all.[69] In the Royal Titles Act 1953,[70] the New Zealand Parliament, for the first time, assented to the royal style and titles to be used by Her Majesty in respect of New Zealand. The preamble recorded the agreed solution.[71] First, there was a need for the royal style and titles of each to:

> . . . reflect more clearly the existing relations of the members of the Commonwealth to one another and their recognition of the Crown as the symbol of their free association and of the Sovereign as the Head of the Commonwealth.

Secondly, there was a need to permit the Commonwealth countries to alter the existing royal style and titles in a way that:[72]

> . . . while permitting the use, in relation to each of those countries, of a form suited to its particular circumstances, would retain a substantial element common to all.

SA de Smith saw the agreement as requiring each Commonwealth realm to include in its form of the royal style and titles:[73]

> (i) an appropriate territorial designation; and
> (ii) as a common element, the description of the Sovereign as Queen of her other realms and territories and Head of the Commonwealth.

He drew an analogy with the blend of elements of unity and diversity agreed upon with regard to citizenship legislation at the Commonwealth conference of experts in 1947.[74]

The 1953 Act assents to the adoption by Her Majesty, for use in relation to New Zealand and all other territories for whose foreign relations her government in New Zealand was responsible,[75] of the following style and titles:

69 SA de Smith "The Royal Style and Titles" (1953) 2(2) Int & Comp LQ 263 at 269.
70 The New Zealand Act was modelled on the Royal Titles Act 1953 (UK) 1 & 2 Eliz II c 9.
71 The United Kingdom, Canada, Australia, New Zealand, the Union of South Africa, Pakistan, and Ceylon.
72 Royal Titles Act 1953, Preamble.
73 de Smith, above n 69, at 270.
74 See de Smith, above n 69, at 270, nn 16 and 17.
75 As to the territories concerned, see Chapter 6 The Letters Patent, the Governor-General and the Realm of New Zealand, under the subheading The territorial reach of the Letters Patent, at 104–106.

> Elizabeth the Second, by the Grace of God Queen of the United Kingdom, New Zealand and Her Other Realms and Territories, Head of the Commonwealth, Defender of the Faith.

It authorised the issue by Her Majesty of Her Royal Proclamation for that purpose.[76] The Queen issued the Proclamation at the Court of St James on 28 May 1953.[77] It was not sealed. At the time there was no New Zealand Seal available for that purpose, a gap that has since been filled.[78] That is where the concerted decision-making about the royal style and titles of Commonwealth realms formally rests, but much has happened since.

Early in 1974, the New Zealand Parliament followed the example of Australia[79] in providing that:[80]

> The royal style and titles of Her Majesty, for use in relation to New Zealand and all other territories for whose foreign relations Her Government in New Zealand is responsible shall be —
> Elizabeth the Second, by the Grace of God Queen of New Zealand and Her Other Realms and Territories, Head of the Commonwealth, Defender of the Faith . . .

Both countries omitted any reference to the Sovereign as Queen of the United Kingdom. In each, the United Kingdom now figures only as one of the Queen's "Other Realms".

The New Zealand Act reflected a desire that the royal style and titles should "reflect more clearly Her Majesty's position in relation to New Zealand and all [its] other territories".[81] In introducing the Bill for the Act, the Prime Minister, the Rt Hon Norman Kirk, explained that Her Majesty, who was then visiting New Zealand, positively welcomed the change which put the emphasis on her role as Queen of New Zealand. The Leader of the Opposition, the Rt Hon JR Marshall, said that the Bill reflected the existing practice of referring to the Queen as "Queen of New Zealand".[82] The country's independent status had become increasingly apparent in its foreign policy and international relations, highlighted as it had been by the decision of the British Government to join the European Economic Community.[83] On 6 February 1974, then known as

76 Royal Titles Act 1953, s 2.
77 Royal Titles Proclamation SR 1953/79. On the same date the Queen also issued Proclamations in respect of the other Commonwealth countries concerned.
78 Seal of New Zealand Act 1977.
79 See Royal Style and Titles Act 1973 (Cth), Schedule.
80 Royal Titles Act 1974, s 2.
81 Preamble.
82 (4 February 1974) 389 NZPD 3.
83 (4 February 1974) 389 NZPD 3.

New Zealand Day, Her Majesty, acting under a power conferred by Parliament to exercise in person any statutory power of the Governor-General,[84] assented to the Bill in person.[85] It was one of the ceremonial highlights of her visit.

In the Royal Titles Act 1974, the New Zealand law-makers, for the first time, focused on the various elements of the royal style and titles. We therefore set out something of their history, as well as the meaning they have come to have today.

The elements of the royal style and titles

"By the Grace of God"

The use of that introductory phrase can be traced back to Anglo-Saxon Kings. Though obviously reflecting the coming to England of Christianity, and the later perception that the Sovereign ruled "under God and the law",[86] the reference to the deity is non-specific. Unlike the title "Defender of the Faith" it does not appear to have been a major source of controversy.

"Queen of New Zealand and Her Other Realms and Territories"

The recognition that, in her person and also as an abstraction, the Queen has a distinct identity as Queen of New Zealand, while remaining Queen of her other realms and territories, is the mainspring of this chapter and of the book as a whole. The historical process that led to the political recognition of this divisibility was described in Chapter 2.[87] It must not be forgotten, however, that the Sovereign is Queen of New Zealand and her other realms because she is Queen of the United Kingdom. There is therefore a practical need for the law of all the realms to take due account of that reality.

"Head of the Commonwealth"

The title "Head of the Commonwealth" was first assumed by Queen Elizabeth II in her Accession Proclamation. Its inclusion reflected the desire of India, as a

84 Royal Powers Act 1953, s 2 and New Zealand Constitution Act 1852 (UK) 15 & 16 Vict c 72. See now Constitution Act 1986, ss 3 and 16.

85 The fact that the Sovereign has given the royal assent in person to a Bill for a New Zealand Act is not apparent from the printed form of the Act.

86 Made famous by Henry de Bracton; *Bracton on the Laws and Customs of England: Volume 2* (translated by Samuel E Thorne, William S Hein & Co, Buffalo (NY), 1997) at 33.

87 The courts also eventually recognised divisibility: see *R v Secretary of State for Foreign and Commonwealth Affairs* [1982] QB 892.

republic no longer owing allegiance to the Sovereign, to remain within the Commonwealth, and to acknowledge the King as "Head of the Commonwealth" and the symbol of the free association of its peoples.[88] The description is generally accepted as being the "common element" to which all of the Queen's realms are committed.[89]

"Defender of the Faith"

In contrast, the title "Defender of the Faith" is long-standing, but it became controversial shortly after it was first used, and remains controversial today. The privilege of using the title was conferred by the Pope on Henry VIII in 1521 for his reputed authorship of an anti-Lutheran treatise. Although the title was later withdrawn by Rome, it was retained by Queen Elizabeth I whose first Parliament recognised her role as the only Supreme Governor of the realm in all things spiritual or ecclesiastical, as well as temporal.[90] The title continued to be used by her successors, including the Protestant Sovereigns who were the Supreme Governor under God of the Church of England — a position the Sovereign still retains in England but not in other parts of the United Kingdom or its territories, or in her other realms.

Since 1952, however, the title "Defender of the Faith" has been seen as optional. Today it is still used only by the United Kingdom, Canada and New Zealand. Australia omitted the title in 1973 but it was retained in New Zealand when Parliament enacted the Royal Titles Act 1974. In the debate on the Bill for the Act, the Leader of the Opposition, the Rt Hon JR Marshall, disclosed that, in the original proposal for the Bill, the title "Defender of the Faith" had been omitted. In view, however, of some reservations within the National Party caucus, and after consultation with the Queen, who was in New Zealand at the time, there had been agreement to retain it.[91] He and the Prime Minister, the Rt Hon Norman Kirk, both noted that, in New Zealand, the phrase had acquired a broader and deeper meaning than its origins might

88 The London Declaration made by the governments of the Commonwealth of Nations on 28 April 1949. Its inclusion in the royal style and titles marked the departure from the old doctrine that the members of what was formerly known as the British Commonwealth were united by their common allegiance to the Crown.

89 See also Chapter 5 The Sovereign in Right of New Zealand: A Personal Touch, around fn 66, at 91, for a discussion of whether the Queen's successor will be the Head of the Commonwealth.

90 Ian Leigh "By Law Established? The Crown, Constitutional Reform and the Church of England" [2004] Public Law 266 at 267.

91 Agreement was a necessary element of the suspension of Standing Orders so as to permit the Bill to be passed through all its stages in a single day. Because the Queen was to be advised to assent to the Bill for the Act in person, the agreement was also seen as respecting the convention that the Sovereign ought not to be involved in controversy over any matter in respect of which she is advised to exercise a royal power by her New Zealand Ministers.

suggest.[92] In New Zealand, however, the title "Defender of the Faith" is not linked in any way to the Church of England or the Anglican Communion, as we shall explain.

The early commitment to freedom of religion

Samuel Marsden launched the first Christian mission to New Zealand in 1814, on behalf of the Church of England's Church Missionary Society (CMS), followed by the Wesleyans in 1823. In 1838 a Roman Catholic Mission under the French Bishop Pompallier was established in the Hokianga, but moved to Kororāreka (Russell) the following year.[93]

Pompallier, fully aware that a British colony was being established, was concerned that religion should not be interfered with, and that "free toleration" would be allowed in "matters of faith". He asked that a public guarantee to this effect be given the Māori, to which Hobson agreed.[94]

We have earlier explained that the law of England was seen as having been brought to New Zealand by the English settlers.[95] Parliament had later provided, with retrospective effect, that English law as it was on 18 January 1840 had become part of the law of the new colony, so far as it was applicable to its circumstances.[96] In 1889, the question of whether English public ecclesiastical law was part of the law of New Zealand came before the New Zealand courts.[97] The Supreme Court (now the High Court) applied the rule enunciated by the Privy Council in *Re the Lord Bishop of Natal*.[98] Denniston J quoted the following passages from the judgment in that case:[99]

> The United Church of England and Ireland is not a part of the constitution in any colonial settlement, nor can its authorities or those who bear office in it claim to be recognised by the law of the colony otherwise than as members of a voluntary association.[100] . . . It cannot be said that any ecclesiastical tribunal or jurisdiction is required in any colony or settlement where there is no established church; and in

92 (4 February 1974) 389 NZPD 1–3.
93 Claudia Orange "The Maori People and the British Crown (1769–1840)" in Keith Sinclair (ed) *The Oxford Illustrated History of New Zealand* (2nd ed, Oxford University Press, Auckland, 1996) at 29.
94 Claudia Orange *The Treaty of Waitangi* (Allen & Unwin, Wellington, 1987) at 53.
95 See Chapter 3 Constitutional Monarchy: Key Concepts, around subheading The Queen as the repository of land and underlying title, at 44.
96 See Chapter 3 Constitutional Monarchy: Key Concepts, around fn 23, at 44.
97 *Baldwin v Pascoe* (1889) 7 NZLR 759. That decision was applied in *Gregory v Bishop of Waiapu* [1975] 1 NZLR 705 (Beattie J).
98 (1865) 3 Moo PCC (NS) 115.
99 At 152.
100 *Baldwin*, above n 97, at 148.

> the case of a settled colony the ecclesiastical law of England cannot for the same reason be treated as part of the law which the settlers carried with them from the Mother-country.

Although the decision in *Natal* has been criticised,[101] the broad conclusion now commonly drawn — that English public ecclesiastical law had no place in the law of the colonies — has become widely accepted.

Having established the basis on which the Sovereign comes to the throne and assumes the titles of the office of the Sovereign in right of New Zealand, we now look at the coronation of Queen Elizabeth II, and at what can be learnt about her role from the commitments she then made.

4
THE CORONATION

The nature of the ceremony

The coronation of Queen Elizabeth II was a religious ceremony conducted on 2 June 1953 by the Archbishop of Canterbury at Westminster Abbey in London, in accordance with the solemn rites of the Church of England. The form of the ceremony has been handed down through the ages, but leaves room for variations that meet contemporary needs, while according with the law and the monarch's own directions. The necessary arrangements were made by a committee of the Privy Counsellors, known as the "Coronation Committee",[102] assisted by a Coronation Joint Committee consisting of representatives of the United Kingdom and other members of the Commonwealth.[103] The ceremony itself followed age-old tradition, but, in her Coronation Oath, the Queen referred by name to all of her realms.

The coronation ceremony began with the Archbishop's symbolic presentation of the monarch to the people, followed by the people's recognition of the monarch. That part of the ceremony reflected the old practice of choosing the monarch through election by the Witan.[104]

Then followed the taking of the Coronation Oath. Addressing the Queen, the Archbishop asked whether Her Majesty was willing to take the Oath:[105]

101 Kenneth Roberts-Wray *Commonwealth and Colonial Law* (Stevens & Sons, London, 1966) at 463.
102 The Order in Council appointing a Coronation Committee for the coronation of Elizabeth II was promulgated in (6 June 1952) 39566 *London Gazette* 3165 at 3166.
103 *Halsbury's Laws of England* Crown and Royal Family, above n 30, at [18].
104 At [18].
105 "The Queen's Coronation Oath" <http://www.royal.uk/coronation-oath-2-june-1953>.

Queen. I am willing.

Archbishop. Will you solemnly promise and swear to govern the Peoples of the United Kingdom of Great Britain and Northern Ireland, Canada, Australia, New Zealand, the Union of South Africa, Pakistan, and Ceylon, and of your Possessions and the other territories to any of them belonging or pertaining, according to their respective laws and customs?

Queen. I solemnly promise to do so.

Archbishop. Will you to your power cause Law and Justice, in Mercy, to be executed in all your judgements?

Queen. I will.

The Queen's promise of good government in all her realms and territories was in the form prescribed by the Coronation Oath Act 1688 (UK).[106] Its words had required only slight adjustment to reflect the recognition of her separate realms and the nature of the modern Commonwealth.[107] Her oath can be seen as a commitment to constitutional rule in all of her realms and as still having powerful symbolism. Deliberately, it has since, in part, been echoed in the oath of office of New Zealand's Governor-General.[108]

Promises in respect of religious matters

The promises the Queen then made in respect of the Protestant religion and the Church of England applied only in respect of the United Kingdom. They had no application to New Zealand, except so far as they gave effect to the Bill of Rights 1689 (UK) and other United Kingdom enactments which are part of the law of New Zealand.[109]

106 1 Will and Mar c 6. That Act is not in force in New Zealand, but the Act of Settlement 1700 (UK) 12 and 13 Will III c 12, s 2 is part of New Zealand law; it requires the taking of the Coronation Oath in the form prescribed in the 1688 Act.

107 The promise required by the1688 Act had referred to the governing of "this Kingdom of England and the Dominions thereto belonging".

108 See Chapter 7 The Office of Governor-General and Commander-in-Chief, around fn 28, at 128–129.

109 Above n 23. In 1910, the original form of the declaration was modified so as to remove what had become recognised as offensive references to Roman Catholics. The 1910 Act was declared to have come into force in New Zealand on 3 August 1910: see Imperial Laws Application Act 1988, s 3(1) and sch 1.

5
ALLEGIANCE TO THE SOVEREIGN IN RIGHT OF NEW ZEALAND

The concept of "allegiance to the Crown"

On the accession to the throne of Queen Elizabeth II, anyone required to pledge allegiance to the Sovereign in right of New Zealand[110] would have taken an oath or made an affirmation to the following effect:[111]

> I, ________ , swear that I will be faithful and bear true allegiance to Her Majesty Queen Elizabeth the Second, Her heirs and successors, according to law. So help me God.

Allegiance to the Crown is a common law concept dating from feudal times. It reflects the reciprocal duties still lying at the heart of the Sovereign's role. Those who owe the Sovereign the duty of loyalty by reason of their allegiance are entitled to her protection. That was also the basis of the reciprocal undertaking given by Queen Victoria in Article III of the Treaty of Waitangi:

> In consideration thereof [the cession of Sovereignty] Her Majesty the Queen of England extends to the Natives of New Zealand Her royal protection and imparts to them all the Rights and Privileges of British Subjects.

The two notions, the cession of sovereignty[112] and the promise of Her Majesty's protection, reflected basic principles of the common law.

The duty of the Sovereign in right of New Zealand to protect those who owe her allegiance must now be met by her New Zealand Government. In carrying it out, the government must protect people's physical safety within the state at a normal, but not an exceptional, level.[113] Outside the state, the duty is met by the exercise of diplomatic protection, now extending not to those who owe allegiance, but to those who are regarded as New Zealand nationals according

110 For a discussion of the divisibility of the Crown see Chapter 2 Building the Modern Constitution, after fn 46, at 24–27.

111 Oaths and Declarations Act 1957, s 17. Under the Constitution Act 1986, s 5(2), the name of the Sovereign as it appears in any enactment is to be updated as required, without the need for a formal amendment. We have allowed ourselves some poetic licence, as this Act did not come into force until 1 April 1958. See also the predecessor provision: Promissory Oaths Act 1908, s 2.

112 As to the acquisition of British Sovereignty over New Zealand, see Chapter 2 Building the Modern Constitution, under the subheading Queen Victoria's acquisition of sovereignty, at 8–10.

113 ECS Wade and G Godfrey Phillips *Constitutional and Administrative Law* (9th ed, Longman Group Ltd, 1977) at 415.

to international law norms. In return for the right to protection, those who owe allegiance to the Sovereign in right of New Zealand have a duty not to commit treason, as defined by law.

The law of treason

The law of treason is aimed at preserving the personal safety of the Sovereign, the physical security of the territory of the State and the effective authority of those who conduct its lawful government.[114] The offence of treason can be committed only by a person who owes allegiance to the Sovereign. Originally, all British subjects, anywhere in the world, were seen as owing allegiance to an indivisible Sovereign and to all of her governments.

In 1947, however, the United Kingdom and the other independent Commonwealth countries agreed that each of them would be free to establish its own citizenship.[115] It had also become clear that allegiance to the Sovereign, as well as citizenship, had to be seen as divisible. In New Zealand, the new citizenship legislation implicitly recognised the narrowed scope of allegiance to the Crown.[116] When the Crimes Act was revised in 1961, the modern reach of "allegiance" was made explicit. Treason and like offences can now be committed only by a person who, at the material time, owed allegiance to Her Majesty the Queen in right of New Zealand.[117]

Who owes allegiance to the Sovereign in right of New Zealand?

Under the common law, all New Zealand citizens,[118] whether they are inside or outside New Zealand, owe allegiance to the Queen in right of New Zealand. So also do aliens who are resident within the Realm of New Zealand, or are outside the Realm, but in circumstances where their families or belongings remain within the Realm, and therefore under the nominal protection of the Sovereign.[119]

114 Crimes Act 1961, s 73.

115 British Commonwealth Conference on Nationality and Citizenship, 1947. The agreed scheme was described in "British Nationality Bill: Summary of Main Provisions" (Cmd 7326, 1948).

116 British Nationality and New Zealand Citizenship Act 1948, s 5.

117 See Crimes Act 1961, s 73, and the definition of "New Zealand" in s 2(1).

118 As to the persons who are New Zealand citizens, see the Citizenship Act 1977. They include the peoples of all parts of the Realm of New Zealand: see further Chapter 6 The Letters Patent, the Governor-General and the Realm of New Zealand, under the subheading What if New Zealand were to become a republic?, at 114–115.

119 *Halsbury's Laws of England* Introduction, above n 26, at [29] and [30].

The oath or affirmation of allegiance

Allegiance does not depend on the taking of an oath or affirmation of allegiance to the Sovereign. But, in certain circumstances, a requirement to take such an oath is imposed by law. Because a requirement to take an oath of allegiance in a form that was unacceptable to those adhering to certain religions was often an instrument of deliberate discrimination or oppression, Parliament, in the United Kingdom and other common law countries, has controlled both the form of an oath of allegiance and the circumstances in which a person is obliged to take it.

In New Zealand, no one can be required or authorised to take the oath of allegiance except by the Oaths and Declarations Act 1957, or by another Act or other source of written law specified in that Act.[120] That is an emphatic statement of the principle that an oath of allegiance should not be required except for good reason. Parliament has imposed an obligation to take an oath of allegiance only on persons appointed to certain high offices, or having other duties or obligations to the Crown which make it appropriate to seek their solemn pledge of loyalty to the Sovereign in right of New Zealand.

The Sovereign in the New Zealand constitution

This chapter has concentrated on aspects of the monarchy which are broadly common to all the Sovereign's realms. In the contexts discussed, the Sovereign's position is much the same or similar in respect of the other Commonwealth realms, especially Canada and the Commonwealth of Australia, which came to nationhood in the same era and have much in common. The Queen herself has shown a distinct preference for keeping her working relationships with all three at a broadly similar level. Originally the United Kingdom itself was the model for the working of the monarchical constitution. Now, however, the constitutional influence is likely to flow in either direction, as long as the affinity remains.

In Chapter 5 we continue the story of the Sovereign in right of New Zealand in that context. The single most significant feature of the Queen's long reign is the direct and personal relationship that has developed between the Sovereign and her realm of New Zealand.

120 Oaths and Declarations Act 1957, s 27 and sch 4. The Act recognises that the Governor-General may be required to take certain oaths by letters patent or some other authority.

CHAPTER 5

The Sovereign in Right of New Zealand: A Personal Touch

1
INTRODUCTION

Queen Elizabeth II is the first reigning monarch to visit New Zealand. A combination of personal visits, modern communications and constitutional developments during her reign has changed the nature of the Sovereign's working relationships with her New Zealand advisers and with New Zealand citizens more generally. Part 2 of this chapter deals with the working relationships linking the Queen with the Governor-General, the Prime Minister and her New Zealand subjects more generally. In Part 3 we consider how New Zealand would be affected by the illness of the Queen or an incapacity that requires a regency, and then look at the issues that may or will arise on the death of the Queen and the accession of her successor.

2
ROLES AND RELATIONSHIPS

Once a Governor-General of New Zealand had ceased to exercise powers, or to carry out representational responsibilities on behalf of the United Kingdom Government, and became answerable, in all respects, to Ministers in New Zealand, it was inevitable that the relationships of the Sovereign, the Governor-General and the Prime Minister would also change.

The Sovereign appoints the Governor-General as her representative in the Realm of New Zealand, but she does so on the New Zealand Prime Minister's advice.[1] Like the Queen herself, the Governor-General, as a general rule, must act in accordance with the advice of the Prime Minister and other Ministers. Accordingly, the main working relationships are those between the Prime Minister and the Sovereign on the one hand, and, on the other, between the Prime Minister and the Governor-General. It is through those channels that the business of the state is carried on, so far as it involves either the Sovereign or the Governor-General. Consequently, the roles of the Sovereign and of the Governor-General tend to run in parallel rather than converge. We now describe these various relationships.

The Sovereign and the Governor-General

The nature of the relationship between the Sovereign and the Governor-General derives its flavour from the unbroken chain of appointments to gubernatorial office going back to 1840. In 1992, the original handwritten manuscript of the Instructions, issued under the seal known as the "Royal Signet" and the "Sign Manual" or signature of Queen Victoria, for the guidance of Captain Hobson and his successors in the Administration of the Colony of New Zealand, were discovered still stored in a safe in Government House in Wellington, as though they might still need to be referred to at any time.[2] Today, for good reason, there is no longer any provision for the Sovereign to provide a Governor-General with Royal Instructions.[3]

The Governor-General no longer has a formal obligation to keep the Sovereign informed about New Zealand affairs. Nevertheless, a direct, informal and confidential channel of communication between the Sovereign and the Governor or Governor-General, which has always existed, is still maintained. If the Governor-General wishes to communicate with the Sovereign, he or she may do so in his or her discretion, without ministerial advice. Some New Zealand Governors-General have made a practice of regularly writing to the Queen about what was happening in New Zealand, and the Queen greatly

1 Letters Patent 1983, cl 1. Note, however, the important qualification that the powers and authorities of the office are without prejudice to the office, powers, or authority of any other person who has been or may be appointed to represent the Sovereign in any part of the Realm of New Zealand.

2 The Royal Instructions of 9 December 1840 were issued to take account of the fact that New Zealand had been erected into a separate colony, and was no longer part of New South Wales: see Chapter 2 Building the Modern Constitution, fn 1, at 10. On 5 November 1992 the Governor-General presented the document to Archives New Zealand: undated note on the nature and importance of the manuscript prepared by Ian Wards, formerly Chief Historian, Historical Publications Branch, Department of Internal Affairs.

3 See below, Chapter 6 The Letters Patent, the Governor-General and the Realm of New Zealand, fn 21, at 102.

appreciates such reports as contributing significantly to the performance of her own role as Queen of New Zealand. In 1991, the Queen decided to reduce the embargo on the release of such correspondence from 60 to 50 years, running from the end of the Governor-General's term of office.[4] When eventually available for scholarly study, the reports seem likely to be an interesting source of information about events in New Zealand and how they were perceived at the time.

The Sovereign and the Prime Minister

In comparison with the long history of the relationship between the Sovereign and a Governor-General, the history of the relationship between the Sovereign and a present-day New Zealand Prime Minister is relatively short. Only since the Balfour Declaration in 1926 have the Prime Ministers of the Commonwealth realms directly advised the Sovereign.[5] In the hard decades of the 1930s and 1940s, there were few opportunities for a New Zealand Prime Minister to build a personal relationship with the King, although, even then, the existence of the relationship was seen by both as having real significance.

In 1937, the New Zealand Prime Minister, Michael Joseph Savage, reluctantly undertook the four-month round-trip by sea to the coronation of King George VI, accepting that it was unthinkable not to attend. He and his accompanying departmental head, Carl Berendsen, went to the Abbey wearing the required black coat, white knee-breeches, gold stockings and sword of court dress. Later, at an Imperial Conference organised by the British Prime Minister, Stanley Baldwin, Savage argued that the Dominions could no longer be expected to accept Britain's foreign policy without question, robustly declaring that the aim of avoiding war at all costs would prove to be a trap.[6]

Savage died in March 1940, and Peter Fraser became New Zealand's wartime Prime Minister. He established a good working relationship with his British counterpart, Winston Churchill, but it was put to the test when Japan entered the war, and Australia and New Zealand became dependent on the protection of the United States. The American President and the British Prime Minister were in close agreement, but smaller allies like Australia and New Zealand felt left out of the decision-making process. The Australian Prime Minister, John Curtin, protested in forthright tones. Fraser expressed his

4 Letter from the Queen's Private Secretary to the Private Secretary to the Prime Minister (4 June 1991).

5 See Chapter 2 Building the Modern Constitution, after fn 53, at 24–28.

6 Gerald Hensley *Beyond the Battlefield: New Zealand and its Allies 1939–45* (Penguin, London, 2009) at 30–33.

concern more carefully, but no less strongly. Wellington and Canberra worked together in trying to make sure that they would have an effective voice.[7]

Gerald Hensley records the deepening crisis as Churchill refused to take any action. One official even began to liken the situation to the quarrel with the American colonies. Then the King weighed in, writing to his United Kingdom Prime Minister:[8]

> His Majesty feels sure you will share his anxiety about the situation which, under the stress of events in the Pacific, may develop in Australia, and to a lesser degree in New Zealand, unless we go some way to meet the wishes of the Dominion Governments.

After some further discussion, Churchill agreed to put the proposals of Australia and New Zealand for a Pacific War Council to President Roosevelt. Eventually, however, the two governments had to accept consultations in London and liaison with the United States at the military level as the best arrangement they could get.[9]

Urging one of his Prime Ministers to meet the concerns voiced by two of his other Prime Ministers clearly came within the King's right and duty to counsel and warn any of his Prime Ministers. There is good reason to believe that his successor, Queen Elizabeth II, sees that right and duty as part of her relationship not only with the Prime Minister of the United Kingdom, but also with the Prime Ministers of her other realms. It seems clear, however, that any expression of her views on the policies or proposed actions of the government of a realm other than the United Kingdom is likely to be focused on matters on which its Prime Minister advises the Sovereign, rather than the Governor-General of the realm concerned. In the nature of things, a New Zealand Prime Minister has limited opportunities to meet with the Sovereign in person, but advantage is taken of all opportunities. It is the practice for a newly appointed Prime Minister to seek an audience with the Queen on his or her first visit to London after taking office, and thereafter as appropriate, taking advantage of the Prime Minister's later visits to London, the Queen's visits to New Zealand, or meetings elsewhere at which both are present. In particular, at Commonwealth conferences attended by the Queen in her capacity as Head of the Commonwealth,[10] she has made a point of meeting with the

7 At 167–174.
8 At 175.
9 At 175–176.
10 See below, this chapter, around fn 65, at 91.

Prime Ministers of as many Commonwealth countries as possible, including the republics as well as the realms.[11]

At the time of the Balfour Declaration,[12] and its further implementation in the Statute of Westminster, King George himself had emphasised the continuing need for the governments of the Dominions to keep the Governor-General informed about the general conduct of the government — a duty recorded in the Letters Patent constituting the office of the Governor-General.[13] In contrast, there has been no express articulation of a similar duty in respect of the Sovereign. Presumably it was assumed that the information would continue to flow through to the Sovereign on the same basis on which it then operated. Inevitably, however, the Governor-General's role would itself change.

After the 1952 accession of Elizabeth II as Queen in right of New Zealand, new and direct lines of communication were established with the Palace. The Queen now receives copies of the regular reports made by officials on the general conduct of the Government of New Zealand. On issues that involve the Sovereign directly, or even indirectly, such as the proposal to substitute appeals to a new Supreme Court for what was then a right of appeal to the Judicial Committee of the Sovereign's Privy Council, the Prime Minister communicated directly with the Queen's Private Secretary or approved the terms of such a communication by the Clerk of the Executive Council. The Clerk also informally notifies the Private Secretary of important matters as they arise. Other Ministers or their departments have no authority to communicate directly with the Palace, except on specific occasions, such as in relation to royal visits, and only with Cabinet Office knowledge and approval.

The Prime Minister's real and active role in advising the Sovereign in right of New Zealand is supported by the close working relationship between the Queen's Private Secretary and the Clerk of the Executive Council. The holders of the two offices go to some trouble to develop and maintain a close working relationship.

The Queen's Private Secretary and the Clerk of the Executive Council

The office of Private Secretary to the Queen has been described as crucial to the working of the modern constitutional monarchy.[14] Like other features of

11 See below, this chapter, fn 65, at 91.
12 See Chapter 2 Building the Modern Constitution, fn 53, at 24–28.
13 Letters Patent 1983, cl 16. See further Chapter 10 Guardian of the Constitution?, under the subheading Strengthening the working relationship, at 226–229.
14 Vernon Bogdanor *The Monarchy and the Constitution* (Oxford, Oxford University Press, 1997) at 197–214.

the constitution, it came into existence in the 19th century, almost by accident. Bogdanor sees the Private Secretary as guarding the constitutional position of the Sovereign by ensuring that he or she is properly informed about matters on which the responsible Ministers may tender advice. He notes that, in supporting the Sovereign's functions, the Private Secretary's allegiance is as much to the institution of the monarchy as to the person who happens to be the Sovereign at a particular time.[15]

The Private Secretary is the personal appointment of the Sovereign, but must be acceptable to the United Kingdom Prime Minister and to senior British civil servants. Today, however, the holder of the office is also Private Secretary to the Queen of New Zealand and the Queen of all her other realms, and must nurture all of those separate constitutional relationships, as well as the Sovereign's relationship with the Government of the United Kingdom. That government, however, has no role in the conduct of the Sovereign's relationship with New Zealand, or any of her other realms.

Those appointed to the office of Private Secretary therefore make sure that they have a good personal understanding of public affairs in each of the Sovereign's realms, and especially of any issues that may affect the Sovereign's relationships with the political leaders and the people themselves in the realm concerned. In that they are supported by the other members of the Sovereign's household.

One way in which the household has sought to maintain a good understanding of the Sovereign's modern constitutional relationships with all of her realms has been the practice during the last 50 years or so of sometimes drawing on the larger realms, Canada, Australia and New Zealand, when recruiting members of the advisory staff in the royal household. Recently, a similar practice has been followed by the household of the Prince of Wales. The appointments, usually for three or four years, may be at least partly funded by the governments concerned. Undoubtedly, the involvement of an officer from one of the other realms contributes to a better understanding within the royal households of the Sovereign's multiple roles. On issues relating to the realm from which the officer comes, he or she can throw light on how that issue is seen within the country concerned. In addition, if an important matter affects all the realms, the three governments will almost certainly consult among themselves before taking a position, especially if it will be necessary for each of them to tender formal advice to the Queen. That kind of coordination accords with her own desire to maintain even-handedness in her dealings with all of her realms.[16]

15 At 205.
16 See, for example, the Sovereign's relinquishment to the Governors-General of the task of signing

At the New Zealand end, the Clerk of the Executive Council has the responsibility of liaising with the Queen's Private Secretary,[17] as well as having a similar but broader range of functions in respect of the Governor-General. The Executive Council itself is the organ of the executive government which formally tenders the advice of Ministers collectively to the Sovereign or the Governor-General.[18] The Clerk of the Executive Council is the holder of an office constituted by the Governor-General in exercise of the prerogative, and is appointed to it by the Governor-General, acting on the advice of the Prime Minister.[19] Since 1967, it has been the practice to appoint the same person as Clerk of the Executive Council and Secretary of the Cabinet,[20] but, although the positions are held concurrently, each appointment is made separately, and the two positions are regarded as distinct. Both offices call for political impartiality. Among other things, the Clerk of the Executive Council has the responsibility of providing the Governor-General, the Prime Minister and the Executive Council with such constitutional advice as may be required. In that respect, therefore, the position is analogous to that of the Private Secretary to the Queen.

The Private Secretary to the Queen and the Clerk of the Executive Council keep in close touch. At the operational level there are also channels of communication between the Queen's Private Secretary and the New Zealand High Commissioner in London, and between the Private Secretary and the Governor-General, or the Official Secretary to the Governor-General, in Wellington. But all matters of policy for which the Sovereign and the Prime Minister have the ultimate responsibility are dealt with in the first instance by the Clerk of the Executive Council. When a matter arises that will be the subject of formal advice from the Prime Minister, such as the appointment of a Governor-General,[21] Her Majesty is consulted informally and confidentially beforehand.

the credentials and letters of recall of the Ambassadors appointed by the other realms: Chapter 8 The Governor-General in the Executive Branch, under the subheading Diplomatic and consular representatives, at 152–153 and Chapter 14 Exercising the Head of State Role, under the subheading The accreditation of diplomats, at 282–286.

17 Cabinet Office *Cabinet Manual 2008* (Department of the Prime Minister and Cabinet, Wellington, New Zealand, April 2008) at [1.31].

18 Letters Patent 1983, cl 7. In virtually all cases, that advice will already have been approved by the Cabinet. In Chapter 8 The Governor-General in the Executive Branch, under the subheading The modern Executive Council, at 158–163, we discuss the constitutional role of the Executive Council.

19 Letters Patent 1983, cl 10. Formerly, the appointment took effect under the Official Appointments and Documents Act 1919, s 2, but, more recently, it has been made by warrant.

20 The Secretary of the Cabinet is appointed under the State Sector Act 1988, s 59.

21 See Chapter 7 The Office of Governor-General and Commander-in-Chief, under the subheading Appointing a Governor-General, at 118–124.

The Sovereign and the people

The division of responsibility

As a matter of law, it would be possible for the Queen to exercise a power delegated to the Governor-General or vested in the Governor-General by statute, even while outside New Zealand. There are, however, few, if any, circumstances in which that might be appropriate. The general principle is that, unless the Sovereign is visiting New Zealand, matters within the powers of the Governor-General should be dealt with by the Governor-General, especially if they are politically controversial and might be seen as involving an element of personal discretion. The rationale for such a principle is that it would be almost impossible for the Sovereign to make, at a distance, the necessary judgement as to the political facts which might justify her action — or inaction — in the particular circumstances. That principle has long been followed when a person in New Zealand exercises the right to petition the Sovereign. It was also seen as applying when a Governor-General of Australia became embattled with a Prime Minister who still retained the confidence of the Lower House of Parliament.[22]

The right to petition the Sovereign

The Bill of Rights of 1689 declares forthrightly:[23]

> That it is the right of the subjects to petition the King, and all commitments and prosecutions for such petitioning are illegal.

New Zealand citizens still avail themselves freely of their right to petition the Sovereign. A former Governor-General, the Rt Hon Sir Michael Hardie Boys, has recorded that the Palace receives quite a number of communications, from all manner of people, about all manner of domestic New Zealand matters. These communications "are referred straight to the Governor-General", the writer being informed that "it is not a matter in which Her Majesty would interfere".[24]

The formula quoted by Sir Michael seems to reflect an age when the Sovereign was formally advised only by her United Kingdom Ministers. In modern times,

22 See the discussion in Chapter 10 Guardian of the Constitution?, under the subheading The dismissal of Gough Whitlam, at 215–216.
23 Imperial Laws Application Act 1988.
24 Michael Hardie Boys "Nodding Automaton? (Some Reflections on the Office of the Governor-General)" (2002) 8 Canterbury Law Review 425 at 428.

the governing principle is simply that New Zealand Ministers must bear the responsibility of advising on the appropriate responses to a petition to either the Sovereign or the Governor-General from someone in New Zealand. That principle has been applied ever since the introduction of responsible government.[25] Certainly, it was recognised in dealing with the petitions that Māori leaders addressed to the Sovereign in the 1880s and later, after the Governor had ceased to have any responsibility for Māori policy, personally or on the instructions of United Kingdom Ministers. Clearly, however, in that case, and no doubt in others, the authors of the petitions were hoping for the active intervention of the Sovereign in person.[26] Today, it would reflect the constitutional position more accurately if New Zealanders petitioning the Sovereign were to be advised that she had referred the petition to her New Zealand Ministers for consideration and any appropriate action.

Royal visits to New Zealand

The Sovereign's visits to New Zealand obviously provide her with the best opportunity of making personal contact with her New Zealand subjects. Although, in the nature of things, such visits cannot be frequent, the Queen and her husband, the Duke of Edinburgh, have paid 10 visits to New Zealand. Between them, other members of the royal family, also, have visited New Zealand 59 times over 63 years.

All official royal visits are made at the invitation of the New Zealand Prime Minister. Naturally, there is usually a good deal of informal consultation before such an invitation is given and accepted. The planning required for a royal visit is intensive. In due course, the Prime Minister will need to approve the programme, and also the final drafts of any significant speeches to be delivered in New Zealand by the Sovereign or another member of the royal family. The cost of an official visit to New Zealand by members of the royal family is met from money appropriated by the New Zealand Parliament.

Exercising constitutional powers during a visit

Once it became known that the newly crowned Queen Elizabeth II would visit as many of her realms as possible during a Commonwealth-wide royal tour, some of the realms, including Canada, Australia and New Zealand, were

25 See Chapter 2 Building the Modern Constitution, under the subheading The Governor's role after 1856, at 18.

26 See Chapter 13 The Crown as a Party to the Treaty of Waitangi in relation to Māori petitions, after fn 18, at 264–268.

interested in the possibility that, during her visit, she might exercise in person some of the powers normally exercised by the Governor-General, under the law of the realm concerned.

In New Zealand, there was no problem with the Queen's exercise of the prerogative powers that the Sovereign had delegated to the Governor-General by the Letters Patent then in force.[27] Under the ordinary law of agency, a person who delegates a power to another can still exercise it in person.[28] By 1953, however, most of the relevant powers, such as the power to assent to a Bill passed by Parliament, and the power to make most Orders in Council, had been codified by statute, and were expressly vested in the Governor-General. Parliament therefore enacted legislation declaring every power conferred on the Governor-General by any Act to be a royal power which is exercisable by the Governor-General on behalf of the Sovereign, and may accordingly be exercised either by the Sovereign in person or by the Governor-General.[29] The provision has since been incorporated into the Constitution Act 1986.[30]

During her first visit in 1954 the Queen opened a new session of Parliament and gave what is still called "the Speech from the Throne". As is customary, that document had been approved by the Prime Minister and announced the government's policy and legislative programme for the coming year.[31] On other occasions the Queen has summoned a meeting of the Executive Council, presided over its business,[32] and exercised statutory powers conferred on the Governor-General in Council to make regulations or a Proclamation. In 1977, on the advice and with the consent of the Executive Council, she exercised the prerogative power to accept the resignation of a Minister, Sir Keith Holyoake, from his office as Minister of State in the Muldoon government.[33] Then, as a prerequisite to the Prime Minister's formal advice that she should appoint

27 Letters Patent Constituting the Office of the Governor-General and Commander-in-Chief of the Dominion of New Zealand 1917, as amended by Letters Patent dated 18 December 1918. By implication, however, certain prerogative powers were, and still are, outside the scope of the powers delegated to the Governor-General, notably the powers to constitute the office of Governor-General and to appoint or dismiss the Governor-General to or from the office.

28 See Peter Watts and FMB Reynolds (eds) *Bowstead and Reynolds on Agency* (20th ed, Sweet & Maxwell, London, 2014) at 6-009; *Morrell v Workers Savings and Loan Bank* [2007] UKPC 3; and *Angove's Pty Co Ltd v Bailey* [2016] UKSC 47, [2016] 1 WLR 3179.

29 Royal Powers Act 1953, s 2. The provision applies to powers vested in "the Governor-General in Council". In 1983 the Executive Council was reconstituted with the express task of advising both the Sovereign and the Governor-General: Letters Patent Constituting the Office of the Governor-General of New Zealand 1983, cl 7.

30 Constitution Act 1986, s 3.

31 Parliament is now formally opened and a Speech from the Throne read only at the first meeting of a new Parliament.

32 As to the constitution and functions of the Executive Council, see Chapter 8 The Governor-General in the Executive Branch, under the subheading The modern Executive Council, at 158–163.

33 As to the power to appoint Ministers of the Crown, see Chapter 8 The Governor-General in the Executive Branch, under the subheading Appointing a Prime Minister and other Ministers, at 160–161.

Sir Keith as the next Governor-General, she signified her informal approval of such an appointment, and announced it publicly.[34] She has also assented to an Act giving effect to the first major modern Treaty settlement,[35] and to other Acts of constitutional significance.[36]

Royal visits are often the occasion for a public display of two other aspects of the Sovereign's constitutional role. Neither role involves the Sovereign's exercise of a power that has a direct effect in the law of the land, but each, in its own way, recognises or reinforces New Zealand's sense of its identity. The first is her role in recognising the notable contributions or achievements of its citizens. The second is her traditional connection with the Defence Force which we consider in Chapters 7 and 14.

The fount of honour

In the course of her reign, Queen Elizabeth II has instituted what is now a comprehensive New Zealand Royal Honours system to replace the British or Imperial honours which New Zealanders were awarded at the beginning of her reign. These include New Zealand awards for bravery, and for long or outstanding service. Unlike many of her other roles, the exercise of the Sovereign's role as the fount of honour has never been the subject of a general delegation to the Governor-General, though the Governor-General may be authorised to play a specific role including in relation to investitures. The New Zealand honours and awards are given by the Sovereign, on the recommendation of the Prime Minister. The Queen signs the documents that each recipient receives and on at least one large public occasion personally invested the recipient with the honour or award concerned. The Royal Victorian Order is an honour that remains in her personal discretion and it is customarily used to acknowledge those who have provided personal service to the Sovereign.

Representing New Zealand in the United Kingdom

In more recent years, as the Queen has undertaken fewer long journeys overseas, she has made known her willingness to represent New Zealand or

34 As to the power to appoint a Governor-General, see Chapter 7 The Office of Governor-General and Commander-in-Chief, under the subheading The Sovereign's informal approval, at 119. As to the choice of a person to be Governor-General and the appointment process, see Chapter 7 The Governor-General in the Executive Branch, under the subheading Choosing a Governor-General, at 118.

35 The Waikato Raupatu Claims Settlement Act 1995. See Chapter 13 The Crown as a Party to the Treaty of Waitangi, under the subheading The Crown's apology to Waikato, at 273.

36 For example, the Royal Titles Act 1974 and Seal of New Zealand Act 1977.

any of her other realms at events of special interest to that realm taking place in London, or other places in the United Kingdom. In her capacity as Queen of New Zealand, she attended the unveiling of the New Zealand War Memorial in Hyde Park,[37] and continues to take part in other New Zealand occasions, both sorrowful and joyful.

Celebrating the country's achievements and sharing its sorrows

New Zealanders have had many opportunities to see, sometimes in dramatic circumstances, that their Sovereign, Queen Elizabeth II, and members of the royal family, are ready to mark in an appropriate way the successful endeavours of the country or its citizens, and just as ready to join in mourning the loss of lives, homes or livelihoods in times of disaster or war.

During the Queen's epic 39-day visit to New Zealand in 1953, there was much to celebrate, but there was also disaster. On Christmas Eve 1953, a railway bridge at Tangiwai, in the central North Island, was destroyed by a lahar from the Mt Ruapehu crater lake. An overnight passenger train between Wellington and Auckland plunged into the swollen river, with the loss of 151 lives. The next day, the young Queen ended what was to become her traditional Christmas broadcast to the world, this time from Auckland, with a message of sympathy to the people of New Zealand. Later, Prince Philip attended a state funeral for many of the victims.

Since those times there have been many messages of congratulation or sympathy. At the time of the death of Te Arikinui Dame Te Ātairangikaahu, the Māori Queen, the Queen of the United Kingdom, as well as the Queen of New Zealand, sent messages of condolence. Before then, during another visit to New Zealand of the Queen and her husband, a destructive cyclone occurred in Niue.[38] Prince Philip accompanied the Premier, Sir Robert Rex (who was then visiting New Zealand), on an overflight of the island to assess the damage. More recently, the Queen's grandson, Prince William, visited New Zealand on her behalf to support the people of Christchurch after a series of destructive earthquakes, and also the grieving relatives of those who lost their lives in the Pike River Mine disaster.

For their part, the Governor-General, the Prime Minister and Parliament, all speaking on behalf of the people of New Zealand, may send messages

37 In March 2006.

38 Niue was then a non-self-governing territory of New Zealand but is now a self-governing state which remains part of the Realm of New Zealand: see further Chapter 6 The Letters Patent, the Governor-General and the Realm of New Zealand, under the subheading The Sovereign in right of the different parts of the Realm of New Zealand, at 110–112.

of congratulation or of condolence to the Sovereign on significant royal occasions. The country was represented by both the Governor-General and the Prime Minister at the funeral of the Queen Mother and, more recently, at the marriage of Prince William to Miss Catherine Middleton.

3
LOOKING AHEAD

The linking thread

In part 3 of this chapter, we discuss several matters that may or will arise in the future, and in some way affect the role of the Sovereign as the Queen of New Zealand. We outline the arrangements in place if the Queen were to become seriously ill or incapacitated, and what will happen on her inevitable death, and the accession to the throne of her heir apparent, the Prince of Wales.

Contingency planning

The Queen's illness or incapacity

There are three sets of circumstances in which the law of the United Kingdom recognises that the Sovereign may be unable to carry out the functions of the office in person, and makes provision accordingly.[39] The first is youth — accession to the throne before attaining the age of 18[40] — a contingency that is not immediately relevant to the circumstances of the royal family. The second is an infirmity of mind or body, or some other definite cause, that makes the Sovereign incapable or unavailable for the time being.[41] The third is illness not amounting to infirmity, or absence, or intended absence, from the United Kingdom, coupled with the need to prevent delay or difficulty in the despatch of public business.[42] In the first and second cases, the law provides for the appointment of a Regent who may exercise all the Sovereign's functions, except those expressly excluded by law. In the present circumstances of the royal family, the heir apparent would become the Regent.[43] In the third case, the law

39 Regency Act 1937 (UK) 1 Edw VII & Geo VI c 16, ss 1–5, as amended by the Regency Act 1943 (UK) 6 & 7 Geo VI c 42, s 1, and the Regency Act 1953 (UK) 2 Eliz II c 1, s 1.
40 Regency Act 1937 (UK), s 1.
41 Section 2.
42 Section 6.
43 Section 3.

provides for the Sovereign to delegate certain specified royal functions to Counsellors of State.[44]

When the earlier statutes were revised in 1937, after the accession of King George VI, they were not applied to any of the then Dominions. In their case it was necessary to take account, not only of the Statute of Westminster,[45] but also of an important practical difference. In the realms other than the United Kingdom, the Governor-General may exercise most if not all of the Sovereign's functions, even if, as a matter of practice, the Sovereign normally exercises some of them in person.[46] That difference materially affects the extent to which the law of the other realms needs to make further provision for the carrying out of the Sovereign's functions, if the Sovereign cannot carry them out herself, or delay would arise in her doing so. Because such a need has seldom, if ever, arisen since the divisibility of the Crown became fully established,[47] it is not one for which many Commonwealth realms have made express provision. In New Zealand, however, the matter was considered in the lead-up to the issue of the current Letters Patent constituting the office of Governor-General in 1983.

A Regent may exercise the functions of the Sovereign in right of New Zealand

Since that time, New Zealand law has provided that, in any circumstance in which a Regent has been appointed in the United Kingdom, the Regent has the power to exercise the royal functions of the Sovereign in right of New Zealand, but without prejudice to the Governor-General's continuing authority to exercise any function within his or her power.[48] The current provision concerning the powers in New Zealand law of a Regent is now to be found in the Constitution Act 1986:[49]

> Where, under the law of the United Kingdom, the royal functions are being performed in the name and on behalf of the Sovereign by a Regent, the royal functions of the Sovereign in right of New Zealand shall be performed in the name and on behalf of the Sovereign by that Regent.

44 Section 6. See further below, this chapter, under the subheading Counsellors of State have no power to act for the Sovereign in right of New Zealand, at 87–88.

45 See Chapter 2 Building the Modern Constitution, under the subheading The Statute of Westminster, at 28–29.

46 See above, this chapter, text following fn 28, at 80 and at 87.

47 See Chapter 2 Building the Modern Constitution, after fn 46, at 24–28.

48 Royal Powers Act 1983, s 4. The United Kingdom Regency Acts ceased to be part of New Zealand law, if indeed they ever were: see s 5. The 1983 Act was repealed and replaced by the Constitution Act 1986: s 28(1) and sch 2.

49 Constitution Act 1986, s 4(1). The existence of the regency does not affect the Governor-General's authority to exercise any power of the Sovereign in right of New Zealand: Constitution Act 1986, s 4(2).

A Governor-General has no power to exercise the prerogative power to revoke or amend the Letters Patent constituting the office of Governor-General,[50] or the power to appoint — or revoke the appointment of — the holder of that office.[51] Those powers are expressly vested in the Sovereign.[52] So also is the power to establish the Seal of New Zealand, an aspect of the prerogative of honour.

The Sovereign herself continues to issue the Statutes, as they are called, constituting the various New Zealand royal honours and awards, and also exercises the power to grant them. The Governor-General may only constitute or grant any honour or award if expressly authorised to do so by the Sovereign, or a Regent. Those, then, are the comparatively few circumstances in which a Regent would need to be called upon to exercise a royal function of the Sovereign in right of New Zealand, but it was seen as important to ensure that the necessary provision was in place.

Recently disquiet has been expressed that it is United Kingdom legislation that determines the rules about regency, with the implication that this is incompatible with New Zealand's self-governing status.[53] As we have explained, however, the authority in respect of New Zealand of any Regent appointed under the law of the United Kingdom is conferred by section 4 of the New Zealand Constitution Act 1986, and that Act alone.

Counsellors of State have no power to act for the Sovereign in right of New Zealand

In 1982, when the applicability of the United Kingdom law providing for a regency was being considered, and the Sovereign's functions in respect of New Zealand were slightly wider, the New Zealand authorities proposed the inclusion of a provision that would allow the powers just mentioned to be exercised not only by a Regent, but also by Counsellors of State, during any period when such Counsellors had been appointed and authorised to act for

50 Letters Patent 1983, cl 18.

51 Clause 2.

52 The former power vested in the Sovereign, acting upon an address of the House of Representatives, and then only for cause, to remove a Judge of the High Court from office is now shared with the Governor-General: Constitution Act 1986, s 23. Since 22 August 2006 it has not been necessary for the Governor-General to obtain leave from the Sovereign before departing from New Zealand in the circumstances formerly prescribed.

53 Grant Parker, Submission to the Constitutional Conversation 31 July 2013 <https://www.parliament.nz/resource/en-nz/50SCJE_EVI_00DBHOH_BILL11999_1_A355672/07b9902bee491a4ade222a99fa5f6d06ab4361d2>.

any purpose, under the law of the United Kingdom.[54] The Queen's Private Secretary, however, noted that there were considerable restrictions on the powers that were delegated to Counsellors of State under United Kingdom law during the Queen's absences from the United Kingdom, and suggested that, with the benefit of modern communications, the few powers exercisable only by the Queen in right of New Zealand could readily be exercised even while she was on tour. He expressed doubt whether, in these circumstances, the Queen would wish to delegate her powers under New Zealand law to Counsellors of State.[55]

In response, the New Zealand officials made the point that Counsellors of State may be appointed if the Queen were to be temporarily disabled by accident or illness, as well as in her absence from the United Kingdom. Although the possibility that a Prime Minister might need to advise the Queen to recall a Governor-General is remote, if that contingency were to arise, it is likely to be both urgent and important. The Private Secretary confirmed, however, that, as envisaged, the Queen, whom he had consulted, would be reluctant to delegate to Counsellors of State the prerogative powers of the Sovereign which are not delegated to the Governor-General.[56] If it were really impossible for the Queen to respond quickly enough, it would probably have become necessary to appoint a Regent. After further discussion among officials, and with the agreement of the Prime Minister, the proposal was not pursued. In his capacity as Clerk of the Executive Council, Patrick Millen commented that:[57]

> . . . this is the first time in my ten years' experience of dealing with the Palace at the informal working level where they have maintained a very firm view contrary to the informal advice they normally accept from New Zealand.

The upshot is that Counsellors of State, appointed under United Kingdom law in the case of the Sovereign's absence from the United Kingdom or her illness, not amounting to incapacity, have no authority to exercise any function of the Sovereign in right of New Zealand.[58]

54 Letter from PG Millen, Secretary of the Cabinet, to the Rt Hon Sir Philip Moore, Private Secretary to the Queen (17 November 1982). See also the Regency Act 1937 (UK), above n 39, s 6.

55 Letter from Rt Hon Sir Philip Moore, Private Secretary to the Queen, to Patrick G Millen, Secretary of the Cabinet (2 December 1982).

56 Letter from Rt Hon Sir Philip Moore, Private Secretary to the Queen, to Patrick G Millen, Secretary of the Cabinet (8 March 1983).

57 Covering note to a formal submission to the Prime Minister dated 28 April on the Constitutional Provisions Bill 1982 (111-1), cl 5.

58 That absence of authority extends to things done by the Queen in right of New Zealand under the Constitution of the Cook Islands — for example, the appointment of the Queen's Representative in the Cook Islands.

Abdication

In some monarchies, such as The Netherlands, it is accepted that an ageing monarch may abdicate, allowing his or her successor to accede to the throne. That has not been the tradition in the United Kingdom. There, it has been the norm that the monarch serves until death. That sense of a duty to serve for the whole of life no doubt contributed to the shock and dismay of other close members of the royal family when King Edward VIII decided to renounce the throne rather than his intended marriage. As the heir presumptive, the young Princess Elizabeth no doubt grew up with a clear sense that the abdication of the reigning Sovereign was not an acceptable option. None of her public statements is better known than the resolution she made in her Cape Town broadcast to the Commonwealth on her 21st birthday:[59]

> I declare before you all that my whole life whether it be long or short shall be devoted to your service and the service of our great imperial family to which we all belong.

The nature of the Commonwealth may have changed since then, but there is no indication of any change in the Queen's resolve. On the 60th anniversary of her accession, 6 February 2012, she released a message echoing her earlier words by dedicating herself anew to the service of the people of the United Kingdom and the Commonwealth.[60]

The death of the Sovereign and the accession of her successor

Loss and renewal

Although one of New Zealand's two national anthems includes the prayerful wish "Long live our noble Queen",[61] the day will inevitably come when the world receives the news that Queen Elizabeth II has died, and that the member of the royal family next in the line of succession has acceded to the throne. In all probability, the heir apparent, the Prince of Wales, will become King in his

59 "A speech by the Queen on her 21st Birthday 1947" <www.royal.uk/21st-birthday-speech-21-april-1947>.
60 "The Queen's Diamond Jubilee message" <www.royal.uk/queens-diamond-jubilee-message>.
61 The second line of "God Save the Queen" which became New Zealand's National Anthem in 1840, and is still used, in conjunction with "God Defend New Zealand". Generally, "God Save the Queen" is used for occasions where Her Majesty the Queen, a member of the royal family, or the Governor-General is officially present, or when loyalty to the Crown is emphasised: <www.mch.govt.nz/nz-identity-heritage/national-anthems/protocols>.

mother's place. The succession will occur automatically in all the Sovereign's realms, just as it did when the Queen herself came to the throne.

The new King's royal style and titles in right of the United Kingdom

It will be for the new King to choose the name by which he wishes to be known, and he will presumably make known to the United Kingdom Prime Minister any views he may have about any other aspect of the royal style and titles which he wishes to assume in right of the United Kingdom. The Cabinet will then approve the form in which the new King's royal style and titles will be set out in the Accession Proclamation. In 1953, the United Kingdom Parliament passed an Act assenting to the adoption by Her Majesty, for use in relation to the United Kingdom and all other territories for whose foreign relations the United Kingdom is responsible, of such style and titles as Her Majesty may think fit. The only condition is that, having regard to the 1952 agreement with the other realms in existence at that time,[62] the royal style and titles used in the United Kingdom must "retain a substantial element common to all".[63]

There is, however, one aspect of the Queen's royal style and titles in respect of the United Kingdom on which the Prince of Wales has spoken publicly about his views, and another title that it would be inappropriate for him to assume unless the members of the Commonwealth are broadly content that he should do so. We have explained how the title "Defender of the Faith" came to be included among the Sovereign's royal style and titles, and what it is now seen to mean. For his part, the Prince of Wales has made known his wish that, on his accession to the throne, the title "Defender of the Faith" should be seen as embracing all faiths, not just one.[64] It seems, however, that the Prince was not contemplating any amendment of the title itself, but rather a reappraisal of what it represents. In an article in *The Telegraph*, the columnist Charles Moore referred to the fact that, in mid-February 2012, the Queen had deliberately chosen a meeting of many faiths at Lambeth Palace to speak publicly about the significance of her historic role as Head of the Church of England. "The concept of our established Church is occasionally misunderstood", she said. By being "woven into the fabric of this country", the Church helps "build a better society". Picking up on the 1994 remarks of the Prince of Wales, Moore saw the Queen, while not admitting as much, as having "quietly modernised

62 See discussion in Chapter 4 The Sovereign in Right of New Zealand: The Institutional Role, fn 73, at 63–65.
63 Royal Titles Act 1953 (UK) 1 & 2 Eliz 2 c 9, s 1.
64 Rodney Brazier "Legislating about the Monarchy" (2007) 66 CLJ 86 at 103, citing J Dimbleby *The Prince of Wales: A Biography* (Little, Brown, London, 1994) at 528–534.

her historic role as Defender of the Faith to that of Defender of Faith".[65] The process will no doubt continue in the reign of her successor.

The title "Head of the Commonwealth" is not hereditary, but is personal to the particular Sovereign. Uncertainties about the nature and purpose of the Commonwealth association itself have provoked a "Commonwealth Conversation" about the future of the role of the Sovereign as Head of the Commonwealth.[66] Although only the realms within the Commonwealth will have to settle the form of the royal style and titles to be adopted by the new King of each realm, he cannot use the title "Head of the Commonwealth" unless that is generally acceptable to all Commonwealth members.

The status of the new King's wife

On 9 April 2005, the Prince of Wales, himself a divorced man, married Mrs Camilla Parker Bowles, a divorced woman. By then, the Prince's first wife, the former Princess of Wales, had died, but he and his second wife announced that she would use the title "Duchess of Cornwall", not "Princess of Wales". Similarly, the Prince suggested that, when he became King, his wife could be known as the Princess Consort, rather than "Queen Consort". The Prince of Wales had apparently been advised that there were no legal obstacles to that course, and, accordingly, that legislation would not be required. The suggestion has provoked a certain amount of comment on the legal status of the Prince's second wife when he himself comes to the throne.

The legal position appears to be as follows. Under the common law of England, the wife of the Sovereign at the time of his accession to the throne becomes the Queen of the realm. As such, she has no legal powers, any more than does the husband of a reigning Queen, but the husband of a female Sovereign has no title other than any he already possesses, unless his wife confers one upon him. Although, however, the Sovereign's wife is legally entitled to be known as "Queen [Name]", she is not obliged to use that title. Nor need she be crowned as Queen at her husband's coronation. On the advice of his Ministers in the United Kingdom, the King may confer on his wife a title other than "Queen", and she may be known by that title without any need for a change in the law.

65 Charles Moore "To defend the Church's role is to defend faith as a whole" The Telegraph (online ed, UK, 17 February 2012) <http://www.telegraph.co.uk/news/religion/9089041/To-defend-the-Churchs-role-istodefend-faith-as-a-whole.html>.

66 The Royal Commonwealth Society *An Uncommon Association — A Wealth of Potential: Final Report of the Commonwealth Conversation* (March 2010) at 39 <www.thecommonwealthassociation.org>.

What will need to happen in New Zealand on the Queen's death?

In New Zealand, the death of Queen Elizabeth II and the accession of her successor will presumably be marked in much the same way as when King George VI died and Queen Elizabeth II acceded to the throne. As explained below, however, there have since been some changes in the relevant New Zealand law.

Formal notification of the Queen's death

When the Queen dies, official advice of her death will be sent to the Governor-General by the Private Secretary to the Queen. It will immediately be passed to the Prime Minister. At the same time, the New Zealand authorities will notify the governments of the Cook Islands, Niue and Tokelau, whose people are New Zealand citizens and owe allegiance to the Sovereign in right of New Zealand. The Cabinet can be expected to meet as soon as practicable, and after that as often as is necessary, to take decisions about the formal and ceremonial steps that it is appropriate to take in New Zealand to mourn the death of the Queen and welcome the accession of her successor.

The effect of the demise of the Crown in New Zealand law

The demise of the Crown now has no effect in the law of New Zealand for any purpose, except to pass the throne to the Sovereign's successor.[67] All the attributes of the Sovereign in New Zealand law become those of the Sovereign's successor.[68] So, in most New Zealand legislation and other official documents, there will be no need to change existing references to the Queen. But although things done before the demise by or in the name of the former Sovereign will remain valid, there is now no provision saving the validity of things done in the old Sovereign's name after the time of the demise and before the demise is publicly notified.[69] The virtually instantaneous nature of modern communications removes any practical difficulty in dealing with this situation, but any document in the Sovereign's name made after the demise must, of course, be made in the name of the new Sovereign, not the old.

67 Constitution Act 1986, s 5(1).

68 Constitution Act 1986, s 5(1). See also s 5(2) under which any reference to the Sovereign in "any document or other instrument in force after the commencement of this Act" is to be read as a reference to the Sovereign's heirs and successors, unless the context otherwise requires. The provision applies to private law documents or other instruments. The Constitution Act entered into force on 1 January 1987: s 1(2).

69 Demise of the Crown Act 1908, s 4 (repealed).

Public observance of mourning

Although there is no longer any legal requirement for a Proclamation to be made on the death of the Sovereign, a formal public notification of her death and of the arrangements for the observance of mourning still seems desirable. It would be appropriate for the Governor-General to make an Order in Council officially recording the Queen's death, and the sorrow of the Government and people of New Zealand, and setting out the arrangements for the observance of public mourning.

The Government of New Zealand will almost certainly make a Proclamation of Accession recognising the accession of the new Sovereign. The Accession Proclamation will serve as an acknowledgement that the new Sovereign is the King of New Zealand and its Head of State and refer to him by the name of his choice as set out in the Accession Proclamation made in the United Kingdom, and his royal style and titles as they are likely to be approved by Parliament for use in the Realm of New Zealand. Of necessity, their form will be provisional. The existing Royal Titles Act 1974 is specific to Queen Elizabeth II. On her death, it will become wholly spent. On the death of the Sovereign, a new Act would be required in order to establish the new royal style and titles. Naturally the concurrence of the governments of the other inhabited parts of the Realm of New Zealand would be a prerequisite to its enactment.

4
THE SOVEREIGN'S INSTITUTIONAL ROLE IN THE NEW ZEALAND CONSTITUTION: AN EVALUATION

The living person of the Sovereign, and the concept of the impersonal and perpetual Crown, inseparable from the living person, remain at the heart of New Zealand's executive government. "The crown translates a woman to a Queen".[70] Our considered view is that, in New Zealand's history, no Sovereign has ever been as focused on all her realms, including the Realm of New Zealand, as the Queen of New Zealand is now.

The Sovereign serves as the symbolic leader of the nation, not only in its times of rejoicing or of trial, but also in its everyday life. That fact allows us

70 "Carol Ann Duffy's poem The Crown: A new poem for the 60th anniversary of the coronation by poet laureate Carol Ann Duffy" *The Guardian* (online ed, UK, 4 June 2013) <www.guardian.co.uk/books/2013/jun/04/carol-ann-duffy-the-crown-poem>.

to catch a glimpse of the person who wears the Crown. It seems likely that a future Sovereign in right of New Zealand will continue to carry out the role of Head of State in accordance with tradition, the circumstances at the time, and the Sovereign's own personal style.

Ordinary citizens respond to opportunities to form — directly or through the news media — impressions of the Sovereign as a living person who shares their own human experience, while still retaining the mystery and majesty of the monarchy.

One story we like happens to express a constitutional truism. It was reported as having been told by the Queen herself, after a visit to Goodenough College in London, a hall of residence for Commonwealth postgraduate students and their families. As the Queen came into the room she heard a small boy calling out excitedly "Which is the Queen? Which is the Queen?" The Queen walked over to him and said, "I am the Queen". Then, she recounted, "This young New Zealander looked me straight in the eye and asked, 'Where is your Crown then?'" "Oh", the Queen replied, "the Crown is far too heavy to wear it every day".

Having discussed the role of the Sovereign as Queen of New Zealand, we now look at how, in 1983, she constituted afresh the office of the Governor-General and Commander-in-Chief, as her representative in her Realm of New Zealand.[71]

71 Letters Patent 1983, cl 1.

CHAPTER 6

The Letters Patent, the Governor-General and the Realm of New Zealand

1 INTRODUCTION

In this chapter we introduce the Governor-General and Commander-in-Chief of the Realm of New Zealand, who is the Sovereign's representative in the Realm. The office of Governor-General is constituted by Letters Patent, a traditional legal instrument.[1] We explain that, in 1983, the Sovereign issued new Letters Patent constituting the Governor-General's office. In part 2 we discuss the reasons for that initiative, the making of the instrument, its legal effect and its relationship to other sources of law. In part 3 we explain why the 1983 Letters Patent, for the first time, described the Governor-General as holding office in respect of the various geographical areas which together comprise the "Realm of New Zealand": New Zealand itself, the self-governing states of the Cook Islands and of Niue, and Tokelau and the Ross Dependency. We explore the significance of the reference to the Realm of New Zealand newly included in the Letters Patent, and stress the fact that its use does not affect the distinct legal and political status of the different parts of the Realm.

1 Letters Patent Constituting the Office of Governor and Commander-in-chief of the Dominion of New Zealand [1908] I AJHR A2 at 14. Letters Patent, literally an open letter, were traditionally used to confer rights or authority, and are still used by the Sovereign to constitute the office of the Governor-General and empower the office-holder.

2
MAKING THE 1983 LETTERS PATENT

The Sovereign reconstitutes the office of Governor-General

On 28 October 1983, Elizabeth II, Queen of New Zealand, signed with Her Regal Hand[2] a document called, in its printed form, "Letters Patent Constituting the Office of Governor-General of New Zealand". In broad outline, the Letters Patent:

- constitute the office of Governor-General and Commander-in-Chief of the Realm of New Zealand;
- provide for the appointment of the Governor-General and the taking and holding of office;
- constitute an Executive Council to advise the Sovereign and the Governor-General on the government of the Realm, and empower the Governor-General to appoint its members;
- authorise the Governor-General to exercise the executive authority of the Realm of New Zealand and confer other powers, including the power to appoint Ministers and other officers; and
- make provision for the exercise of the Governor-General's powers if the office is vacant, or the Governor-General is, for any reason, unable to exercise them.

That description looks straightforward, but it conceals some important matters. We deal first with the overarching conceptual issues, including the question of who advises the Sovereign about how the office of the Governor-General should be constituted. We then consider "the Realm of New Zealand" comprising the five countries or territories within the sovereignty of the Queen in right of New Zealand.

2 See the testimonium clause at the end of the document. It has been suggested that the document was not signed by the Queen: Gavin McLean *The Governors: New Zealand's Governors and Governors-General* (Otago University Press, Dunedin, 2006) at 16. That, however, was a misapprehension arising from the fact that the printed document does not reproduce the Queen's signature. The Queen signed the original document at the top right-hand corner of the first page. The Prime Minister, RD Muldoon, countersigned the document at the foot of the last page.

Instruments empowering and instructing Governors

Ever since Queen Victoria issued a Commission to Captain Hobson as Governor,[3] the Sovereign has made continuous provision for the office of Governor or Governor-General of New Zealand, and has conferred certain powers on its holder. These instruments have been issued in the exercise of a prerogative power vested in the Sovereign. In law it is known as the prerogative constituent power. At first, the prerogative instruments were carefully tailored to the circumstances of New Zealand, and dovetailed with the statute law. Immediately after the conferment of representative government by the New Zealand Constitution Act 1852 (UK),[4] a new instrument constituting the office of Governor of New Zealand was issued, together with Royal Instructions. The Constitution Act had reserved certain constitutional functions to the Sovereign, except so far as she might delegate them to the Governor. The new Letters Patent, issued at the same time, delegated to the Governor some of the Sovereign's functions under the 1852 Act. To that extent, the instrument had effect as subordinate legislation.

From then on, however, an ever-widening gap developed between the words of the Letters Patent and accompanying Royal Instructions and the other laws and practices that affected the way in which the institutions established by the Letters Patent functioned in practice. One factor was the evolutionary nature of the relevant constitutional conventions. These shaped the two key relationships: that between the Governor and his New Zealand Ministers; and that between the self-governing colony (later the Dominion of New Zealand) and the Government of the United Kingdom.[5] The formal instruments were periodically updated to take some account of the developments in both areas, but were seldom fully up to date. At the same time, the prerogative instruments originally written specifically for New Zealand were gradually replaced by instruments in a common form for all the self-governing Dominions. They did not necessarily fit well with all the New Zealand legislation.

It was not until the early 1960s that the New Zealand authorities began to realise that, after 1931, the responsibility for updating the Letters Patent had moved from London to Wellington. In 1976, the Prime Minister's Department asked Alison Quentin-Baxter to review the work already done and to bring it to a conclusion. The resulting 1980 Report led to the 1983 Letters Patent

3 See Chapter 2 Building the Modern Constitution, fn 1, at 12.

4 15 & 16 Vict c 72.

5 For an explanation of Dominion status see Chapter 2 Building the Modern Constitution, under the subheading Dominion status, at 24–30.

which replaced earlier Letters Patent and associated documents issued by King George V in 1917.[6]

Like its predecessor, the 1983 instrument was made by the Sovereign in the exercise of what is known as the prerogative constituent power. In New Zealand, that aspect of the royal prerogative is used only to constitute the office of the Sovereign's representative. It is therefore not well known, although, as we show in this and later chapters, its exercise for that purpose is the basis of New Zealand's executive government.

Essentially, the structure originally established to give New Zealand responsible government in 1856 has changed little. But the setting in which the constitutional actors operate and the expectations which influence their behaviour have changed vastly.

Putting the current instrument in place

The Letters Patent of 1917 had been signed by King George V, countersigned by Sir George Shuster on behalf of the Secretary of State for the Colonies, and sealed with the Great Seal of the United Kingdom. A draft of the instrument would have been approved by the Privy Council, the body through which United Kingdom Ministers have traditionally advised the Sovereign on matters pertaining to the colonies.

By the 1970s, the New Zealand authorities were looking for a way in which New Zealand Ministers, exclusively, could tender advice to the Sovereign in her capacity as Queen of New Zealand. In 1977, with the need for new Letters Patent in mind, Parliament passed an Act assenting to the establishment by Her Majesty and her successors of the Seal of New Zealand, for use on instruments made by the Sovereign or the Governor-General on the advice of a New Zealand Minister in the Executive Council or otherwise.[7] The Queen established the Seal of New Zealand by a Proclamation made at Wellington on 28 February 1977.[8]

The 1980 Report had explained that, on a matter as important as the reconstitution of the office of the Governor-General, it would not be appropriate for the Sovereign to be advised by the New Zealand Prime Minister alone. The preferred option was for Her Majesty herself to make an Order, acting on the advice and with the consent of the Executive Council while visiting

6 Alison Quentin-Baxter *Review of the Letters Patent 1917 Constituting the Office of Governor-General of New Zealand: Report* (Cabinet Office, Wellington, 1980) [1980 Report].

7 Seal of New Zealand Act 1977, ss 2 and 3.

8 The Seal of New Zealand Proclamation SR 1977/29.

New Zealand. That was not practicable. Instead, the Governor-General, acting on the advice and with the consent of the Executive Council, requested Her Majesty to make new Letters Patent while still in London. A draft of the proposed new Letters Patent was attached to the request.

As the name suggests, Letters Patent are in the form of an open letter addressed to all who read them, and are written in the first person, as if by the Queen herself. The drafting style of the new instrument, particularly when it came to the formal provisions, was modelled on that of the 1947 Canadian Letters Patent, then the most recent precedent. To the extent that they are cast in the traditional form, these provisions have been described as "quaint, and certainly belonging to a century other than the 21st".[9]

Since their making in 1983, the Letters Patent have been amended twice, in each case because it was necessary to take proper account of newly made changes to the statute law.[10] On each occasion the opportunity was taken to update the instrument in other ways. Essentially, however, the instrument remains in its original form.

Part of the law of the Realm of New Zealand

On 1 November 1983, the Letters Patent constituting the office of Governor-General took effect as part of the law of the Realm of New Zealand, "comprising New Zealand, the self-governing state of the Cook Islands, the self-governing state of Niue, Tokelau, and the Ross Dependency".[11]

As a first step in making the instrument, a draft was approved by the Leader of the Opposition and the Leader of the Social Credit Party, which was also represented in Parliament at the time. Later, they approved the procedure that would be followed to give the Letters Patent legal force. The governments of the self-governing states of the Cook Islands and of Niue also signified their informal approval of the draft. It was then submitted for the informal approval of the Queen.

Once that approval had been received, the governments of the Cook Islands and of Niue signified their formal approval.[12] An Order in Council was then made requesting Her Majesty's signature.[13] The Queen signed the Letters

9 Tony Angelo "The Letters Patent" [2007] NZLJ 5 at 6. The comment referred to the Letters Patent (2006) Amending Letters Patent Constituting the Office of Governor-General of New Zealand (SR 2006/219) which had maintained the style of the 1983 Letters Patent it had amended.
10 See, for example, Constitution Act 1986, Supreme Court Act 2003.
11 Letters Patent 1983, cl 19.
12 See Letters Patent 1983, Preamble, 7th recital.
13 Order in Council made on 26 September 1983.

Patent in London on 28 October 1983. The instrument was then returned to New Zealand, countersigned by the Prime Minister, the Rt Hon Robert Muldoon, and sealed with the Seal of New Zealand.

By special request, and as an exception to the general rule that the Sovereign signs only one copy of a legal instrument, the Queen signed the Letters Patent in duplicate. One copy is held in the Cabinet Room.[14] It is to be wondered, however, whether the Ministers of the Crown, who regularly make their most important decisions there, are aware that the document nearby is the formal source of their authority as Ministers, and also of some of their powers.

Legal and policy issues

The structure of the 1983 Letters Patent took account of some overarching legal and policy considerations. The first was the limited nature of the prerogative constituent power. By the 1980s, it could not be used to make any provision affecting Parliament or the courts. Provision for those branches of government had long been made by statute. Essentially, therefore, the Letters Patent are concerned with the executive branch of government. Within that ambit, the focus is on the office of Governor-General, and things directly linked to that office, such as the Executive Council.

Secondly, although the Letters Patent do not say so expressly, the powers they confer must always be exercised in accordance with the unwritten rules of New Zealand's constitution. We refer, of course, to constitutional conventions. The instrument contains a pointer to this basic principle by constituting an Executive Council "to advise Us and Our Governor-General", and describes the members of the Executive Council as "Our responsible advisers".

The third consideration was the need to take account of the relationship between the Letters Patent and the statute law, a matter we now discuss.

The Letters Patent and the statute law

The general principles apply

The Letters Patent are legislation, but they are legislation of a special kind. By definition, they are "regulations" for the purposes of references to that term

14 Situated in the Executive Wing, Parliament Building, and more commonly known as the Cabinet Room. The second signed copy is held by Archives New Zealand.

in the statute law.[15] And, because they are made in the exercise of the royal prerogative, the Letters Patent have the same relationship to Acts of Parliament as an exercise of other prerogative powers.

Acts of Parliament and the Letters Patent can and do sit comfortably side by side as sources of the law. But the Letters Patent cannot amend an Act of Parliament, or do, or authorise the doing, of anything inconsistent with such an Act. Nor can they do anything which only Parliament can do, such as to impose, or grant immunity from, a tax, or appropriate the expenditure of public money. From earliest times, therefore, Parliament has made separate provision for the payment of the salary of the Governor or Governor-General out of New Zealand's public revenues.[16]

Although the making of Letters Patent provided an opportunity to harmonise the new instrument with the statute law then in force, they recognise that statute law is unlikely to remain static:[17]

> Our Governor-General shall do and execute all the powers and authorities of the office according to —
>
> . . .
>
> Such laws as are now or shall hereafter be in force in Our Realm of New Zealand or any part thereof.

That direction is reiterated in other clauses, and potentially applies to every provision of the instrument. It is a direction to give effect to the Letters Patent consistently with any relevant statute law.

15 At the time of their making, the 1983 Letters Patent were "regulations" for the purposes of the Regulations Act 1936, s 3, which had required their publication in the *Statutory Regulations* series. See now the Acts and Regulations Publication Act 1989, s 2 which defines "regulations" by importing the definition of "regulations" in s 2(d) of the Regulations (Disallowance) Act 1989. That definition includes "an instrument made under . . . the Royal Prerogative and having the force of law in New Zealand". Initially, however, the Letters Patent were not "regulations" for the purposes of the Acts Interpretation Act 1924, s 4 which defined "regulations" as meaning "regulations made by the Governor-General in Council". The 1989 definition of "regulations" was prospectively substituted for that definition, but the substitution was not retrospective. The Interpretation Act 1999, ss 4 and 29(d), however, applies that definition retrospectively to the 1983 Letters Patent, including amendments made from time to time.

16 The need for a colony to bear the expenses of its own government was a basic principle of British colonial policy. The New Zealand Constitution Act 1852 (UK), above n 4, therefore included a permanent appropriation of £2,500 in payment of the Governor's salary: s 64 and Schedule. We have not sought to trace the authority made for that purpose in the years after New Zealand became a separate colony and before the 1852 Act took effect. As to the provision now made by the Governor-General Act 2010, see Chapter 7 The Office of Governor-General and Commander-in-Chief, under the subheading The Governor-General's salary and expenses, at 126–127.

17 Clause 4(b). See also the qualifications in the concluding provisions of cl 1 and the chapeau to cl 11, the form of the Governor-General's oath of office in cl 6(b), and the word "lawfully" in cl 10; and Letters Patent 1917, cl 2.

Statutes need to be understood in their context

In commenting on the substantive provisions of the Letters Patent in this and other chapters, we take account of many statutory provisions. It should not be assumed, however, that if something is provided for in an Act of Parliament, the statutory provision always supersedes the Letters Patent. Sometimes, the prerogative is preserved, expressly or by implication. Sometimes, the statutory provision is merely declaratory, included so as to give a full picture, but without affecting the force of the Letters Patent as the primary source of the law.

That is particularly true of some provisions of the Constitution Act 1986. For example, that Act provides that "[t]he Governor-General appointed by the Sovereign is the Sovereign's representative in New Zealand".[18] That provision, however, is purely descriptive. It does not supersede — in the sense of making unnecessary — the provision made in the Letters Patent that the holder of the office shall be appointed by the Sovereign,[19] and shall be "our representative in our Realm of New Zealand".[20] That remains the substantive operative provision.

A single, self-contained document

The 1983 Letters Patent take the form of a single document which is self-contained. In contrast with the 1917 Letters Patent,[21] the 1983 instrument was not accompanied by Royal Instructions. The essential purpose of Royal Instructions was to specify how far the Governor or Governor-General was required to exercise his powers and authorities as directed by Ministers in the United Kingdom, while otherwise being required to act in accordance with the advice of Ministers in the colony or Dominion concerned.

As time went on, it had become clear that there was a third possibility. In some circumstances the Governor-General was expected or permitted to act, not as instructed or advised, but in his own deliberate judgement. By 1917, the Royal Instruction had been pared back to a common-form requirement to:[22]

18 Section 2(1).
19 Clause 2.
20 Clause 1. See *Constitutional Reform: First and Second Reports released by the Minister of Justice, the Hon. Geoffrey Palmer* (Department of Justice, Wellington, 1986) at [3.7].
21 Clause 1.
22 Royal Instructions 1917, cl 5. The Instructions also reflected other aspects of the former colonial relationship in less dramatic ways that stemmed from their role as subordinate legislation for the purposes of the New Zealand Constitution Act 1852 (UK), above n 4, s 56.

> . . . be guided by the advice of the Executive Council, but if in any case [the Governor-General] shall see sufficient cause to dissent from the opinion of the said Council, he may act in the exercise of his powers and authorities in opposition to the opinion of the Council, reporting to Us without delay, with the reasons for his so acting.

There was a masterly silence about what might happen next.

By 1980, this Instruction, and the provision under which it had been given, raised two issues. The first was the scope, under the current constitutional conventions in New Zealand, of a Governor-General's basic duty to accept and act on the advice tendered by the responsible Ministers. We pursue that matter in later chapters. The immediate question, however, was whether provision for the giving of Royal Instructions to the Governor-General[23] still had any place in the constitutional arrangements of an independent Commonwealth realm. Analysis of the governing principles and an examination of the current practice both showed clearly that it did not.

The Balfour Declaration and the Statute of Westminster had established that the Governor-General was in the same relationship with his Ministers as was the Sovereign in the United Kingdom with his.[24] Ministers in the United Kingdom no longer had any part in a Governor-General's appointment, or for that matter his recall, let alone the way in which the Governor-General performed the duties of the office. Conversely, the Governor-General of a realm no longer had a right to appeal to the Sovereign, and through the Sovereign to Ministers in the United Kingdom, if disquieted by the advice received from Ministers in the realm concerned.

From then on, it has been clear that the Sovereign would be able to give Instructions to a Governor-General only on the advice of the Prime Minister in the realm concerned. For that reason, everything that the Sovereign needs to say to a Governor-General can be included in the instrument constituting the office itself. That instrument may be a stand-alone document, as in Canada, or a comprehensive constitution, as in the realms that came to nationhood after World War II. None of those instruments makes any provision for the giving of Royal Instructions. By 1980, it was clear that, in New Zealand, too, that established model should be followed. Accordingly, the 1983 Letters Patent are a self-contained, stand-alone instrument that does not provide for the giving of Royal Instructions.[25]

23 Royal Instructions 1917, cl 2.

24 See Chapter 2 Building the Modern Constitution, fn 58, at 24–28.

25 In making new Letters Patent in 1984, the Government of the Commonwealth of Australia followed that and the earlier precedents and repealed the existing Royal Instructions.

We now look at the use in the 1983 Letters Patent of the new term, "the Realm of New Zealand". The instrument itself provides that it is subject to the law of the part of the realm concerned. We explain why this provision was necessary and what the notion of the single Realm of New Zealand signifies today.

3
THE LETTERS PATENT AND THE REALM OF NEW ZEALAND

"Our Realm of New Zealand"

A new description

For the first time, the 1983 Letters Patent described the Governor-General as holding office in a geographical area called the "Realm of New Zealand". The expression itself was an extrapolation from the words of the Sovereign's royal style and titles as prescribed by the Royal Titles Act 1974:[26]

> Queen Elizabeth the Second, . . . Queen of New Zealand and Her Other Realms and Territories . . .

The clear implication is that New Zealand is itself a "realm", comprising all the countries and territories within the territorial sovereignty of the Queen in right of New Zealand. The Royal Titles Act was — and still is — part of the law of every part of the realm thus conceived.[27]

The territorial reach of the Letters Patent

The 1917 Letters Patent had applied to the geographical areas which, from 1840 on, the Sovereign had declared to have been "brought within the boundaries of" New Zealand. They then comprised New Zealand itself, including its outlying islands, and the more distant Cook Islands and Niue which had been annexed to the Crown in 1901. By 1980, however, a number of developments posed real questions about the geographical areas to which new Letters Patent should apply.

26 Royal Titles Act 1974, s 2.
27 Section 3.

In 1923, the Governor-General of New Zealand had been made the Governor of the Ross Dependency,[28] a wedge-shaped slice of the Antarctic continent claimed by the United Kingdom Government to be "part of Her Majesty's possessions".[29] On behalf of the Sovereign, a Secretary of State issued an Instruction that, in exercising the functions of Governor of the Ross Dependency, the Governor-General was to be guided by the advice of the New Zealand Executive Council.[30]

Then, in 1925, Tokelau, a group of three small South Pacific atolls then known also as the Union Islands, were detached from the Gilbert and Ellice Islands — the United Kingdom colony to which they had been annexed.[31] The Governor-General of New Zealand was appointed as Governor of Tokelau. His powers in that capacity were delegated to the High Commissioner of Western Samoa, the senior New Zealand official in what was then a League of Nations Mandated Territory administered by New Zealand.[32]

Although New Zealand administered Western Samoa, as it was then known, under the Mandate, and later under a United Nations Trusteeship Agreement, Samoa was never brought within the sovereignty of the Crown. Accordingly, the Governor-General had no authority under the 1917 Letters Patent in respect of Samoa. The jurisdiction conferred by the Mandate was, however, vested in the Sovereign,[33] and Parliament invested the Governor-General with certain statutory powers.[34] On 1 January 1962, Parliament recognised the independence of Samoa.[35]

The responsibilities of the Governor-General in respect of the Ross Dependency and Tokelau were exercised on the advice of New Zealand Ministers. Those Ministers originally regarded their authority as that of an agent, acting on behalf of the United Kingdom Government. By the end of World War II, however, it was apparent that changes in the relationships between the Sovereign and the British Dominions recorded in the 1926 Balfour Declaration and the 1931 Statute of Westminster had made the Crown divisible in reality, although that was yet fully to be acknowledged. Because the Governor-General was advised in respect of both the Ross Dependency and

28 Ross Dependency Boundaries and Government Order 1923.

29 Preamble and cl 1.

30 Despatch number 178 dated 9 August 1923, preserved in the Archives of the Governor-General (reference G.484/3).

31 Union Islands (No 1) Order 1925 and Union Islands (No 2) Order 1925.

32 Union Islands (No 2) Order 1925. The Order was subsequently amended by s 3(3) of the Samoa Amendment Act 1947.

33 Western Samoa Order 1920, made by His Majesty with the advice of His Privy Council on 11 March 1920.

34 Samoa Act 1921.

35 Western Samoa Act 1961, s 3.

Tokelau solely by New Zealand Ministers, New Zealand had been invested with an exclusive constitutional responsibility for both.

On 1 January 1949, Tokelau, with the agreement of the United Kingdom Government, was declared to form part of New Zealand.[36] No such declaration has ever been made in respect of the Ross Dependency, but events were to confirm the exclusive and plenary nature of New Zealand's domestic law responsibility. On 1 December 1959, New Zealand signed the Antarctic Treaty.[37] In order to give effect to the treaty in domestic law, Parliament then enacted the Antarctica Act 1960. Among other things, the Act provided for the trial and punishment in New Zealand of any person who, in the Ross Dependency, had done or omitted any act that would have been a crime if it had been done or omitted in New Zealand.[38] The Antarctica Act can be seen as New Zealand's exercise of territorial sovereignty in respect of the Ross Dependency, consistently, however, with the carefully drafted treaty provisions.

At San Francisco in 1945, New Zealand's Prime Minister, Peter Fraser, had taken a leading part in the drafting of the United Nations Charter provisions about non-self-governing territories. His government decided that although the Cook Islands and Niue had been brought within the boundaries of New Zealand, both, together with Tokelau, were "Non-self-governing" countries for the purposes of Chapter XI of the United Nations Charter. Accordingly, New Zealand accepted the relevant Charter obligations in respect of all three territories. They included the obligation "to develop self-government" in respect of each.[39]

The Cook Islands became self-governing on 4 August 1965.[40] A decade later, Niue was ready to follow suit, and became self-governing on 19 October 1974.[41] Those landmark developments revealed an element of divisibility even within the legal person of the Queen in right of New Zealand, originally regarded as a unitary entity. The new status of the Cook Islands and Niue as "self-governing states" clearly raised the question whether new Letters Patent should continue to apply to them, as the 1917 Letters Patent still did.

36 Tokelau Act 1948, s 3.
37 The Antarctic Treaty 402 UNTS 71 (signed 1 December 1959, entered into force 23 June 1961).
38 Antarctica Act 1960, s 3.
39 Charter of the United Nations, art 73(b).
40 Cook Islands Constitution Act 1964, ss 1(2) and 4; Cook Islands Constitution Act Commencement Order 1965 SR 1965/128.
41 Niue Constitution Act 1974, s 1(2); Niue Constitution Act Commencement Order 1974 SR 1974/286.

Replacing an outdated concept

The events just described clearly show that New Zealand's relationships with each of the countries or territories concerned no longer depended on whether or not it had been brought within the boundaries of New Zealand. Although the relevant enactments are still part of New Zealand law,[42] the so-called "boundaries" or "limits" are not borders which themselves signify the extent of New Zealand's territorial jurisdiction.[43] They are simply straight lines of latitude and longitude enclosing certain islands or island groups for the purpose of identifying them. In most, if not all, cases the island or island group concerned had already been brought within the sovereignty of the Crown. Bringing territory within the boundaries of New Zealand did, however, serve an essential purpose. In the years before New Zealand's adoption of the Statute of Westminster, it gave the New Zealand Parliament the necessary authority to make laws for its governance.[44]

That did not mean, however, that the laws applying to mainland New Zealand would necessarily have to apply to the country or territory that had newly been made part of New Zealand. This was never the case in respect of the Cook Islands or Niue. They were always administered under separate sets of laws. Since 1947, however, Parliament has had the "full power to make laws".[45] There is no longer a shadowy restriction on their territorial reach. But Parliament itself has now irrevocably empowered the Cook Islands and Niue each to take itself out of the reach of laws made by the New Zealand Parliament, and both, in effect, have done so. In each, however, the executive authority continues to be vested in the Sovereign in right of New Zealand. Each still has some kind of constitutional connection with her representative in New Zealand, the Governor-General, although the Cook Islands now has its own "Queen's Representative". Both still had a constitutional connection with New Zealand that, it was thought, should continue to be recognised in the Letters Patent.

The 1980 Report recommended that the Letters Patent constituting the office of Governor-General should take effect not only in New Zealand law, but also

42 See, for example, the New Zealand Boundaries Act 1863 (UK) 26 & 27 Vict c 23 which bears the long title "An Act to alter the boundaries of New Zealand", and, in the Preamble, recites that it is expedient to alter the "limits" of the Colony of New Zealand. The Act is part of the laws of New Zealand: Imperial Laws Application Act 1988, s 3(1) and sch 1.

43 Compare the different meaning of "limits" in the expressions "territorial limits of New Zealand", "limits of New Zealand", or a similar expression when used as a territorial description. Those expressions are defined as meaning the outer limits of the territorial sea of New Zealand: Interpretation Act 1999, s 29.

44 Originally Parliament could make laws only for the territorial area described as "New Zealand".

45 See Chapter 2 Building the Modern Constitution, text following fn 68, at 29.

in the law of the Cook Islands, Niue, Tokelau and the Ross Dependency. For that purpose, all five states or territories should be regarded as continuing to be parts of a single "Realm of New Zealand". The new instrument would, however, need to take full account of the different sets of laws, usually referred to as "legal systems", in each part of the realm, including the different arrangements for the governance of each, already in place or likely to be introduced within the foreseeable future. That was the approach in drafting the new instrument. We now explain the consequences for the interpretation of the 1983 Letters Patent, generally, and in the law of each part of the realm.

The need to take account of the laws in all parts of the Realm

The 1983 Letters Patent provide that the Governor-General and Commander-in-Chief[46] is the representative of the Sovereign "in and over Our Realm of New Zealand". The Governor-General has, and may exercise, in the whole of the Realm, the powers and authorities conferred by the Letters Patent. Those general provisions are made subject to two overriding conditions.

First, the role of the Governor-General as the Queen's representative in the Realm of New Zealand is:[47]

> without prejudice to the office, powers, or authorities of any other person who has been or may be appointed to represent Us in any part of Our Realm of New Zealand and to exercise powers and authorities on Our behalf.

That saving provision takes account, in particular, of the role of the Queen's Representative in the Cook Islands, and also the fact that, since 1924, the Governor-General has held a separate appointment as the Governor of the Ross Dependency. We describe the implications of those roles below.

Secondly, as already mentioned, all the powers and authorities conferred on the Governor-General by the Letters Patent in respect of the Realm are governed by the general qualification "except as may be otherwise provided by law".[48] That law may be the law of any part of the Realm. The relevant provision requires the Governor-General to exercise the powers and authorities of the office in accordance with ". . . such laws as are now or shall hereafter be in force in Our Realm of New Zealand or any part thereof".[49]

46 In this book, the "Governor-General and Commander-in-Chief" is referred to as the Governor-General, unless the context otherwise requires.
47 Clause 1.
48 Clause 1.
49 Clause 4.

The same principle is reflected in the oath for the due execution of the office. The Governor-General promises faithfully and impartially to serve the reigning Sovereign and the people of the Realm of New Zealand ". . . in accordance with their respective laws and customs".[50] The Governor-General's roles are therefore distinct and different in respect of each part of the Realm.

The Realm of New Zealand in the constitution

The references in the 1983 Letters Patent to "the Realm of New Zealand" are sometimes misunderstood. The Realm was simply a way of referring to all, or to any one or more, of the five countries or territories over which the Sovereign in right of New Zealand reigns. In respect of the Ross Dependency, the role of the Governor-General has always been a large one, at least on paper. In respect of the Cook Islands, the Governor-General's role is now very small. In Niue, the Governor-General is the Sovereign's representative, but that does not give him or her the same role as that of the Sovereign's representative in New Zealand. Tokelau, technically a "non-self-governing" territory for the purposes of the Charter of the United Nations, is different again.

The fact that the Governor-General has some role in respect of each part of the Realm was seen as making it desirable for the Letters Patent to be part of the law of every part. In the law of each part, however, the 1983 instrument has a very different effect. The Realm is therefore the sum of its parts, not an entity in itself. On its face, the term is merely a drafting device, avoiding the need to list all the parts on every occasion, with the qualification that the term also means "any one or more of those parts, as the case requires". Historically, the Realm of New Zealand is the outcome of the distinctive legal and political relationships between New Zealand and each of the other parts of the Realm. Those other parts have no direct links with one another.

To some extent, however, the concept of the Realm of New Zealand has taken on a life of its own. The role of the Sovereign in right of New Zealand as Queen of all parts of the Realm can be seen as more than the recognition of a distant monarch. The common Sovereign symbolises the shared experiences and continuing status of the peoples of the Realm. Its populated parts are the homes of Polynesian peoples of the South Pacific. All were affected, in greater or lesser measure, by the explorers, traders and settlers from Europe and elsewhere who arrived on their shores. All parts of the Realm were annexed by the British monarch, colonised under the New Zealand flag, and affected by the received English law as well as that enacted in New Zealand. Everyone

50 Clause 6.

who now belongs to any part of the Realm has, as of right, the status of a New Zealand citizen. Those factors give the Realm of New Zealand a reality going well beyond the words of the Letters Patent which gave the Realm a constitutional role.

At the same time, it is important to understand, not only what the Realm of New Zealand is, but also what it is not. The references in the Letters Patent to the Realm of New Zealand do not mean that New Zealand is a federal state. There is no Prime Minister or government of the Realm. Nor do Acts of the New Zealand Parliament become part of the law of the self-governing state of the Cook Islands or the self-governing state of Niue unless the law of the state concerned so provides.

The Government and Parliament of New Zealand do, however, have legislative and executive authority in respect of Tokelau and the Ross Dependency, but each of those territories also has its own legal system, conferring real legislative and executive powers in the case of Tokelau and nominal powers in the case of the Ross Dependency. Accordingly, nothing can be seen as "the law of the Realm" unless, by a law-making process that its own law recognises, it has become the law of every part. In making the 1983 Letters Patent in the exercise of the prerogative constituent power, the Sovereign exercised the only legislative power that is common to the law of all parts of the Realm.

Although the executive authority of each part of the Realm is vested in the Queen in right of New Zealand, she is separately advised in respect of New Zealand and each of the two self-governing states. That principle, however, has to operate within the parameters of another: the Sovereign has a single adviser in respect of each of her realms.

The Sovereign in right of the different parts of the Realm of New Zealand

Once it had been recognised that the Crown is divisible, as among the Sovereign's different realms, it was also recognised that she must be able to look to a single adviser in respect of each. The convention first emerged in respect of the long-established federal states. In Canada, the Sovereign is represented not only by a Governor-General, but also by a Lieutenant Governor in each province. Similarly, in Australia, she is represented by the Governor-General, and also a Governor in each state. Those offices reflect the fact that the Canadian provinces and the Australian states were once separate colonies, each having its own relationship with the Sovereign. Even so, the Sovereign now acts only on the advice of the Prime Minister of Canada or of Australia as the case may be.

That practice is sometimes rationalised on the basis that the Canadian provinces and the Australian states are not "Sovereign independent countries",[51] but that formulation simply reflects the chain of events since 1926, when the governing principle was first enunciated: "[I]t is the right of the Government of each Dominion to advise the Crown in all matters relating to its own affairs."[52]

It was once usual to regard "sovereign independence" as a main criterion for "full membership" of the Commonwealth. On that basis, the units of a federal state did not qualify as separate members of the Commonwealth. "Sovereign independence" is now a rather dated way of referring to statehood in international law, and "full" membership of the Commonwealth no longer figures in discussions about eligibility to become a Commonwealth member. Even so, statehood is still relevant.

Although three parts of the Realm of New Zealand, the Cook Islands and Niue, as well as New Zealand itself, are "states" at international law, the Cook Islands and Niue remain freely associated with New Zealand, and are parts of a single "Realm of New Zealand". Constitutionally, the Prime Minister of New Zealand is not, however, the Prime Minister of the Realm. He or she cannot speak for a self-governing state. Each has a Prime Minister or a Premier of its own.

The principle remains that Her Majesty cannot be expected to determine the allocation of responsibilities as among the different parts of what remains a single realm. There must be someone with the authority to speak for the Realm as a whole, and able to advise the Sovereign on the status of its individual parts. History, as well as the law of some, but not all, parts of the Realm of New Zealand, has given that task to the Prime Minister of New Zealand. As will be seen, it has been necessary to work out a way of reconciling that accepted practice with the principle that the Head of Government in a self-governing state like the Cook Islands or Niue has the right to advise the Sovereign directly on a matter relating solely to that state. What may now be regarded as the governing conventions are explained below.

On matters concerning the Sovereign that affect each part of the Realm in the same way, and on which it is essential to maintain uniform law in all parts of the Realm (such as a change in the royal style and titles), the Prime Minister of New Zealand speaks to the Sovereign on behalf of the Realm, but only after

51 Letter from the Private Secretary to the Queen, Sir Philip Moore, to the Governor-General of New Zealand, Sir Arthur Porritt (26 December 1970).

52 "Report of the Inter-Imperial Relations Committee of the Imperial Conference of 1926" (Cmd 2768, 1926) at 5.

consulting the governments of the self-governing states and, more recently, the government of Tokelau as well.[53]

In the days before the self-government of the associated states, it was the practice to ensure that any change in New Zealand law on matters of that kind would take effect also in the law of the Cook Islands, Niue and Tokelau. That course is no longer possible in respect of the Cook Islands, and can occur in respect of Niue only at its request and with its consent, given by Act — a procedure now rarely undertaken, if at all. Even in respect of Tokelau, the direct application of a New Zealand Act may not necessarily be the preferred option.

In the constitutions or other laws of all three, however, a reference, express or implied, to "the Sovereign in right of New Zealand" can be seen as importing by reference any change that may be made in New Zealand law in respect of the Sovereign, if it is clearly pertinent to her role in all parts of the Realm. On that basis, it can be seen as unnecessary expressly to amend the local law (although that would still remain an option). For that reason, it is all the more important that, before the New Zealand Parliament makes any such changes to its own law, the New Zealand Government should observe what can be regarded as a constitutional convention requiring prior consultation with the other parts of the Realm.

The practice just described cannot, however, be seen as applying to a change to the law of New Zealand that would bring to an end the Sovereign's role as New Zealand's Head of State. As a matter of law, the constitutions of the Cook Islands and of Niue can be changed only by the people of the self-governing state concerned, and the law of Tokelau should not be so changed unless its people so wish. The people of the other parts of the Realm have the same right as the people of New Zealand to decide the future of their constitution.

4
CONCLUSIONS ON THE SOVEREIGN AND THE GOVERNOR-GENERAL'S ROLE IN THE DIFFERENT PARTS OF THE REALM

The diverse countries and territories

We have shown that New Zealand is the hub of the Realm. The Governor-General is essentially a New Zealand organ of government, advised by New Zealand

53 An assurance to that effect was given in the Joint Centenary Declaration of the Principles of the Relationship between New Zealand and the Cook Islands, 11 June 2001, cl 3(2).

Ministers, and the role performed by the holder is woven into the fabric of the constitution as a whole. That said, each other part of the Realm has (notionally in the case of the Ross Dependency) its own governmental institutions. In these the Governor-General plays a greater or lesser part. Generally speaking, the Governor-General still acts on the advice of New Zealand Ministers, with two exceptions. First, the constitution of the self-governing state of Niue gives the Governor-General a distinct role, acting on the advice of his or her Niue Ministers. Secondly, under its own constitution the self-governing state of the Cook Islands now has its own Queen's Representative, but the Governor-General, acting on the advice of the New Zealand Prime Minister, plays a part in transmitting to the Sovereign the advice of the Prime Minister of the Cook Islands on appointments to that office.

Although the Letters Patent are part of the law of all the parts of the Realm of New Zealand, they have effect in each part only so far as consistent with its other law. While therefore having greater or lesser practical relevance in the parts of the Realm other than New Zealand, the Letters Patent signify that, in those parts too, the Governor-General remains an essential link with the Sovereign in right of New Zealand.

The exercise of the Sovereign's power to issue Letters Patent constituting the office of Governor-General of the Realm of New Zealand is now the only way of making law for all parts of the Realm. The organs of government the Letters Patent constitute and the powers they confer are, however, primarily concerned with the governance of New Zealand. That is not surprising, in view of the history of the Realm and New Zealand's role as its core part.

The Realm of New Zealand now and in the future

The Realm of New Zealand is made up of five countries or territories each with its own distinct but overlapping legal system. The main unifying factor is that, under its own law, each country or territory that is part of the Realm is within the territorial sovereignty of the Queen in right of New Zealand. The executive authority of each is vested in the Sovereign. All the peoples of the Realm therefore owe allegiance to that Sovereign, and, although that allegiance is no longer the legal basis of their citizenship, all, under New Zealand law, are New Zealand citizens. The single Sovereign is a symbol of their shared rights and responsibilities. The Sovereign is now, to a greater or lesser extent, separately advised in respect of each part of the Realm.

What if New Zealand were to become a republic?

The peoples of the other populated parts of the Realm should be seen as free to make their own decisions about whether they wish to maintain or bring to an end their present allegiance to the Sovereign, however unprecedented it may be to have to find a way of accommodating the decisions of such small communities. Here we consider briefly a different aspect of a scenario in which New Zealand or, for that matter, another populated part of the Realm, chooses to bring its people's allegiance to the Sovereign to an end. Such a situation would call for a cool-headed first reaction and a careful analysis of where the people's real interests lie.

First, a change in the location of territorial sovereignty over any part of what is now the Realm would not in itself bring the relationships between New Zealand and the other part or parts of the Realm to an end.[54] Neither would a change in the form of the government of any part of the Realm. The concept of common allegiance to the Sovereign in right of New Zealand would of course disappear, and with it the use of the word "realm", as a way of describing the present collective grouping. Although it is not easy to think of any other name or description that could be used in its place, that is not the real issue.

The changes just mentioned would not change the history or the nature of the present-day relationships between New Zealand and each of the other parts of the former Realm. Nor would those changes affect the rights and obligations inherent in those relationships. Among them, the shared New Zealand citizenship, and with it New Zealand's continuing commitment to the well-being of its citizens, whether in New Zealand itself or in whichever part of the former Realm they may be, would have an even greater significance. The question of how that might best be recognised would become important.

The Sovereign in right of New Zealand is a common element in the constitutional law of every part of the Realm. That, however, is not true of the shared citizenship, which is essentially the product of the law of New Zealand. Even so, the right of the peoples of all parts of the Realm to be and remain New Zealand citizens already has a constitutional dimension. The international law of human rights recognises the right of every person to have a nationality, and not to have that nationality taken away.

In order to act as a truly unifying factor, the right to New Zealand citizenship of the peoples of what are now the other parts of the Realm of New Zealand

54 See further Andrew Townend "The Strange Death of the Realm of New Zealand: The Implications of a New Zealand Republic for the Cook Islands and Niue" (2003) 34 VUWLR 571.

would need to be expressly recognised. The right of the governments of the states and territories concerned to be consulted about all matters affecting the content or the administration of New Zealand's citizenship law would need to be spelt out. So too would the rights and duties of citizenship itself, as they appertain to both the citizens and the governments under which those citizens live. Then, the symbolism of the common allegiance to the Sovereign in right of New Zealand could be seen as having been replaced by the recognition of the shared New Zealand citizenship as the mainspring of the relationship.[55]

Having explained generally the legal status and content of the Letters Patent and how they are made, and the new concept introduced in the 1983 Letters Patent of a Realm of New Zealand comprising different territories and countries, each with their own constitutional status, we next consider the provision made in the Letters Patent for the office of Governor-General itself.

55 The consequences for the other parts of the Realm of an initiative to give New Zealand a republican constitution are touched on in the Afterword, under the subheading The other parts of the Realm of New Zealand, at 312–313.

CHAPTER 7

The Office of Governor-General and Commander-in-Chief

1 INTRODUCTION

In this chapter we discuss the office of the Governor-General. We begin by describing how appointments to the office are made, and the ways in which the political neutrality of the office is sought to be maintained. We then consider the more vexed question whether the designation of the Governor-General's title as Commander-in-Chief currently confers on the holder of the office any attributes that the Governor-General does not already possess. Finally, we consider the role of the Administrator of the Government in ensuring that there is always someone available to exercise the powers and perform the functions associated with the office. In doing so, we describe the nature of the office itself.

2 THE OFFICE OF GOVERNOR-GENERAL

The office of Governor-General and Commander-in-Chief

The constitution of the office

In the 1983 Letters Patent, the Queen in right of New Zealand reconstituted the office of Governor-General of New Zealand, using the words:[1]

1 Clause 1.

> We do hereby constitute, order and declare that there shall be, in and over Our Realm of New Zealand . . . a Governor-General and Commander-in-Chief . . . who shall be our representative in our Realm of New Zealand.

We begin by explaining the significance of the title thus conferred on the holder of the office.

The compound title

In making provision for a "Governor-General and Commander-in-Chief", the Sovereign constituted what is a single office, although the compound title recognises that, originally, the office had two facets. Today, however, except in a formal context, or one specifically associated with the armed forces, the title "Governor-General" is usually thought of as encompassing the essentially ceremonial role of "Commander-in-Chief". We follow that usage in this book, but, later in this chapter, we discuss, and find to be unfounded, a supposition that the Commander-in-Chief has unspecified powers in addition to those possessed by the Governor-General.

The title "Governor-General"

The early practice was to vest the government of British colonies in a "Governor". The federation, first of the Canadian colonies, then of the Australian colonies, and, eventually, of the former English and Dutch colonies in South Africa, led to the introduction of the new title "Governor-General". Initially the title merely signified a gubernatorial appointment at the central government level, while leaving in place the existing Governors or Lieutenant Governors of the former colonies that had become the provinces or states of the newly minted federal state. Later the title "Governor-General" came to be associated with Dominion status.

In New Zealand the elevation of the Governor to Governor-General was made in recognition of New Zealand's contribution to the Imperial forces in World War I. When the new 1917 Letters Patent reached Wellington, the Governor, Lord Liverpool, was hastily sworn in as Governor-General, to coincide with the opening of Parliament.[2] It has since become the invariable practice in all the independent Commonwealth realms to designate the Queen's representative as "Governor-General".

2 On 28 June 1917.

Appointing a Governor-General

Appointments are made by the Sovereign

The Governor-General is appointed by the Sovereign, by a legal instrument known as a Commission. Like the Letters Patent themselves, the Commission must be sealed with the Seal of New Zealand. Not spelt out in the 1983 Letters Patent or anywhere else, is the unwritten constitutional convention that, in appointing a Governor-General, the Sovereign acts on the advice of the New Zealand Prime Minister. In signification of that fact, the Commission, once signed by the Sovereign, is countersigned by the Prime Minister. That is a formal indication that the Prime Minister and the other members of his or her government are collectively responsible to Parliament for advising the appointment. As we later show, the Leader of the Opposition will also have been involved.

Choosing a Governor-General

Even after the Prime Minister's right to recommend a person of his own choosing had long been recognised,[3] New Zealand Governors-General had been mainly upper-class Englishmen selected from a list which the United Kingdom authorities put forward at New Zealand's request. Such appointments were interspersed with those of Governors-General who had been born or brought up in New Zealand but had made their permanent homes in Britain, at the time of their appointment. In comparison with Canada and Australia, New Zealand was slow to look for a Governor-General from within its own community.

That pattern changed with the appointment of Sir Denis Blundell in 1972. It is now well established that the Governor-General will be a man or a woman who is a New Zealand citizen living permanently in New Zealand. Although some choose to leave New Zealand for a time after their appointments have ended, they no longer "sail away" as they once did. Most have sooner or later resumed a role as a member of the New Zealand community. In the past, one or two Prime Ministers have cherished the hope that a suitable member of the royal family might be persuaded to accept the office, but there has been no sign that any such member is in fact interested and available. Today such an appointment would be politically controversial and unlikely to be seriously considered.

3 Gavin McLean *The Governors: New Zealand's Governors and Governors-General* (Otago University Press, Dunedin, 2006) at 188.

The practice of appointing the Governor-General from among New Zealand residents has led to changes in administrative practice and heightened public interest in the making of the choice.

The Sovereign's informal approval

It is well established that, before formally advising the Sovereign to appoint a Governor-General, the Prime Minister must seek her informal approval of the proposed appointment. Until that informal approval has been given, the identity of the proposed appointee is kept secret. The governing principle is that the Queen ought not to be presented by any of her Prime Ministers with a *fait accompli*.[4] The proposed appointment[5] is kept confidential until it is officially announced by the Prime Minister and the Palace, simultaneously. Such an approach obviously precludes any public discussion about the suitability of a person under consideration, although there will always be some media speculation. There is, however, one well-established principle which helps to ensure that the person who becomes Governor-General will carry out the functions of the office in an appropriate way: the Governor-General must remain above politics.

Once the government of New Zealand had been fully placed in the hands of Ministers responsible to Parliament, constitutional convention required the Governor and the Governor-General, like the Sovereign herself, to remain aloof from party politics. That convention was relatively easy to honour as long as the Sovereign's representative was a person with no previous involvement in the country's political life. But with the appointment of born-and-bred New Zealanders to the office of Governor-General, the convention would come under pressure.

On Monday 7 March 1977, a press release issued from the royal yacht, *Britannia*, then moored in Lyttelton Harbour, announced that the visiting Queen had been graciously pleased to give her informal approval to the appointment of a former Prime Minister, Sir Keith Holyoake, to succeed Sir Denis Blundell as Governor-General. The appointment would be for three years, not the usual five. The Prime Minister, the Rt Hon Robert Muldoon, immediately issued his own statement, welcoming the announcement as a fitting culmination of an unparalleled career.

4 Letter from the Rt Hon Sir Philip Moore, Private Secretary to the Queen, to Patrick Millen, Clerk of the Executive Council (5 July 1979).

5 The confidentiality of the relevant information is protected by the Official Information Act 1982, s 9(1) and (2)(f)(i) and (iv).

Neither statement mentioned that Sir Keith, although no longer Prime Minister, was still a Member of Parliament and serving as a member of both the National Government's Executive Council and the Cabinet. Although he had been appointed Minister of State, without a portfolio, and to that extent had withdrawn from the political fray, he was still entitled to take part in all of the government's decision-making. Later the same day, Sir Keith himself announced that he was immediately relinquishing the office of Minister of State and would resign his seat in Parliament as soon as practicable. The damage, however, had already been done.

Even before the appointment had been announced, there had been leaks. Commentators had criticised the proposed appointment as a breach of the constitutional principle that the office of Governor-General is above party politics. To make matters worse, the Leader of the Opposition, Mr Bill Rowling, had not been told of the appointment in advance but learnt of it from the radio. Mr Muldoon recognised that this omission had been a breach of the accepted practice of informing the Leader of the Opposition before the public announcement and subsequently apologised, explaining that he had not been able to reach Mr Rowling by telephone over the preceding weekend. That was not enough, however, to mollify the Opposition or the public.

Some people also read sinister implications into Sir Keith's three-year term (apparently reflecting the fact that he had already reached the age of 73), instead of the usual five years. Would this become the standard practice in future and thus give a newly elected government the opportunity of replacing the outgoing Governor-General with one of its own choosing? A general election was due at the end of the year. The Deputy Leader of the Labour Party, Bob Tizard, suggested that, if elected, a Labour Government would advise the Queen to recall Holyoake, but Rowling, more statesmanlike, realised that such a step would politicise the office of Governor-General even further.

More generally, the press clippings reveal a vigorous flow of critical comment on what was widely seen as a breach of constitutional principle. The criticism came from a wide variety of sources and continued over an extended period, from the time of the announcement in early March until at least the end of May. Few commentators were able to pinpoint exactly why the constitution required the Governor-General to be free of any involvement with party politics. But that was clearly regarded as the governing principle.

Some thought that a former politician would never be able to act impartially in a situation involving a conflict of the interests of the different political parties. Others noted that, in Canada and Australia, former politicians had discharged their responsibilities as Governor-General without any difficulty. They thought that, as a distinguished former Prime Minister, Sir Keith would make a good Governor-General, if only it had become clear before his appointment that he had already severed all links with the party he had formerly led. A Heylen poll[6] showed that only 26 per cent of New Zealanders approved of the appointment of a party politician as Governor-General, but 44.7 per cent were satisfied with the appointment of Sir Keith, while 42.9 per cent were not.[7]

The 1980 Report on what became the 1983 Letters Patent suggested that the controversy over Sir Keith's appointment did not reflect a constitutional principle that a person who has held high political office should not be appointed Governor-General.[8] It was, however:[9]

> . . . a clear indication that, in the eyes of most New Zealanders, the Governor-General must be a person who will carry out the duties of his office impartially. It could therefore be said to be contrary to convention to recommend the appointment of anyone who, avowedly or by implication, is in the pocket of the government making the recommendation. The further principle deducible from the events of 1977 is that any alteration in the constitutional arrangements relating to the office of Governor-General (and, it is submitted, the appointment of Sir Keith Holyoake did, in the circumstances, amount to an alteration)[10] ought not to be undertaken without consultation with the Opposition, and, if the alteration is sufficiently important, without an opportunity for the public to be informed and to make its opinion known.

As was to be expected, Sir Keith Holyoake is recorded as never displaying, during his time in office, any political partisanship.[11] Behind the scenes, however, remedial measures were soon being discussed. They have led to greater openness about the appointment process itself, and, within it, to a more orderly approach aimed at restoring public confidence that the Governor-General will always carry out the functions of the office impartially, and in an otherwise appropriate way. In an era of mixed-member proportional representation the requirement of the appearance of impartiality in the Governor-General has almost certainly become even more important.

6 Taken on 26 March 1977.
7 As noted in Gavin McLean, above n 3, at 299.
8 Alison Quentin-Baxter *Review of the Letters Patent 1917 Constituting the Office of the Governor-General of New Zealand: Report* (Cabinet Office, Wellington, 1980).
9 The extract is quoted in Gavin McLean, above n 3, at 300.
10 Muldoon sought to justify the appointment as comparable with Sir George Grey's participation in New Zealand's politics, eventually as Prime Minister, after serving for two terms as Governor, but the two cases were not comparable.
11 At 301.

The current practice in making an appointment

After the former Prime Minister, Mr Muldoon, had so manifestly failed to observe what was then the accepted practice of giving the Leader of the Opposition, Mr Rowling, advance notice of the appointment of Sir Keith Holyoake shortly before its announcement, it became Muldoon's considered view, expressed to both his own advisers and to the Palace, that the Leader of the Opposition ought to be informed of a proposed appointment, in strictest confidence, before the Queen was asked to give it her informal approval. In due course, Muldoon informed Rowling, whom he had sworn to secrecy on his Privy Council oath, that he proposed to recommend to the Queen that a High Court Judge, the Hon Sir David Beattie, be appointed to succeed Sir Keith.

From then on, the Prime Ministers who have succeeded him have followed the same course. The implication is that informing the Leader of the Opposition before the Queen's approval has been given has a real significance. Although the action is carefully described as "informing", not "consulting", it is accepted that only a foolhardy Prime Minister would proceed with a proposed appointment that evoked a well-founded objection by the Leader of the Opposition.

When the Labour Prime Minister, David Lange, informed the Leader of the Opposition, Jim McLay, in confidence, that he proposed to recommend the appointment as Governor-General of Paul Reeves, the Anglican Bishop of Auckland and Primate and Archbishop of the Church of the Province of New Zealand, he explained that Archbishop Reeves would not use his ecclesiastical styles or titles while in office, nor would he exercise a priestly function in any public way. On its announcement, Mr McLay congratulated Archbishop Reeves on his appointment, welcomed the decision to appoint a Māori, but disclosed the reservations he had earlier expressed to the Prime Minister. These were, first, a possible conflict between Sir Paul's responsibilities as the Queen's representative and those of an ordained priest. They also concerned his recent strong public statements on the nuclear issue, the Treaty of Waitangi and sporting contacts with South Africa. Mr McLay said:[12]

> It is the wish and expectation of the Opposition that Archbishop Reeves now leaves such issues for others to debate.

Clearly, he was firing a warning shot across Sir Paul's bow.

After New Zealanders had voted in a 1993 referendum to change their voting system from the traditional first-past-the-post (FPP) method to mixed-member

12 Press Statement (29 March 1985).

proportional representation (MMP), the Prime Minister, the Rt Hon Jim Bolger, was asked a question in Parliament about the procedure for the appointment of the next Governor-General. He indicated that the procedure for making a new appointment would follow the procedure used in previous years.

The procedures used to appoint Dame Catherine Tizard as Governor-General involved consideration by the government of possible nominees, followed by a stage of information and confidential inquiries to see if the proposed nominee was available, and informal advice to the Queen and the Opposition of the nominee. Once a formal offer was made and accepted, a formal submission was made to the Queen recommending that the proposed appointee be the next Governor-General. The appointment was then simultaneously announced by the Palace and the government.

The 1994 parliamentary question to Mr Bolger was clearly prompted by the likelihood that, after the 1996 general election to be held under the MMP electoral system, there might well be no single party with a parliamentary majority. All parties wanted the next Governor-General to be a person well-equipped to play whatever part might be appropriate. Before seeking the Queen's informal approval, Mr Bolger informally notified the Leader of the Opposition, Ms Helen Clark, of his intention to propose the appointment of the Hon Sir Michael Hardie Boys, a Judge of the Court of Appeal. After receiving the Queen's informal approval but before advising her to make the formal appointment, he also made the proposed appointment known, in confidence, to the leaders of the other parties then represented in Parliament.

It appears that Prime Ministers have since resumed the earlier practice of giving advance notice of the projected appointment of a Governor-General only to the Leader of the Opposition. Other party leaders are notified very shortly before the announcement, if at all.[13] Even so, it can be said that a Governor-General is appointed by the Sovereign on the recommendation of a Prime Minister who is acting with the broad support of the House.

Other criteria for appointment as Governor-General

As well as the need for the appointee to be above politics, some other criteria have been identified. The person appointed to the office of Governor-General must have the ability to represent New Zealand at the Head of State level, both in New Zealand and overseas. He or she must be able to meet with other Heads of State and their representatives, and to take part in a wide range of formal

13 See for a news report on the process adopted in relation to the current Governor-General <http://www.radionz.co.nz/news/political/299679/reddy-for-a-new-governor-general-appointment-process>.

ceremonies, including those involving the Defence Force. As the country's leading citizen, the Governor-General also needs to be a person who will enjoy meeting and mixing with all New Zealanders on a wide variety of occasions. These range from the formal investiture of royal honours, as the Sovereign's representative, to less formal meetings, not only at Government House, but all over the country. There appears to be a growing perception that, in exercising the Head of State role, a Governor-General should give non-partisan but inspirational leadership to the nation in ways that ring true for each.

Finally, the Governor-General needs to be someone of high personal standing and good character. It is important that there should be nothing in his or her background that would cause damage to the office if it were to become known to the public. That point is illustrated by the eventual resignation in 2003 of the Australian Governor-General, Peter Hollingworth, a former Anglican Archbishop of Brisbane, who found it impossible to retain office after his alleged lack of rigour in ridding the church of paedophiles had become the subject of public discussion.

So far, New Zealand has been cautiously innovative in making appointments to the office. If it is to retain the interest and support of the public, that approach needs to continue.

The Governor-General holds office "during pleasure"

After the prospective appointment of a Governor-General has been announced but well before his or her entry into the office, the Prime Minister, through the Clerk of the Executive Council, negotiates with the Governor-General to settle what are known as "Terms of Appointment". Among other things, these specify the term for which the Governor-General is expected to serve, usually five years. Although the agreed term of office expresses the shared expectation of the parties, it is still subject to the Sovereign's pleasure, as the Letters Patent and the Commission appointing the Governor-General to the office provide.[14]

An appointment "during pleasure" is the traditional way of signifying that, unless the appointee dies in office, the appointment remains in force until terminated. It is implicit that an appointment during pleasure may be terminated at any time without assigning any reason for the termination. Theoretically,

14 Compare the carefully worded provision in the Governor-General Act 2010, s 5(3) specifying the period for which the Governor-General's salary is payable. Despite the reference to a Governor-General's "terms of . . . appointment" in s 11(1) of the Act, it is clear from the context that the Governor-General's "term of office" referred to in s 5(4) is the period specified in s 5(3), not the period provided for in the Governor-General's Terms of Appointment.

the person so appointed does not have the same freedom to withdraw his or her services, but a request to be relieved of the office would almost certainly be met.

It is not uncommon for a Prime Minister to ask a Governor-General to remain in office for somewhat longer than the agreed term, to avoid a clash with some other event of national importance — for example, the time at which a general election must be held. If the Governor-General agrees, the Prime Minister, as a courtesy, asks the Sovereign to approve the proposed extension. Once she has signified her agreement, the extension is announced, after the Leader of the Opposition has been informed in confidence immediately beforehand. The "extension", however, requires no change in the Governor-General's Commission. The holding of office "during pleasure" permits the period in office to be adjusted as required.[15]

In the days when a Governor-General arrived in New Zealand and departed at the conclusion of his term, the Commission of an arriving Governor-General contained a clause revoking the appointment of his predecessor. In theory, there was always a Governor-General in office, but, when the departing Governor-General left New Zealand, the Chief Justice or the next most senior judge took office as Administrator of the Government until the new Governor-General had arrived and been sworn in.

Now that the Governor-General is always a New Zealand resident, the Prime Minister advises the Sovereign to revoke an incumbent Governor-General's Commission as from a named date, usually that foreshadowed in the Terms of Appointment. The office then becomes vacant, so the Administrator assumes its functions and powers. A few weeks later, on the specified date, the Commission of the incoming Governor-General will take effect. On or shortly after that date the Governor-General completes the formalities prescribed in the Letters Patent and assumes the duties of the office.

As a matter of law, the Sovereign has the power, at any time, to recall the Governor-General. That was illustrated by the abrupt recall of Sir George Grey in 1867. Then, however, New Zealand Governors and Governors-General were appointed and recalled on the advice of United Kingdom Ministers, not the Prime Minister of New Zealand. Since 1926, there has been a clear constitutional convention that, in appointing or recalling a Governor-General, the Sovereign acts on the advice of the Prime Minister of the realm concerned.[16]

15 The legal position in respect of the Governor-General is sometimes wrongly assumed to be the same as that in respect of the Queen's Representative in the Cook Islands who holds office for a finite term of three years. If, as is not unusual, the outgoing Queen's Representative is to be reappointed, the Queen issues a new Commission.

16 See above, this chapter at 118.

An assessment of whether, in present-day New Zealand, the Governor-General and the Prime Minister could ever find themselves on a collision course and, if so, whether the Governor-General would then be justified in dismissing the Prime Minister, or the Prime Minister would be justified in advising the recall of the Governor-General, is considered in the course of our closer look at the relationship between them in Chapters 9 and 10.

The Governor-General's salary and expenses

Arrangements for the payment of the salary and expenses of the Governor-General which properly acknowledge the independence and dignity of the office have been long in the making and there have been significant problems along the way. The present practices are provided for in the Governor-General Act 2010. By that Act, Parliament removed the existing permanent appropriation for the Governor-General's salary and allowances from the Civil List Act,[17] and made new provision for that purpose. It did so on the recommendation of the Law Commission, which had concluded that such a step would enhance the perception of the apolitical nature of the Governor-General's constitutional role, and bring New Zealand into line with Australia and Canada.[18] Under the new Act,[19] the Governor-General's salary continues to be paid at a rate determined by the Remuneration Authority,[20] and his or her allowance for official expenses is still payable at a rate fixed by Order in Council.[21] Those and all payments to a former Governor-General or his or her spouse or partner continue to be authorised by a permanent appropriation.[22] There are, however, some important changes.

The Governor-General's salary is now subject to income tax.[23] The Governor-General's allowance now covers only expenses of a personal nature directly attributable to the office, such as the need for suitable clothing for both the Governor-General and his or her spouse or partner, and is a good deal smaller than it used to be.[24] To offset that, however, the Governor-General Act now includes two new permanent appropriations.

17 Since repealed and replaced by the Members of Parliament (Remuneration and Services) Act 2013.
18 Law Commission *Review of the Civil List Act — the Governor-General* (NZLC R112, 2009) at [1.2].
19 The Governor-General Act 2010 came into force on 23 November 2010: s 2.
20 Section 5.
21 Section 6.
22 Section 12.
23 Income Tax Act 2007, s RD5, as amended by the Governor-General Act 2010, s 24; Income Tax Act 2007, s CW16, as inserted by the Governor-General Act 2010, s 23; Goods and Services Tax Act 1985, s 6(3)(c)(i), as amended by the Governor-General Act 2010, s 21.
24 At the time of writing the allowance is $30,000: Governor-General (Allowance) Order (No 2)

The permanent appropriation for the Governor-General's programme covers expenses incurred to meet the costs of the Governor-General in:[25]

> ... carrying out his or her duties of office in New Zealand (such as the costs of, and incidental to, travel of the Governor-General, staff of the Governor-General, and his or her family members, and the costs of hosting functions and events, as part of the Governor-General's programme).

These are matters within the control of the Governor-General. A second permanent appropriation covers the costs of the Governor-General in carrying out the duties of the office outside New Zealand (such as undertaking international travel at the government's request) and also the costs of travel for the purpose of enabling the Governor-General designate to have the customary audience with the Sovereign.

Although the two permanent appropriations do not specify a particular amount, the Public Finance Act 1989 requires each expense to be managed and accounted for in the same manner as an expense incurred in accordance with an Appropriation Act.[26] The operating budget for the two Government Houses and the salaries of staff continue to be funded through Vote Prime Minister and Cabinet.[27]

Entitlements after leaving office

After ceasing to hold office a Governor-General is entitled to an annuity and other benefits. The Law Commission has explained that these recognise both the contribution made to the country by the former Governor-General and his or her spouse or partner and also the fact that their period of service will almost certainly have ongoing consequences. A former Governor-General is expected to maintain the dignity of the office and ensure that any future employment or other activity befits the status of the office formerly held. He or she is also likely to have ongoing obligations such as continuing to be the Patron of organisations with which they have been associated, responding to correspondence, delivering speeches and attending as guests on state occasions.

2011 SR 2011/251, r 3. See also the Explanatory Note to that Order, and NZLC R112, above n 18, at [3.9] and [3.10].

25 Governor-General Act 2010, s 13.

26 Public Finance Act 1989, s 11(2). The estimated amount to be incurred in each financial year must be reported in the Estimates and the actual expenditure incurred must be reported in the annual report of the Department administering the appropriation: NZLC R112, above n 18, at [2.5].

27 NZLC R112, above n 18, at [2.3].

The Governor-General's Commission

The future Governor-General's audience with the Sovereign is the first formal step in entering on the duties of the office. It marks his or her transition to the new role. Once the Governor-General designate has been honoured by the Sovereign, and with the date on which he or she will take office already settled, the next step is to prepare the new Governor-General's Commission, and for the Prime Minister to recommend that the Commission be signed by Her Majesty.[28] On its return to New Zealand it is countersigned by the Prime Minister and sealed with the Seal of New Zealand.

The Commission is addressed to "our Trusty and Well-beloved" Governor-General by his or her name. It follows closely the terms of the Letters Patent. It directs the new Governor-General, as soon as convenient after the date it takes effect, and before entering on any of the duties of the office, to cause the Commission to be publicly read. Immediately after that, the Governor-General must take the required oath of allegiance and the oath for the due execution of the office of Governor-General.[29] The Commission ends by enjoining Ministers of the Crown, other officers and all the inhabitants of the Realm of New Zealand to take notice of the Commission and comply accordingly. The scene is thus set for the public ceremony known as the swearing-in of the Governor-General.

In 2006, the form of the Governor-General's oath of office was amended so as to include an express promise to serve the people of the realm.[30] The oath now reads as follows:[31]

> I, [*name*], swear that, as Governor-General and Commander-in-Chief of the Realm of New Zealand, comprising New Zealand; the self-governing states of the Cook Islands and Niue; Tokelau; and the Ross Dependency, I will faithfully and impartially serve Her [*or* His] Majesty [*specify the name of the reigning Sovereign, as thus:* Queen Elizabeth the Second], Queen of New Zealand [*or* King of New Zealand], Her [*or* His] heirs and successors, and the people of the Realm of New Zealand, in accordance with their respective laws and customs. So help me God.

28 See Letters Patent 1983, cls 2, 5 and 6.
29 Letters Patent 1983, cl 5.
30 This initiative was taken in response to a suggestion made by the Hon Sir Anand Satyanand, while serving as Governor-General.
31 Letters Patent 1983, cl 6.

The promise to observe the relevant "laws and customs"[32] (which echoes the promise made by Queen Elizabeth II in the Coronation Oath) is the closest a New Zealand Governor-General could feasibly come to the promise to "uphold the constitution" now included in the oaths taken by the Governors-General of some of the "new" Commonwealth monarchies.

We consider now the more vexed question of the significance of the designation Commander-in-Chief in the Governor-General's title.

The title "Commander-in-Chief"

In retaining provision in the 1983 Letters Patent for a "Governor-General and Commander-in-Chief", the Sovereign constituted what is a single office, although the compound form of the name by which it is called recognises that, originally, the office had two facets. Here we consider whether the designation "Commander-in Chief" now confers on the holder of the office any attributes that the "Governor-General" does not already possess. The 1980 Report[33] concluded that the answer to that question was "No". That conclusion has been strengthened by what has happened since.

The 1980 Report recommended that Letters Patent should place the main stress on the office of Governor-General, but the office itself should continue to be constituted as that of the "Governor-General and Commander-in-Chief". That recommendation could have been based simply on the long history of the compound title, had it not been for a provision in the Defence Act 1971 then in force:[34]

> The Governor-General, by virtue of being Commander-in-Chief of New Zealand, shall have such powers and may exercise and discharge such duties and obligations relating to the Armed Forces as pertain to the office of Commander-in-Chief.

The Report traced the history of that provision to legislation enacted in 1865, almost certainly on the initiative of the Governor, Sir George Grey, then actively involving himself in the conduct of the wars against the Waikato Māori and their supporters. On at least one occasion, in July 1865, after the British commander, General Cameron, had refused to attack Weraroa pā, Grey

32 "The Queen's Coronation Oath" <http://www.royal.uk/coronation-oath-2-june-1953>. It must also include the upholding of such customary law as may be recognised in any part of the Realm.

33 Alison Quentin-Baxter *Review of the Letters Patent 1917 Constituting the Office of the Governor-General of New Zealand: Report* (Cabinet Office, Wellington, 1980).

34 Defence Act 1971, s 4(3), and see now the Defence Act 1990, s 6(1).

had personally taken command of colonial volunteers and two detachments of Imperial forces, and had led the attack himself.[35]

Until 1865, legislation authorising the raising of troops within New Zealand had invested "the Governor" with all the requisite powers. Under an 1862 Act passed after the introduction of responsible government, all the powers vested in the Governor were required to be executed with the advice of the Executive Council.[36] The new Acts passed in 1865 still vested in the Governor the power to raise forces, and also to call them out for a particular purpose, but there was no longer any reference to the Executive Council. In words very close to those that have remained part of New Zealand law ever since, each Act provided as follows:[37]

> The Governor shall be the Commander-in-chief . . . and shall have all the powers and may exercise and discharge all the duties and obligations appertaining to the office of Commander-in-chief . . .

The 1865 Acts had also equated the orders of the Commander-in-Chief with those of an officer.[38]

In 1868, Governor Grey was recalled. He had by then fallen out not only with the commander of the Imperial forces, but also with his responsible advisers in New Zealand and the Colonial Secretary in London. The last of the Imperial forces left New Zealand in 1870. Although some later Governors or Governors-General had also had earlier careers in the armed forces, none of them ever attempted to assume any sort of military role. At the invitation of the government of the day, however, one or two contributed their specialised experience to the designing of coastal defences[39] or the functioning of a War Cabinet at a time of heightened need.[40]

Surprisingly, Governor Grey's legacy still lives on in the statute law. A study of the defence legislation enacted after 1865 suggests that, out of an abundance of caution, the later law-makers simply assumed that it was necessary

35 Ruth Fletcher "The Governor as Commander-in-Chief" (1943) 2 Historical Studies Australia and New Zealand 209 at 219.
36 Colonial Defence Force Act 1862, s 231.
37 Militia Act 1865, s 5 and Volunteer Force Act 1865, s 8.
38 Militia Act 1865, s 41 and Volunteer Force Act 1865, s 38.
39 While Governor, Lieutenant-General Sir William Jervois, who had experience in designing British harbour defences, put forward acceptable proposals for coastal defences in New Zealand: Gavin McLean, above n 3, at 109.
40 After the crippling of the United States Pacific Fleet at Pearl Harbor and the loss of the British warships *Prince of Wales* and *Repulse*, the New Zealand War Cabinet sought expert advice on its functioning from the Governor-General, Air Marshall Sir Cyril Newall, previously Chief of Air Staff in the United Kingdom: Gerald Hensley *Beyond the Battlefield: New Zealand and its Allies 1939–45* (Penguin, London, 2009) at 165.

or desirable to perpetuate the statutory provision appointing the Governor as the Commander-in-Chief, and, in that capacity, conferring on him the "powers ... duties and obligations" appertaining to the Commander-in-Chief.[41] In the 1950s, separate Acts in respect of each of the three services no longer purported to confer the office of Commander-in-Chief on the holder of what had become, in 1917, the office of Governor-General and Commander-in-Chief. They simply provided that "[t]he Governor-General, by virtue of his appointment as Commander-in-Chief of New Zealand, shall have all the powers and may exercise and discharge all the duties and obligations ... appertaining to the office of Commander-in-Chief".[42]

The Defence Act 1971 repealed Acts pertaining to the three services and replaced them with a single Act containing the substantive provision reproduced at the beginning of this section. The 1980 Report[43] concluded that, although the statutory provision by which Sir George Grey had tried to justify his active participation in the wars had survived continuously as part of New Zealand law for 150 years, it did not serve any necessary or useful purpose. Other provisions of the Defence Act conferred on "the Governor-General",[44] or the "Governor-General in Council",[45] a number of specific powers in respect of the armed forces. The Letters Patent, too, would continue to empower "the Governor-General and Commander-in-Chief" to exercise all relevant prerogative powers in respect of the armed forces, and a separate provision of the Defence Act expressly protects those prerogative powers against supersession by the statute.[46]

Accordingly, any other "powers ... duties and obligations appertaining to the office of Commander-in-Chief" had to be found — if they could be found

41 Militia Act 1870, s 5; Volunteer Act 1881, s 3; Defence Act 1886, s 5; Defence Act 1909, s 5.

42 New Zealand Army Act 1950, s 15; Royal New Zealand Air Force Act 1950, s 14; Navy Act 1954, s 8. The Defence Act 1964 aimed at greater coordination of the three services at the most senior level. Section 6 simply provides that nothing in that Act derogated from the powers, duties, and obligations conferred by any of the Service Acts on the Governor-General as Commander-in-Chief.

43 Alison Quentin-Baxter *Review of the Letters Patent 1917 Constituting the Office of the Governor-General of New Zealand: Report* (Cabinet Office, Wellington, 1980).

44 Then defined as "the Governor-General of New Zealand" and as including "the Administrator of the Government". The Administrator was defined as "authorised by law to perform all or any of the functions of the Governor-General whenever the office of Governor-General of New Zealand is vacant or the holder of the office of Governor-General is for any reason unable to perform all or any of the functions of the office of Governor-General": Acts Interpretation Act 1924, s 4, definitions of "Governor-General" and "Administrator" as amended in 1983 No 22. When the 1924 Act was replaced by the Interpretation Act 1999, "Governor-General" and "Administrator" were no longer defined. "Governor-General" must now be seen as meaning the Governor-General and Commander-in Chief appointed by the Sovereign: Constitution Act 1986, s 2(2), and the Letters Patent 1983, cl 1. As to the authority of an Administrator to exercise the powers of the Governor-General, see now Constitution Act 1986, s 3(b).

45 Then defined in the Acts Interpretation Act 1924, s 4. See now the definition of that term in the Interpretation Act 1999, s 29.

46 Defence Act 1971, s 4(4). See now the Defence Act 1990, s 6(2).

at all — within the four corners of New Zealand statute law and subordinate legislation. And, if there were any such provisions, they would have the force of law in their own right. There would be no need to look to any unspecified powers, duties and obligations said in the Defence Act to be vested in the Commander-in-Chief. The Report concluded that the Defence Act provision was "devoid of substantive effect", and that when opportunity offered, consideration should be given to its repeal.

Defence Act 1990

The finding in the 1980 Report about the effect of the provision so long perpetuated in successive Defence Acts was subsequently cited as authoritative.[47] In 1990, however, a new Defence Act was enacted. The provision authorising the exercise of such attributes as the Governor-General possesses as Commander-in-Chief was re-enacted without change. It remains in force at the time of writing.[48] But, since the recommendations were made in the 1980 Report, the role of the Governor-General as Commander-in-Chief has twice been brought into the public domain. The first occasion concerned involved the power of the Governor-General and Commander-in-Chief to act as the review authority of last resort in relation to military wrongdoing; the second was an attempt by officers to justify their conduct by claiming a "higher loyalty" to the Commander-in-Chief. We look at what was said in each context about the role of the Governor-General as Commander-in-Chief.

Commander-in-Chief as review authority of last resort

Captain Bradley, a former naval officer, exercised his right to complain to the Governor-General and Commander-in-Chief as a last resort on the ground "that his honour, integrity or professional standing [had] been impugned".[49] He subsequently applied to the High Court for the judicial review of the decisions made by two Governors-General. The Court held that although the power and duty of review was conferred on the Governor-General and Commander-in-Chief, that office was representative of the Sovereign, and its holder for the time being acted on behalf of the Sovereign. Whether required

47 See, for example, *Laws of New Zealand* Defence: Warfare (Reissue 1) (online ed) at [17] n 8; Matthew Palmer "Legal Analysis of New Zealand Defence Legislation" in DK Hunn *Review of Accountabilities and Structural Arrangements between the Ministry of Defence and the New Zealand Defence Force* (New Zealand Government, Wellington, 30 September 2002) Annex F <http://www.defence.govt.nz/assets/Uploads/hunn-review.pdf> at 51 [*Hunn Review*].

48 Defence Act 1990, s 6(1).

49 Per Defence Act 1971, s 50 and DCO 19/1976, cl 6.

to act on advice or to act "personally", the continuity of the office was not affected by changes to the identity of the holder.[50] The decision impliedly rejected the view that the "Commander-in-Chief" had a role distinguishable from that of the Governor-General. The Court can be seen as taking the view that the Governor-General and Commander-in-Chief was exercising a royal power — one that, under the Constitution Act, the Sovereign could have exercised herself.[51]

A third Governor-General, Dame Catherine Tizard, then reviewed the complaint. She issued a press statement explaining that, following the decision of the High Court, the Minister of Defence had referred the case to her for further investigation. As Commander-in-Chief, she had appointed the Rt Hon Sir Duncan McMullin, a former Judge of the Court of Appeal, to act as her Commissary to hear the case. On the basis of his report, she had granted the measures of relief she then outlined.[52] So far as we are aware, the press release was the first time that the exercise of the role of the Governor-General and Commander-in-Chief as the Defence Force appeal authority of last resort had been brought into the public domain.

The Defence Act 1990 still gives servicemen the right to make a complaint.[53] A Defence Force Order implements that right.[54] It gives the force of law to the New Zealand Defence Force Human Resources Manual.[55] The inclusion of the whole manual in a Defence Force Order gives the force of law to a number of explanatory statements that would otherwise be merely policies, practices and procedures not having legal effect.

The "Governor-General"[56] is now named as the review authority of last resort. There is no reference to the "Commander-in-Chief".

50 *Bradley v The Governor-General and Commander-in-Chief* HC Auckland M1864/89, 28 February 1991 at 18. Earlier, in *Bradley v Attorney-General* [1988] 2 NZLR 454 (HC) at 462, the Court had found that "the Governor-General's position as Commander in Chief is constitutional only and the real powers of appointment, command and administration are exercised through the statutory provisions which I have referred to". Although in *Bradley v The Governor-General and Commander-in-Chief* the earlier decision was not referred to, the word "constitutional" appears to have been used to describe the position as set out more fully in the later case.

51 Constitution Act 1986, s 3.

52 Press Release (31 July 1992, Government House, Wellington).

53 Defence Act 1990, s 49.

54 As to the power to make such Orders, see Defence Act 1990, s 27. As to the provision for the redress of complaints by such a Service authority and in such a manner as may be prescribed in Defence Force Orders, see Defence Act 1990, s 49.

55 Defence Force Order 3, signed at Wellington on 23 November 2009 by Lieutenant General J Mateparae and last amended on 5 April 2012, Part 13: Suggestions, Complaints and Grievances, paras [13.2.18]–[13.2.63].

56 That is now the normal way of referring to the Governor-General and Commander-in-Chief in primary and secondary legislation.

The Defence Force Order contains the following statement:[57]

> In constitutional terms the Governor-General's role in investigating complaints is exercised personally rather than on the advice of a responsible Minister. Complaints forwarded, or made, to the Governor-General will be investigated by:
> (1) The Governor-General personally, or
> (2) A commissary appointed by the Governor-General for the purpose.

The claimed absence of ministerial responsibility in respect of the Defence Force complaints process represents a departure from an important constitutional principle. There is no obvious reason why the principle of ministerial responsibility which applies to the exercise of the prerogative of mercy should not apply also in the case of appeals by members of the armed forces. As well as the right to seek judicial review of the exercise of the complaints review process, services personnel have an acknowledged right to take any matter to a Member of Parliament.[58] There ought to be a Minister with responsibility to Parliament for the conduct of the complaints review process, at least when it goes beyond the military level and reaches the Governor-General and Commander-in-Chief. In our view, responsibility for the due exercise of the review power should be seen as resting with the Minister of Defence.

A higher loyalty to the Governor-General as Commander-in-Chief?

The second occurrence throwing some light on the role of the Governor-General and Commander-in-Chief was an inquiry by the State Services Commissioner into standards of behaviour within the Defence Force. One issue was whether:[59]

> . . . some members of the Armed Forces believed they had a higher loyalty — to the Queen, through the Governor-General, who is Commander-in-Chief — which might cause them to work actively against Government policies which seemed to them detrimental to New Zealand defence interests.

57 Defence Force Order 3, above n 55. It appears, however, that in the case of Captain Bradley, the Minister of Defence sent to the Governor-General his third request for a review.
58 Defence Force Order 3, above n 55, at [13.2.25]–[13.2.26].
59 Douglas White QC and Graham Ansell "Review of the Performance of the Defence Force in Relation to Expected Standards of Behaviour, and in Particular the Leaking and Inappropriate Use of Information by Defence Force Personnel" (20 December 2001) <www.ssc.govt.nz/defence-force-report-dec-02> [White/Ansell Review] at [9.4].

The question arose because of increasing government disquiet about the handling of Defence documents and information, including "leaks" to members of the parliamentary Opposition. The State Services Commissioner, who was already investigating some wider issues,[60] appointed a Review Team to report separately on this aspect of the inquiry.

The Review Team had been informed that, at the time in question, the "higher loyalty" thesis had been voiced quite widely among members of the Defence Force.[61] But on the basis of the interviews it conducted with a total of 75 persons, many of them members of the Defence Force, it found "virtual unanimity":[62]

> ... [w]hile their oath of allegiance was to the Sovereign, their loyalty was solely to the Government of the day.

While some may have seen a "higher loyalty" as an excuse for their conduct, the Review Team did not believe that it was "a significant element of motivation".[63]

As well as conducting interviews, the Review Team considered relevant documentary material. This had included a Crown Law Office opinion on the constitutional relationship between the Defence Force and the government of the day.[64] The opinion stated that the Governor-General had powers relating to the armed forces by virtue of being Commander-in-Chief of New Zealand, but noted that those powers essentially related to the consideration of certain complaints, as well as some largely ceremonial matters.[65]

In addressing the "statutory role" of the Governor-General as Commander-in-Chief,[66] the Review team did not think there was any serious ambiguity but thought that the role should be clarified:[67]

60 Hunn *Review*, above n 47.

61 On separate occasions each of us has heard the thesis put forward in conversation by a (different) member of the armed forces.

62 White/Ansell Review, above n 59, at [67] (emphasis in original).

63 At [69].

64 At [14.4].

65 Ellen France, Deputy Solicitor-General, Opinion dated 23 November 2001, Appendix 5 to the White/Ansell Review, above n 59, at [10]. The ceremonial matters, however, appear to relate to the undivided role of the Governor-General and Commander-in-Chief. The holder of that office is entitled to be accorded the dignities and respect inherent in the office — for example, the right to receive the Royal Salute from a military guard of honour: *Laws of New Zealand* Defence, above n 47.

66 At [70]. The office of "Governor-General and Commander-in-Chief" is in fact constituted by the Sovereign: Letters Patent 1983, cl 1. It seems therefore that the "statutory role" must be taken as a reference to the meaning and effect of s 6(1) of the Defence Act 1990.

67 At [138.1].

> The powers of [the office of Commander-in-Chief] in New Zealand (quite unlike those of, say, the US President as Commander in Chief) are strictly limited in scope. We suggest that clearer statutory definition of the Commander in Chief's role and powers would remove any grounds for misinterpretation, deliberate or otherwise.[68]

A single office with undifferentiated powers

For the reasons already explained, we do not support that suggestion. In our opinion, the person appointed as the Governor-General and Commander-in-Chief of New Zealand is the holder of a single office with roles and powers that are not derived from one or other part of its compound title but from the office as a whole.[69] As a matter of law, it is not possible to regard some powers as belonging to the office of Governor-General and others to a separate office of Commander-in-Chief. The longevity of the statutory provision first enacted in 1865 has created the impression that there are two divisible offices, but that is not, and has never been, the case in New Zealand.

The 1983 Letters Patent constituted the office of the Governor-General and Commander-in-Chief and clarified that later references to the "Governor-General" refer to the holder of that compound and indivisible office. In all other contexts references to the "Governor-General" should be read in that sense. The Sovereign has expressly empowered the Governor-General thus defined to exercise "the executive authority of New Zealand", as well as "all the things belonging to the office of Governor-General".[70] The authority thus conferred includes the authority to exercise, both inside and outside New Zealand, all the Sovereign's prerogative rights and powers in respect of the armed forces, so far as they are part of New Zealand law.

Certain aspects of what were formerly prerogative powers in respect of the armed forces have been spelt out in statutory form, with or without modifications. That process will no doubt continue, although there are policy questions about how far the broad prerogative powers of the executive branch of government to deploy the armed forces ought to be codified by law, or their exercise be considered by Parliament before or after the event.

Meantime, Parliament should repeal section 6(1) of the Defence Act 1990 and should not replace it. When that has been done, a colourful episode in New Zealand's 19th-century constitutional and military history will no

68 At [70].

69 We discuss further the relationship between the Governor-General and the Defence Force in Chapter 14 Exercising the Head of State Role, under the subheading The New Zealand Defence Force, at 302–305.

70 Letters Patent 1983, cl 3.

longer be reflected in the statute law, and the law itself will no longer convey the misleading impression that there are powers vested in the Commander-in-Chief, as distinct from the Governor-General, when in reality that is not the case.

As was apparent from the Court's remarks in *Bradley*, the office of the Governor-General continues even as the office-holders change. Of equal importance is that there is always someone able to fulfil the role — even if in an acting capacity. We consider now who is empowered to act when the Governor-General is not available at any particular time.

The Administrator of the Government

Ensuring the continuity of the office of Governor-General

The Governor-General has the wide-ranging prerogative and statutory powers discussed in this and other chapters. If he or she is not readily available to exercise such a power when the need arises, there must always be someone else who can. Accordingly, the legal arrangements constituting the office of the Governor-General always include provision for continuity and succession. The 1983 Letters Patent provide that, whenever the office of Governor-General is vacant, or the holder of the office is for any reason unable to perform all or any of the duties of the office, the Chief Justice of New Zealand must act as the Administrator of the Government with the power to perform all or any of the functions of the office. If, however, there is not a Chief Justice who is able to act, then the next most senior available judge must do so.[71]

Unless inconsistent with the context, references in the 1983 Letters Patent to the Governor-General include the Administrator.[72] Although this chapter focuses on the Administrator's role within New Zealand, it should not be forgotten that the Administrator exercises the role of the Governor-General in respect of all parts of the Realm of New Zealand.[73] The 1983 Letters Patent provide that while the Administrator is performing all or any of the functions of the office:[74]

71 Clause 12. After the entry into force of the Supreme Court Act 2003, cl 12 as originally enacted was amended by Letters Patent (2006) Amending Letters Patent Constituting the Office of Governor-General of New Zealand (SR 2006/219), cl 3.

72 Clause 12.

73 For example, the Administrator has acted as the representative of the Sovereign in respect of the self-governing state of Niue.

74 Letters Patent 1983, cl 14. The provision was based on the 1917 Letters Patent, cl 12, authorising a Governor-General to appoint a Deputy.

> . . . the powers and authorities of Our Governor-General shall not be abridged, altered, or in any way affected, otherwise than as We may at any time hereafter think proper to direct.

An action taken by the Administrator cannot be challenged in the courts on the ground that a situation had not arisen in which the Governor-General was unable to act.[75] The Letters Patent, however, could not authorise the Administrator to exercise powers conferred on the Governor-General by the statute law of New Zealand. That was something that only Parliament could do. The authorisation is now included in the Constitution Act 1986.[76]

On the first occasion on which the Chief Justice or any other judge acts as the Administrator, and before entering on any of the duties of the office, he or she must take the oaths required to be taken by the Governor-General.[77] The oaths are to be administered by another Judge of the High Court in the presence of at least two members of the Executive Council.

When is an Administrator required to act?

A vacancy in the office of Governor-General will be self-evident. Normally a vacancy will occur in the period between the revocation of the Commission of an outgoing Governor-General and the entry of his or her successor to the duties of the office.[78] A vacancy would also occur if the Governor-General were to die in office.

The Letters Patent also recognise that the Administrator may need to exercise "all or any" of the powers of the Governor-General if the holder of the office is "for any reason" unable to perform a particular function. The reason for the "inability" is not material. On at least one occasion, the Administrator has been advised to execute a particular instrument, although the Governor-General was available, but was unable to act in the particular case because of the likely public perception that she had a personal interest. Instead, the Chief Justice, as the Administrator, was advised to sign an instrument reappointing the Governor-General's husband to a statutory board.[79]

75 Constitution Act 1986, s 3B (2). The original provision was the Administrator's Powers Act 1983, s 3.

76 Constitution Act 1986, s 3B(1). In its present form the provision authorises an Administrator to "perform a function or duty imposed on the Governor-General, or exercise a power conferred on the Governor-General", thus applying to statutory functions, duties and powers, and also those rooted in the royal prerogative. So far as it refers to prerogative powers, however, and thus overlaps the Letters Patent 1983, cl 12, the section must be taken as declaratory. Compare the definition of "Governor-General" or "Governor" in the Acts Interpretation Act 1924, s 4.

77 See above, this chapter, fn 31, at 128.

78 See above, this chapter, under the subheading The Governor-General's Commission, at 128.

79 Dame Silvia's husband Peter Cartwright was appointed to the ACC appeal authority.

Inability to perform some or all of the duties of the office could also arise from the illness of the Governor-General or for some other reason. Not surprisingly, however, the most common reason is absence from New Zealand. But the absence of the Governor-General does not in itself mean that it is necessary to call on the Administrator. Usually, if the Governor-General's presence is urgently required in the capital,[80] he or she will be able to return fairly quickly from most parts of mainland New Zealand or even from further afield, and would be expected to do so. That may sometimes be impracticable or inappropriate, especially if the Governor-General's absence is for the purpose of carrying out his or her functions elsewhere. So when, exactly, will the Administrator need to be called upon?

The 1983 Letters Patent gave to the Administrator the additional duty of filling in for the Governor-General during short absences in neighbouring countries — a task which would formerly have been given to a Deputy under earlier versions of the Letters Patent.[81] Under the new arrangement, the Governor-General no longer needs to have "departed from [New Zealand]"[82] before the Administrator can enter on the duties of the office. Long before the plane has taken off, it is likely to have become impracticable for the departing Governor-General to carry out some if not all of the functions of the office. For that reason there is an administrative discretion to set the time at which the Administrator should have both the authority and the legal duty to act in the Governor-General's place.

Even if the Governor-General were still to be in the country at the time of the changeover, that would have no legal or constitutional significance. A 1985 newspaper article with the banner headline "Viceregal Double-Up" reported the delay of the Governor-General's flight to Antarctica beyond the time at which the Administrator had assumed office as if the overlap were a breach of constitutional principle,[83] but, after the entry into force of the 1983 Letters Patent, that suggestion no longer contained even the grain of truth it might once have had. The Cabinet Office advises Ministers and departments when the Administrator will be fulfilling the Governor-General's functions by issuing a Cabinet Office Notice.

80 The circumstances in which the Executive Council may meet without the Governor-General being present, or even without any of its members being physically in the same place, are discussed in Chapter 8 The Governor-General in the Executive Branch, under the subheading Meetings of the Executive Council, at 161.

81 The Chief Justice or another senior judge could then be appointed in that capacity.

82 Letters Patent 1917.

83 "Viceregal Double-up" *The Evening Post* (New Zealand, 19 November 1985).

A possible conflict with judicial responsibilities?

The practice of appointing the Chief Justice or next most senior judge to act for a non-existent, absent or indisposed Governor or Governor-General was introduced in colonial times as a matter of expediency. The practice has been retained in Canada and New Zealand,[84] and in some, if not all, of the smaller realms because it is convenient, inexpensive, and, so far at least, does not seem to have given rise to practical difficulties.

Even so, the question is sometimes asked whether it is constitutionally proper for the role of the Governor-General, who is part of both the executive and the legislative branches of government, and has important royal powers in respect of the judiciary, to be carried out by the Chief Justice. Is that arrangement consistent with the constitutional doctrine of the separation of powers? Could it mean that the Chief Justice or other senior judge may be faced with a real or apparent conflict of interest if he or she is involved in the making of primary or secondary legislation that later needs to be interpreted and applied by the court, or needs to act in some other conflicting capacity?

The principle of the separation of powers was raised directly in a Canadian case concerning the validity of an Act to which the royal assent had been given by a Judge of the Supreme Court who was at the time acting as the Deputy of the Governor-General.[85] The Federal Court of Appeal upheld the legality of the power thus conferred, while recognising that in some people's minds it might raise the question whether it was desirable, in the context of the separation of powers, on the ground that a judge who had given the royal assent to an Act might subsequently be required to consider its constitutional validity.[86] At the administrative level, however, the Canadian Privy Council Office considered that, in such a case, there is no real conflict of interest because, as Administrator or Deputy of the Governor-General, the Chief Justice or other Judge of the Supreme Court must act on the advice of the Privy Council, and has no personal responsibility for the exercise of the powers concerned. This does not, however, take into account the, albeit remote, possibility that in an extreme case the Administrator may have to act in his or her personal discretion (a matter which we discuss in Chapter 10).

84 In Australia, all state Governors hold dormant commissions to act as Administrator. Usually, the longest-serving Governor will become the Administrator if the need should arise.

85 Constitution Act 1867, s 14. See also Letters Patent Constituting the Office of Governor General of Canada 1947, cl 8. Canada retains the practice of appointing an Administrator only if the office of Governor-General is vacant or the Governor-General is incapacitated or absent from the country for more than 30 days. In the case of shorter absences, however, the Governor-General appoints a Deputy who is authorised to exercise all the Governor-General's powers except the power to dissolve Parliament.

86 *Kassongo Tunda v The Minister of Citizenship and Immigration* [2001] FCA 151.

In New Zealand, some care is taken to avoid even the perception of a conflict of interest, but sometimes this is not possible. Concerns were raised, for example, when the Administrator executed the Canterbury Earthquake (Local Government Act 2002) Order (No 2) 2011 made under the controversial Canterbury Earthquake Recovery legislation.[87] The Order could well have become the subject of legal challenge. As a matter of principle, the current arrangement is not ideal, although it is hard to think of an appropriate and workable alternative.

Another worry from the practical viewpoint is the demand made on the time of a Chief Justice who now leads the country's highest court. The problem is the greater because Governors-General now travel overseas on official business more often than they once did. If it became clear that the Chief Justice's ability to preside over sittings of the Supreme Court was seriously affected, then some change would need to be made, perhaps by recognising that it would be appropriate for a senior Judge of the Court of Appeal to act as Administrator if the Chief Justice or other Supreme Court Judge were unable to do so, by reason of a sitting of that court.

3
IN CONCLUSION

In this chapter we have shown how a Governor-General is chosen, ways in which the political neutrality of the office is preserved, and how continuity of government is achieved. We also confirmed that the powers inherent in the office are those of the Sovereign and are therefore unaffected by the compound title of Governor-General and Commander-in-Chief. In chapters 13 and 14 we discuss further the Governor-General's role — in the constitutional relationship between the government and Māori, as representative of the Head of State in foreign relations, and in maintaining relationships with other sections of the New Zealand community (including the Defence Force). First, however, we consider the more taxing questions of what role a politically neutral Governor-General does and should play in the operation of New Zealand's executive government,[88] and in the legislative[89] and judicial branches of government.[90]

87 Canterbury Earthquake Recovery Act 2010.

88 Chapter 8 The Governor-General in the Executive Branch, Chapter 9 Finding and Changing a Prime Minister, Chapter 10 Guardian of the Constitution?.

89 Chapter 11 The Governor-General in Parliament.

90 Chapter 12 The Governor-General in the Judicial Branch.

CHAPTER 8

The Governor-General in the Executive Branch

1 INTRODUCTION

Most New Zealanders understand that "the Government" consists of the Ministers of the Crown drawn from the governing party or parties in Parliament. Few of them, however, realise that, as a matter of law, the authority to govern belongs to the Sovereign, and is delegated to the Governor-General, and through the Governor-General to Ministers and their officials. In exercising their delegated authority Ministers and Officials usually act in the name of "the Crown". That chain of constitutional authority is a fundamental element of New Zealand's democratic government. In Chapter 5 we discussed the Sovereign's delegation of her executive authority through the Governor-General to the government of the day, making the point that it not only has the authority to govern, but also the duty to do so. In this chapter we consider the implications of the way in which the 1983 Letters Patent currently provides for the exercise of her executive authority in New Zealand itself, as distinct from the Realm as a whole.

2 CONSTITUTING THE EXECUTIVE

The written law and the unwritten rules

In the 1983 Letters Patent, the Sovereign authorises and empowers the Governor-General:[1]

1 Letters Patent 1983, cl 3.

> a) to exercise on Our behalf the executive authority of . . . New Zealand, either directly or through officers subordinate to our Governor-General; and
> b) to do and execute in like manner all things that belong to the office of Governor-General.

The Governor-General is required to do and execute the executive authority in accordance with the Letters Patent, his or her Commission of appointment and the relevant law.[2]

The Sovereign also constitutes an Executive Council "to advise Us and Our Governor-General in the Government of Our Realm of New Zealand". The Executive Council consists of:[3]

> those persons who, having been appointed to the Executive Council from among persons eligible for appointment under the Constitution Act 1986,[4] are, for the time being Our responsible advisers.

The Sovereign authorises and empowers the Governor-General "from time to time in Our name and on Our behalf, to appoint . . . to hold office during pleasure . . . all such Members of the Executive Council, [and] Ministers of the Crown . . ." (among others) "as may be lawfully . . . appointed by Us".[5]

By the Letters Patent, the Sovereign establishes the executive branch of government. There is no more detailed provision in the written law. Implicit is the constitutional principle that the executive powers and functions vested in the Sovereign and delegated to the Governor-General must, as a general rule, be exercised by, or on the advice of, Ministers. Subject to any relevant law, they may act themselves or advise the Governor-General to do so, directly or through the Executive Council.

In accordance with a further convention, however, Ministers act, or advise the Governor-General to act, only with the express or implied authority of the Cabinet. And, for both their own actions and their advice to the Governor-General, Ministers are collectively responsible to Parliament. That constitutional principle gives rise to another: a government may continue to

2 Clause 4.
3 Clauses 7 and 8.
4 Constitution Act 1986, s 6. The section contains a transitional provision that allows a government to be formed immediately after a general election from among persons who were candidates at that election even though the relevant writ has not been returned or the outcome of the election is contested, but must become a Member of Parliament within 40 days beginning with the date of the appointment.
5 Clause 10.

govern only as long as it has the confidence of a majority in Parliament on issues of confidence and supply.

In this and the following two chapters we trace this chain of constitutional authority in more detail.

3
DEFINING THE GOVERNOR-GENERAL'S POWERS AND AUTHORITIES

Delegating the Sovereign's executive authority

The executive authority of New Zealand is vested in the Sovereign in right of New Zealand. In respect of New Zealand, the Queen has broadly the same kind of authority to govern as she has in respect of the United Kingdom and her other realms. Earlier, we described the evolutionary political process through which the former British colony became one of the Sovereign's independent realms.[6] Here we look at the parallel administrative and legal process through which the whole of the Sovereign's executive authority became exercisable by the Governor-General, acting on the advice of New Zealand Ministers.

Colonial Governor to Dominion Governor-General

The Governor of a British colony was never seen as invested with the whole of the Sovereign's authority in respect of the colony, but only with the authority expressly or impliedly conferred by the instruments constituting his office. That spelt out the particular things that the Governor was authorised to do. Over time, the fact that these instruments emanated from the Sovereign, coupled with the supervision and control of the Colonial Office, brought about an element of uniformity in the practice observed.[7]

When Captain Hobson was appointed as the first Governor and Commander-in-Chief of the separate colony of New Zealand, the standard practice had to be adapted. The most significant functions and powers of the office had been separately conferred by a Charter issued under the authority of an Act of

6 See Chapter 2 Building the Modern Constitution.

7 Kenneth Roberts-Wray *Commonwealth and Colonial Law* (Stevens & Sons, London, 1966) at 337.

Parliament, constituting New Zealand as a separate colony.[8] Hobson's Commission of appointment, however, included what had already become a standard formula. It required him to "do and exercise all things in due manner that shall belong to your said Command". He was to do those things in accordance with the Instructions given to him by or under the authority of the Sovereign and in accordance with any relevant law.

Gradually, as responsible government was put in place, the instruments constituting the offices of Governors or Governors-General became less tailored to their individual circumstances, including any relevant statute law, and took a more or less common form. By then, Governors or Governors-General in the self-governing colonies, and later the British Dominions, were required to act exclusively on the advice of their responsible Ministers in respect of the internal affairs of the Dominion concerned. The traditional authority and duty of the Governor-General of a Dominion to "do all things belonging to the office of Governor-General" had come to be seen as a grant of the constitutional authority to exercise all of the Sovereign's executive authority and powers in respect of the Dominion concerned.

"Imperial interests" had become limited to all aspects of foreign policy and international trade, relations with foreign states, treaty-making and the making of war and peace. On those matters the Governor or Governor-General, if required to act, did so on the instructions of United Kingdom Ministers.[9] In consequence, the external affairs powers of what was seen as an indivisible empire were therefore seen as being outside the Governor-General's authority.

That perception coloured the interpretation of "the things belonging to the office of Governor-General" conferred on a Governor-General by the Letters Patent constituting the office. That was the perception even in the Commonwealth of Australia, where a constitution enacted by the United Kingdom Parliament appeared on its face to have conferred a comprehensive executive authority on the Governor-General.[10] The earlier Canadian constitution had put the main emphasis on the executive authority of the Sovereign herself,[11] so the extent of a Governor-General's executive authority to exercise it depended on the terms of the delegation. The New Zealand constitution, which was earlier still, had not made any provision at all for

8 "Charter for erecting the Colony of New Zealand, and for creating and establishing a Legislative Council and an Executive Council" issued on 16 November 1840, reproduced in WD McIntyre and WJ Gardner (eds) *Speeches and Documents on New Zealand History* (Oxford University Press, Oxford, 1971) at 54–56.

9 See Chapter 2 Building the Modern Constitution, under the subheading Responsibility for foreign relations and trade, at 22.

10 Commonwealth of Australia Constitution Act 1900 (UK) 63 & 64 Vict c 12, ss 2 and 61.

11 Now known as the Constitution Act 1867 (UK) 30 & 31 Vict c 3, s 9.

the executive branch of government. That had been left to the prerogative instruments constituting the office of — eventually — the Governor-General, and to constitutional convention.[12]

The Governors-General of the independent realms

After 1926, the United Kingdom Government and those of the self-governing Dominions accepted that, on all matters, external as well as internal, the Sovereign would in future act only on the advice of the Prime Minister of the Dominion concerned. Already, the Dominions had been accepted as separate members of the international community and were beginning to exercise their own treaty-making powers.[13]

In the period between the wars, none of the Dominion governments appears to have become concerned about any disjunction between the powers formally granted to their Governors-General by the Sovereign, in the Letters Patent constituting their offices or otherwise, and those which their governments were beginning to exercise in practice.

Towards the end of World War II or shortly after its conclusion, that changed. Both Australia and Canada sought some further clarification of the extent to which the Governor-General had acquired the authority to exercise, on the advice of local Ministers, certain powers vested in the Sovereign and formerly exercised by or on the advice of United Kingdom Ministers.

In the same period, New Zealand brought its constitution into line with the constitutional law and conventions of the Commonwealth, so far as they concerned the power of the United Kingdom Parliament to make law for New Zealand, and the plenary nature of the New Zealand Parliament's own power to make laws. But, with no need to reconcile any disparity between the statutory sources of its constitution and the powers conferred on the Governor-General by the Letters Patent, it otherwise did nothing to ensure that they were in harmony with one another. The Letters Patent constituting the office of the Governor-General and the associated royal instruments remained in the form in which they had last been issued in 1917, when the status of the Governor had been raised to that of Governor-General.

From 1947 on, new independent members of the Commonwealth came into being, most of them with constitutions made in Whitehall, rather

12 Even now, the only substantial provision of the Constitution Act 1986, so far as it deals with the executive branch, is the requirement in s 6 that Ministers of the Crown must be Members of Parliament.

13 See Chapter 2 Building the Modern Constitution, around fn 52, at 25.

than Westminster, for the country concerned. The constitutions of the new Commonwealth monarchies were self-contained and in a more or less common form. They declared that the "executive authority" of the newly independent state was vested in the Sovereign, and delegated that authority to the Governor-General, and, through the Governor-General, to Ministers and officials. The office of Governor-General was itself constituted by the constitution. Clearly, those provisions alone were seen as authorising the government of the newly independent state to exercise all the external affairs powers of the Sovereign, in respect of the state concerned, as well as the powers pertaining to its internal government. Nothing more was required.

Like Canada, Australia and New Zealand, most of the new Commonwealth monarchies continued for some time to obtain the signature of the Queen herself to a number of instruments pertaining to the state's external relations and made in her name. But, at the signing of the ACP–EEC Convention of Lomé of 28 February 1975, a treaty in Heads of State form, the Queen of the United Kingdom contracted with herself as Head of State of some of the other Commonwealth monarchies. The necessary "Full Powers"[14] were apparently signed by Governors-General in the exercise of the powers conferred by the constitutions of the country concerned. That incident demonstrated that the practice of continuing to seek the signature of the Queen, as Head of State, for certain instruments exercising the external affairs power was not to be taken as indicating that Governors-General did not have the requisite authority.

The New Zealand solution

Having described the situation when work began on updating the 1917 New Zealand Letters Patent, we now look at the issues considered in deciding how the requisite authority should be conferred on the Governor-General by a new instrument. The 1980 Report[15] expressed the view that, by one route or another, the "things belonging to the office of Governor-General of New Zealand" had come to include the full range of executive powers, including the external affairs powers. While the new instrument should recognise the scope of the Governor-General's authority more explicitly, care should be taken not to cast doubt on the efficacy of the practices that were already being followed. That objective could be accomplished by a delegation of

14 "Full Powers" are documents authorising a representative of a state to sign an international treaty on behalf of that state.

15 Alison Quentin-Baxter *Review of the Letters Patent 1917 Constituting the Office of Governor-General of New Zealand: Report* (Cabinet Office, Wellington, 1980) [1980 Report].

authority in general terms, rather than a specific delegation of the external affairs power. As to the form of a general delegation or grant of authority, the 1980 Report made a number of recommendations.

First, problems arising from the possible non-availability of the Sovereign to sign a New Zealand document did not need to be dealt with in the Letters Patent. They should be met by applying to New Zealand the appropriate provisions of the Regency Act 1937 (UK). Secondly, the 1980 Report recommended that the new Letters Patent should include the following provision delegating to the Governor-General the Sovereign's authority in respect of New Zealand:

> Except as otherwise provided by law, the executive authority of New Zealand may be exercised on the Sovereign's behalf by the Governor-General.

While there were some uncertainties about exactly what "the executive authority of New Zealand" would encompass, it would certainly include the whole of the foreign affairs power, thus clarifying the matter of greatest concern.

Prerogatives in respect of Parliament?

The main uncertainty about the scope of New Zealand's "executive authority" was whether it included any of the Sovereign's prerogative powers in respect of Parliament, as distinct from the executive branch. That question might have more importance than it otherwise would, because the Governor-General's former statutory power to "summon" Parliament had been repealed in 1956, apparently in the mistaken belief that every aspect of the power to "summon" Parliament was covered by the Governor-General's separate statutory powers to issue the writs for a general election and also to "fix the time and place" for a meeting of Parliament.

Historically, however, the "summoning" of the United Kingdom Parliament by the Sovereign was a prerequisite for its members' ability lawfully to meet, and, "in Parliament assembled", to make new laws. It was not impossible, therefore, that the question of whether the New Zealand Parliament had been lawfully summoned could become an issue. If the Sovereign had once had a prerogative power to summon the New Zealand Parliament, and that power had survived its embodiment in the statute law, or had been superseded but had been revived by the repeal of the statute, then the Governor-General needed a clear power to exercise it.[16]

16 The power to summon Parliament is now conferred on the Governor-General by the Constitution Act 1986, s 18.

Principally for that reason, and with the benefit of Canadian precedent, the 1980 Report recommended that the Sovereign's conferment on the Governor-General of the power and duty to exercise New Zealand's executive authority should be supplemented by a further clause on the following lines:

> . . . and for greater certainty but not so as to restrict the generality of the foregoing, to do and execute in like manner all things that may belong to his office.

Effect was given to both recommendations in the 1983 Letters Patent.[17] The two grants of authority clearly overlap. Neither limits the other. Specific powers conferred on the Governor-General by later clauses of the Letters Patent are seen as falling into one or both of the broader grants of authority already conferred in general terms. From this point on, however, in discussing the nature of the broad authority conferred on the Governor-General by the Letters Patent, we use "executive authority" as an all-embracing term. We will begin by explaining its meaning.

The authority and the duty to govern New Zealand

Exercising New Zealand's "executive authority"

In authorising the Governor-General to exercise the executive authority of New Zealand, the Sovereign is delegating her own authority to the Governor-General. In accordance with general principle, the delegation does not deprive the Sovereign of the right to exercise that authority herself. The Sovereign not only *authorises* and *empowers*, but also requires the Governor-General to *do* and *execute* all the powers and authorities of the office, including the exercise of New Zealand's executive authority.[18] The traditional language may not bring out the force of this duty quite as clearly as the similar requirement in the Australian constitution: the executive power of the Commonwealth exercisable by the Governor-General "extends to the execution and maintenance of this Constitution, and of the laws of the Commonwealth".[19] Even so, the two provisions have the same thrust. As well as conferring the authority to act, they *require* the Governor-General to do so. New Zealand's system of responsible government means that the main burden of that duty further devolves upon Ministers and their officials.

17 Clause 3.
18 Clause 4.
19 Commonwealth of Australia Constitution Act 1900, above n 10, s 61.

The nature of executive authority

The authority to exercise the "executive authority" of New Zealand confers the right to exercise certain powers and perform certain functions and also a duty to do so if that is desirable or necessary. But it is not in itself the *source* of legal powers. A government authorised to exercise the executive authority has the right and the duty to govern. In doing so it may well be necessary or desirable to exercise particular legal powers. But the powers themselves must be found elsewhere, in the law of the land.

That point was made clear by the High Court of Australia in discussing the effect of the authority to exercise the "executive power of the Commonwealth" conferred by section 61 of the constitution:[20]

> It [section 61] enables the Crown to undertake all executive action which is appropriate to the position of the Commonwealth under the Constitution and to the sphere of responsibility vested in it by the Constitution. It includes [the exercise of] the prerogative powers of the Crown, that is powers accorded to the Crown by the common law.

Accordingly, the conferral of "executive authority" on the Governor-General gives the Governor-General, Ministers and officials the right to exercise legal powers conferred on the Sovereign or the Crown by or under an Act of Parliament or by the common law, including the royal prerogative.

The 1983 Letters Patent also contain a general instruction that the authority it confers on the Governor-General must be executed in conformity with the Letters Patent and the Governor-General's Commission of appointment, and also with:[21]

> [s]uch laws as are now or shall hereafter be in force in Our Realm of New Zealand or any part of it.

That is a reminder that the Letters Patent are and remain subject to the statute law in force at the material time. The principle is a general one, but has particular importance in respect of the exercise of prerogative powers, so far as they are part of New Zealand law.

20 *Barton v Commonwealth* (1974) 131 CLR 477 at 498 per Mason J, cited by Leslie Zines *The High Court and the Constitution* (5th ed, Federation Press, Annandale (NSW), 2008) at 343, but with our interpolation.

21 Clause 4.

The Letters Patent are, in effect, the conduit by which the Sovereign authorises the Governor-General, and, through the Governor-General, New Zealand Ministers, to exercise or enjoy, with some relatively minor exceptions, "all the functions, duties, powers, authorities, rights, privileges, and dignities belonging to the Crown".[22] While the Crown's attributes themselves came to New Zealand by virtue of the reception of English law, the authority of a New Zealand government to exercise them is vested in the Governor-General, acting in accordance with ministerial advice.

Certain powers not delegated to the Governor-General

Certain powers are not conferred on the Governor-General but remain with the Sovereign. By implication, the prerogative constituent power, which the Sovereign exercises in making the Letters Patent constituting the office of Governor-General, has not been delegated to the holder of that office. Nor has the power conferred by the Letters Patent to appoint and recall a Governor-General. It seems clear also that there has been no general delegation to the Governor-General of the prerogative of honour.[23]

The authority to exercise particular powers

The 1983 Letters Patent authorise the Governor-General to exercise certain powers (the source and substance of which must be found in the relevant law) either as part of New Zealand's "executive authority" or as "things belonging to the office of the Governor-General" or both. They also confer two specific powers on the Governor-General: the power to exercise the prerogative of mercy (discussed in Chapter 11) and the power to make certain appointments,[24] consistently with the specified conditions. These last we now discuss.

The Governor-General's power to make appointments

The Letters Patent authorise and empower the Governor-General to exercise the prerogative power to constitute certain offices under the Crown, and to make appointments to them, under the Seal of New Zealand.[25] In exercising

22 Constitution Act 1986, s 5(1).

23 While there is no judicial authority on the matter, it seems clear that the prerogative of honour is not part of the "executive authority" of New Zealand.

24 Letters Patent 1983, cl 10.

25 The need to affix the seal means that it is not possible to dispense with the need for a warrant or other written instrument of appointment as permitted by the Official Appointments and Documents

the power, it is not the practice to constitute an office separately and then to appoint its holder. Appointment to a named office is regarded as constituting the office itself.

All appointments made by the Governor-General in the exercise of the authority thus conferred are held during pleasure. Historically, the Sovereign's freedom to dismiss its servants (including Ministers) at will was claimed to be necessary in the public interest. That approach has long been modified by statute in the case of most appointments to the New Zealand public service. Indeed the idea of being a "servant" at all has fallen into disfavour, although, as a legal concept, it still plays a part. Members of the New Zealand armed forces still serve "during pleasure", on the ground that the contingencies of battle may require the instant dismissal of anyone from a Private to a General. An element of contingency is also inherent in the roles of most if not all of the officers now listed as those whom the Governor-General has an express power to appoint and an implied power to dismiss.[26]

We now discuss the powers to make specific appointments. Although members of the Executive Council and Ministers are first in the list, their appointment is governed by important constitutional principles and is discussed separately in Chapter 9.

Diplomatic and consular representatives

The Governor-General is expressly authorised to appoint New Zealand diplomatic and consular representatives in the exercise of the prerogative power to appoint officers to the service of the Crown.[27] Under the Foreign Affairs Act 1988,[28] the Governor-General has a parallel statutory power to appoint "heads of mission" and "heads of post", which appears to cover the field of the prerogative power. Even so, the 1988 Act expressly preserves any prerogative power or authority of the Crown in existence on the date of its enactment.[29]

The appointment of a New Zealand diplomatic or consular representative by the Governor-General under New Zealand's domestic law is only the first step. In order to assume the diplomatic or consular offices to which they have been appointed, "heads of mission" and "heads of post" need to be furnished with

Act 1919, s 2. Since 1977, that seal has been available for use on instruments made by Her Majesty, or by the Governor-General, on the advice of New Zealand Ministers: Seal of New Zealand Act 1977, s 3.

26 See also the Interpretation Act 1999, s 12. The Letters Patent are an "enactment" for the purposes of that Act. See the definition of that term and of "regulations" in s 29.

27 Letters Patent 1983, cl 10.

28 Foreign Affairs Act 1988, ss 4 and 5. For the definitions of "head of mission" and "head of post", see s 2.

29 Section 13.

credentials which they will present to the appropriate authority in the receiving state. Until quite recently, the Sovereign herself continued to issue the credentials of New Zealand Ambassadors and Consuls, but, as authorised by the Letters Patent, that responsibility is now exercised by the Governor-General as part of New Zealand's executive authority.[30]

Judicial appointments not now included

Until 1983, the Governor-General was expressly authorised to appoint judges and justices of the peace. That had reflected the more or less common form that the Letters Patent had by then assumed. In New Zealand, however, all judges have always been appointed in the exercise of an authority conferred by a statute. The relevant enactment safeguards their independence by providing that they hold office during good behaviour. Similarly, justices of the peace have long been appointed under statutory provisions which provided for their tenure of office. For those reasons, judges and justices of the peace are no longer included in the list of offices to which the Governor-General may make appointments in exercise of the prerogative.

Other necessary officers

Finally, the Governor-General has express authority and power to constitute and appoint such "other necessary Officers as may be lawfully constituted or appointed by Us".[31] The need for such appointments to be made under the Seal of New Zealand suggests that, although the power to constitute and appoint other officers is open-ended, it should be exercised only for the purpose of making appointments to high office. The practice bears out that contention. Other offices constituted and appointed by the Governor-General include the Solicitor-General, the Clerk of the Executive Council and the Secretary of the Cabinet.

It follows that the power to make appointments specifically delegated to the Governor-General cannot be taken as reflecting the full scope of the prerogative power to make appointments to the service of the Crown. The executive authority of New Zealand must be taken as including a wider power to make such appointments, exercisable either directly by the Governor-General or through subordinate officers.

30 See Chapter 14 Exercising the Head of State Role, under the subheading Issuing the credentials of New Zealand diplomats, at 282–284.

31 Letters Patent 1983, cl 10.

The devolution of authority on other actors

The Governor-General's executive authority may be exercised "either directly, or through officers responsible to our Governor-General".[32] The constitutions of most of the post-war Commonwealth realms included such a provision. Its inclusion resulted from a general policy of giving a new-born independent realm a constitution that codified, to a greater extent than formerly, the underlying rules and principles on which a Westminster constitution is based.

The phrase itself only hints at the structure it reflects. Like the Sovereign, the Governor-General must, as a general rule, act on the advice of Ministers, and the public service departments under ministerial direction. For some purposes, however, the Governor-General, Ministers and members of the public service are, in law, all "servants of the Crown". In practice, the authority to govern has been seen by the courts as, in some circumstances, devolving upon the other constitutional actors, in ways that reflect that hierarchy, without any need for sub-delegation.[33]

A picture of the relationships between a Governor-General and his or her Ministers will, we hope, unfold as we work through other aspects of the Letters Patent and the constitutional principles they reflect. We now look at things from the other direction: what do the Letters Patent say about the responsible advisers of the Sovereign and the Governor-General? Again, for what seemed good reason, the way in which the relationships work in practice is not spelt out in the instrument itself.

4
THE GOVERNOR-GENERAL'S RESPONSIBLE ADVISERS

The tradition of an advisory body

New Zealand's early Executive Council

Traditionally, the Governor of a British colony was advised by an Executive Council. The practice can be traced back to the constitutions of the North American colonies before the revolution. They had provided for the Governor to be advised by a body analogous to the Privy Council in England, the body

32 Letters Patent 1983, cl 3.

33 Janet McLean *Searching for the State in British Legal Thought* (Cambridge University Press, New York, 2012) at 222–223 and above Chapter 3 Constitutional Monarchy: Key Concepts, under the subheading The Queen and Crown as a corporation, at 40–44.

that traditionally advises the Sovereign. The practice was maintained in the second phase of British colonisation.

The 1840 New Zealand Charter provided for an Executive Council "to advise and assist the Governor". It was to consist of such persons as were named or designated in the Governor's Instructions.[34] As there directed, Governor Hobson appointed as members of the Executive Council his three most senior permanent officials, the Colonial Secretary, the Attorney-General and the Colonial Treasurer.[35]

The impact of responsible government

In Chapter 2 we described the way in which New Zealand attained, first, an elected legislature, and not long afterwards, responsible government. From then on, at least on matters concerning its internal affairs, the Governor was advised by members of the Legislative Assembly who, for the time being, had the support of a majority in the House of Representatives. The way in which this change was made throws considerable light on the present character of the Executive Council, and also of a new body, the Cabinet, that came into being at the same time.

As the Secretary of State for the Colonies had explained, the conventions governing the operation of responsible government rested on "usage only".[36] On 7 May 1856, even before there had been any change in the Royal Instructions, but after the General Assembly had provided that they would be entitled to pensions, the officials who had been members of the Executive Council resigned their offices.[37] Governor Thomas Gore Browne, having made known his intention of acting in accordance with the advice of his responsible advisers,[38] then appointed to the vacant offices the member of the Legislative Assembly who appeared to have the confidence of a majority, and two of his supporters.[39] In that way the Executive Council came to consist of members of what would become known as "Parliament" who had, for the

34 Above n 8.

35 Queen Victoria's Royal Instructions dated 5 December 1840, cl 30.

36 Chapter 2 Building the Modern Constitution, fn 21, at 15.

37 The Colonial Secretary and the Colonial Treasurer resigned, but later, on the advice of the newly constituted Executive Council, the Governor terminated the appointment of the Attorney-General, who was on leave in England, and appointed a member of the Legislative Assembly in his place: Despatch from Governor Gore Browne to the Rt Hon Henry Labouchere, Secretary of State for the Colonies (8 May 1856).

38 Chapter 2 Building the Modern Constitution, fn 30, at 19.

39 Despatch of 8 May 1856, above n 37. For a time, however, as the Governor's Instructions required, the Senior Officer of Her Majesty's land forces in New Zealand remained a member of the Executive Council: Instructions to Governor Thomas Gore Browne dated 9 February 1855, cl 18.

time being, the support of a majority. Immediately, the role of the Executive Council changed.

On 23 May 1856, the Governor reported an understanding reached with his "responsible advisers" that:[40]

> questions of ministerial policy are not to be brought before the Executive Council which will only be convened for purposes required by law to be approved in Council, or when it may be thought necessary to hold consultations unconnected with party views.

In that way, the Governor's control over policy-making in respect of New Zealand's internal government came to an end.[41] In future the Executive Council would have a purely formal role. The government's policies would be made by a new body — the Cabinet.

Cabinet government

The new members of the Executive Council appointed in 1856 quickly became known as "Ministers". They immediately adopted the British conventional practice of meeting privately, without the Governor, as the Cabinet.[42]

Earlier, we have touched on how the traditional council in which the Sovereign met with his or her Ministers transformed into the modern Cabinet. The great political changes that took place in England in the mid-19th century, such as the widening of the franchise after 1832 and the redistribution of seats in the House of Commons, would alter the relationship between the Sovereign and his or her Ministers. That, in turn, led to changes in the nature and role of political parties. The choice of a Prime Minister and his tenure of the office became matters for the House of Commons, not the Sovereign.

Those developments shaped the relationship between the executive and the legislature. Bagehot, writing early in the second half of the century, famously described the "efficient secret" of the English constitution as "the close

40 Despatch, Governor Gore Browne to Labouchere, 25 May 1856 (GBPP 1860/2718 at 224). That despatch suggests that the understanding may have stemmed, at least in part, from the fact that the Senior Military Officer was still a member of the Executive Council.

41 As to the responsibility for Māori policy, see Chapter 2 Building the Modern Constitution, under the subheading Responsibility for Māori affairs and land, at 18–22; and Chapter 13 The Crown as a Party to the Treaty of Waitangi, under the subheading The Transfer of Responsibility for "Native Affairs", at 260–263.

42 KJ Scott *The New Zealand Constitution* (Oxford University Press, Oxford, 1962) at 65.

union, the nearly complete fusion, of the executive and legislative powers".[43] He attributed this relationship to the role of the Cabinet as:[44]

> a *hyphen* which joins, a *buckle* which fastens, the legislative part of the State to the executive part of the State.

It was the mid-19th-century model which, in 1856, the New Zealand political leaders set out to emulate.

The modern Cabinet

In New Zealand today, Cabinet is the "central decision-making body of executive government".[45] Still the product of convention, not law, the Cabinet does not exercise powers. Its role is to make policy decisions, or sometimes to confirm, possibly with changes, decisions provisionally made elsewhere, by an individual Minister, a Cabinet committee, or in other, less formal ways. Legal powers, whether statutory or stemming from the common law including the prerogative, are still exercised either by individual Ministers or by the Governor-General. In the last-mentioned case the Governor-General acts either on the advice of an individual Minister or on the collective advice of the Executive Council. Often, and always in the case of things required to be done by the Governor-General, acting "on the advice and with the consent of the Executive Council", the decision to exercise a particular power will first have been made or confirmed by the Cabinet.

The Cabinet is chaired by the Prime Minister who exercises both power and influence. Even so, in the opinion of the Rt Hon Sir Geoffrey Palmer, a constitutional lawyer who has also held office as a member of Cabinet and, for a time, as Prime Minister, Cabinet has remained a highly collective and effective decision-making body.[46] It has done so partly because Cabinet procedures are orderly, clearly set out, and efficient, and partly because:[47]

> [i]n New Zealand Cabinet works not only administratively but politically, and it has continued to do so because successive Prime Ministers have found it of value.

43 Walter Bagehot *The English Constitution* (Collins, London, 1963) at 65.
44 At 68 (emphasis in original).
45 Cabinet Office *Cabinet Manual 2008* (Department of the Prime Minister and Cabinet, Wellington, New Zealand, April 2008) at [5.2].
46 Geoffrey Palmer "The Cabinet, the Prime Minister and the Constitution" (2006) 4 NZJPIL 1 at 15. Sir Geoffrey was comparing the Cabinet in New Zealand with the modern Cabinet in the United Kingdom.
47 At 19.

Cabinet is at the heart of executive government. That fact has implications for the role of the Governor-General in New Zealand's constitution, as we now show.

The modern Executive Council

Given the centrality of Cabinet, is an Executive Council still required? On the introduction of responsible government, the functions of the Canadian and Australian equivalents of the Executive Council suffered the same kind of downgrading as in New Zealand. The institutions themselves survived, however, not least because they were provided for in constitutions that were difficult to amend. The constitutions of the post-war Commonwealth realms, in contrast, make no provision for an Executive Council.

Instead, the post-war constitutions typically provide for a Cabinet consisting of the Prime Minister and such other Ministers as the Prime Minister may designate from time to time. The functions of the Cabinet are simply to advise the Governor-General in the government of the country concerned. It is implicit that, in a realm without a separate Executive Council or the equivalent, a statutory power such as that to make regulations would be vested in the Governor-General "acting on the advice and with the consent of the Cabinet". Cabinet ceased to be the creature of convention. It had been constituted by the constitution itself.

In revising New Zealand's 1917 Letters Patent, one issue was whether to retain the Executive Council or, instead, to vest its advisory functions directly in the Cabinet. At an early stage, however, it had been concluded that, because the concept "the Governor-General in Council" was in such extensive use throughout the statute book, and generally in constitutional discourse, it would be politically impossible, for the foreseeable future, to do away with the Executive Council altogether. Instead, some of those involved suggested reconstituting the Executive Council so that the Governor-General would no longer be required to preside over its meetings or even to attend.

The 1980 Report concluded that, although arguments could be made in support of such a course, it would be misconceived. The Executive Council is merely an advisory body. The powers exercisable by "the Governor-General in Council" belong to the Governor-General, not to some kind of corporate body. If the Governor-General was not to have any working relationship with the Executive Council, but was merely required to sign the instruments that the Executive Council had approved, there would be little point in retaining the Executive Council itself. The Executive Council was therefore retained as, in effect, a "dignified part of the constitution", to use Bagehot's words.[48]

The present-day Executive Council

In the 1983 Letters Patent, the Sovereign constitutes an Executive Council:[49]

> to advise Us and our Governor-General in the Government of Our Realm of New Zealand.

Essentially, the Executive Council is an organ of New Zealand's executive government. Although the Letters Patent as a whole are part of the law of every part of the Realm, they are subject to the law in force in each part.[50] The Executive Council is not an organ of government in the two self-governing states, the Cook Islands and Niue. The constitution of each makes different provision for the conduct of the executive branch of government.[51]

The opening statement that the Executive Council advises the Sovereign and the Governor-General was designed to send an important signal. It is the first step in making it clear in the written law that both have a general duty to act only on ministerial advice.

Composition of the Executive Council

The Letters Patent go on to provide as follows:[52]

> The Executive Council shall consist of those persons who, having been appointed to the Executive Council from among persons eligible for appointment under the Constitution Act 1986, are for the time being Our responsible advisers.

The provision has two elements. First, it identifies those who are eligible for appointment. Appointees must be Members of Parliament or, if not already declared elected, must have been a candidate at a general election immediately before being appointed. In that second case, the appointee must vacate office if he or she has not become a Member of Parliament within 40 days.

48 See Bagehot, above n 43, at 4–5.
49 Clause 8.
50 Chapter 6 The Letters Patent, the Governor-General and the Realm of New Zealand, after fn 47, at 108.
51 Clause 7 of the Letters Patent 1983 has a minimal application to the two self-governing states of the Cook Islands and of Niue which have their own constitutions but are part of the Realm: see Chapter 6 The Letters Patent, the Governor-General and the Realm of New Zealand, after fn 49, at 108.
52 Clause 8.

Originally, only persons who had already become Members of Parliament were eligible for appointment.[53] As amended in 1987 to refer to the Constitution Act provision, the clause now permits the speedy taking of office by a newly elected government, without any need to wait for the return of the election writs. We describe the events that lead to the inclusion of that provision in Chapter 9.

Secondly, the provision contains a clear statement that the members of the Executive Council are the responsible advisers of the Sovereign and the Governor-General. That role is the counterpart to their own general duty to act only on ministerial advice. The present practice is to appoint as members of the Executive Council the Prime Minister and all eligible persons whom the Prime Minister intends to recommend for appointment to offices that will entitle them to use the title "Minister". It is unusual, however, to appoint all Ministers as members of the Cabinet. Ministers outside the Cabinet are able to have the same full responsibility for portfolios as those Ministers within Cabinet. Cabinet Ministers are bound by the principle of collective responsibility. According to the Cabinet Manual, Ministers outside Cabinet are subject to selective ministerial responsibility in relation to their portfolios only.[54] The position of Ministers outside of Cabinet is likely further to crystallise and to be the subject of political agreement.

Appointing a Prime Minister and other Ministers

All Ministers are appointed by the Governor-General in the exercise of the prerogative power to make appointments to the service of the Crown. While the Governor-General must normally exercise that power on ministerial advice, the appointment of a Prime Minister is an act logically prior to the operation of that duty. In its place, the Governor-General must look to the governing constitutional conventions.

The office of Prime Minister is itself the product of convention. The changed relationship between the Sovereign and Parliament after the 1688 revolution gradually led to the recognition that, among the Sovereign's Ministers, one of them needed to assume a leadership role. By the early 19th century, the term "Prime Minister" — originally used in a derogatory sense to describe a Minister regarded as seeking to exercise too much power — was beginning to be used by the *The Times* to describe what had, by then, become an accepted political reality. In colonial New Zealand, however, the leader of the government was

53 Electoral Act 1979, s 9.
54 *Cabinet Manual*, above n 45, at [1.24] and [2.26]–[2.28].

at first known as the "Premier". The title "Prime Minister" was first used in 1906,[55] when New Zealand was on the eve of officially becoming a "Dominion".

When one of the party leaders has succeeded in forming a government after a general election, a formal appointment ceremony is held, even if the composition of the government has not greatly changed. The Governor-General formally appoints the Prime Minister designate as an Executive Councillor, and then as Prime Minister. Then, on the Prime Minister's advice, the Governor-General appoints the other members of the Executive Council. Similarly, on the advice of the Prime Minister, the Governor-General appoints to their respective ministerial offices the members of the Executive Council who are to be members of the Cabinet and those who are to be Ministers outside Cabinet but still receiving portfolios. In general, the authority vested in a Minister by virtue of his or her portfolio may be exercised by any other member of the Executive Council.[56] We look more closely at the constitutional principles governing the choice of a Prime Minister in Chapter 9.

Meetings of the Executive Council

The Letters Patent refer only obliquely to the fact that, in keeping with the purpose for which the Executive Council is constituted, the Governor-General, though not a member of the Executive Council, normally attends the meetings of the Council unless prevented from doing so by the other duties of the office or by some other cause such as ill health. If present, the Governor-General presides. It is implicit that, if the Governor-General is not present, one of its members, normally the most senior Minister present, will preside. To constitute a quorum, at least two members of the Council, exclusive of any member presiding, must be present throughout the whole of the meeting at which its business is despatched.

In a situation of urgency or emergency, the "presence" of members (and by implication that of the Governor-General or other member presiding) may be achieved by any method of communication that allows each member to participate effectively during the whole of the meeting. That provision, inserted in 2006, permits the speedy exercise of any statutory power vested in the "Governor-General in Council".[57] The "Governor-General in Council"

55 The title "Prime Minister" was first used by William Hall-Jones who held office after the death of Richard Seddon until the return to New Zealand of Sir Joseph Ward, Seddon's designated successor.

56 Constitution Act 1986, s 7.

57 The Interpretation Act 1999, s 29 defines that expression as meaning "the Governor-General acting on the advice and with the consent of the executive council". The other elements of the detailed provisions formerly set out in the Acts Interpretation Act 1924, s 23 were not re-enacted. They may, however, be taken as a guide to the applicable principles.

may also exercise any prerogative power that is part of New Zealand law. In short, the emergency powers available to the state can be activated by the Governor-General and two Ministers, or by any three Ministers, at any time of the day or night, as long as they are in communication with one another.

In the absence of a statutory requirement to obtain the advice and consent of the Executive Council, constitutional convention may provide guidance as to whether, in exercising a particular power, the Governor-General should be advised by the Executive Council or simply by the responsible Minister. Ministers themselves must act only under the general direction or with the express approval of the Cabinet, and the public service, acting within the departmental structure, must have the express or implied authority of the responsible Minister.

The Clerk of the Executive Council

The Clerk of the Executive Council is the senior official responsible for advising on and helping to conduct the New Zealand Government's relationships with both the Sovereign and the Governor-General.[58] That wide-ranging role developed naturally, although not inevitably, from the Clerk's direct responsibility to the Prime Minister and the Governor-General for servicing the Executive Council and providing such advice as may be required from time to time on constitutional matters. The offices of Clerk of the Executive Council and Secretary of the Cabinet are usually held by the same person.[59]

The Governor-General's role in executive government

Traditionally, colonial Governors used their authority to decide when a meeting of the Executive Council should be held and what matters should be included in the agenda, as a means of exerting considerable practical control over their constitutional advisers. As we have shown, however, Governors in New Zealand lost that power immediately after the introduction of responsible government. The modern business of the Executive Council is essentially formal and usually comprises the exercise of a statutory power, to make regulations or appointments or to perform some other formal act. Occasionally the Executive Council may need to advise the Governor-General to exercise a prerogative power.[60]

58 Chapter 5 The Sovereign in Right of New Zealand: A Personal Touch, after fn 17, at 74.

59 *Cabinet Manual*, above n 45, at [1.30]–[1.34]. As to the role of the Secretary of the Cabinet, see [5.77]–[5.80]. As to the appointment process for both offices, see [5.81].

60 The making or amendment of Letters Patent constituting the office of Governor-General is one example.

The policy decision to exercise the power concerned will already have been made or approved by the Cabinet. These days, the Executive Council usually meets regularly, on the day of or day after a Cabinet meeting. Through the Clerk, the Prime Minister can control the agenda, but it is usually uncontroversial. The day before the meeting the Governor-General receives copies of the instruments to be approved by the Council before their signature.

With the possible complexities of a general election under the MMP voting system in mind, the three successive Governors-General appointed in or after 1996 have all been persons "learned in the law". Lawyers are not in the habit of signing legal documents without reading them first, and they are not willing to sign them if they happen to contain an obvious mistake. It is fair to say that, as a result, there has been a needed tightening-up of the process of making delegated legislation. The Minister responsible will be well briefed on why it is needed, and on the processes of consultation that have taken place before the Governor-General is advised in the Executive Council to give it the force of law. We do not suggest, however, that a recent Governor-General, a former Chief of Defence Force, should have been ready to maintain standards with his sword. The Governor-General has no responsibility for exercising general quality control over the actions of the executive, although that may be an incidental benefit of their involvement.

It is, in fact, not easy to say what role the Governor-General has — or ought now to have — in the exercise of New Zealand's executive authority, the task with which the holder of the office is charged, nominally at least. The Governor-General's responsibility is conditioned by the equally important governing principle we now discuss.

The duty to act on ministerial advice

Signposts, but not a road map

The statements in the Letters Patent that the Executive Council is constituted to advise the Queen and the Governor-General in the government of the Realm of New Zealand, and that the members of the Executive Council are their responsible advisers, are as close as the Letters Patent come to spelling out the constitutional conventions that define the role of the Governor-General. Care was taken to avoid any suggestion that the duty to act on ministerial advice is unqualified, but there are reasons why the statements in the Letters Patent do not give a full picture.

The Letters Patent have never been seen as a place in which to articulate the basic principle that Ministers are responsible to Parliament for the advice they give to the Governor-General or to the Sovereign. In most cases, that responsibility is collective, meaning that it engages the responsibility of the government as a whole. There are, however, some exceptions to that rule. The Minister of Justice has a personal responsibility for advising on the exercise of the prerogative of mercy. Those decisions are seen as needing to be "kept out of politics". Conversely, the Prime Minister, acting alone, may advise the Governor-General to dissolve Parliament. That right, along with the freedom, or in some circumstances a duty, to tender resignation from office, can be seen as the tools which a Prime Minister may or ought to use to maintain the government's majority support in Parliament or, if that is in doubt or lost, to give some other Member of Parliament the opportunity to form a government.

Taken together, the two conventions, the Governor-General's duty to act on ministerial advice and ministerial responsibility to Parliament for the advice given, have transformed the exercise of the executive authority vested in the Sovereign and delegated to the Governor-General into the modern democratic form of government that New Zealanders enjoy today. There are, however, some qualifications to the duty of the Governor-General to act in accordance with the advice of Ministers. That is another respect in which the Letters Patent, read in isolation, give an incomplete picture. The omission was deliberate, and it is useful to explain the reasons.

Codifying the Governor-General's constitutional discretions?

In making the 1983 Letters Patent, it was understood that the Governor-General still had both prerogative and statutory powers in the exercise of which the constitutional conventions may permit or even require the exercise of an element of personal responsibility. But, even by the standards of that time, the 1917 Royal Instructions had given the Governor-General what appeared to have been an unduly wide discretion to dissent from the opinion of the Executive Council.[61] For good reason, the new Letters Patent no longer make any provision for the issue of Royal Instructions. Once it had been made clear in the Balfour Declaration of 1926 that the Sovereign would, in the future, act solely on the advice of the Prime Minister of the Dominion concerned, there was no longer any basis on which the Sovereign, acting on the advice of United Kingdom Ministers, was able to issue Royal Instructions. From then on, new Letters Patent constituting the office of Governor-General ceased to be accompanied by Royal Instructions.

61 See cl 5 of the 1917 Royal Instructions.

That was the reason why the 1983 Letters Patent revoked the 1917 Royal Instructions and did not replace them. Although some commentators take the view that the revocation of the Royal Instructions also revoked any discretion to act otherwise than on the advice of Ministers, we think that view is not soundly based. The Royal Instructions cannot be interpreted as if they were a statute, conferring a legal power. If a statute is repealed, the power is lost. The Royal Instructions simply informed the Governor-General of the discretion he was seen as having in 1917 to act otherwise than on the advice of Ministers who have majority support in Parliament. They did not confer the discretion itself. We explain below that, in later chapters, we have taken an initiative to clarify the current constitutional principles over a wide field. The information supplied in 1917 is evidence of the thinking at that time, but the withdrawal of that information in 1983 for a reason unconnected with its substance throws no light on what the situation was then or is now.

The immediate question in making what became the 1983 Letters Patent constituting the office of Governor-General was whether it would be a suitable vehicle in which to codify the constitutional responsibilities of the Governor-General and the Prime Minister, assuming that objective were to be agreed upon. The 1980 Report concluded that it would not. The Governor-General might need to make a principled judgement about the exercise of both prerogative and statutory powers. As a prerogative instrument having the force of law, and potentially reviewable by the courts, the Letters Patent were not a suitable place in which to record understandings having purely conventional force about how and when the Governor-General would exercise those powers.[62]

As recommended in the 1980 Report, the 1983 Letters Patent do not go beyond the reference to the advisory role of the Executive Council and the fact that the Ministers who are its members are the constitutional advisers of the Sovereign and the Governor-General. That statement was seen as sufficient recognition of the underlying constitutional principle. The Governor-General must act on the advice of Ministers except in the rare cases where he or she may have an element of personal responsibility to make a principled decision. That approach accorded with that taken in the Letters Patent then in force in Canada[63] and Australia.[64]

62 1980 Report, above n 15, at [151]–[154].

63 The Canadian Letters Patent of 1942 record only the basic principle that the Governor-General acts on the advice of Ministers, without including any reference to constitutional discretions.

64 The Australian instrument required only that the Governor-General was to exercise his powers and authorities "in due manner".

The duty to keep the Governor-General informed

Alongside the Governor-General's duty to act on ministerial advice is the countervailing duty on Ministers to keep the Governor-General informed. We explained how the Balfour Declaration of 1926 led to the recognition that the Governor-General's relationship with his Ministers would be essentially the same as that between the Sovereign and his Ministers in the United Kingdom. He would no longer be the representative of His Majesty's Government. King George V is credited with foreseeing that this change in the Governor-General's role might lead to his isolation from his Ministers. It was therefore agreed that:[65]

> . . . a Governor-General should be supplied with copies of all documents of importance and in general should be kept fully informed as is His Majesty the King in Great Britain of Cabinet business and public affairs.

There, the Sovereign gives regular weekly audiences to the Prime Minister, and has the opportunity to discuss matters with the Prime Minister before a decision is made.

In New Zealand, however, there seems never to have been a practice of giving all Cabinet papers to the Governor-General, and no such practice was initiated in 1926 or subsequently. Nor, it appears, has there ever been a tradition that the Prime Minister should pay a weekly call at Government House. Nonetheless, the duty to keep the Governor-General informed became a standard provision of the post-war independence constitutions of Commonwealth monarchies. On that basis, the following provision was included in the 1983 Letters Patent:[66]

> Our Ministers of the Crown in New Zealand shall keep Our Governor-General fully informed concerning the general conduct of the Government of Our said Realm, so far as they are responsible therefor, and shall furnish Our Governor-General with such information as he may request with respect to any particular matter relating to the Government of Our said Realm.

The duty to keep the Governor-General informed was laid on Ministers generally rather than on the Prime Minister, because the principle in the United

65 "Report of the Inter-Imperial Relations Committee of the Imperial Conference of 1926" (Cmd 2768, 1926) at [IV (b)].

66 Clause 16.

Kingdom is that all Ministers have access to the Sovereign on matters concerning their portfolios. It seems, however, that Ministers' offices now communicate with the Governor-General through the Clerk of the Executive Council rather than directly with Government House.[67]

The current practice is that the duty of keeping the Governor-General informed on a regular basis falls to the Clerk of the Executive Council rather than the Prime Minister or any other Minister.[68] At least one recent Governor-General has commented publicly that he usually learnt of important new government policy initiatives from the news media, but his tone was one of resignation rather than complaint.

In Chapters 9 and 10 we take a fresh look in the modern era at the whole subject of the Governor-General's constitutional powers, duties, and responsibilities for exercising legal powers otherwise than in accordance with advice, as well as the rights, duties and responsibilities of other political actors. Governments are led by Prime Ministers who now — and most probably in the future — will need the support of more than the members of their own political party in order to maintain confidence and supply. They cannot always secure the passage of legislation unless they negotiate the support of other political parties, usually on a case-by-case basis.

In that changed political and constitutional setting, the content and the role of the relevant constitutional conventions need to be reassessed. We will try to identify what now seems to have become settled practice, and also the areas where there still appear to be uncertainties or gaps. Then it will be possible to see whether New Zealand's constitutional machinery, so far as it concerns the duty of the Governor-General to act on the advice of Ministers and any glosses on or exceptions to that duty, is in good working order.

67 *Cabinet Manual*, above n 45, at [1.34].
68 See Chapter 5 The Sovereign in Right of New Zealand: A Personal Touch, around fn 17, at 79.

CHAPTER 9

Finding and Changing a Prime Minister

1
SETTING THE SCENE

In this chapter we examine the role of the Governor-General in finding a Prime Minister who has majority support in Parliament. The process of forming a government after a general election is now well established, largely due to the careful work of officials in the lead-up to the first MMP general election and in the period immediately following. What should happen if the government were later to be defeated in Parliament is much more controversial and there is little or no New Zealand precedent or practice. The Governor-General's discretion to *dismiss* a Prime Minister whose government still has the confidence of Parliament will be discussed separately, in Chapter 10.

We begin this chapter with a discussion of the respective roles of law and constitutional convention as they govern the expectations of both the Governor-General and the Prime Minister then in office, after a general election. We consider first the scenarios in which the New Zealand principles and practice are relatively well established, before moving to areas of greater uncertainty involving the possibility of a mid-term dissolution of Parliament and an early election. In the absence of relevant New Zealand experience, we draw on Commonwealth codifications as well as underlying principle. Finally, we consider the possibility of further codifying the constitutional conventions as they apply across the whole area, and produce our own attempt.

The legal powers

This chapter concerns the Governor-General's exercise of two very ordinary legal powers. The first is a power to appoint the Prime Minister. The second is a power to dissolve Parliament and call a general election. Our main purpose is to identify the basis on which each power is exercised in the relevant circumstance. The essential question is: "Who really makes the decisions, and on what grounds?" First, however, we need to explain the sources and the nature of the powers themselves.

The power to appoint a New Zealand Prime Minister is vested in the Sovereign. In the Letters Patent 1983, the Governor-General is expressly authorised to exercise the prerogative power to constitute the Executive Council and to make appointments to it on behalf of the Sovereign.[1] As a matter of law, the Prime Minister and other Ministers are servants of the Crown who hold office "during pleasure".[2] The Governor-General accordingly has an implied common law power to dismiss the Prime Minister at any time.[3] Ordinarily, the question of dismissal never arises, because convention requires Prime Ministers to tender their resignations in certain circumstances. Historically, a subject could not refuse to act in the Crown's service if so required. Once appointed to office, the Crown servant could not unilaterally bring that service to an end. A Crown servant could, however, ask to be relieved of office. Accordingly, a present-day Prime Minister who wishes, or is obliged, to step down "tenders" his or her resignation to the Sovereign or the Governor-General. Only when the Sovereign or the Governor-General signifies that the tendered resignation has been accepted does the Prime Minister's tenure of office come to an end.

The Governor-General also has an express statutory power to dissolve Parliament. The power is now exercised by the making of a Proclamation which takes effect as soon as it is publicly announced, either by publication in the Gazette or by being publicly read by a person acting with the Governor-General's authority.[4] The second option means that, if necessary, Parliament can be dissolved orally, and very quickly. It was once usual for the Governor-General to prorogue Parliament — in other words, to suspend it temporarily — before dissolving it, but that is no longer done.[5] If the Governor-General dissolves Parliament, he or she must, within seven days, issue a writ to the Electoral Commission requiring it to make all the necessary arrangements for a general election.[6]

1 Letters Patent 1983, cl 10.
2 See Chapter 8 The Governor-General in the Executive Branch, under the subheading New Zealand's early Executive Council, at 152.
3 Section 12(a) of the Interpretation Act 1999 makes explicit that a power to appoint includes a power to dismiss.
4 Constitution Act 1986, s 18(2).
5 David G McGee *Parliamentary Practice in New Zealand* (3rd ed, Dunmore Publishing, Wellington, 2005) at 51.
6 Electoral Act 1993, s 125.

Constitutional discretions

Decisions to appoint the Prime Minister and to dissolve Parliament are sometimes said to involve the "reserve powers" of the Governor-General. For a number of reasons, however, the term "reserve powers" is now inappropriate, as some contemporary commentators point out.[7] We do not propose to use it ourselves, but, because the term continues to be used, we need to explain briefly the range of ideas that it connotes.

When New Zealand acquired responsible government in 1856, the Governor ceased to govern the country but still had the role of protecting Imperial interests. To that end, Lord Durham had recommended that certain matters should remain outside the field of ministerial responsibility. Instead, they would be reserved to the Governor, acting on the instructions of United Kingdom Ministers. Inevitably, the existence of those "reserved powers" became inextricably entwined with the essentially separate question of how far the Governor, as the Sovereign's representative, had the powers or discretions exercisable in the United Kingdom by the Sovereign herself. Although the United Kingdom authorities always recognised that a Governor's personal responsibilities went beyond the protection of Imperial interests, there was a good deal of confusion about how much discretion a Governor or Governor-General had to act without instructions.

It may be better to talk about the Governor-General's "constitutional discretions", rather than "reserve powers", but that would suggest a focus on the role of the Governor-General, to the exclusion of the other constitutional actors, especially the Prime Minister. We therefore prefer not to give a generic label to our field of inquiry. Instead we look in turn at some possible sequences of events, and at the rights and duties of all the office-holders who share the responsibility of making the constitution work.

A Prime Minister is appointed in the exercise of a prerogative power, while Parliament is dissolved in the exercise of statutory power. The fact that the royal prerogative was the original source of both powers may explain the genesis of notions about the existence of a discretion, but in our view, nothing necessarily follows from that. If there is still an element of discretion, the conditions of its exercise must now be looked for in the constitutional conventions exclusively. We now turn our attention to that all-important source.

7 See Philip A Joseph *Constitutional and Administrative Law in New Zealand* (4th ed, Thomson Reuters, Wellington, 2014) at 726.

In determining what such conventions might be, the New Zealand Cabinet Manual has been something of a trailblazer.[8] The Cabinet Manual plays an important role in helping to ensure that politicians and the news media in particular, as well as the wider public, have an understanding of the likely position of the Prime Minister immediately after a general election. Starting as a collection of the practices and procedures regulating the decision-making processes of the executive branch of government, it has evolved to become also "a primary source of information on New Zealand's constitutional arrangements, as seen through the lens of the executive branch of government".[9] The Manual is an authoritative statement of the relevant constitutional conventions as they are currently understood. It does not purport itself to effect change, but aims to record incremental change as it occurs.[10] Sometimes it is used to record expectations, as in the lead-up to the first election under mixed-member proportional representation (MMP), when it was amended to include an up-to-date picture of how the Governor-General expected a Prime Minister to be chosen if, as was likely, none of the political parties won a majority of the seats.[11]

The actual experience of coalition and minority government, particularly in the 1996–1999 period, made it desirable to set out further authoritative guidance on the constitutional principles. What has now become Chapter 6 of the Manual, dealing with Elections, Transitions, and Government Formation, was almost entirely rewritten to incorporate the principles that would guide the Governor-General during the government formation period or a mid-term political crisis. These guidelines were based largely on the public speeches, between 1996 and 1998, of the then Governor-General, Sir Michael Hardie Boys.[12] They are a major source on which we have ourselves drawn. Hardie Boys himself took full account of modern experience in countries with voting systems based on proportional representation, but he also looked back to the older, well-established principles of the Westminster monarchical constitution. In the next part we discuss the main issues. Some are now well settled but others are yet to be clarified definitively.

8 Cabinet Office *Cabinet Manual 2008*. At the time of the 2010 general election in the United Kingdom, the New Zealand *Cabinet Manual* was used as a guide as to what should happen if, after a general election, no one party had won a majority of the seats. Subsequently, a United Kingdom Cabinet Manual was produced, with an acknowledgement of the ground-breaking role of the New Zealand Cabinet Manual.

9 *Cabinet Manual*, above n 8, foreword by Helen Clark at xv.

10 Foreword at xv. See also Rebecca Kitteridge "The Cabinet Manual: Evolution with Time" (paper presented at the 8th Annual Public Law Forum, March 2006), available at <www.dpmc.govt.nz/sites/all/files/reports/the-cabinet-manual-evolution-with-time.pdf>.

11 Marie Shroff was Clerk of the Executive Council and Secretary to the Cabinet at the relevant time.

12 See Kitteridge, above n 10, at 9.

2
FINDING A GOVERNMENT AFTER AN ELECTION

The Governor-General's role after a general election

The general election and its outcome

After issuing a writ for an election,[13] the Governor-General plays no further part in the electoral process.[14] The outcome of the election determines who is a Member of Parliament,[15] and therefore who may be or remain a Minister and a member of the Executive Council.[16] That is as far as the statute law extends. All other implications of the outcome of a general election, for the Governor-General, the Prime Minister, his or her Cabinet, other political leaders and Members of Parliament generally are governed solely by constitutional convention.

While the votes are being counted on election night, the Governor-General is in the same position as other citizens, learning of the election results through the news media, and possibly of the Prime Minister's concession of electoral defeat.

An earlier version of the constitutional convention required a Prime Minister whose government has clearly been defeated at a general election to tender his or her resignation from office immediately, without first meeting Parliament. The convention was born in the United Kingdom in 1868 when the Prime Minister, Benjamin Disraeli, realised that, in the new political situation created by the widening of the franchise, the outcome of the general election had become decisive. If an Opposition party won more than half the seats, it would have been pointless for the defeated Prime Minister to remain in office until Parliament could meet. Instead, he immediately tendered his resignation to the Sovereign, and advised her to call first on the Leader of the Opposition, as the member of the House most likely to be able to form a government. From then on, the Members of Parliament observed strict party loyalty. It was a clear demonstration of the way in which an "instant" constitutional convention can arise when the political environment is changed.[17]

The convention was observed in New Zealand from 1890, as party-based governments became the norm. During the long periods when one or other of two main political parties was able to form a majority government, it usually

13 Electoral Act 1993, s 125.
14 Section 129.
15 Section 27.
16 Constitution Act 1986, s 6.
17 Ivor Jennings *Cabinet Government* (3rd ed, Cambridge University Press, Cambridge, 1959) at 7.

became clear very shortly after a general election whether or not the existing Prime Minister would be able to remain in office. If there was to be a change of government, it was also clear who would be the next Prime Minister. Subject only to the need, in the period between 1950 and 1986, to wait about two weeks for the election results to be confirmed, there was usually no difficulty in complying with the constitutional convention that a Prime Minister defeated at a general election must immediately tender his or her resignation without waiting to meet Parliament.

If, however, the outcome of a general election left it unclear whether the existing government retained enough support to remain in office, it was accepted that the new Parliament should meet as soon as possible. Then, the fate of the existing government would be settled by the outcome of the motion of no confidence in the government that would inevitably be moved by the Leader of the Opposition, and perhaps also the leaders of other Opposition parties. That happened in New Zealand in 1912 and again in 1928. In both cases, Parliament effectively confirmed the decision of the electors. In each case the Prime Minister tendered his resignation, and those of his Ministers. The Governor in the first case, and the Governor-General in the second, then invited the leader of the main Opposition party to form a new government.

The current New Zealand practice is to avoid a time lag between the tender of a Prime Minister's resignation and its acceptance, if that is at all possible. There is, however, always the possibility that a Prime Minister's tendered resignation will not be accepted immediately. Until it is accepted, a tendered resignation has no effect. In certain situations, a time lag between the tender of a Prime Minister's resignation and its acceptance may be unavoidable, as we show later in the chapter.

The effect of MMP

The MMP voting system changed the dynamics of general elections. It became unlikely — although not impossible — that a single party would win a majority of the seats. Coalition and support arrangements will usually have expired with the previous Parliament. Unless one of the main political parties wins considerably more seats than the other, the leaders of both may try to form a government. So, although it may not be clear whether the Prime Minister will again be able to form a government with majority support, the existing government will not clearly have been defeated. In that situation the Prime Minister will not be obliged to tender his or her resignation and is likely to remain in office. The government will, however, have a duty to observe the caretaker convention as long as its support in Parliament remains unclear.

The existing government must remain in office

The situation just described occurred at the 1996 election at which no party won a majority of seats and the government, led by the Prime Minister, the Rt Hon Jim Bolger, then the Leader of the National Party, had not clearly been defeated. A basic principle of the parliamentary constitution is that the Sovereign must not be left without advisers. Accordingly, Mr Bolger had a constitutional duty to remain in office until he or another political leader was able to form a government with the necessary support in Parliament. He therefore had no constitutional obligation to tender his resignation or otherwise indicate that he conceded defeat, and he did not do so.

The caretaker convention

During the eight-week period before it was known which party leader would succeed in forming a government, the Bolger government operated in accordance with what had by then become known as the caretaker convention. The notion that a country has a "caretaker" Prime Minister or government signifies that its executive government is being carried on in a temporary or provisional way during a period when it is not possible to put a "regular" government in place. In particular, the term is often used to describe the arrangements applying in transition periods, between the defeat of one elected government and the entry into office of another. The need for formal caretaker arrangements has become greater as proportional representation systems have lengthened the time needed after a general election to form and install a new government. At the same time, the complexity and reach of modern government has made it essential to have clear understandings about who, as one commentator put it, is "minding the shop".[18]

Because an outgoing government must continue to carry out the task of governing until the incoming government is appointed, the purpose of caretaker conventions is to ensure that, so far as possible, the caretaker government does not make significant new commitments that would tie the hands of a future government, perhaps irrevocably.

The New Zealand version of the caretaker convention began to evolve well before the adoption of MMP. Under earlier statutory provisions, a new government could not be sworn in until the writs certifying the election of

18 Anne Tiernan *Caretaker Conventions in Australasia: Minding the Shop for Government* (ANU E-Press (Centre for Governance and Public Policy), 2007), available at <http://epress.anu.edu.au/anzsog/caretaker/pdf_instructions.html>.

the prospective Prime Minister and other Ministers had been returned. That meant a delay of about two weeks after the election. Usually, that delay did not matter, but in 1984 it did. The Prime Minister, the Rt Hon Sir Robert Muldoon, had been defeated at the "snap" general election he had impulsively called, but was still in office. The incoming Prime Minister was the Leader of the Labour Party, David Lange. The prospective change of government provoked a run on the New Zealand dollar, and the Governor of the Reserve Bank advised both political leaders that an urgent devaluation was necessary. That required the making of an Order in Council, and the outgoing Prime Minister's cooperation.

Muldoon immediately announced publicly that he did not propose to devalue. The Deputy Prime Minister and Attorney-General at the time, the Rt Hon Jim McLay, has recently published an account of how, with the support of other senior Ministers, he was able to persuade Muldoon to accept that he had a constitutional duty to act in accordance with the wishes of the incoming government.[19] Among other things, he told Muldoon of a recent devaluation by an outgoing government in Australia at the request of its successor. In his later account he acknowledges that the precedent had not been an exact parallel, but it had been enough. Reluctantly, Muldoon agreed to devalue, referring publicly to "the constitutional position". In Chapter 10 we discuss another element in this drama which bears on the role of the Governor-General in encouraging Prime Ministers to behave constitutionally. Because, however, Muldoon agreed to act in accordance with the incoming government's wishes, nothing further was required.

McLay immediately issued a press statement which included the following assertion:[20]

> That, having been defeated in an election, and during the transition period, an outgoing government should
>
> - undertake no new policy initiatives; and
> - act on the advice of the incoming government on any matter of such great constitutional, economic or other significance that it cannot be delayed until the new government formally takes office — even if the outgoing government disagrees with that course of action.

The New Zealand version of the "caretaker convention" had been born, in a form that suited an immediate need.

19 Jim McLay "1984 and All That" (2012) 10 NZJPIL 267.
20 At 277.

The incoming Labour Government took steps to change the law, so that the same problem could not arise again. The Constitution Act now permits a new government to be appointed after a general election, even if the election writs have not been returned. Before long, however, the decision to move to the MMP voting system made it necessary for the first of McLay's two principles — the duty of the incumbent government to avoid new policy initiatives in the post-election period — to apply in a rather different political situation, and in an expanded form.

The present-day guidelines on the application of the caretaker convention are now set out in the Cabinet Manual. They are seen as applying in three sets of circumstances. The first arises after a general election when it is clear that there will be a change of government and the identity of the new Prime Minister is known, but the incoming government has not yet been sworn in.[21] The second arises if a government cannot be formed until after the return of the election writs, and is now the more likely. Only when the final distribution of seats becomes known can the identity of the incoming Prime Minister, and the composition of his or her government, be determined. The Cabinet Manual also makes it clear that the caretaker convention may apply after a government's defeat in Parliament.[22] We discuss in part 3 of this chapter the application of the caretaker convention to a mid-term defeat.[23]

For the moment, however, we wish to sound a note of caution about the interpretation of the caretaker convention in situations where it is not known which party or parties will be able to form a government. In discussing the handling of significant or potentially controversial issues, including new policy initiatives or changes to existing policy that might limit the freedom of action of an incoming government, the Cabinet Manual provides that, if a decision cannot be deferred or some temporary or holding arrangement made, it should be taken "only after consultation with other political parties, to establish whether the proposed action has the support of a majority in the House".[24]

Majority support, however, suggests a need for something more than reluctant acquiescence. In 1993, the Solicitor-General, JJ McGrath,[25] wrote an opinion on the operation of the caretaker convention when it is not known who will be the next Prime Minister.[26] McGrath suggested that a caretaker government "can, and at times must, take urgent decisions of major constitutional or economic importance", and "should endeavour to reach a degree

21 *Cabinet Manual*, above n 8, at [6.19(b)].
22 At [6.20].
23 See below, this chapter, under the subheading Early dissolutions of Parliament, at 182ff.
24 *Cabinet Manual*, above n 8, at [6.20].
25 Sir John McGrath is now a retired Judge of the Supreme Court.
26 The Prime Minister, Mr Bolger, issued a press release on 7 October 1994, making the opinion public.

of consensus with other parties which reflects support of the House for the proposed action". That rather more nuanced formulation puts the emphasis on finding a broadly acceptable way of dealing with an urgent problem, but without any need for a counting of heads.

Publicly announced support

Having established that the Sovereign is never to be left without advisers and that if the result of the election is unclear the Prime Minister continues to govern under the caretaker convention, we return now to the question of how the Governor-General is to ascertain which political leader is able to form a government. In public speeches and statements before the first MMP election, the Governor-General, Hardie Boys, enunciated various principles which have since been characterised by the Cabinet Office as having the force of constitutional convention.[27] Sir Michael's starting point was that the formation of a government is a political decision and must be arrived at by politicians. As Governor-General, he saw the task as that of ascertaining where the support of the House of Representatives lay. In a multi-party system Hardie Boys saw as irrelevant the fact that one of the main parties may have won more seats than the other, if neither had a majority. For that reason he rejected suggestions that he should first invite the leader of the party winning the largest number of seats to try to form a government, and so on, down a list of the parties in the order of the number of seats won by each. Unless it had won a majority of the seats, the number won by each had no bearing on its ability to attract coalition partners or pledges of support on issues of confidence. Evidence of broader political support was what mattered.

Communicating with party leaders

Although the Governor-General does not play an active part in the negotiation of coalition or support agreements, it is desirable that there should be a recognised channel of communication between the Governor-General and the party leaders. That would facilitate the exchange of information in either direction, if that should prove desirable. The leaders themselves also need access to technical advice about the Governor-General's expectations concerning the nature and form of coalition or support agreements. The Governor-General would not necessarily have to meet with party leaders until a new government had been formed.

27 *Cabinet Manual*, above n 8, at [6.39].

The Clerk of the Executive Council acts as the constitutional link between the Governor-General and party leader. The Clerk acts as the Governor-General's agent and intermediary, impartially and in the strictest confidence, from the time the election results become available until the Prime Minister is either confirmed in office, or has tendered his or her resignation and a new Prime Minister has been appointed.[28] This dovetails with the Clerk's other role in facilitating the transition process upon any change of Prime Minister, whether or not it is also a change of government.[29]

Parliament must meet

The Constitution Act provides that, after a general election, Parliament must meet not later than six weeks after the day fixed for the return of the writs.[30] In practice, that means about eight weeks after the date of the general election. The Prime Minister can, of course, advise the Governor-General to summon Parliament to meet at an even earlier date.[31] The provision was enacted before MMP had been thought of, but, in that context, it has had a significant effect.

After the first MMP general election took place on 12 October 1996, Parliament had to meet no later than Friday 13 December. The New Zealand First Party entered into parallel negotiations with National, the party in office, and Labour, the main Opposition party. On 10 December, New Zealand First publicly announced that it would be joining National in a coalition government. On the same day, the Prime Minister publicly confirmed that a coalition agreement had been reached, and the Labour Party conceded that it could not form a government. On 11 December, the Prime Minister personally confirmed to the Governor-General that, on the basis of the agreement reached, he would be able to form a government that would have the confidence of the House. A coalition agreement was then signed.

On the same day, as required by law, Commissioners appointed by the Governor-General formally opened Parliament.[32] The State Opening of Parliament and the Speech from the Throne duly followed on 12 December. The new government had not then been sworn in, so the Speech from the Throne had to be tailored accordingly, but that situation was not unprecedented. Hardie Boys described the timing as "unquestionably tight".[33] He considered that the meeting of Parliament had clearly operated as an informal deadline for

28 *Cabinet Manual*, above n 8, at [6.41].
29 At [1.30]–[1.34].
30 Constitution Act 1986, s 19.
31 Section 18.
32 Section 19.
33 Rt Hon Sir Michael Hardie Boys "Continuity and Change" (Harkness Henry Lecture, 31 July 1997).

the government formation process. The novelty of the process for all concerned had meant that it had taken longer than might be expected in the future. That expectation has since been borne out.

Appointing a Prime Minister and the other Ministers

The 1996 general election did not in fact lead to a change of Prime Minister, but, in view of the formation of a new coalition government, Mr Bolger and all his existing Ministers thought it appropriate to tender their resignations. The leaders of the two coalition parties made decisions about which of their MPs should be appointed as members of the Executive Council and as Ministers inside or outside Cabinet, and the portfolios each should hold. The members of the new government were sworn in.

Under MMP, the basis on which a political leader claims to have majority support, at least on issues of confidence, needs to be clear. The voters and the public generally have the right to know what agreements have been reached between political parties, and the general thrust of each. If necessary, the Governor-General would need to be satisfied that the relevant parties had made clear and public agreements which provided a firm basis on which to appoint a new Prime Minister. Any uncertainties in a proposed agreement would therefore need to be clarified, but otherwise the Governor-General is unlikely to make a judgement about the content of a coalition or support agreement or its likely durability.

The approach to the formation of a government fashioned in 1996 has proved to be a sound model for what should happen after any general election. There have, however, been some significant developments. Of most constitutional interest are the confidence and supply agreements which Labour made in 2005 with both United Future and New Zealand First. Each agreement entitled the leader of the party concerned to be appointed as a Minister outside Cabinet with responsibility for certain portfolios. It was agreed that both would have individual and collective responsibility to Parliament, along with all other Ministers, for matters within their respective portfolios, but otherwise they would be free to support or oppose the government as they thought fit, except on issues of confidence, including supply.

That has proved to be an ingenious arrangement which rewards the support parties with some real power, but allows them to criticise the government's policies on other issues. That is especially important in the critical period before an approaching general election, when all parties wish to distinguish themselves, not only from Opposition parties, but also from others of the same political complexion.

In 2008 the National Party Leader, John Key, made similar arrangements with ACT, United Future and the Māori Party, enabling him to form a National-led minority government, and to do so again in 2011. In 2013 the leader of United Future, Hon Peter Dunne, resigned his portfolios when it was alleged that there had been leaks of confidential documents from his office, but the support agreement remained in force. In the following year, Dunne was reinstated to the Cabinet with somewhat different portfolios.

It is a cardinal principle of the constitution that a Prime Minister cannot govern alone, but must be able to attract the loyal support of sufficient colleagues who are willing to serve under his or her leadership as members of the Cabinet. The collective responsibility to Parliament owed by all members of the Cabinet is seen as tempering the exercise of public power. For that reason, a Prime Minister is sworn in only when he or she can advise the Governor-General whom to appoint as the other members of the Cabinet. A Prime Minister may, however, at any time advise the Governor-General to dismiss a Minister. That puts the Prime Minister in a powerful position.

Although the Ministers appointed under support arrangements have limited collective responsibility to Parliament, their offices, like those of other Ministers, clearly stand or fall with the government as a whole. Support agreements, as distinct from coalition agreements which require Ministers belonging to the participating parties to accept collective responsibility for all of the government's acts and omissions, seem to have become the standard way of forming a government in the MMP environment.

In the MMP era, the role of the Governor-General in appointing a Prime Minister has been made much less mysterious. In the example we have discussed, a government was able to be formed before Parliament was required to meet. If that informal deadline is not met, that is by no means a disaster, and, in the next part, we look at what would then happen.

The government meets Parliament

Demonstrating Parliament's support

After a general election, the traditional formalities associated with the opening of the new Parliament include the Governor-General's Speech from the Throne. That speech is written by the government and outlines its legislative programme, and its policies generally, during the parliamentary session.[34]

34 Since 1993–1996 the norm has been for a single session to last the whole life of Parliament (from the first sitting until prorogation or dissolution).

In response, a government member moves the Address in Reply. The debate on that address, which is, in effect, a general debate, provides an opportunity for the Opposition to move an amendment to the address stating that the House has no confidence in the government. It is usual for the Opposition to move such an amendment, whether or not it has any realistic possibility of bringing down the government.

The fact that a coalition government, or a government dependent on a support agreement, formally appointed by the Governor-General, is then able to win a confidence vote in Parliament is, in effect, a seal of approval which marks as completed the Governor-General's task of appointing or reappointing a Prime Minister and government.

What if a government loses a confidence vote?

A general election result might produce a situation in which the existing government has not been clearly defeated, but neither the Prime Minister nor any other political leader has been able to form a government with the necessary support before the date on which Parliament must meet. Although that scenario is unlikely, it is not fanciful. And, contrary to what is sometimes supposed, it would not produce any kind of constitutional crisis or even a political one.

In the case of the United Kingdom, the expectations of a Prime Minister in such a situation have been set out in the Cabinet Manual produced after the 2010 general election. It contains the following provision:[35]

> **Parliaments with no overall majority in the House of Commons**
> 2.12 Where an election does not result in an overall majority for a single party, the incumbent government remains in office unless and until the Prime Minister tenders his or her resignation and the Government's resignation to the Sovereign. *An incumbent government is entitled to wait until the new Parliament has met to see if it can command the confidence of the House of Commons*, but is expected to resign if it becomes clear that it is unlikely to be able to command that confidence and there is a clear alternative.

There is no equivalent provision in the New Zealand Cabinet Manual, but that must be mainly because it is so long since a Prime Minister has been in such a position. If the government is found to have lost the confidence of the House,

35 UK Government *The Cabinet Manual* (1st ed, October 2011) at [2.12] (emphasis added) <https://www.gov.uk/government/uploads/system/uploads/attachment_data/file/60641/cabinet-manual.pdf>.

it seems clear that the Prime Minister should tender his or her resignation. That was what Thomas Mackenzie did in 1912, and Gordon Coates in 1928. It is essential then that the newly elected Members of Parliament should then have a further opportunity of finding a new government. In 1912 and 1928, a new Prime Minister was able to form a government. But, especially in 1928, there could have been a stalemate.

There is an outside possibility too that a newly formed government might lose the initial confidence vote. A coalition or support agreement cobbled together by inherently incompatible parties might quickly fall apart. Once again, there may be an attempt to find an alternative government. If, on either of these scenarios, a government still cannot be found then there should be a dissolution of the existing Parliament and a new election called. The only remaining question is how such a dissolution should come about.

During the last hundred years, the circumstances in which an early dissolution of a Parliament should be possible or required has been a contentious constitutional issue in the United Kingdom, Canada and a number of Australian jurisdictions. Prime Ministers have tended to request early dissolutions as a way of prolonging the lives of their governments. Traditionally, the Sovereign or a Governor-General is seen as having a discretion to refuse a Prime Minister's request for an early dissolution, but are there really any circumstances in which it would be both right and practicable for them to do so? The practice suggests otherwise. In part 3 of this chapter we explore those questions.

3
EARLY DISSOLUTIONS OF PARLIAMENT

The different scenarios

This part focuses on a Prime Minister's request to the Governor-General to dissolve Parliament before it has reached the end of its term. A Prime Minister might make such a request in a range of circumstances including: after a vote of no confidence when Parliament first meets; after a mid-term defeat in a confidence vote in Parliament; and in the event that a Prime Minister wants to go to an early election on the date of his or her choosing. In this part we focus on the latter two scenarios but the general principles also apply to the first scenario.

Advising a dissolution

We begin with matters that are well established. As was once the case in all the Sovereign's other realms, the Governor-General has the legal power to dissolve the New Zealand Parliament at any time. The dissolution can be made to take effect very quickly if that should be necessary. There is a fundamental constitutional convention that the Governor-General may take that step only on the advice of the Prime Minister. When Queen Victoria, in her anxiety to prevent the passage of Gladstone's Home Rule Bill, spoke of dissolving Parliament on her own responsibility, without the Prime Minister's advice, Lord Salisbury put the matter in what Jennings saw as "its proper perspective":[36]

> A dissolution by the Queen, against the advice of her Ministers, would, of course, involve their resignation. Their party could hardly help going to the country as the opponents of royal authority; or, at least as the severe critics of the mode on which it had been exerted. . . . There must be *some* hazard that, in the end, such a step would injure the authority of the Queen.

If the Governor-General considers that Parliament should be dissolved but the Prime Minister refuses to advise that step, the Governor-General's only option is to take the drastic course of dismissing the Prime Minister and appointing another who will give the necessary advice.

Originally, it was the practice in the United Kingdom for a Prime Minister to have the support of the Cabinet before asking the Sovereign to dissolve Parliament, but that changed during World War I. From then on it was generally accepted, in the Dominions as well as in Britain, that a Prime Minister is not obliged to have the support of the Cabinet in advising the Governor-General to dissolve Parliament. It is now well established that the Prime Minister may act alone in *advising* a dissolution. Traditionally, a Prime Minister's right to advise a dissolution was seen as a useful way of maintaining party discipline, but, in New Zealand, it seems not to have been used in that way.[37]

A discretion to refuse a dissolution?

While a Prime Minister could advise a dissolution, it seems to have been generally accepted that the Sovereign or a Governor-General had a discretion in

36 Ivor Jennings *The Law and the Constitution* (5th ed, University of London Press, London, 1959) at 413–414 (emphasis in original).

37 RS Milne *Political Parties in New Zealand* (Oxford University Press, London, 1966) at 159.

deciding whether to act on that advice. The existence of such a discretion is reflected in the statutory codifications of the Governor-General's power to dissolve Parliament. They use the word "may", rather than "shall" or "must". For the same reason, a Prime Minister is often described as "requesting" a dissolution, rather than "advising" one.

Given the perception that the Sovereign or a Governor-General had a discretion to *refuse* a requested dissolution, it was natural to suppose that constitutional conventions must have developed, to guide them in its exercise. But although there have been many suggestions about the circumstances in which a request should be refused, their application involved what could at best be only an intelligent guess about the outcome of future events. An added complication was the belief that a Governor or Governor-General in a colony or Dominion, answerable for so long to the Colonial Secretary on at least some issues, had a wider discretion to refuse a dissolution than the Sovereign himself.

In 1950 Britain, the possibility that the Prime Minister, Clement Attlee, who had been returned to power with a very small majority, might ask the King for a dissolution in an attempt to increase the support for his party, became the subject of discussion in letters to *The Times*. Among them was a letter later revealed to have been written by the Private Secretary to King George VI, Sir Alan Lascelles. In discussing the Prime Minister's possible request for a dissolution he took the view that:[38]

> the Sovereign, if he so chooses, may refuse to grant this request. . . . [but] no wise Sovereign would deny a dissolution to his Prime Minister unless he were satisfied that: (1) the existing Parliament was still vital, viable, and capable of doing its job; (2) a General Election would be detrimental to the national economy; (3) he could rely on finding another Prime Minister who would carry on his government, for a reasonable period.

For a time that formulation was regularly cited as authoritative. Gradually, however, the meaning of the criteria in point (1) was acknowledged to be unclear, and, in applying the tests referred to in points (2) and (3), it was questionable whether the Sovereign was as well placed as his Prime Minister to assess the impact of a general election on the national economy or whether another stable government could be found from within the existing Parliament. It was becoming apparent that the question whether there should be an early

38 *The Times* (London, 2 May 1950), reproduced in Geoffrey Wilson *Cases and Materials on Constitutional and Administrative Law* (Cambridge University Press, Cambridge, 1976) at 22–23.

dissolution of Parliament was predominantly a political one. Accordingly, it was questionable whether it was a decision in which a politically neutral Sovereign or Governor-General ought to be involved.

What the practice shows

It is useful to identify the main considerations which, over the years, have been seen as relevant. First, there is no historical basis for supposing that a Prime Minister whose government has lost its majority in Parliament no longer has the same right to ask for a dissolution as one whose government continues to command majority support.

There is, however, a practical reason for making a distinction between a request for a dissolution by a Prime Minister who continues to have the support of a majority in Parliament and one who does not. If the Sovereign or the Governor-General were to decline the request, a Prime Minister with majority support would almost certainly tender his or her resignation, and it would not be possible for any other political leader to form a government. The Sovereign or the Governor-General therefore has no option but to grant the requested dissolution. It is not that the Prime Minister with majority support is seen as having a *right* to a dissolution, but rather that there is no practical way of refusing such a request.

A Prime Minister who has lost majority support in Parliament on an issue of confidence is obviously in a different position. But while that deprives the defeated government of the constitutional right to remain in office, it does not follow that another party leader will necessarily be willing or able to form a government. The leader of an Opposition party would have to attract the support of defectors or other parties in a new political marriage of convenience. The feasibility of doing so would depend on the political situation at the time.

That is why it may not be possible or wise for the Sovereign or a Governor-General to refuse a dissolution to a Prime Minister whose government has been defeated in Parliament. The Lascelles convention,[39] as it is sometimes called, had acknowledged that, before taking that step, the Sovereign would need to be satisfied that another government could indeed be found from within the existing Parliament. In 1926, the Governor-General of Canada, Lord Byng, thought he had assessed the situation correctly, but, in the event, he had not.

39 At 22–23.

The facts of the King–Byng controversy, as set out by Jennings, were as follows:[40]

> At the Canadian general election of 1925 the Conservative party had a small majority over the Liberal party, but the Liberal Government believed that it could continue to govern with the aid of smaller groups. Threatened with a vote of censure nine months later, the Liberal Prime Minister asked for a dissolution. Lord Byng, as Governor-General, refused on the ground that the Conservative party could form a government. The Prime Minister thereupon resigned and the Conservative party took office but was defeated within a week and advised a dissolution, which was granted. At the general election the Liberals gained a majority and again resumed office.

That dispassionate account gives no hint of the bitterness with which Mackenzie King accused the Governor-General of political bias and the United Kingdom Government of political interference in Canada's affairs. Although he had the opportunity to appeal to the voters that he had sought, he had been deprived of the opportunity of doing so as Prime Minister, a recognised political advantage. After his party had won the general election and his triumphant reappointment as Prime Minister, King insisted that no Sovereign would have acted as Lord Byng had done, and pressed for a reformulation of a Dominion Governor-General's role. At the Imperial Conference of 1926, it was acknowledged that the relationship between a Governor-General and the Prime Minister of a Dominion was no different from that between the Sovereign and the Prime Minister of the United Kingdom.

Jennings considered that, in 1926, Lord Byng's case had been very strong — meaning that he had solid grounds for believing that another government could be found within the existing Parliament — but also noted that, for more than a hundred years, there had been no clear case in which the Sovereign had denied a dissolution to a United Kingdom Prime Minister who had requested one. There was, nevertheless, "a persistent tradition" that the Sovereign could refuse a dissolution if the "necessary circumstances arose", but he added that it was difficult to see what those circumstances would be.[41]

40 Jennings, above n 37, at 427.
41 At 427.

The impossibility of exercising a discretion

The position can now be summarised. A request for a dissolution by a Prime Minister with majority support cannot be refused, for the reason that it would not be possible to form another government from the existing Parliament. If the government has been defeated in Parliament, and the Prime Minister asks for a dissolution, that request can be refused only if the Governor-General is satisfied that another member of the existing Parliament is able to form a government. In that event, the defeated Prime Minister will tender his or her resignation, the Governor-General will accept it, and will appoint the new Prime Minister. If the incoming government has the confidence of the House, all will be well. But if that should prove not to be the case, the Governor-General will face real difficulties, including the accusation of having breached the duty to maintain political neutrality.

Given these dynamics, there may not be a viable basis on which a Governor-General can refuse a request for an early dissolution of a Parliament. It should not be forgotten, however, that a possible need and the ability, *during the parliamentary term*, to change a government which no longer has the confidence of Parliament is a main strength of the parliamentary constitution.

Request by a Prime Minister whose government has lost the confidence of Parliament

Historically at least, the situation of a Prime Minister whose government has formerly enjoyed the confidence of Parliament but has then been defeated in a confidence vote has been seen as being different from that of a Prime Minister who has been defeated by a confidence vote on the first meeting of Parliament after a general election.

Despite the conceptual differences between the two situations, they raise some of the same issues. After a government's defeat in Parliament, should there *always* be an opportunity, before an early dissolution, to see whether another government can be found from among its members? Then, the question arises of how long should the search continue? Finally, if the search is unsuccessful, how should the necessary dissolution be triggered? We discuss now the considerations which a Governor-General should take into account in responding to a request for a dissolution of Parliament by a Prime Minister whose government has been defeated in a confidence vote.

New Zealand has no modern experience of such a situation. The last time that a dissolution was sought and granted after a government's defeat in

Parliament was in 1887. Robert Stout's government was defeated in the House on proposed tariff legislation and other financial proposals. Stout sought and was granted a dissolution by the Governor, Sir William Jervois. At the ensuing general election, Stout lost his seat in Parliament. Since then, no New Zealand Premier or Prime Minister has sought a dissolution after a defeat in Parliament. The reason is simple. There have been no such defeats.[42] In the FPP environment, the party discipline which developed after the first Liberal Party government came to power in 1891 was strong enough to prevent any dissenters from bringing down their governments, although some occasionally took advantage of a situation in which they could show their disaffection, while leaving the government in power.

Confidence votes

One explanation for the paucity of the New Zealand experience is that governments are seen as having the confidence of Parliament as long as they have not been defeated in what is recognised as being a confidence vote,[43] and in the New Zealand Parliament the opportunities for a vote of confidence are relatively rare.

Confidence votes initiated by the government

The government may at any time take the initiative in putting to a vote the question of whether it continues to enjoy the confidence of Parliament, and may do so in a variety of ways. It may, for example, declare that it will treat a forthcoming vote on a matter before the House to be an issue of confidence.[44] That has the effect of putting pressure on its possibly wavering supporters, as well as providing an opportunity for the Opposition. After the event, it may regard an adverse vote it has suffered as an indication that it no longer enjoys the confidence of Parliament.[45] The Prime Minister may also, at any time, move a positive vote of confidence in the government. It took that step in 1998, after the break-up of the former majority coalition government.

42 Although Atkinson in 1881 tendered his resignation after the candidate his government had nominated for the office of Speaker failed to be elected. McGee, above n 5, at 98.
43 At 95.
44 At 98.
45 At 98.

Confidence votes not controlled by the government

McGee makes the point that, unlike some other Parliaments, the House of Representatives has no tradition of allowing the Opposition, at any time, to move a motion of no confidence in the government, and then of the government finding a time to debate the motion.[46] The Address in Reply debate, in response to the Governor-General's Speech from the Throne on the opening of a parliamentary session, affords one such opportunity.[47] Others are the debate on the Prime Minister's statement when the House first meets in its second and third years, the annual Budget debate and any Imprest Supply debate.[48] There are therefore at least four occasions in each year when the Opposition can move an amendment expressing a want of confidence in the government, as it often does.[49]

A government's ability to raise and spend money — the ability to "obtain supply" — has always been seen as fundamental to its survival. So although the Opposition may not have moved a "want of confidence" amendment to an Imprest Supply or an Appropriation Bill,[50] any vote at the second or third reading of such a Bill is regarded as a test of Parliament's confidence in the government. So also is a vote on any provision of a Bill setting the annual tax rates. All such votes engage any coalition or support party's assurance of support on issues of "confidence or supply". It follows that, like the passing of a no-confidence motion, a failure to pass a "supply" Bill in the form proposed by the government would signify just as clearly that the government had lost the confidence of Parliament.

Conceptually, Parliament is the forum in which the Opposition may hold the government to account. At first sight the limited opportunities it will have in any one year directly to move a motion of no confidence in the government may seem undemocratic. That impression may be heightened by the fact that no New Zealand government has suffered a mid-term defeat in Parliament in the last 130 years. It must be remembered, however, that the government's job is to govern if it can for the whole of the parliamentary term — at present only three years. It can therefore be strongly argued that the constitution should be weighted towards the continuity, during that short period, of both the government and the Parliament.

46 At 97. He points out, however, that, on rare occasions, such a step has been taken.

47 See above, this chapter, text following fn 32, at 178.

48 An Imprest Supply Act authorises the government to incur operating expenses and make capital expenditure in advance of the entry into force of an Appropriation Act (which gives statutory force to the Budget) for any financial year.

49 McGee, above n 5, at 97.

50 There may be more than one such Bill in a financial year.

Given the current three-year parliamentary term, the limited opportunities to move a motion of no confidence, and that in New Zealand unfinished parliamentary business does not automatically lapse upon prorogation, we think it unlikely that a Prime Minister would request that Parliament be temporarily suspended, or prorogued,[51] in order to avoid a vote of no confidence (as occurred under the Harper government in Canada).[52] If such a request were to be made, the situation would be similar to that following a request for an early dissolution.

The responsibilities of the Prime Minister and the Governor-General

The question of where the confidence of the House lies is a matter, not of parliamentary procedure on which the Speaker can rule, but of political judgement. McGee sees the Governor-General as having the ultimate responsibility of determining whether the government possesses the confidence of the House.[53] At the same time, he regards it as a fundamental constitutional requirement that a Prime Minister whose government has lost the confidence of the House must resign or seek a general election, and sees that constitutional convention as supported by the Governor-General's power to dismiss a Prime Minister.[54] The constitution vests the ultimate power in the Sovereign or her representative but requires the political actors to ensure that it never needs to be exercised.

Professor Joseph has persuasively argued that the onus should be on the political parties to demonstrate that any mid-term impasse is irretrievable, leaving no option but to have recourse to a general election. The Governor-General would be right to refuse a dissolution until that onus has been discharged, and there is no longer any possibility of a political accord. The objective is to maintain continuity of government throughout the full term of a Parliament. That would meet the perceived public interest in the avoidance of frequent and unwanted general elections.[55]

51 See Constitution Act 1986, s 20. The power to prorogue used to be exercised before the general election but it is no longer required. The Governor-General now summons a new Parliament by Proclamation in conjunction with the dissolution of the old Parliament. This is to indicate parliamentary continuity. The death of the Sovereign does not dissolve Parliament as used to be the case under UK law: see Constitution Act 1986, s 5(2).

52 See Lorne Sossin and Peter H Russell (eds) *Parliamentary Democracy in Crisis* (University of Toronto Press, Toronto, 2009).

53 McGee, above n 5, at 96.

54 At 95.

55 Philip A Joseph "Commentary on Alison Quentin-Baxter 'Implications for the Governor-General'" in *The Constitutional Implications of MMP* (Dunmore Press, Wellington, 1998) 96 at 126.

As it happened, developments in the first Parliament elected under the MMP voting system gave the Governor-General, Sir Michael Hardie Boys, good reason to think about the possibility that, after the breakdown of the coalition between National and New Zealand First, the minority government led by the Rt Hon Jenny Shipley might be defeated in Parliament, and the Prime Minister might then ask for a dissolution. As things turned out, the Shipley government overcame its difficulties and continued to retain the confidence of Parliament, but Hardie Boys subsequently spoke publicly about the courses of action he might have taken if the government had lost its majority support. Here we discuss the points of principle that Hardie Boys identified, and the possibilities he had contemplated if the government had been defeated in a confidence vote.

Significance of confidence votes

In his November 1998 address, Hardie Boys explained that when the coalition between National and New Zealand First collapsed in August 1998, he had thought it important to be able to look back at the votes of confidence earlier won by the Shipley-led government. Once the ability to govern no longer depended simply on the number of seats a party had in Parliament, the winning of successive confidence votes confirmed a government's right to be appointed to office and to remain in power.

The government had in fact won an implied vote of confidence on 11 August, but that was before the collapse of the coalition. The storm first broke on 12 August, and the government's position remained potentially in doubt until 30 August, when the Prime Minister announced the composition of the new National-led minority government. The next day, four new Ministers were appointed, and various other portfolios were reallocated. On 8 September the Prime Minister took the initiative in moving a positive motion of confidence in the government. This the government duly won. In his public address Sir Michael said:[56]

> In initiating this vote of confidence, the Government acted responsibly and democratically. Its legitimacy — which might otherwise have been open to question — was established beyond doubt. In my view the Government's decision to test the confidence of the House at an appropriate time established an important precedent that will provide sound constitutional guidance to political leaders confronted by the same situation in the future.

56 Rt Hon Sir Michael Hardie Boys "Governing under MMP: the Constitutional and Policy Challenges" (Institute of Policy Studies Seminar, Wellington, 1998).

Sir Michael's statements leave no room for a Governor-General actively to intervene in what is a political controversy, or to attempt to force the issue if the government's support in Parliament should become unclear. In that event, the Governor-General might intimate to the Prime Minister, and, with his or her agreement, to the leaders of the other political parties,[57] that he or she is looking to them to clarify the political situation as quickly as possible, but that is all.

It seems clear that the Governor-General would leave it to the Prime Minister to decide whether it was desirable to force the issue by moving a positive motion of confidence in the government. That remains a political decision. There are probably moments in the life of any government when feelings are running so high that, if such a motion were voted on at that moment, it might well result in the government's defeat. But the constitution does not require it voluntarily to place its neck on the block. There are occasions during the political year when the Opposition is entitled to move a motion of no confidence, and sometimes does (as we have outlined). Otherwise, there is a constitutional bias towards the maintenance of the status quo. That is no bad thing, given the short parliamentary term. A political crisis putting the government's support in issue must be disposed of promptly, but, unless the Opposition is in a position to force the issue in Parliament, the initiative remains with the government.

Request for a dissolution after defeat in House

The possibility of such a defeat is recognised in the Cabinet Manual as one of the circumstances in which a government would be bound by the caretaker convention.[58] Too much, however, should not be read into that fact, or into the further statement in the Cabinet Manual that the Prime Minister is the Governor-General's principal adviser "as long as the government commands the confidence of the House".[59] It does not follow that, because the government has lost the confidence of the House, the Prime Minister no longer has the right to advise the Governor-General to dissolve Parliament. The caretaker convention should not be seen as depriving the Prime Minister of either authority or responsibility. The constitutional principle is that the Prime Minister remains

57 Any communication to the leaders of other parties would almost certainly be made through the Clerk of the Executive Council. See Chapter 8 The Governor-General in the Executive Branch, under the subheading The Clerk of the Executive Council, at 162.

58 *Cabinet Manual*, above n 8, at [6.17].

59 At [2.4].

the Governor-General's principal adviser as long as he or she is in office, subject, however, to the caretaker convention, so far as it applies at the time, and requires the Prime Minister to consult with other party leaders before tendering advice on matters of policy.

In 1998, the Governor-General had recognised unequivocally that a Prime Minister whose government had been defeated in Parliament would have the option of requesting a dissolution of Parliament as an alternative to tendering his or her resignation. Although Shipley's government had survived, he chose to share with the public the possibilities he had contemplated if the government had been defeated. Hardie Boys referred to the fact that:[60]

> [t]he Leader of the Opposition [Helen Clark] said publicly during the events of August that if the minority Government proved unsustainable, she would not wish to try to form a Government, but would prefer an election. Had the minority Government failed to obtain the confidence of the House, that indication would have been pivotal in my mind in determining whether to allow an opportunity for an alternative government to be formed or whether an election should be called.

It would no doubt have been inappropriate for the Governor-General to say more. In our view, however, his concluding sentences reflect important principles which are becoming established in other parliamentary systems.

The first such principle is that there ought to be an early dissolution if so decided by what has been described as a "super-majority" in Parliament. The Scotland Act 1998 has so provided. In 2011, the United Kingdom Parliament adopted the same rule.[61] It seems clear that if in 1998, the National Government had been defeated in the House of Representatives, and the Prime Minister had then asked for an early dissolution, the Governor-General would have taken account of the public statement of support for a dissolution by the Leader of the Opposition, and granted the dissolution. In those circumstances, the dissolution would have had the support of both the main parties.

The Governor-General had, however, contemplated the possibility that, if the government were defeated, the Opposition might not have favoured a dissolution. In that event, the Governor-General would apparently have been willing to "allow an opportunity for an alternative government to be formed".[62] The idea of such a delay is reflected in the statutory rules of some Australian

60 Hardie Boys "Governing under MMP", above n 57.
61 Fixed Term Parliaments Act 2011 (UK), s 2(1) and (2).
62 Hardie Boys "Governing under MMP", above n 57.

states and territories and also in Scotland and, most recently, the United Kingdom. In the countries where legislation recognises there is a duty or at least an opportunity to see if another government can be found, before the Parliament is dissolved, the time allowed for that purpose varies quite widely. In the Australian jurisdictions, one week is the norm.[63] In the United Kingdom, the cut-off point is two weeks.[64] In Scotland it is four weeks.[65] In all the jurisdictions, however, it is provided that if, after the government's defeat in Parliament, a new government has not been found within the prescribed period, the Parliament will dissolve by operation of law.

In New Zealand, where there is no such legislation, would a delay in responding to the Prime Minister's request come within the ambit of a Governor-General's constitutional discretion? A delay would have the great advantage of providing an opportunity to see if another government could be found from within the existing Parliament. If another government cannot be found, the Prime Minister would then be granted the asked-for dissolution, and would go into the general election in that capacity. If feelings were running high, no doubt the shadow of the King–Byng controversy would be likely to loom darkly. For that reason, politicians and the public may prefer the suggested approach to be put in place through legislative change, rather than by a reformulation of the constitutional conventions, as we later propose. Whichever form such rules may take, the time for spelling out the suggested rules is before, not after, a New Zealand government is defeated in the House.

As a first step, the Cabinet Manual should set out what would become new constitutional conventions guiding the Governor-General in responding to a Prime Minister's request for an early dissolution, after his or her government has suffered a mid-term defeat in Parliament. The conventions would set out the circumstances in which the Governor-General should grant the request, and those in which he or she should "delay" a decision until there has been an opportunity to see whether a new government can be found from among the existing members. The purpose of the delay and its likely duration should therefore be explained.

It would not, however, be enough simply to submit the new rules for the approval of the Cabinet. Although it can be strongly argued that their content is within the scope of the Governor-General's existing discretion, the formulation of "rules" is an initiative in which all Members of Parliament should have the opportunity to participate. Although the possibility of a government's

63 Constitution Fixed Term Parliaments Amendment Act 1993 (NSW).
64 Fixed Term Parliaments Act 2011 (UK), s 2(3) and (5).
65 In Scotland, the First Minister must resign and the Parliament must nominate a First Minister afresh after the general election.

mid-term defeat in Parliament may seem remote, it is an important element of the parliamentary constitution. While there may not be any existing machinery for discussing the proposed rules on a non-partisan basis, an analogy can be drawn with the process for revising the Standing Orders of the House of Representatives. All Members of Parliament and also members of the public are invited to make submissions to the Standing Orders Committee. The members of that committee usually endeavour to find a consensus, instead of taking decisions by majority vote.[66]

It may become desirable, however, to enact legislation, instead of relying on conventional rules. The November 2013 report of the Constitution Advisory Panel included the following recommendation:[67]

> [T]he Government should set up a process, with public consultation and participation, to explore a fixed election date in conjunction with any exploration of a longer [parliamentary] term.

Any proposal for a fixed election date would, of course, need to identify the circumstances in which an early general election would still be required. As has been recognised in other Commonwealth jurisdictions, including the United Kingdom and Scotland, the government's mid-term defeat in Parliament is one of those circumstances, unless another government has been found.

The responsibility of formally advising the Governor-General to dissolve Parliament should not be seen as falling within the scope of the caretaker convention. Although the government may be operating in that mode, the Prime Minister continues to have rights and duties — there are likely to be elements of both, depending on the circumstances. It is not relevant that, by then, the Prime Minister may already have tendered his or her resignation. If advised to dissolve Parliament, the Governor-General could wait for a time before doing so. Statutory rules already ensure that a general election will follow.[68]

Will the general election have the desired result, and lead to the formation of a government that has the necessary support in Parliament? Experience elsewhere suggests that, if it is necessary to have an early dissolution, followed by a general election, there is likely to be some redistribution of the seats in Parliament. The parties themselves may change their leaders, form pre-election

66 McGee, above n 5, at 118.
67 Constitution Advisory Panel *New Zealand's Constitution: A Report on a Convention* (Ministry of Justice, Wellington, 2013) at 48.
68 Electoral Act 1993, s 125.

coalitions, or signify in advance their support for one or other of the larger parties on confidence issues. The composition of the new Parliament is therefore likely to be significantly different from that of the old.

In the period leading up to the general election and afterwards, the Prime Minister must remain in office, at the head of the government which is operating in accordance with the caretaker convention, until the general election has been held and a Prime Minister and government can be appointed from among the members of the newly elected Parliament. At that point the Governor-General accepts the outgoing Prime Minister's tendered resignation and appoints the incoming Prime Minister. The process as a whole enables the political leaders and their supporters to make a fresh start in finding a government which has the confidence of a majority in Parliament. It is a key feature of the Parliamentary constitution, distinguishing it from other forms of democratic government.

Manipulation of an electoral date

The manipulation of an electoral date by a Prime Minister who still has the confidence of Parliament has not occurred in New Zealand because the three-year term of Parliament does not allow much opportunity for a Prime Minister to use the date of the next general election for party political advantage. The desire to hold a general election at an advantageous time has not been totally absent, but it operates within narrow bounds. In general, the political parties themselves are not keen to face the disruption and considerable expense of a general election any more often than they have to. Government majorities are often relatively small, and political survival is seen as requiring tight party discipline. Despite those limiting factors, some Prime Ministers have been willing to take what advantage they could of a particular situation, but there is no perception that the electoral system is regularly abused. Even minority governments with slender majorities on confidence issues have so far remained stable. It would be wrong, therefore, to suggest that there is a need for the sweeping reforms which have been put in place elsewhere.

Our conclusion is that, in general, New Zealand Prime Ministers respect what can be seen as an expectation by the public that, unless there is good reason to shorten the full term of Parliament by a month or two, a government will complete the three-year term for which it has been elected. Any tendency to delay the announcement of a general election date or to seek a manifestly early dissolution of Parliament for party political gain would probably provoke a backlash. Accordingly, there is no present need for any change.

That said, the Constitution Act vests in the Governor-General the power to dissolve Parliament before the expiration of its three-year term.[69] New Zealand constitutional convention (as codified in the Cabinet Manual) recognises that a Governor-General is not in a position to refuse a dissolution to a Prime Minister who has the confidence of Parliament. The length of the New Zealand parliamentary term is to some extent a live constitutional issue[70] (though not itself within the scope of this book). If the life of a Parliament were to be lengthened, there is a possibility that, over time, the political actors might behave differently from the way they behave now. We mention that, not to discourage any change in the term of Parliament, but simply to make the point that, if such a change were to lead to a change in political behaviour, the present conclusions may also need to be reassessed.

4
NEW ZEALAND PRINCIPLES FOR APPOINTING AND CHANGING A PRIME MINISTER

The form of new principles

It seems desirable that, initially at least, the governing principles we have identified or suggested should remain in the form of constitutional conventions. Their reformulation would not involve the drawing of any dividing line between a codification of the existing conventional rules and their "progressive development".[71] We do not foresee any immediate need for legislation, although that could change if there were changes to other aspects of the constitution, especially the length of the parliamentary term, as mentioned above. Obviously, the more far-reaching the change, the greater the need to make sure that the constitution remains an integrated whole, and that any formulation of it is internally consistent. It must also be accessible to the people who live under it.

The appointment and eventual replacement of a Prime Minister marks the birth and the death of a government that, while in office, had the authority to govern, as long as all the relevant constitutional requirements were complied with, from the first moment of its existence until the last. In New Zealand, the constitutional responsibility for securing that compliance is shared among the

69 Constitution Act 1986, s 18.
70 It was one of the Terms of Reference of the New Zealand Constitution's Review: see <www.ourconstitution.org.nz>.
71 Compare to the Statute of the United Nations International Law Commission.

constitutional actors — the Governor-General, the Prime Minister and the other Ministers, as well as the other Members of Parliament. We now set out our conclusions about how that responsibility is shared. Some of those principles are well established, and can be expressed in a form that is sanctioned by long and widespread usage. Some, however, are based on the findings and conclusions set out earlier in the chapter, and take into account the developments that have occurred in other Commonwealth monarchies. Elements of innovation are inevitable, especially in the absence of recent New Zealand experience.

As we have explained, we see the principles as having the force of constitutional convention. As such, they are a source of enduring principle, but the details have an element of flexibility, allowing new problems to be solved consistently with principle but in innovative ways. The rules should therefore be read in that light, and not as if they were rules of law. Our purpose is simply to show how the constitution already works, or could be made to work, within the full range of political situations which it is reasonable to envisage in the MMP environment.

The New Zealand Principles

APPOINTING AND CHANGING A PRIME MINISTER

1. If the Prime Minister has tendered his or her resignation from office, the Governor-General must appoint as Prime Minister a Member of Parliament who is the leader of a political party and whom the Governor-General, taking into account his or her public statements and those of other political party leaders but otherwise acting in his or her judgement, considers able to form a government which has the support of a majority of the members of the House of Representatives on issues of confidence (referred to as a government having "the necessary support").

2. If a Prime Minister whose government has the necessary support advises the Governor-General to dissolve Parliament on a date earlier than the date on which Parliament would otherwise expire, the Governor-General must dissolve Parliament accordingly.

3. A Prime Minister who, at any time, has tendered his or her resignation from office to the Governor-General must remain in office until the Governor-General accepts his or her resignation and appoints another Prime Minister who has the necessary support.[72]

72 If the Prime Minister is gravely ill or has died or has ceased to be a Member of Parliament, it can

4. A government which remains in office when it does not clearly have, or after it has lost, the necessary support in Parliament must govern in accordance with the caretaker convention.

5. After a general election, a Prime Minister whose government has, at that election, lost the necessary support must tender his or her resignation to the Governor-General. If, however, the government's support remains in doubt, the Prime Minister need not tender his or her resignation but may remain in office without doing so until such time as he or she is either confirmed in office in accordance with paragraph 1, or is required to tender his or her resignation in accordance with this paragraph, whichever occurs first.

6. If, when Parliament first meets after a general election, the government led by the Prime Minister then in office[73] is defeated in a confidence vote —

(a) the Prime Minister must tender his or her resignation to the Governor-General; and

(b) the members of Parliament must endeavour to form another government which has the necessary support.

7. If in any other circumstance the government led by the Prime Minister is defeated in a confidence vote, the Prime Minister must either —

(a) tender his or her resignation to the Governor-General; or

(b) request the Governor-General to dissolve Parliament.

8. If, in accordance with paragraph 7, the Prime Minister requests the Governor-General to dissolve Parliament, and, before or immediately after the request is made public, the Leader of the Opposition publicly expresses a preference for a dissolution, the Governor-General must accede to the Prime Minister's request and dissolve Parliament accordingly.

9. In the absence of a publicly expressed preference for a dissolution, of the kind referred to in paragraph 8, the Governor-General, acting in the exercise of his or her judgement, may, instead of making a decision on the request for a dissolution, defer that decision until a later named and publicly announced date (referred to as

be expected that the party to which he or she belonged will designate, in accordance with its internal rules, an Acting Prime Minister who will perform the duties of the office until a successor is appointed.

73 The expression "then in office" refers to a Prime Minister in any of the following situations: one whose support, after a general election, has not been determined; one who has already tendered his or her resignation; and one who, after a general election, has been confirmed in office or has been newly appointed.

the "named date") by which, in his or her opinion, it should be possible to ascertain whether a government which has the necessary support can again be found within the existing Parliament. The Members of Parliament must then endeavour to form, before the named date, a government which has the necessary support.

10. If, before the date named, a Member of Parliament succeeds in obtaining the necessary support (referred to as the "incoming Prime Minister") —

(a) the request for a dissolution lapses;

(b) the Prime Minister whose government was defeated in Parliament (referred to as the "outgoing Prime Minister") must tender his or her resignation (even if he or she is also the incoming Prime Minister), and the Governor-General must accept it; and

(c) the Governor-General must then appoint (or reappoint) the incoming Prime Minister, in accordance with paragraph 1.

11. If the Governor-General has deferred a decision on a request for a dissolution until a named date, and, before that date, an incoming Prime Minister has not been found, the Governor-General must grant the Prime Minister's request for a dissolution and dissolve Parliament accordingly.

12. If, in any other circumstance —

(a) the Prime Minister has tendered his or her resignation; and

(b) the Members of Parliament have been endeavouring to form a government but an incoming Prime Minister has not been found; and

(c) a period of time has elapsed which the Governor-General, acting after consultation with the Prime Minister, the Leader of the Opposition and other political leaders but in the exercise of his or her judgement, considers to have been sufficient in the circumstances —

the Governor-General must so inform the Prime Minister. The Prime Minister must then advise the Governor-General to dissolve Parliament, and the Governor-General must dissolve Parliament accordingly.

CHAPTER 10

Guardian of the Constitution?

1
THE PURPOSE OF THIS CHAPTER

In Chapter 9, we discussed the part the Governor-General plays, or might need to play, in appointing a Prime Minister, and eventually in accepting that Prime Minister's resignation, interwoven as it is with the political processes of forming and changing a government. In this chapter, our focus is on whether the Governor-General has rights or responsibilities in respect of the policies and decisions of a government in office. Does a Governor-General have the same right as the Sovereign "to be consulted . . . to encourage . . . [and] to warn"[1] the Prime Minister, especially if the proposed action has constitutional implications? And could there be circumstances in which the Governor-General would be justified in "changing his or her advisers"? That is how the Governor-General's refusal to act on the Prime Minister's advice or dismissal of the Prime Minister is euphemistically described.

It is appropriate to ask those questions because it is not the practice in New Zealand for the Prime Minister, in person, to keep the Governor-General regularly informed about the policies and proposed actions of the government. It is also more than a hundred years since two Governors in succession persisted in their refusal to act on the advice tendered by the Executive Council, until, eventually, the Secretary of State for the Colonies found that their refusal was unjustified. No New Zealand Premier or Prime Minister has ever been dismissed from office. In Canada, however, a Governor-General has refused to act on a Prime Minister's advice to dissolve Parliament, and a Governor-General of Australia has dismissed the Prime Minister, despite the fact that, in each case, the Prime Minister had majority support in Parliament at the time.

1 See Chapter 5 The Sovereign in Right of New Zealand: A Personal Touch, after fn 5, at 76.

The possibility that a New Zealand Governor-General would do such things may seem unlikely, but it has never been ruled out. Our inquiry is therefore focused on whether the current situation is satisfactory or whether it should be clarified or changed.

The description of the Governor-General's role as the "guardian of the constitution" was used by some Australian and New Zealand Governors-General and other commentators after the 1975 dismissal of the Australian Prime Minister, Gough Whitlam, by the Governor-General, Sir John Kerr. In more recent times the description has become part of the language of scholarly inquiry into the present-day constitutional role of a Governor-General.[2] That is the context in which we use it in the title to this chapter, and in the conclusion we reach.[3]

In part 2 we look at the origin and nature of the current New Zealand practice in two main areas: the duty of Ministers to keep the Governor-General informed and the Governor-General's duty to act in accordance with ministerial advice. Although they are separate issues and will be discussed separately, they are obviously connected. The better-informed the Governor-General is about the background to the government's policy initiatives, the less concern he or she is likely to have in implementing them, in accordance with ministerial advice. The Governor-General is often advised to make an Order in Council or an appointment to a high office, or to assent to a Bill passed by Parliament. On a rare occasion, however, even a Governor-General with a good understanding of the background might be concerned about whether the government's proposed action conforms to constitutional principle. Would the Governor-General ever be justified in refusing to act on the government's advice, or even in replacing the existing Prime Minister with another?

Our inquiry into those questions takes us back to the early years of responsible government. From the beginning, the settler governments, focused as they were on the acquisition of land from its Māori owners, did what they could to circumvent the Governor's continuing responsibility for "native affairs". The Colonial Office required the Governor to supervise a colonial government in observing the basic principles of the constitution, a responsibility that was not required in London. Ministers responded by keeping the Governor at arm's length, so far as that was possible. Although the reasons for their reserve have long been forgotten, the political culture it nurtured lives on today.

2 See, for example, Harshan Kumarasingham *Onward with Executive Power: Lessons from New Zealand 1947–57* (Institute of Policy Studies, School of Government, Victoria University of Wellington, Wellington, 2010) ch 2; Cheryl Saunders *The Constitution of Australia: A Conceptual Analysis* (Hart Publishing, Oxford, 2011) at 161.

3 See below, this chapter, under the subheading Is the Governor-General the guardian of the constitution? at 224.

In part 3 we argue that the constitutional conventions no longer positively authorise a Governor-General to change his or her advisers. In extreme cases in which the constitution is itself at stake, such a power may still be contemplated. But given that the exercise of such a power would risk the continuing tenure in office of the Governor-General and also possibly put the office of the Governor-General and the monarchy itself at risk, other things need to change to make the Governor-General's constitutional role more meaningful. We recommend that steps should be taken to enable the Governor-General and the Prime Minister to establish a more positive working relationship. We recommend the explicit recognition that the Governor-General may discuss with the Prime Minister in confidence any aspect of government policy or actions. Both the Governor-General and the Prime Minister each need to have a good understanding of what the other is trying to achieve. We see a closer relationship, not as reflecting any kind of supervisory role on either side, but as enabling the Governor-General to provide non-partisan leadership to the country and its people, in parallel with the Prime Minister's political leadership.

With that introduction to the chapter as a whole, we now return to those early years of responsible government and their lasting legacy.

2
THE THEORY AND THE PRACTICE

A formative experience

On the introduction of responsible government in 1856, the Governor, Colonel Thomas Gore Browne, insisted on retaining the responsibility for "native affairs".[4] His policies and actions immediately gave rise to tensions in his relationship with his Ministers, although subsequently Gore Browne and, on his appointment for a second term as Governor, Sir George Grey, were at one with the government in embarking on the wars, first in Taranaki and later in the Waikato.[5] In the course of the campaign, Grey fell out with the commanding officer of the Imperial forces, with the Colonial Office in London, and finally with his own Ministers. By the time the fighting ended, Grey had been recalled. In 1870 the Governor ceased to have responsibility for any

4 See Chapter 2 Building the Modern Constitution, under the subheading Responsibility for Māori affairs and land at 18–22 and Chapter 13 The Crown as a Party to the Treaty of Waitangi, under the subheading The Transfer of Responsibility for "Native Affairs", at 260–263.

5 Alan Ward *A Show of Justice: Racial "Amalgamation" in Nineteenth Century New Zealand* (Auckland University Press, Auckland, 1973) at 115, 131 and 158–159.

aspect of the country's internal government. From then on, Premiers and then Prime Ministers seem to have been determined to keep Governors and, later, Governors-General, well away from any participation in the government's policy-making processes.

Twenty years after the government had assumed the full and exclusive responsibility for the internal government of the country, the then Governor, Sir Arthur Gordon,[6] gave a friend in England a catalogue of the changes in the Governor's working relations with his Ministers:[7]

> (1) Twenty years ago . . . the business done [at Cabinet meetings] was . . . reported to the Governor by the Prime Minister. Now, not the slightest hint of Cabinet proceedings is allowed to reach the Governor.
> (2) One was allowed free intercourse with all the Ministers. All communications now pass through the Premier exclusively.
> (3) Though the ultimate decision, of course, rested with Ministers, all questions were freely discussed with the Governor. His opinion was listened to, and sometimes taken. Now, unless his signature is required, no matter is mentioned to him, and then only in the shape of "advice" which must be taken.
> (4) [The Governor complained that he was asked to sign documents *after* they had already been acted upon, a practice that has since been remedied].
> (5) The Governor was the *sole* medium of communication between the local and home governments. Now, all the larger colonies have an "Agent General" in London, who communicates direct with the C.O.,[8] and none of whose correspondence with the local government is ever seen by, or mentioned to, the Governor.
> (6) The Governor's despatches were simply an affair between himself and the Home Govt. They were of course liable to be published, and he might, if he chose, communicate them to his Ministers, but the claim of the local Ministers as a matter of right to see them was refused, time after time, by the Secretary of State. Now, they not only see all, but affect practically to dictate those written from [here].
> (7) The Governor exercised a *personal* command over the Militia and Volunteers, as Commander in Chief. It was subject, of course, to the general control of the Government, but was real and afforded some employment. Now, the control of the armed forces is so completely in the "Defence Minister", that not even the Governor's formal approval is required for any matter related to it . . .

6 Sir Arthur Gordon was the Governor of New Zealand from 19 November 1880 to 24 June 1882.

7 From the Stanmore Papers, quoted by DK Fieldhouse "Autochthonous Elements in the Evolution of Dominion Status: The Case of New Zealand" (1962) 1(2) Journal of Commonwealth Political Studies 85 at 89–92; and reproduced in WD McIntyre and WJ Gardner (eds) *Speeches and Documents on New Zealand History* (Oxford University Press, Oxford, 1971) at 242 (emphasis in original).

8 The Colonial Office.

Most of the matters the Governor complained about were inevitable outcomes of fully responsible government and the fact that the self-governing colonies were "growing up", but the determination to keep the Governor well away from every aspect of policy-making is a lasting legacy of the Governor's earlier attempt to retain the responsibility for "native affairs".

The 20th-century developments

The Imperial Conference of 1926 had recognised that the Governor-General occupies the same position in all essential respects as the Queen in Britain, and should no longer act as the representative of the United Kingdom Government or as the channel of communication between that government and the government of the Dominion concerned. King George V is said to have been concerned that, in these different circumstances, the Governor-General would no longer be kept informed about the policy initiatives of the Dominion governments. The Inter-Imperial Relations Committee reported as follows:[9]

> It was recognised by the Committee . . . that a Governor-General should be supplied with copies of all the documents of importance and in general should be kept as fully informed as is his Majesty the King in Great Britain of Cabinet business and public affairs.

There was a clear implication that the purpose of keeping the Governor-General informed was to enable him or her to discuss the government's policy initiatives with the Prime Minister of the day.

The question of keeping the Governor-General informed was eventually put to a New Zealand Prime Minister, Sidney Holland, after his National Government had entered into office in December 1949. The Head of the Prime Minister's Department, AD McIntosh, explained that, in New Zealand:[10]

> . . . the Governor-General is not informed of Cabinet proceedings. In the United Kingdom, and it is understood also in other Commonwealth countries, the King or his representative, as the case may be, is kept advised. He receives copies of Agenda,

9 "Report of the Inter-Imperial Relations Committee of the Imperial Conference of 1926" (Cmd 2768, 1926), para IVb.

10 AD McIntosh to Sidney Holland, 2 December 1949, AAFD 816/1A 10/1, Archives New Zealand/ Te Whare Toku o Tuhituhinga o Aotearoa, Head Office, Wellington, cited by Harshan Kumarasingham *Onward with Executive Power: Lessons from New Zealand 1947–57* (Institute of Policy Studies, Victoria University of Wellington, Wellington, 2010) at 49.

> of papers and of the Minutes of the Cabinet discussion. It is for consideration whether or not some such regular advice should not be instituted here.

The suggestion that the Governor-General should be more fully advised about the government's policy initiatives was not taken up, then or later.

In the older Dominions, including New Zealand, the performance of that duty had been left to constitutional convention, but in the later written constitutions of most, if not all, of the newly independent Commonwealth monarchies, a duty to keep the Governor-General informed had been spelt out. The 1980 Report recommended the inclusion in the New Zealand Letters Patent of what is now the following provision:[11]

> Our Ministers of the Crown in New Zealand shall keep Our Governor-General fully informed concerning the general conduct of the Government of Our said Realm, so far as they are responsible therefor, and shall furnish Our Governor-General with such information as he may request with respect to any particular matter relating to the Government of Our said Realm.

The implementation of that duty

Although the 1980 Report had explained the background to the new provision, nobody seems to have realised that a change of practice on the part of Ministers was called for, and no such change has occurred. In the main, the duty of keeping the Governor-General informed is therefore carried out by officials. Much the same information is given also to the Queen.[12] Officials, however, do not wish to give any impression that they are analysing or commenting on government policy and this must affect the substance of what is conveyed and the quality of the exchange. From time to time, the Prime Minister, or the Clerk of the Executive Council, on the Prime Minister's behalf, will write to the Governor-General about a government initiative which bears directly on the office, but there is still no practice of sharing Cabinet papers or the minutes of Cabinet meetings.

On that note we turn to another concept which has affected the relationship between the Governor-General and Ministers.

11 Letters Patent 1983, cl 16, as recommended in Alison Quentin-Baxter *Review of the Letters Patent 1917 Constituting the Office of Governor-General of New Zealand: Report* (Cabinet Office, Wellington, 1980) [1980 Report] at 175.

12 See Chapter 5 The Sovereign in Right of New Zealand: A Personal Touch, under the subheading The Sovereign and the Prime Minister, at 77.

The duty to act on ministerial advice

The 19th century

In Chapter 2 we discussed New Zealand's acquisition of representative government and the immediate request of the elected members of the House of Representatives for responsible government as well. That request had quickly been granted. The settler governments had a very clear understanding that, from then on, the Governor would have a constitutional duty to act on ministerial advice. The main exception to that principle in the first decade of responsible government was the Governor's retention of the responsibility for "native affairs". When, in 1863, the United Kingdom Government relinquished that responsibility, the settlers were informed that the Governor would still have a constitutional discretion to act otherwise than in accordance with the advice of his Ministers.

The Secretary of State for the Colonies, the Duke of Newcastle, set out the parameters. On all colonial affairs the Governor would "generally" be bound to give effect to the policies proposed by Ministers and for which they would be responsible. The exceptions included not only Imperial interests and matters at variance with the pledges on the faith of which Her Majesty had acquired sovereignty over New Zealand. They also included policy recommendations which appeared to the Governor to be "clearly disastrous", and on which, "in the interests of the colonists themselves", he should appeal from the government advising him to the General Assembly, and from the General Assembly to the constituencies.[13]

In other words, in certain prescribed circumstances the Governor should refuse to act on the advice which his Ministers had tendered. The Premier would then be likely to tender his resignation, but, if he did not do so, the Governor should dismiss him, and look for a new Premier from within the existing Parliament. If the incoming Premier could not form a government from within the existing Parliament, he should advise an immediate dissolution which the Governor would grant.[14]

Putting the Governor's discretion to the test

There was always going to be uncertainty about what the Governor would regard as a "disaster" of the government's own making. Nearly three decades later, a Governor, and then his successor in the office, saw themselves as justified

13 See Chapter 2 Building the Modern Constitution, after fn 35, at 20–22.
14 See further Chapter 9 Finding and Changing a Prime Minister.

in refusing to act on the Premier's advice to make the recommended number of appointments to what was then the Upper House of Parliament, the Legislative Council. The Council, established by the New Zealand Constitution Act 1852,[15] was the colonial equivalent of the House of Lords. It, too, was expected to act as a brake on the law-making function of the House of Representatives. The Governor, acting on the advice of Ministers, had a delegated, and later a statutory, authority to make the appointments to the Legislative Council, initially for life. In 1891 the term of office of future members was reduced to seven years. There was no upper limit on the total number of members at any one time.

From the beginning, successive governments sought to "stack" the Legislative Council by filling it with their own supporters, who would remain in office long after the government which had advised their appointment had been defeated. After the defeat in 1890 of Harry Atkinson's government by the newly formed Liberal Party government, and before tendering his resignation, Atkinson advised the Governor that he should himself be appointed to the Legislative Council, along with five others, in order to strengthen the "conservative" composition of the Upper House. The Governor, the Earl of Onslow, made the appointments accordingly. In 1891 the new Premier, John Ballance, advised the appointment to the Legislative Council of 12 Liberal members. Onslow refused, on the ground of "swamping". The matter was still unresolved in June 1892 when the Earl of Glasgow became Governor. He tried to maintain the stance of his predecessor, but the matter was referred to the Colonial Secretary, Lord Ripon, who rejected the "swamping" allegation, especially as the Liberal Government had already passed legislation reducing the terms of new members of the Legislative Council to seven years.

The Governor to observe some further limits

Lord Ripon's despatch in response to the Governor's refusal to make the advised appointments to the Legislative Council is chiefly important for the further guidance he then gave about the exercise of the Governor's constitutional discretion. One paragraph in particular strikes us as having lasting value. The language may be that of the 19th century, but the principle it sets out is valid today:[16]

15 15 & 16 Vict c 72.

16 Despatch to the Earl of Glasgow from the Secretary of State, Lord Ripon, 26 September 1892, GBPP 1893/76 at 39, CO 209/252 at 113, 203–207, as reproduced in *Speeches and Documents on New Zealand History*, above n 7, at 256.

> 7. . . . I think it right to add that a question of this kind . . . presents also a constitutional aspect, which should be considered on broad principles of general application. When questions of a constitutional nature are involved, it is especially . . . the right of the Governor fully to discuss with his Ministers the desirability of any particular course that may be pressed upon him for his adoption. He should frankly state the objections, if any, that may occur to him; but if, after full discussion, Ministers determine to press upon him the advice which they have already tendered, the Governor should, as a general rule, and when Imperial interests are not affected, accept that advice, bearing in mind that the responsibility rests with Ministers, who are answerable to the Legislature, and, in the last resort, to the country.

That paragraph established two important limitations. First, it is not the Governor's role to question the wisdom or otherwise of an action his Ministers have advised him to take unless that action conflicts with some basic constitutional principle. Secondly, even if does, the Governor's first step is to discuss its implications with the Prime Minister, in an attempt to reach a meeting of minds. If, after such a discussion, the Prime Minister maintains the advice, the Governor should, as a general rule, act in accordance with it because the government is answerable to Parliament and ultimately to the voters.

Obviously, it is not very often that a Governor-General thinks it necessary to question the advice of Ministers. Our own observation is that, on the one or two occasions in which the Governor-General is known to have done so, the Prime Minister was ready to regard the question as the first step towards a refusal to act on the advice.[17] Lord Ripon had taken the opposite view. Usually, a discussion with the Prime Minister will be the only step the Governor-General can take. That is because a constitutionally elected government has to be free to make the decisions and take the ultimate responsibility for them. That principle is still at the heart of the constitution. We return later in the chapter to the importance of confidential discussion between the Governor-General and the Prime Minister about the government's policy initiatives, especially if they will later become the subject of formal advice.

17 One example is the reaction of the Prime Minister, Peter Fraser, to the response of the Governor-General, Sir Cyril Newall, to advice to commute a sentence of flogging, recounted in Keith Sinclair *Walter Nash* (Auckland University Press, Auckland, 1976) at 204, cited by RQ Quentin-Baxter "The Governor-General's constitutional discretions: An essay towards a re-definition" (1980) 10 VUWLR 289 at 312.

Refusing to act on advice or dismissing the Prime Minister

Pragmatism rather than principle

In 1892, Lord Ripon went on to consider whether, after the discussion and the Prime Minister's decision to maintain his advice, the Governor could still refuse to act on it:[18]

> 8. A Governor would, however, be justified in taking another course if he should be satisfied that the policy recommended to him is not only in his view erroneous in itself, but such as he has solid grounds for believing, from his local knowledge, would not be endorsed by the Legislature or by the constituency.
> 9. In so extreme a case as this, he must be prepared to accept the grave responsibility of seeking other Advisers; and I need hardly add, very strong reasons would be necessary to justify so exceptional a course on the part of the Governor.

Like Newcastle 20 years earlier, he only hinted at what the "other course" was. By that time, all the emphasis was on the expediency of a refusal to act on the tendered advice. The Governor should do so, only if he was confident that a new and different government could be formed from within the existing Parliament or, at worst, after a general election. We spell out below the hinted-at actions and their consequences. By the end of the 19th century, there were perceived limits to the feasibility of a colonial Governor's refusal to act on ministerial advice.

The Royal Instructions

Lord Ripon's statement of principle was in fact a commentary on the new Royal Instruction to the Governors of all the self-governing colonies. Earlier in 1892, the Colonial Office had attempted to bring the working of the Letters Patent constituting the office of Governor into line with what had already become the actual practice in the colonies.[19] The new Instruction read as follows:[20]

> In the execution of the powers and authorities vested in him, the Governor shall be guided by the advice of the Executive Council, but if, in any case he shall see

18 [1893] I AJHR A7a at 23.
19 Ruth Fletcher "The Governor as Commander-in-Chief" (1943) 2 Historical Studies Australia and New Zealand 209 at 221.
20 Royal Instructions to the Governor of New Zealand passed under the Royal Sign Manual and Signet, 26 March 1892, reproduced in *Speeches and Documents on New Zealand History*, above n 7, at 257–258.

> sufficient cause to dissent from the opinion of the said council, he may act in the execution of his said powers and authorities in opposition to the opinion of the Council, reporting the matter to Us without delay, with the reasons for his so acting.
>
> In any such case it shall be competent to any Member of the said Council to require that there be recorded upon the Minutes of the Council the grounds of any advice or opinion that he may give upon the question.

The 1892 formulation of the right to act "in opposition to the opinion" of the Executive Council remained part of the Royal Instructions to New Zealand Governors and Governors-General until 1983. After 1892, however, no New Zealand Governor or Governor-General seems to have invoked the right to act in opposition to the advice of his or her Ministers. By 1892, Lord Ripon was already taking a pragmatic view about the wisdom of such a step. A refusal to act, or action "in opposition to the opinion" of a Prime Minister, would almost certainly lead a Prime Minister to tender his or her own resignation, and those of the other Ministers. The Governor's dismissal of the Prime Minister and the refusal to act on the Prime Minister's advice need to be considered together because they would likely produce the same result. In either case the Governor would be left without advisers and must therefore appoint a new Prime Minister.[21]

The 20th-century developments

The first quarter of the 20th century would bring about major changes of perception. The United Kingdom Government's assumption that a Governor-General needed to control the elected governments of the self-governing colonies more firmly than did the Sovereign in the United Kingdom would be discarded; the United Kingdom itself would have to confront whether the Sovereign could intervene to prevent the passing of the Bill granting Home Rule to Ireland; and the Prime Ministers of the Dominions would be recognised as having the exclusive right to advise the Sovereign on all matters, including the appointment — or the recall — of a Governor-General. In each of the "old Dominions" that now remain — Canada, Australia and New Zealand — the exercise of the Governor-General's constitutional discretions would become an issue. We now look more closely at those developments.

21 As discussed in Chapter 9 Finding and Changing a Prime Minister.

The Balfour Declaration

The Imperial Conference of 1926 was dominated by the flow-on effects of the refusal by the Governor-General of Canada, Lord Byng, to grant a dissolution of Parliament to the Prime Minister, Mackenzie King. We discussed that aspect of the Canadian experience in Chapter 9.[22] The Balfour Declaration adopted at the Conference spelt out the fact that:[23]

> . . . the Governor-General of a Dominion is the representative of the Crown, holding in all essential respects the same position in relation to the administration of public affairs in the Dominion as is held by His Majesty the King in Great Britain . . .

Subsequently, it was made clear that, in appointing — or by implication recalling — a Governor-General, the Sovereign acted on the advice of the Prime Minister of the Dominion concerned.

The fact that a Commonwealth Prime Minister with majority support in Parliament can advise the immediate recall of the Governor-General has altered the dynamics of the relationship between a Governor-General and Prime Minister. A Governor-General had become even more vulnerable than the Sovereign. It has long been well understood that the Sovereign's failure to act in accordance with the advice of a Prime Minister whose government has majority support in the House of Commons would put at risk the future of the monarchy itself. A Governor-General who acted in the same way would put themselves, as well as the constitution, at risk, and, if they gave the Prime Minister an inkling of their intentions, the axe would be likely to fall before they had had time to act.

The United Kingdom faces Irish Home Rule

The reality that the King might put the monarchy in danger emerged clearly during the discussions in the United Kingdom in 1913–14 about the passing of a Bill which would grant Home Rule to Ireland. By then the entry into force of the Parliament Act 1911 had deprived the House of Lords of its former veto power. For the first time there was a real prospect that such a Bill would become law after it had been passed only by the House of Commons and then received the royal assent. The Conservative Party and its supporters pleaded

22 See Chapter 9 Finding and Changing a Prime Minister, fn 41, at 186.
23 See Chapter 2 Building the Modern Constitution, fn 58, at 27.

for the Sovereign's intervention. In his Memorandum on the King's position, the Prime Minister, Herbert Asquith, wrote:[24]

> The Sovereign undoubtedly has the power of changing his advisers, but it is relevant to point out that there has been, during the last 130 years, one occasion only in which the King has dismissed the Ministry which still possessed the confidence of the House of Commons. This was in 1834, when William IV (one of the least wise of British monarchs) called upon Lord Melbourne to resign. He took advantage (as we now know) of a hint improvidently given by Lord Melbourne himself, but the proceedings were neither well-advised nor fortunate. The dissolution which followed left Sir R[obert] Peel in a minority, and Lord Melbourne and his friends in a few months returned to power, which they held for the next six years. The authority of the Crown was disparaged, and Queen Victoria, during her long reign, was careful never to repeat the mistake of her predecessor . . .

Asquith then described the unfortunate consequences for the Crown if the King were to be seen as intervening in any political controversy on one side or the other.

King George V replied:[25]

> While you admit the Sovereign's undoubted power to change his advisers, I infer you regard the exercise of that power as inexpedient and indeed dangerous. Should the Sovereign *never* exercise that right . . . ?

Asquith replied that for the King to dismiss Ministers might entail consequences "very injurious to the authority of the Crown".[26] One of the King's advisers, Lord Esher, denied that the King could refuse assent to the Bill, but considered that "the King still possesses the power to dismiss his Ministers, but not of dictating policy, whether in the form of a dissolution of Parliament or otherwise".[27] The King replied that although he might not have any constitutional responsibility, he could not allow bloodshed among his loyal subjects without "exerting every means in his power" to avert it.[28] Asquith then expressed surprise and hoped that the King would not think of refusing assent to the Bill, which would "inevitably prove disastrous to the Monarchy".[29]

24 Ivor Jennings *The Law and the Constitution* (5th ed, University of London Press, London, 1959) at 408.
25 At 408–409 (emphasis in original).
26 At 409.
27 At 409.
28 At 409.
29 At 409.

Jennings comments that, although Asquith's arguments were compelling as far as they went, he did not make the further point that the King would have the right to dismiss his Ministers only if he had reason to believe that, although their policy had the approval of a majority in the House of Commons, it did not have the approval of a majority of the voters. If that was his belief, and he was concerned about the situation, then he should have insisted that his Ministers advise a dissolution. If they did not wish to do so, they would probably have resigned, but, if they did not, he could dismiss them and appoint other Ministers who would so advise. Jennings questioned, however, whether the monarch was really in a position to judge in advance the outcome of a general election. In any case, that was not a matter in which the Sovereign should become involved.[30]

Jennings makes the important additional point that every government makes decisions that would not be approved by the electorate if they were voted upon individually, a process that is neither practicable nor desirable.[31] Nor is it a valid argument that, if Home Rule were granted to Ireland, a later government would not be able to take it away. That was true of many government policies, whether or not specifically endorsed by Parliament.[32] While the King had done his best to act impartially, that was not possible when feelings were running so high. If World War I had not intervened and George V had dismissed his Ministers, a strong republican party would probably have emerged.[33]

On that basis, Jennings, writing in 1959, concluded that the reigning monarch, Elizabeth II, should let the constitution function in the normal manner, but she:[34]

> would be justified in refusing to assent to a policy which subverted the democratic basis of the Constitution by unnecessary or indefinite prolongation of the life of Parliament, by a gerrymandering of the constituencies in the interests of one party, or by fundamental modification of the electoral system to the same end. She would not be justified in other circumstances; and certainly the King would not have been justified in 1913.

The clear inference was that, unless the government was trying to change the constitution in a way that would give the party in power an unfair advantage, political controversy should be allowed to take its course.

30 At 409–410.
31 At 810.
32 At 411.
33 At 411.
34 At 412.

An Australian Governor-General dismisses the Prime Minister

The dismissal of Gough Whitlam

In 1975 the Governor-General of Australia succeeded in changing his Prime Minister in circumstances that, on their face, came a fair way towards complying with the conditions laid down before the turn of the century by Lord Ripon and others. Was the Governor-General vindicated by the fact that the government led by the new Prime Minister he had appointed, after dismissing his predecessor, won a victory at the ensuing general election?

A dispute had arisen in the Australian Federal Parliament in 1974. In the Lower House, the Labor Government, led by the Prime Minister, Gough Whitlam, had majority support, but the Opposition parties, led by Malcolm Fraser, had the support of a majority in the Upper House. There, the Opposition refused to allow a vote on the supply Bills. With a recent election mandate behind him, the Prime Minister declined to act on the Governor-General's repeated suggestions that he should advise a double dissolution of both Houses of Parliament. The government was forced to plan for reductions in public services and makeshift arrangements for the payment of public servants when supply ran out.

Without taking Whitlam into his confidence but after communication with the Queen, the Governor-General had secretly prepared a letter dismissing Whitlam from office. When Whitlam again refused to act in accordance with the Governor-General's request that he advise a double dissolution, and asked for the use of the telephone[35] — clearly with the intention of advising the Queen to recall the Governor-General — Sir John Kerr presented him with the signed letter of dismissal. Kerr then appointed Fraser as the Prime Minister. As the leader of a minority government, Fraser advised an immediate dissolution which Kerr granted. In due course, Fraser and his supporters won the general election and he was then able to form a majority government.

Did the Governor-General's startling and subsequently much debated action demonstrate that in an extreme case, a Governor-General may be able to change his or her advisers without putting at risk the constitution itself? We think not. Many Australians were deeply disquieted by the Governor-General's dismissal of a Prime Minister whose government commanded the support of a majority in the House of Representatives. It was argued that Kerr was justified in preparing secretly to dismiss Whitlam because Whitlam would otherwise himself have

35 This request is disputed in Jenny Hocking's account in *The Dismissal Dossier: Everything you were never meant to know about November 1975* (Melbourne University Press, Carlton (Vic), 2015).

acted first, and advised the Queen to recall the Governor-General.[36] But many Labor supporters saw Kerr as having acted in support of the Opposition's unjustified action in withholding supply from a government which retained majority support.

Subsequent attempts to clarify the Governor-General's discretions

In 1985, at a meeting in Brisbane of the Australian Constitutional Convention, an attempt was made to identify the constitutional conventions that govern the exercise of the "reserve powers" of the Governor-General, including the power to dismiss the Prime Minister. Michael Crommelin records that the Convention was unable to achieve any resolution of what was a highly contentious issue, especially when discussed in that open-ended way. He explains that the Structure of Government Committee had put forward various proposals, including one that the power to dismiss may be exercisable if the government was "involved in a gross and patent breach of the basic principles of the Constitutional System" that was not justiciable, or, for some other reason, could not be resolved by the courts. On that issue, however, the level of disagreement was so high that neither the Structure of Government Committee nor the Convention itself proposed any principle or practice regulating the exercise of the dismissal power.

Crommelin also records that, in December 1985, the Commonwealth Government established a Constitutional Commission to carry out a fundamental review of the constitution. The Commission recognised the reserve power of the Governor-General to dismiss the Prime Minister, but recommended that this power should be exercised only following the adoption of a resolution of the House of Representatives that the government no longer has the confidence of the House. The discretion was needed in case the defeated government did not tender its resignation or take some other appropriate action reflecting the absence of majority support.[37] Our own observation is that this very limited proposal must be seen as a clear rejection of a Governor-General's right, in any circumstance, to dismiss a Prime Minister whose government continues to enjoy the confidence of a majority in the House of Representatives. It was, however, only a recommendation. When next Australians debated the Governor-General's "reserve powers", this rejection had been lost to sight.

36 The constitutional turmoil surrounding the Whitlam government was not forgotten: see Gareth Evans (ed) *Labor and the Constitution 1972–1975: Essays and Commentaries on the Constitutional Controversies of the Whitlam Years in Australian Government* (Heinemann, Richmond (Vic), 1977). See also Michael Crommelin, below n 41.

37 The other possibility would be the Prime Minister's request that the Governor-General should grant a dissolution: compare Chapter 9 Finding and Changing a Prime Minister, fn 59, at 192.

An Australian republic?

Twenty years after Whitlam's dismissal, on 7 June 1995, the then Prime Minister, Paul Keating, the Leader of the Labor Party, put forward a well-developed proposal that Australia should become a republic.[38] Keating did not link his proposal for a republic with the 1975 dismissal of Whitlam. He saw the relationship between the two Houses of the Federal Parliament as an issue that would have to be resolved, but not as part of the proposal for a republic. Surprisingly, he saw the President of an Australian republic as automatically inheriting the Governor-General's "reserve powers". The Leader of the Opposition, John Howard, doubted whether that would be the case, unless the republican constitution so provided.[39] We come back to that question in the Afterword.

What has been described as the "Republic Model . . . put to the 1999 referendum" stated that:[40]

> the President might independently use a power which was formerly "a reserve power of the Governor-General" [as long as its use was] in accordance with the constitutional conventions relating to the exercise of that power.

The outcome of the referendum was a decisive "No" in all the Australian states and territories except the Australian Capital Territory. Although there is no way of ascertaining the reasons why a majority of the voters rejected the proposal for a republic, commentators have suggested that the constitutional turmoil surrounding the Whitlam government's dismissal had not been forgotten. The idea of vesting in the President the Governor-General's "reserve powers" in an undefined form therefore had little appeal.[41] The proposal that Australia should become a republic, its form, and its rejection by a majority of the voters rekindled, rather than settled, the debate about the course followed in 1975 by the Governor-General, Sir John Kerr. There is still debate about whether he exercised his undoubted legal power in a constitutional way.[42]

38 PJ Keating "An Australian Republic: The Way Forward" (House of Representatives, 7 June 1995), available at <http://australianpolitics.com/1995/06/07/an-australian-republic-the-way-forward.html>.

39 John Howard "Response to Paul Keating's 'An Australian Republic: The Way Forward'" (House of Representatives, 8 June 1995), available at <http://australianpolitics.com/1995/06/08/howard-response-to-republic-proposal.html>.

40 Brenton Holmes *Tracking the push for an Australian republic* (Parliamentary Library, 2013) at 38, available at <http://parlinfo.aph.gov.au/parlInfo/download/library/prspub/2394055/upload_binary/2394055.pdf;fileType=application/pdf>.

41 Michael Crommelin "Governor-General and the Republic: Powers of the Head of State" (2015) 38 MULR 1118 at 1125.

42 See, for example, Hocking, above n 35.

The situation in New Zealand

A redefinition of the constitutional conventions?

We now return to New Zealand and to perceptions of the role of the Governor-General in the period which began in 1975, when Robert Muldoon became Prime Minister, and ended only on his resignation, immediately before the appointment of his successor, in 1984. The New Zealand Governor-General, too, came near to dismissing the Prime Minister, but by that time his government no longer had the confidence of a majority in Parliament. The incident demonstrated, however, that the legal power to dismiss a Prime Minister remains in place in New Zealand.

In 1980, Professor RQ Quentin-Baxter published an article, "The Governor-General's constitutional discretions".[43] Quentin-Baxter explained why attempts to dogmatise about the nature and extent of the reserve powers of the Governor-General were apt to end badly:

> The legal fact is that if the . . . Governor-General dismisses a Prime Minister, or refuses advice to dissolve Parliament, or withholds assent from a Bill, the courts and every civil power will give effect to that action. The political fact is that the use of these Draconian measures causes the constitution to shudder, and may set in train evolutionary or revolutionary forces. The constitutional fact is that any exercise of a reserve power is evidence that a constitutional convention has been broken, because only such a breach on the part of ministers can justify resumption of personal power by the Sovereign['s] . . . representative.

Quentin-Baxter reached a sobering conclusion:

> Accordingly, the reserve powers are never without value when the possibility of their exercise causes a government to pause and think, and perhaps to conduct a dialogue with the Governor-General; but they are never fully successful if an impropriety, on one side or both, leads to their actual use.

Quentin-Baxter therefore proposed that, by agreement, perhaps recorded in a resolution of the House of Representatives, some of the long-standing formulations of the constitutional conventions could be "redefined". Essentially, his proposals were aimed at making it unnecessary for a Governor-General to contemplate dismissing a Prime Minister whose government had the support of Parliament, or refusing to act on such a Prime Minister's advice. To that end,

43 RQ Quentin-Baxter, above n 17.

the Governor-General and the Prime Minister should each have clear rights and duties which would come into play if a matter of "constitutional principle" was at stake. They would not be triggered by a dispute about policy. That was a matter which the government in power should be free to determine from time to time. The proposed principles can be summarised as follows.

If the Governor-General is of the opinion that a course of action proposed by the government and opposed by a segment of public and parliamentary opinion:

- raises a question of constitutional principle;
- was not put before the voters at the most recent general election; and
- that fact is not outweighed by any existing or pending emergency —

the Governor-General may bring the situation to the attention of the Prime Minister. It shall then be the duty of the Prime Minister:

- to defer or modify the proposed course of action so as to meet the Governor-General's concern; or
- to tender his or her resignation; or
- to advise a dissolution of Parliament.

Quentin-Baxter hoped that such a constitutional convention would enable the Governor-General to put an effective brake on a legislative or executive proposal that would be inconsistent with constitutional principle and had not been put before the voters at a general election. It would have the advantage of doing so without raising the spectre of the dismissal or resignation of a Prime Minister whose government still had majority support in Parliament. The Prime Minister might therefore be willing to take account of the constitutional issues in an appropriate way. The tender of the Prime Minister's resignation while the government itself remained in office would signal its readiness, under other leadership, to take a conciliatory course.

Clearly, however, Quentin-Baxter was aware that a Prime Minister might choose to regard the Governor-General's warning, not as good reason for a strategic retreat, but as the opening salvo in a fight to the finish. In that case, the Prime Minister would tender his or her resignation, and those of the other Ministers. The Governor-General, left without advisers, would have to appoint a new Prime Minister — presumably the Leader of the Opposition — who would not have majority support and would therefore have to advise an immediate dissolution. The Governor-General's position would be the same as it would have been if he or she had dismissed the Prime Minister. It was, however, more likely that the Prime Minister would simply advise the Sovereign to recall the Governor-General. Quentin-Baxter proposed that, in that event, there should be a requirement of at least a month's delay before a more amenable Governor-General could enter on the duties of the office.

A product of its time

Rereading Quentin-Baxter's proposal more than 30 years after it was made, it becomes apparent that it was a product of its time. It was a response to a widely shared perception that, if the government was led by a Prime Minister whose party commanded substantial majority support in Parliament, New Zealand's unwritten and uncontrolled constitution was extraordinarily vulnerable. The Prime Minister, Sir Robert Muldoon, had boasted publicly that, if he woke up one morning with a bright idea, he could have it endorsed by the Cabinet by mid-morning, put it into the House in the afternoon and have it become law by midnight. He saw such speedy law-making as entirely proper. The three-yearly general elections were the only constitutional safeguard that the country required.[44] Quentin-Baxter referred to the fact that others, too, had seen the New Zealand constitution as insufficiently protected. Woodhouse J, then a member of the Court of Appeal, had published an article arguing that "the time has come for New Zealand to reduce its constitution to writing supported by a Bill of Rights".[45] In the same period, Cooke J suggested that an Act of Parliament might be so contrary to constitutional principle that no court would be willing to regard it as law.[46]

Quentin-Baxter's article was tabled in Parliament along with the 1980 Report on the 1917 Letters Patent constituting the office of Governor-General, in support of the recommendation that new Letters Patent should not deal with the relationship between the Governor-General and the Executive Council. Both documents agreed that principles governing the relationship should be left to constitutional convention. The Muldoon government accepted that part of the recommendation so far as it went.

The 1892 formulation of the right of the Governor and later Governor-General to act "in opposition to the opinion" of the Executive Council which was still part of the Royal Instructions at the time was subsequently revoked by the 1983 Letters Patent, along with the Royal Instructions as a whole. There was no longer a need or a place for Royal Instructions, once the Sovereign in

44 Gerald Hensley *Final Approaches: A Memoir* (Auckland University Press, Auckland, 2006) at 321.
45 Cited by RQ Quentin-Baxter, above n 17, at 312.
46 *Taylor v NZ Poultry Board* [1984] 1 NZLR 394, 398 (CA).

right of New Zealand was no longer advised by United Kingdom Ministers, but solely by the New Zealand Prime Minister.[47]

But, as the 1980 Report acknowledged, the revocation of the Royal Instructions would not, in itself, dispose of the question whether the Governor-General still possessed a residual constitutional discretion to refuse to act on ministerial advice. It explained that the matter ought not to be dealt with in new Letters Patent which would have the force of law. The Governor-General's constitutional discretions should continue to be guided by constitutional convention. Accordingly, the current 1983 Letters Patent simply describe the Executive Council as consisting "of those persons who, having been appointed to the Executive Council from among persons eligible for appointment under the Constitution Act 1986 [namely, Members of Parliament in New Zealand], are, for the time being, Our responsible advisers".[48] That statement was seen as a sufficient indication of the underlying constitutional principle. The Governor-General must act on the advice of Ministers except in the rare cases where he or she may have an element of personal discretion. The same approach had been taken in the Letters Patent then in force in Canada[49] and Australia.[50]

The Muldoon government, however, was not disposed to take up the question of redefining the conventions themselves.[51] As long as he remained Prime Minister, Muldoon himself remained truculent, even after his government had been defeated at a general election.

A possible dismissal of the Prime Minister

In his last days in office, the actions of Sir Robert Muldoon, the outgoing Prime Minister, led the Governor-General, the Hon Sir David Beattie, for what appears to have been the first time in New Zealand's history, to recognise the possible need to dismiss the Prime Minister from office. We have earlier told the story of how, in 1984, Muldoon's government was defeated at a general election but the incoming Labour Prime Minister, David Lange, was unable to be appointed to office until the outcome of the election had been formally declared. That meant a delay of about two weeks. Meantime, there had been a run on the New Zealand dollar and Lange had accepted the advice

47 1980 Report, above n 11.

48 Clause 8.

49 The Canadian Letters Patent of 1942 recorded only the basic principle that the Governor-General acts on the advice of Ministers, without including any reference to constitutional discretions.

50 The Australian instrument citation required only that the Governor-General was to exercise his powers and authorities "in due manner".

51 Constitutional Provisions Bill, Report of the Statutes Revision Committee (9 August 1983) 451 NZPD 1276, 1277–1278; Second reading (5 October 1983) 453 NZPD 2826–2828, 2878–2880, 2832–2833.

of the Governor of the Reserve Bank immediately to devalue the currency. The necessary Order in Council had to be made by the outgoing government. Muldoon had publicly refused to take that step, but the Deputy Prime Minister, Jim McLay, was at length able to persuade Muldoon that, until the changeover took place, he had a constitutional duty to act in accordance with the caretaker convention requiring him to implement the policies of the incoming government.[52]

The part of the story we have not yet told is that McLay had informed Muldoon that, if he remained unwilling to make the Order in Council, McLay and the other senior Ministers would resign from the Cabinet. McLay also told Muldoon that, through the Clerk, he had already informed the Governor-General of the action that the Ministers would take, and that, if the Governor-General dismissed the Prime Minister, McLay would be willing to serve as interim Prime Minister. His government would operate in accordance with the caretaker convention until Lange could be appointed to office. The Governor-General later let it be known to McLay that, if the Prime Minister had not accepted the need to implement the incoming government's policy, the Governor-General would have dismissed him from office.

A summing-up

The incident showed that the Governor-General not only has the legal power to dismiss a Prime Minister, but would be prepared to exercise it if the Prime Minister were to refuse to act in accordance with an important constitutional convention. It should be noted, however, that, by that time, Muldoon was not a Prime Minister whose government had majority support in Parliament. The possibility of dismissing a New Zealand Prime Minister whose government continues to have majority support in Parliament seems not to have arisen since the argument about the number of members to be appointed to the Legislative Council in 1892. On that occasion, the Colonial Secretary found that the evil the Governor was trying to prevent was outweighed by the likely consequences of a refusal to act on ministerial advice.

In a similar situation a modern Governor-General would be entitled to seek outside advice from anyone willing to provide it, but that would not necessarily be helpful in maintaining a sense of proportion in a worrying situation. At such a time, a Governor-General would be bound to have a sense of responsibility, but there is little or nothing to give them reliable guidance about how they should act. That is the position in New Zealand today.

52 See Chapter 9 Finding and Changing a Prime Minister, after fn 19, at 174–177.

3
A TIME FOR ASSESSMENT AND CHANGE

The needs and opportunities

Within the executive branch of government there is a division of labour. The political executive, comprising the Prime Minister and the other members of the Cabinet, has the responsibility for the exercise of executive authority and is answerable to Parliament and the electorate. The non-executive role of the Governor-General, with its commitment to political neutrality, is more elusive. If, in the years ahead, that division of labour is to survive and prosper, it needs to be nurtured. It should not thoughtlessly be subjected to strain. We argue that the time has come for a public acknowledgement that almost nothing is now left of the colonial concept that the Governor-General is a constitutional watchdog, with a residual responsibility for the constitutional propriety of the government's policies and actions. The ultimate outcome of the attempted exercise of such a responsibility is likely to be the resignation or dismissal of the Prime Minister, despite the fact that he or she is still the leader of a government which has majority support in Parliament. Whatever the eventual outcome in Parliament and at a general election, the Governor-General's intervention would be seen by a large section of the community as a breach of the duty to remain politically neutral. Major constitutional change would be likely to follow.

Intervention by the Governor-General would be a high-risk strategy for all concerned, as well as potentially for the constitution itself. Given that risk, we make the case for refocusing attention on what is usually an accepted aspect of a Governor-General's role. In contrast to the position in the United Kingdom, New Zealand Prime Ministers do not meet regularly in private with the Governor-General. Though opportunities for formal interaction exist at meetings of the Executive Council over which the Governor-General presides,[53] and communication no doubt takes place informally, generally speaking, the Governor-General and the Prime Minister inhabit different spheres.

53 See Chapter 8 The Governor-General in the Executive Branch, under the subheading Meetings of the Executive Council, at 161.

Is the Governor-General the guardian of the constitution?

The background

We begin by asking whether the Governor-General is the guardian of the constitution with a residual responsibility for the propriety of a government's policies. The expression "guardian of the constitution" was used by some Australian and New Zealand Governors-General and other commentators in the late 20th century to describe the Governor-General's role. They did not spell out its implications. Most seem to have used the description as a way of meeting the very real difficulty of explaining what a Governor-General does. While some Governors-General may have been aware that the role of guardian might require them to consider the exercise of a discretion to change their advisers, others may not. We see the question whether the Governor-General is the guardian of the constitution as needing to be considered in a broader context. We therefore look at whether the Governor-General has any wider role in preventing or remedying an abuse of governmental power or dealing with some other unwanted situation. That will provide a broader basis for determining the nature of the Governor-General's role.

The power to appoint or dismiss a Prime Minister

The Governor-General has the legal power to appoint, and also to dismiss, a Prime Minister. The power to appoint a Prime Minister is used routinely, every time there is a change of government. In Chapter 9, we discussed the Governor-General's exercise of the power to appoint a Prime Minister on the first coming to power of a new government. The governing principle is that a government which has the confidence of Parliament has the right to remain in office. A Prime Minister who heads a government which has the confidence of Parliament should be dismissed only if he or she needs to be relieved of the office for some personal reason, and is not able, or has failed, to take the usual step of tendering his or her resignation. A Prime Minister who has lost the confidence of the House, and will not tender their resignation or seek a dissolution, may be dismissed by the Governor-General.

The Governor-General has no other emergency powers

It is sometimes suggested that the Governor-General has some other residual power which he or she could exercise in an emergency, particularly an emergency that prevents the constitutionally appointed government from functioning normally. As Wade and Phillips explain, however, although the

Crown has some emergency powers under the prerogative, those powers are generally too uncertain for the executive to rely on them.[54] Most common law countries therefore make statutory provision for the exercise of emergency powers in a range of foreseeable situations.[55] To avoid the risk of the abuse of a wide emergency power, the modern practice is to confer emergency powers on a sectoral basis, and limit them to the likely needs of the particular kind of emergency.[56]

The statute law is likely to empower the executive to declare a state of emergency, to exercise additional powers not ordinarily available, and to make emergency regulations which may override the ordinary law. In wartime, Parliament is likely to give the executive the power to make a wider range of emergency regulations. In peacetime, however, the authorising statute will provide safeguards. Parliament will be required to meet promptly if it is not already in session. There will be a time limit on the period for which a state of emergency may continue, and provision for its renewal only for a limited period, and perhaps only with the consent of Parliament. The constitution or other law may also limit the extent to which emergency regulations may derogate from fundamental rights and freedoms. If a statute or emergency regulation confers powers on the Governor-General, then, expressly or implicitly, the Governor-General will be required to exercise the powers on ministerial advice in the ordinary way.

In some other realms, or former realms, where emergencies have been caused by the unlawful or unconstitutional actions of the government or by the overthrow of the constitution itself, or both, Governors-General have done what they could to save the situation and return the country to constitutional government. In the nature of things, however, a constitution cannot make provision for its own overthrow. A Governor-General will be likely to find themselves acting outside the constitution and the law. If lawful government is restored, the courts may find the unlawful actions of the Governor-General and others to have been justified, or may excuse them, on the ground of their necessity. The doctrine of necessity is not, however, a direct source of legal authority or powers.

Once Parliament is again functioning in the normal — or in what may have become the "new normal" — way, it may pass an Act of Indemnity, and retrospectively validate some or all of the unlawful actions taken. It may also grant the Governor-General and others immunity from any criminal or

54 ECS Wade and G Godfrey Phillips (eds) *Constitutional and Administrative Law* (9th ed, Longman Group Ltd, London, 1977) at 513.

55 In the case of New Zealand see, for example, Defence Act 1990, ss 9 and 10.

56 See Law Commission *Final Report on Emergencies* (NZLC R22, 1991) at [4.8]–[4.11].

civil liability. It is also possible that the illegal or unconstitutional actions of the Governor-General or others may eventually be recognised as having established a new constitutional order. These possibilities, and perhaps others, reflect the overriding importance of preserving the territorial integrity of the state and the safety and well-being of its people. We mention them only to show that there will always be limits to a Governor-General's constitutional powers.[57]

The idea that, as Commander-in-Chief, the Governor-General has unspecified legal powers has been perpetuated in the Defence Act, but, as we have explained in Chapter 7, it remains without foundation.

Drawing the conclusions

If legal powers are conferred on the Governor-General, they must be exercised on ministerial advice in the usual way. Beyond that, the good offices of a Governor-General might in some situations be able to preserve constitutional government. The Governor-General will always endeavour to uphold the constitution and the law, and will encourage the government to do the same, but, unlike a court, a Governor-General cannot make a determination that a government's actions are unconstitutional. He or she may ask a question or express a view, but that is all. When the government has taken account of any views the Governor-General may have expressed, and whether or not it has modified its own earlier proposals, the Governor-General must then act in accordance with its advice as tendered in its final form. That was the clear implication, once the Prime Minister had assumed the responsibility for advising the Sovereign to appoint or recall a Governor-General, notwithstanding the fact that the Governor-General retains the legal power to appoint or dismiss a Prime Minister.

That does not mean that a present-day Governor-General has only a passive role. On the contrary, freeing the Governor-General of the role of ultimate constitutional guardian opens up the possibility for a more dynamic working relationship with the Prime Minister and other Ministers.

Strengthening the working relationship

Given that the practical value of the residual discretion is not necessarily to operate as a veto but rather as a mechanism by which to cause a Prime Minister

57 It used to be emphasised that a Governor-General is not a Vice-Roy who, conceptually, has all the powers and dignities of the Sovereign. A Governor-General has always been seen as having only the powers conferred on the holder of the office, plenary though they may be.

to pause, we think that the traditional emphasis on the Governor-General's "watchdog" image with a power of dismissal is misplaced. It would be better to focus on developing a more significant working relationship between the Governor-General and the Prime Minister. The substance of any communication between them should remain confidential, but the fact that they communicate should become an accepted aspect of the relationship. An initiative to that end is both possible and desirable. It is possible because the constitutional climate is now very different from what it was in 1984. It is no longer necessary to look to the Governor-General as perhaps able to act as a last line of defence against the impetuous actions of a government with a large, single-party majority in Parliament. Other power-limiting and procedural constitutional mechanisms such as MMP, the New Zealand Bill of Rights Act 1990, judicial review, the Waitangi Tribunal and the Official Information Act 1982 are well in place. The operation of such mechanisms could no doubt continue to be improved but that is beyond the scope of our inquiry.

There needs now to be a deliberate initiative to establish a direct line of communication because it seems that neither the early New Zealand Premiers nor the later Prime Ministers have ever been in the habit of discussing with the Governor or the Governor-General in confidence the government's proposed policies and actions, as the United Kingdom Prime Minister does with the Queen. It is not that such a relationship once existed but later came to an end: no such relationship seems ever to have been put in place. The Premier and later the Prime Minister met with the Governor or the Governor-General whenever there was a particular reason to do so, but, as the reasons became fewer, they met less often. By the time that there was almost never a reason to meet, except in the Executive Council or on some other state occasion, or socially, no one realised that a practice which would have been of value had never been put in place.

For a long time there were particular reasons for the Prime Minister to meet in private with the Governor and later the Governor-General. Until 1926, the Sovereign's representative remained formally responsible for "Imperial interests".[58] The Prime Minister and he would have met in private on that account. In 1926, that formal basis for keeping in touch was swept away, but the Governor-General remained the channel for communication with the United Kingdom Government and the New Zealand High Commissioner in London. On the outbreak of World War II, separate channels of communication were established, but, during the war, the government remained in close

58 See Chapter 2 Building the Modern Constitution, under the subheading The Governor's role after 1856, at 18.

touch with Governors-General who still had links with the United Kingdom establishment.

Peace came and, eventually, a change of practice. There were few, if any, practical reasons for the Prime Minister and the Governor-General to be closely in touch. Successive Governors-General have themselves made a point of arranging social occasions which give them the opportunity to get to know the Prime Minister and other Ministers, and to discuss with them in private their policies and aspirations for the country and its government. Those occasions, however, are not a substitute for a more formal arrangement. The 1983 Letters Patent recognises the duty of Ministers to keep the Governor-General informed,[59] but, as we have shown, the formal recognition of that duty came too late to be the catalyst for a closer working relationship.

Acknowledging a right

In our view, the right to be kept informed implies that the Governor-General also has a right to discuss with the Prime Minister any aspect of the government's policies and actions. But such a right has never been acknowledged explicitly. We therefore recommend that the Governor-General's right to speak privately with the Prime Minister about any aspect of the government's policies and actions should be put beyond doubt.

Once it is made clear that the Governor-General no longer has a constitutional discretion to act otherwise than in accordance with the advice of a Prime Minister whose government continues to have a constitutional right to govern, the Prime Minister will have nothing to fear in discussing with the Governor-General the policy issues facing the government, or the advice which the Prime Minister or the Executive Council has tendered or is likely to tender. The Prime Minister should consider any concerns the Governor-General may have, and may think it right to put them to the Cabinet. If the Governor-General has a concern on constitutional grounds about the advisability of a course of action proposed or advised by the Prime Minister, an acceptable solution or compromise may emerge. But if, after further consideration, the Prime Minister maintains his or her earlier advice, the Governor-General will have a constitutional duty to act on it. In that way, the constitution draws on convention and the good sense of the constitutional actors to harmonise what could otherwise become their competing powers. We reach a similar

59 Letters Patent 1983, cl 16; Cabinet Office *Cabinet Manual 2008* (Department of the Prime Minister and Cabinet, Wellington, New Zealand, April 2008) at [1.16].

conclusion in Chapter 11 in considering the Governor-General's function of giving the royal assent to Bills.

It would be implicit that, if the Governor-General wished to discuss a particular matter with the Prime Minister as soon as possible, he or she would ask the Prime Minister to call at Government House as soon as is mutually convenient. Such a request is not likely to be made often, if at all, but the right to make it is important, along with the Prime Minister's duty to comply. A Governor-General would, however, be wise to make such a request only if there is a real and urgent need for a meeting. If such a request were to be made routinely, the duty to comply with it would soon be ignored.

The news media should see meetings between the Governor-General and the Prime Minister as the normal functioning of the constitution. They should not be taken as a sign of tensions or disagreement, any more than are the United Kingdom Prime Minister's meetings with the Queen. Anything said by either the Governor-General or the Prime Minister in the course of such a meeting must of course remain confidential, unless they decide otherwise.[60] If the conversations were to become the subject of public speculation or comment, the political neutrality of the Governor-General would be compromised, perhaps irreparably.

All that is formally required to implement the Governor-General's right to discuss matters with the Prime Minister, as proposed in this section, is a short statement of principle in the Cabinet Manual. Such a statement is necessary, not only to confirm a right which might otherwise be disputed, but also to keep the people of New Zealand informed about how their constitution works.

Spelling out the constitutional conventions

Our recommendations

The Cabinet Manual records the duty of Ministers to keep the Governor-General informed.[61] The Manual should further provide that the Governor-General has the right to discuss with the Prime Minister any matter concerning the government of New Zealand. Those matters would include any advice to the Governor-General tendered by Ministers. The Cabinet Manual should provide that, if the government has the constitutional right to govern, and there is no personal reason affecting the ability of the Prime Minister to

60 There would be good reason for withholding information about the matters discussed at such a meeting "to the extent necessary to protect the confidentiality of communications by or with the Sovereign or her representative": Official Information Act 1982, s 9(1) and (2)(f)(i).

61 *Cabinet Manual*, above n 59, at [1.16].

carry out the responsibilities of the office, the Governor-General does not have a constitutional discretion to act otherwise than in accordance with the advice of the Executive Council, the Prime Minister, or another Minister acting with the Prime Minister's authority. Nor, in those circumstances, does the Governor-General have a constitutional discretion to dismiss the Prime Minister from office.

The proposed statement of principle in the Cabinet Manual would leave intact the Governor-General's legal power to appoint or dismiss a Prime Minister. In a circumstance depriving the Prime Minister of the physical or mental capacity or the personal qualifications to remain in office, the Prime Minister would have a duty to tender his or her resignation. If for any reason that did not happen, the Governor-General would have a duty to dismiss the Prime Minister. Such a dismissal would not usually bring about a change of government, although a change of Prime Minister might raise a question about the survival of a coalition or support agreement. The Governor-General would usually be acting with the knowledge and the consent, or at least the acquiescence, of the Deputy Prime Minister and other senior Ministers. As in the case of a Prime Minister's death in office, an Acting Prime Minister might be appointed to carry out the duties of the office until the completion of the party's process for electing a new leader, and confirmation that the new leader is able to form a government that will have majority support.

The New Zealand principles

Our proposed restatement of the principles in a form designed to achieve the recommended outcomes is set out below. Because the principles involve elements of reform, they should not be included in the Cabinet Manual unless they have been considered, not only by the government, but also by the Opposition, and any independent parties as well as by the public. The government should, however, assume the responsibility for proposing their inclusion, in the same way as it is responsible for the periodic revision of the Standing Orders of the House of Representatives. A consensus should be the goal.

RELATIONSHIP BETWEEN THE GOVERNOR-GENERAL AND MINISTERS

1. Ministers must keep the Governor-General fully informed concerning the general conduct of the government, and must furnish the Governor-General with such information as he or she may request with respect to any particular matter relating to the government.[62]

62 Letters Patent 1983, cl 16.

2. The Governor-General may discuss with the Prime Minister, in confidence, any aspect of the government's policies or actions in carrying out its responsibilities for the executive government of New Zealand, or in participating in any parliamentary proceeding.

3. The Governor-General exercises the powers and duties of the office on the advice of the Executive Council, the Prime Minister, or another Minister acting with the authority of the Prime Minister, unless, in the particular case, the Governor-General is required by law or by a constitutional convention to act on the advice of some other person or authority, or in the exercise of his or her judgement.

4. During a period when the government led by the Prime Minister enjoys the confidence of the House of Representatives, and the Prime Minister is able and qualified to remain in office, the Governor-General has no constitutional discretion to act otherwise than in accordance with ministerial advice, or to dismiss the Prime Minister from office.

5. Paragraph 4 does not affect the legal power of the Governor-General to appoint or dismiss a Prime Minister or the Governor-General's duty to exercise that or any other power in accordance with any other law or constitutional convention.[63]

63 See further Chapter 9 Finding and Changing a Prime Minister on appointing a Prime Minister.

CHAPTER 11

The Governor-General in Parliament

1
INTRODUCTION

Up until now, we have been focused primarily on the Sovereign's and Governor-General's role in relation to the executive branch of government. The English constitution did not originally contemplate a separation of powers. At the time of personal rule, the Sovereign was the locus of *all* of the branches of government, but now the connections between the Sovereign and Parliament and the Sovereign and the judicial branch are in large part symbolic. In this chapter we identify the most important roles which the Sovereign by her Governor-General still plays in relation to legislative matters. We explore what it means for the Sovereign and the legislature together to constitute Parliament — focusing on the Sovereign's assent and consent to legislation.

2
THE QUEEN IN PARLIAMENT

In formal constitutional terms, Parliament is comprised of both the House of Representatives and the Sovereign. This is reflected in section 14(1) of the Constitution Act 1986. What, if anything, follows from that? In the first section below, we explain the Sovereign's most well-known, but perhaps least well-understood, role in assenting to legislation. This is the requirement for the Sovereign (or her representative) to assent before a Bill becomes law. The careful wording of the Constitution Act 1986 tells us nothing about whether, or under what circumstances, she may *refuse* or withhold her assent to a particular Bill:

Section 16 Royal Assent to Bills

A Bill passed by the House of Representatives shall become law when the Sovereign or the Governor-General assents to it and signs it in token of such assent.

This was a deliberate change from section 56 of the New Zealand Constitution Act 1852 (UK) which expressly gave the Governor-General the discretion to refuse assent. The majority of the Officials Committee,[1] which in 1986 considered changes to the 1852 Act, thought section 56 was misleading and gave the impression that the Governor-General had an unfettered discretion to refuse consent when "[i]n fact, by long-standing constitutional convention, the Governor-General acts in this matter on the advice of a Minister of the Crown".[2] The Officials Committee added that "[i]n all but the most extraordinary circumstances the refusal of assent would be unthinkable. It would immediately produce a constitutional crisis of the first order."[3]

The work of the Officials Committee was conducted with very little public attention, participation or fanfare. Even so, it was the issue of how the assent power should be framed which provoked the only dissenting view in its report. A minority thought that the power to refuse assent should be expressly retained.[4] While it accepted that there is a convention that the Governor-General acts on advice, it thought that the proposed wording would change the law in an unacceptable way and that it was conceivable that the responsible Ministry might advise against the royal assent being granted.[5] The majority view nevertheless prevailed and the explicit statutory power to refuse assent was removed. The modern formulation in section 16 of the Constitution Act 1986 leaves unsaid whether and, if so, when assent can be withheld. Those questions remain something of a constitutional mystery.

The last time the Sovereign exercised a personal discretion to refuse assent was in 1707–08 during the reign of Queen Anne in relation to a Scottish Militia Bill.[6] On that occasion, the refusal was in fact with the approval of

1 Department of Justice *Constitutional Reform: Reports of an Officials Committee* (Wellington, New Zealand, 1986).
2 At 3.46.
3 At 3.47.
4 At 3.50.
5 There is only one known instance where the Premier advised the Governor not to assent to a Bill: Premier Sir George Grey advised the Governor (the Marquis of Normanby) to refuse assent to the Land Bill 1877. The Bill had been passed through the two Houses under the previous administration and the new Premier did not support it. The Governor, however, declined to follow the Premier's advice in that instance and assented to the Bill. See "Despatches from the Secretary of State to the Governor of New Zealand" [1878] AJHR A02 at 13–14. See the discussion of this in Philip A Joseph *Constitutional and Administrative Law in New Zealand* (4th ed, Thomson Reuters, Wellington, 2014) at 324, in particular fn 129. See also John Lochiel Robson *New Zealand: The Development of its Laws and Constitution* (Stevens & Sons, London, 1954) at 40.
6 See, for example, William McKay (ed) *Erskine May's Treatise on the Law, Privileges, Proceedings*

her Ministers and without objection from the Commons and Lords.[7] As is the case with so many of the Sovereign's powers, the power to assent has, over time, been moderated by constitutional convention. The personal power of the Sovereign has been ceded to the representative claims of the House of Commons now for hundreds of years. That is an important element of what constitutes a *constitutional* monarchy. The fact that Sovereigns and Governors-General have at times been sorely tempted to refuse assent — and in relation to *major* constitutional issues — for example, King George V during the Home Rule crisis[8] — only serves to reinforce the strength of the conventional position that, despite his or her own views of the matter, the Sovereign invariably assents to Bills passed by the legislature. Bagehot's 19th-century view of the matter is uncompromising:[9]

> [T]he Queen has no [legislative] veto. She must sign her own death warrant if the two Houses unanimously send it up to her.

The mechanics of assent

The Sovereign's assent in person in the UK House of Parliament was given for the last time in 1854.[10] Since then the practice has been for the Lord Chancellor to send a list of Bills which are ready for royal assent to the Sovereign. All that is put before the Sovereign is the short title to the Bill. Assent is signified either by Letters Patent signed by the Sovereign to which the short titles of Bills are attached as a schedule,[11] or by Commissioners who declare the Sovereign's assent to both Houses at the time of prorogation of Parliament in accordance with a standard formula. Royal assent is separately notified to the House by the Speaker of each House sitting separately.[12] *Erskine May*, the leading

and Usage of Parliament (23rd ed, LexisNexis UK, London, 2004) at 654, fn 2 [*Erskine May*]. For a history of the English practice see Graham John Wheeler "Royal Assent in the British Constitution" (2016) 132 LQR 495.

7 ECS Wade and G Godfrey Phillips *Constitutional and Administrative Law* (9th ed, Longman, London 1977) at 17. In 1870s New Zealand, the Governor *granted* assent to a Bill against the advice of the Premier Sir George Grey. The Governor's actions were subsequently approved by London. See Anne Twomey "The Refusal or Deferral of Royal Assent" (Sydney Law School, Legal Studies Research Paper No 07/58, August 2007) at 5. Bogdanor suggests that an implied veto threat by George III prevented the progress of an India Bill that had already passed the Commons: Vernon Bogdanor *The Monarchy and the Constitution* (Oxford University Press, Oxford, 1997) at 12.

8 Draft Letter by George V dated 31 July 1914, cited in Wade and Phillips, above n 7, at 229.

9 Walter Bagehot *The English Constitution* (Fontana ed, Collins, London 1963) at 98 (originally published 1867).

10 *Erskine May*, above n 6, at 654, fn 2, though she retains that right.

11 For the standard wording of the Letters Patent see Francis Bennion "The Modern Royal Assent Procedure at Westminster" at <www.francisbennion.com>.

12 *Erskine May*, above n 6, at 654. Assent for a Bill for aids and supplies is declared in the words

United Kingdom text on parliamentary practice, does not even discuss the possibility of the Sovereign's refusal.[13] In any event, the mechanics by which the Sovereign's assent is signified have the effect of removing the focus on her person, and direct avenues for the tendering of ministerial advice on whether or not to assent. Such procedures are not designed to enable the Sovereign's personal scrutiny of the contents of Bills.

In New Zealand, the Governor used to attend the last session of Parliament in person and would grant royal assent to all of the Bills presented during the session and then prorogue the Parliament. That practice ceased in 1875. In contrast with the United Kingdom, however, Bills are still presented for the Sovereign's or Governor-General's signature before they become law. After a Bill has received its third reading, the Clerk of the House of Representatives certifies the copies as the version of the Bill which was passed by the House[14] and presents two copies to the Attorney-General (the Crown's first legal adviser). The Attorney-General certifies that the Bill "does not contain anything that would require the withholding of royal assent"[15] — a procedure which originated from a time when the New Zealand legislature did not enjoy full law-making power and Royal Instructions to the Governor listed areas in which the Governor should reserve his assent (of which more later).[16] This certificate is now treated as *pro forma*.[17]

Copies of Bills are then presented to the Prime Minister to advise the granting of the Governor-General's assent. David McGee describes the Prime Minister as performing the "political act of assent".[18] The Clerk arranges for the Bills to be presented for the Governor-General's signature which then constitutes the "legal act of assent".[19] On a few special occasions coinciding with the Queen's visits, she has personally signified her assent to New Zealand legislation.[20]

In New Zealand, in contrast to the United Kingdom, copies of Bills (as opposed to a list of their short titles) are physically presented for the Sovereign's or Governor-General's signature before they become law, and following the Prime Minister's advice. The Governor-General has perhaps

"La Reyne remercie ses bons sujets, accepte leur benevolence, et ainsi le vault" ("the Queen thanks her good subjects, accepts their kindness and thus wishes it"). For all other public and private Acts the formula is "La Reyne le vault" ("the Queen wishes it").

13 Above n 6.

14 It is conceivable that the Clerk could withhold certification if the proper processes were not met.

15 RQ Quentin-Baxter "The Governor-General's constitutional discretions: An essay towards redefinition" (1980) 10 VUWLR 289 at 298.

16 David G McGee *Parliamentary Practice in New Zealand* (3rd ed, Dunmore Publishing, Wellington, 2005) at 392.

17 There is a standard form cover sheet into which the name of the Bill is inserted. We discuss below whether the Attorney-General could refuse to certify, after fn 51 at 243.

18 McGee, above n 16, at 392.

19 At 392.

20 Royal Titles Act 1974, Seal of New Zealand Act 1977, Waikato Raupatu Claims Settlement Act 1995.

understandably remained the focus of petitions and litigation seeking to prevent signature to unpopular laws. The symbolism of the Queen's signature to the Waikato-Tainui settlement legislation may have helped keep alive a belief in the Sovereign's personal interest and involvement in the substance of legislation. The Governor's historical role in regulating the limits of the New Zealand legislature's law-making power, too, seems to have remained part of New Zealand's constitutional memory. We turn first to the historical practices.

New Zealand Constitution Act 1852 (UK): reservation, amendment and disallowance

As we have already mentioned, section 56 of the New Zealand Constitution Act 1852 (an Act of the United Kingdom Parliament) expressly empowered the Governor to assent to a Bill, to refuse assent, or to "[reserve a] bill for the signification of her Majesty's pleasure". Section 56 also gave the Governor power to make amendments he thought "needful or expedient" and by message to return the Bill with such amendments to the legislators. For a short time the Governor also had power to disallow Bills made by the provincial legislatures.[21]

In exercising these powers, the Governor was bound by the provisions of the New Zealand Constitution Act 1852 itself and by his Royal Instructions.[22]

Such procedures were aimed primarily at protecting the United Kingdom's Imperial interests, at ensuring legal uniformity and consistency (for example, in relation to divorce laws around the empire), and at supervising the conduct of the colony (including, in particular, in relation to "native affairs"). Such powers need to be understood against the background of the United Kingdom Parliament's continuing power to legislate for New Zealand and of a common law rule that laws repugnant to the laws of England were invalid.[23]

Disallowance

Before the New Zealand legislature became fully self-governing (and, at least formally, for some time thereafter), its legislation was subject to reservation and disallowance. Section 58 of the New Zealand Constitution Act 1852

21 New Zealand Constitution Act 1852 (UK) 15 & 16 Vict c 72, s 29. Some 266 Provincial Bills were disallowed. See John E Martin "Refusal of Assent — A Hidden Element of Constitutional History in New Zealand" (2010) 41 VUWLR 51 at fn 3.

22 For examples of the terms of the Royal Instructions see Martin, above n 21, at 53 and 54.

23 The common law rule was clarified and narrowed in its scope by the Colonial Law Validity Act 1865 (UK) 28 & 29 Vict c 63.

declared the Sovereign's power to disallow any Act passed by the colonial legislature. Having received the Governor's assent, all laws were referred to the United Kingdom Secretary of State and could be disallowed within two years of their passing. Sovereigns did not exercise power in their personal discretion but rather on the advice of United Kingdom Ministers.

The disallowance power was used throughout the colonies during the 19th century and whenever the Government of the United Kingdom took a different view on the merits of a legislative measure from that of local legislatures. As practice developed and responsible government of the colonies became better established, a constitutional convention emerged that the power of disallowance could only be used when the United Kingdom's Imperial interests were affected and not in relation to laws of local significance. What counted as local or Imperial also shifted during that time. Well before the power of disallowance was removed, the convention developed that it should not be exercised.[24]

The power of disallowance was exercised in New Zealand in relation to the Waste Lands Act 1856 and for the last time in 1877 to disallow the Indemnity Act 1866 which would have granted wide immunities to persons "acting in suppression of native insurrection".[25] If the New Zealand legislature were willing to amend a measure, however, formal disallowance was not always necessary. Amendments negotiated between London and Wellington were preferred.

The disallowance procedure in section 58 of the New Zealand Constitution Act 1852 remained in force even after the Statute of Westminster Adoption Act 1947, but by then New Zealand had stopped sending legislation to the Secretary of State in the United Kingdom, rendering the practical exercise of the disallowance power difficult.[26] The formal legal power to disallow legislation was not removed until the enactment of the Constitution Amendment Act 1973. In introducing the amending legislation, the then Attorney-General Dr Martyn Finlay stated that: "These provisions have long since ceased to have any relation to constitutional realities."[27]

For our purposes it is important to emphasise that disallowed Acts had all received the Governor's assent. The Sovereign did not take a personal decision

24 Conference on the Operation of Dominion Legislation and Merchant Shipping Legislation 1929 [1930] I AJHR A6 at 5.

25 John Martin's work, above n 21, helpfully clarifies matters. Previous accounts differed or were incomplete. See Kenneth John Scott *The New Zealand Constitution* (Clarendon Press, Oxford, 1962) at 46; John Lochiel Robson *New Zealand: The Development of its Laws and Constitution* (1st ed, Stevens & Sons, London, 1954) at 49. Compare John Lochiel Robson *New Zealand: The Development of its Laws and Constitution* (2nd ed, Stevens & Sons, London, 1967) at 63.

26 Robson (1967), above n 25, at 64.

27 New Zealand Constitution Amendment Act 1975 2nd Reading (1973) 388 NZPD 5235–5237.

to disallow, but acted on the advice of United Kingdom Ministers exercising Imperial oversight.

Reservation

Perhaps more interesting were the powers given to the Governor under the New Zealand Constitution Act 1852 (UK) to "reserve" Bills "for the signification of her Majesty's pleasure". The Governor was *obliged* to reserve Bills in relation to certain matters and enjoyed a discretion in relation to others. The obligatory power to reserve was another means of Imperial oversight. Certain provisions of the Constitution Act 1852 were automatically reserved from change, including those relating to the salary of the Governor and the sum allocated for native purposes.[28] Also reserved was section 73 of the Constitution Act 1852 which enshrined in statute the Crown's right of pre-emption (Article II of the Treaty of Waitangi), and section 71 which provided for Māori customary law to prevail over both English and colonial law in districts set aside for that purpose (a power which was never utilised).[29]

In practice, reservation powers allowed the intervention of the United Kingdom Government in the New Zealand legislative programme at three points: in its instructions to the Governor about which classes of legislation were to be reserved (section 57);[30] in the advice tendered to the Crown by United Kingdom Ministers about the giving and withholding of assent to Bills actually reserved; and in the form signifying royal pleasure upon the reserved Bill.[31] In addition to such political checks, the New Zealand legislature was legally constrained: it did not have the capacity to make valid laws with extraterritorial effect (such as measures relating to shipping,[32] and certain aspects of immigration and trade); and there was always the potential for a law to be found by a court to be repugnant for inconsistency with the "laws of England"[33] (a vague legal test). No reserved Bill would have force until the Sovereign's

28 This had the effect of freezing the allocation for native purposes. The 1857 Amendment to the Constitution Act automatically reserved 21 sections.

29 This provision was repealed in 1862. Hanna Wilberg concludes that the "main enduring effect of the reserved provisions was simply to lock in the imperial Crown's supervisory powers in general; they did not include any effective protection for Treaty rights in particular" though the disallowance of the Indemnity Act in 1877 would appear to indicate some limited effectiveness. See Hanna Wilberg "Facing Up to the Original Breach of the Treaty?" [2007] NZ Law Review 527 at 535.

30 Royal Instructions required the Governor to reserve Bills according to their subject matter until 1907: see Robson (1967), above n 25, at 61. Classes included divorce, discipline of the armed forces, rights of absentee British subjects, Bills previously disallowed.

31 1926 Imperial Conference Report [1927] I AJHR A6.

32 In addition ss 735 and 736 of the Merchant Shipping Act 1894 (UK) 57 & 58 Vict c 60 also required shipping legislation to be reserved.

33 See DB Swinfen *Imperial Control of Colonial Legislation 1813–1865: A Study of British Policy towards Colonial Legislative Powers* (Clarendon Press, Oxford, 1970) at 53–63.

assent had been notified. Two reserved Bills failed to obtain royal pleasure after 1900.[34]

The *discretionary* power in the Governor to reserve or amend legislation was controversial especially in relation to whether the Governor acted on the advice of United Kingdom or New Zealand Ministers. Robson suggests that after 1892 the Governor was required to accept the advice of his New Zealand Ministers in relation to discretionary reservations unless Imperial interests were affected and "save in the most exceptional circumstances".[35] In practice, though, "New Zealand Ministers were sensitive to the wishes of the Imperial government and were prepared to amend Bills to which the Imperial Government objected".[36]

John Martin records that in addition to the two instances in which the British Government disallowed Acts which had already received the Governor's assent, there were five occasions on which it notified that it would refuse assent to reserved Bills: the Native Territorial Rights Act 1858 (which would have allowed for direct settler purchase of Māori land circumventing the Crown's right of pre-emption), the Picton Railway Bill 1861, The Governor's Salary Bill 1867, the Extradition Bill 1873 and the Administration Bill 1878). On six further occasions the Bills became void after assent was withheld for two years and on numerous occasions amendments were negotiated.[37]

Amendments

Section 56 of the New Zealand Constitution Act 1852 also gave the Governor power to delay assent and by message return a Bill to the House with proposed amendments. Even after disallowance had fallen into disuse, New Zealand governments maintained what had come to be seen as the useful practice of advising the Governor or Governor-General to introduce or propose amendments to a Bill by means of a Governor or Governor-General's message to Parliament. That became the standard way in which a government introduced or proposed amendments to a Bill. The Shipping and Seamen Amendment Bill 1948, for example, after submissions had been made to a select committee, was returned to the House with proposed amendments by a message from the Governor-General. The same happened with a Bill to amend the Licensing Act in 1949.[38] In both cases the amendments were advised by the New Zealand

34 Robson (1967), above n 25, at 61.
35 At 61.
36 Robson (1954), above n 25, at 37.
37 Martin, above n 21, at 55.
38 In that case the Governor-General's message was referred to the committee and the amendments proposed by the Governor-General were considered the next day.

government of the day.[39] The government defended the manner in which the amendments had been introduced on the basis that it would be easier for lawyers to find all the amendments in one place rather than to have them scattered throughout various miscellaneous Bills. Ronald Algie, the Member of Parliament for Remuera at the time, rejected that rather opportunistic rationale. He argued that the power of reservation in section 56 was spent and should no longer be used, given the constitutional changes wrought by New Zealand's adoption of the Statute of Westminster, asking: "Why should we concede to our Governor-General a power over our Parliament which is greater than the King himself would claim with regard to the Imperial Parliament?"[40]

Why indeed? Algie's arguments eventually won the day. By the time the Governor-General's legal power to propose a Bill or amendment to a Bill by a message to Parliament was formally repealed by the New Zealand Constitution Amendment Act 1973, the procedure had long fallen into disuse.

Algie had the right side of the constitutional argument. Powers to introduce Bills, and, in particular to introduce amendments, through an exceptional process without possibility of debate properly belong to a period before the New Zealand legislature became fully self-governing. They can only be understood as part of the New Zealand legislature's gradual emergence as a law-making body with a full power to make laws. The former practices of the colonial era do not indicate a place for the Governor-General's personal involvement in the legislative process, other than the continuing function of signing a Bill passed by Parliament in signification of the royal assent.

Amending errors

The Governor-General's power in section 56 of the New Zealand Constitution Act 1852 had also been used by the Governor-General to correct slips and errors. The Officials Committee in 1986 considered whether the Governor-General's power to return Bills to the House with suggested amendments for the purposes of correcting minor slips and errors should be revived, especially given the speed at which legislation was often passed and the absence of a second chamber. It concluded that the convenience of such a power was not sufficient justification.

The Standing Orders of the House of Representatives now confer a power on the Clerk to make minor corrections before the fair copies proceed to royal

39 (1948) 283 NZPD 3148–3152.
40 (1948) 284 NZPD 4303–4309.

assent.[41] Nevertheless, occasionally mistakes will be missed. McGee gives two examples.[42] The New Zealand practice suggests that any remaining errors (such as the wrong copy being sent for assent) should be cured by further legislation rather than by the Governor-General's withdrawal or revocation of assent. Once the assent to an Act has been given, the Act is treated as valid, but it is not necessarily in force. The default rule is that the Act comes into force the day after assent.[43] Fortunately, many modern statutes name a later date on which they come into force — allowing time for administrative and other measures to be set in place. This also gives time for corrections to be made before an Act comes into force.

In 1976 the Australian Governor-General rescinded his purported assent because the Bill presented had not passed through both Houses. The Attorney-General advised that the assent had "no effect in law" and therefore could be validly revoked.[44] This happened again in 2001 when the Bill which had received assent did not include all of the material agreed to by both Houses.[45] McGee suggests that assent may be revoked in New Zealand should there be a fundamental error in the manner and form by which the presented Bill has been passed, and failing action by the House of Representatives.[46] This could be on the advice of the Attorney-General. Our view is that it is unlikely to come to that, given the Clerk's and the Attorney-General's role in preparing Bills for assent (discussed below).

A constitutional safeguard?

We turn now to consider whether the requirement of royal assent could ever be used as a constitutional safeguard in the modern constitution.

The courts

There have, in recent times, been legal challenges which have sought to prevent a Bill from being presented to the Governor-General for his or her signature.

41 Standing Order of the House of Representatives 2011, SO 312: "Verbal or formal amendments: In preparing the bill for the Royal assent, amendments of a verbal or formal nature may be made and clerical or typographical errors may be corrected in any part of the bill by the Clerk."

42 McGee, above n 16, at 393. One was the Sharebrokers Bill 1872: (1872) 12 NZPD 18; and the other the Electoral Act Amendment Bill (No 3) 1996: (1996) 553 NZPD 11302–11303.

43 Interpretation Act 1999, s 8.

44 C Harris (ed) *House of Representatives Practice* (5th ed, Department of the House of Representatives, Canberra, 2005) at 396. See also McGee, above n 16, at 393–394.

45 McGee, above n 16, at 393.

46 At 393.

In *Smith v Attorney-General*, Ellis J suggested that "in some extreme situation superior Courts could indicate that the Governor-General should not consent [sic] to a particular Act".[47] Though the actual claim was ultimately unsuccessful, in *Westco Lagan Ltd v Attorney-General*,[48] McGechan J suggested that the courts were able to entertain an inquiry into whether the correct procedures (manner and form requirements) have been followed in the enactment of legislation and in a proper (and presumably exceptional) case could intervene to prevent assent from being given.

McGechan J's suggestion in *Westco Lagan* that judges could possibly prevent a Bill from being presented for assent provoked a strong reaction from the Parliamentary Privileges Committee. It considered that the submission of a Bill for royal assent was a proceeding of Parliament in relation to which the courts are constitutionally restrained from intervening by article 9 of the Bill of Rights 1689 (UK). It argued that under Standing Order 309, when the Clerk submits a Bill for assent he or she is effectively transmitting a Bill from one part of Parliament to another. Parliament has for centuries been jealous of its powers to regulate its own procedures. In addition, the House has its own checks on the compliance of Bills with the law.

McGechan J's indication of a willingness to preserve for the judges a potential role in intervening before a Bill is presented for assent in an exceptional case is in many ways similar to the Governor-General's potential power to refuse assent to Bills itself. There may be some value served in framing an additional potential constitutional safeguard even if it is one reserved for the most exceptional circumstances and it is never used. But if the real concern in *Westco* was to prevent the passing of a law that breached individual rights in a more "routine" way (the substantive controversy being whether the claimants had been denied proper compensation for breach of contract), then there are other, better, ways to ensure that this does not happen. A Bill of Rights giving judges the power to invalidate legislation would be one such mechanism.

The Governor-General and other actors

Despite the fact that the power to refuse assent has for hundreds of years been constrained by constitutional convention and that legal attempts to stop the Governor-General from giving assent have been consistently unsuccessful in New Zealand, the idea that the Governor-General's personal discretion to

47 *Smith v Attorney General* HC Wellington CP 950/89, 11 June 1990 at 6.
48 [2001] 1 NZLR 40 (HC).

refuse assent serves as an effective kind of constitutional safeguard seems to persist in the public imagination. The Officials Committee which drafted the Constitution Act 1986 said that "[i]n all but the most extraordinary circumstances the refusal of assent would be unthinkable. It would immediately produce a crisis of the first order."[49]

Joseph suggests that the power might exist in two circumstances: where to grant the royal assent would be unlawful (for example, where a Bill extending the term of Parliament has not received the 75 per cent majority required by the Electoral Act 1993); or where government legislation seeks to usurp representative democracy.[50]

These two circumstances raise distinct constitutional issues. In situations in which the House of Representatives has not followed its own procedures or has not been properly constituted, then a refusal of assent is not properly viewed as a breach of the convention that the Governor-General ought to act on advice, and neither does it squarely raise separation of powers arguments. Rather, it raises a prior question of whether the Bill presented for assent has "been passed by the House of Representatives".[51] In such a case the Clerk of the House and the Attorney-General potentially exercise critical constitutional roles in ensuring that a Bill does not proceed to assent. Though the Attorney-General's certificate is now largely anachronistic, it could still arguably be withheld if the Attorney-General were to take the view that the House of Representatives was not lawfully constituted to pass the measure.[52] The Clerk is also required to form an independent judgement about whether the Bill has been passed by the House. The judges too may potentially assert a role as indicated by McGechan J in *Westco* — not interfering in the proceedings of Parliament as the Privileges Committee alleged, but defining how Parliament must be constituted in relation to a certain question.[53] In such a case, the Governor-General would be acting as part of the Parliament rather than the executive and would be unlikely to be acting alone.

The second scenario identified by Joseph where the question of a refusal to grant assent may arise is when a fundamental premise of democracy is put at risk (for example, removing access to the courts). This example raises the question more squarely whether the Governor-General could ever refuse

49 *Constitutional Reform: Reports of an Officials Committee*, above n 1, at 3.47.
50 Joseph, above n 5, at 742–743.
51 Constitution Act 1986, s 16.
52 There are instances in Australia of Attorneys-General using the procedure to delay Bills for politically partisan reasons — but this is a misuse of the procedure. We are grateful to Tim Workman from the Office of the Clerk of the House of Representatives for information about this practice.
53 See, for example, *Attorney-General for New South Wales v Trethowen* [1932] AC 526 (PC) at 540–541. Fogarty J in *Taylor v Attorney-General* [2016] 3 NZLR 111 assumed the judicial enforceability of entrenched provisions.

to assent in his or her own discretion or against advice. Even in this kind of case, the Attorney-General potentially has an opportunity to exercise an independent judgement about whether the Bill contains (in the words of the Attorney-General's certificate) "anything that requires the withholding of assent". An advantage of emphasising the constitutional role of the Attorney-General, the Queen's first legal adviser, is that it multiplies the sites of possible "advice" to the Governor-General.[54] This strengthens the Governor-General's arm and also makes it politically more difficult for a Prime Minister to advise the recall of a Governor-General who has indicated his or her likely refusal of assent.[55]

We would emphasise, however, that these powers are only ever likely to be exercised, or threatened, in the *most extreme* cases. The more commonly imagined scenario involves a Governor-General with enormous popular or very strong sectional support refusing on a point of principle to assent to legislation perceived to be unjust. If a Governor-General were so to refuse in such circumstances, a determined government of the day could advise the Sovereign to dismiss the Governor-General and to appoint another person to the office who is likely to be more amenable to its wishes. Such challenges to the neutrality of the Governor-General's office would likely place the survival of the institution of the monarchy and Governor-General itself at risk. Alternatively, it might be thought that the Governor-General ought in these circumstances to "get in first" and dismiss the government. However, the Governor-General's power to do so is itself constrained by constitutional convention, as we discussed in Chapter 10. Such an action too would place the neutrality and potential survival of the Governor-General's office at risk.

If the Governor-General's power to refuse assent is a safeguard then it is an unreliable one and one that could not be used often and perhaps only once. If there is a need felt to stop substantively unjust or discriminatory laws from being passed or taking effect, there are other constitutional mechanisms better able to achieve this, which take us beyond the scope of this book.

Consent to Bills

In the previous section, we have been talking about the assent to Bills. This is to be differentiated from the *consent* procedure. The Sovereign's consent is required before certain Bills are allowed to proceed in the House. This

54 The Clerk's role could also be enhanced for this kind of scenario.

55 See Chapter 10 Guardian of the Constitution?, under the subheading The dismissal of Gough Whitlam, at 215.

is currently recognised in Standing Order 313 of the House of Representatives. It requires that:

> **313 Members' bills, local bills, and private bills affecting rights or prerogatives**
> No Member's bill, local bill, or private bill that contains any provision affecting the rights or prerogatives of the Crown may be passed unless the Crown has, by message, indicated its consent to that provision.

A critical question is what exactly are the rights and prerogatives of the Crown. The scope of the requirement is potentially quite broad. Legislative measures affecting honours, pardons, the disposition of Crown lands or other property rights, *bona vacantia* (abandoned) property passing to the Crown, the Crown's *parens patriae* (supervisory) role in relation to trusts, the conduct of war, passports, and the royal succession are all potentially covered by this requirement. In the past, for example, messages from the Governor-General have been conveyed to the Speaker signifying the Crown's consent to debate the Pardon for Soldiers of the Great War Act 2000, the Tauranga District Council (K Route Toll) Empowering Act 2000 affecting the disposition of Crown land or other property rights, and the Eden Park Trust Act 1955. We have not been able to find any examples in New Zealand of refusals of consent. That is not surprising. The government of the day is likely to advise the granting of consent to its own legislative proposals; and granting consent to a private member's or local Bill does not indicate approval of the measure or that the government would support it.

A similar procedure has achieved some recent limited notoriety in the United Kingdom. Consent is required in the United Kingdom for a wider range of matters than in New Zealand, including matters relating to the Queen's *personal* property, the royal household, and the Duchy of Lancaster. The Prince of Wales's consent as the Duke of Cornwall is also sometimes required. The idea of the Sovereign personally enjoying special legal privileges over property has attracted criticism.[56]

Another criticism of the procedure in the United Kingdom has been that it is the government of the day which advises consent. The Queen, on the advice of the government of the day, controversially declined her consent for debate on a private member's Military Action Against Iraq (Parliamentary Approval)

56 See, for example, Steven Swinford "Royal consent is 'arcane' and could be abolished, MPs say" *The Telegraph* (online ed, UK, 26 March 2014) <www.telegraph.co.uk/news/uknews/queen-elizabeth-II/10722828/Royal-consent-is-arcane-and-could-be-abolished-MPs-say.html>; and Robert Booth "Ministers accused of exploiting royal veto to block embarrassing legislation" *The Guardian* (online ed, UK, 15 January 2013) <www.theguardian.com/uk/2013/jan/15/ministers-exploited-royal-veto-legislation>.

Bill. This effectively stopped parliamentary debate on the United Kingdom's involvement in Iraq.[57] The advice was in breach of a convention requiring the government to advise the Crown to consent to a Bill even when the government does not support the measure.

In New Zealand no similar controversies have arisen. Unless it can be shown still to serve a useful purpose, we recommend that the consent procedure should be abandoned in New Zealand. There is already protection of the Crown's prerogative against inadvertent legislative erosion in section 27 of the Interpretation Act 1999. It provides that no enactment binds the Crown unless the enactment expressly provides that the Crown is bound by the enactment. The Parliamentary Counsel Office regularly considers these issues when deciding whether to include an express provision binding the Crown. Statutes which relate to large areas of prerogative power typically include a proviso protecting the prerogative. The Foreign Affairs Act 1988, section 13, for example, provides that:

> Nothing in this Act extinguishes any power or authority that, if this Act had not been passed, would be exercisable by virtue of the prerogative of the Crown.

A summing-up

The Sovereign's role in assenting to a Bill before it becomes law is the last significant remnant of the idea of the Queen or King in Parliament. The Sovereign or her representative has never refused assent contrary to advice in New Zealand, or for hundreds of years in England. The constitutional memory of a Sovereign's power to refuse assent goes back to a time before the New Zealand legislature had full law-making power and when the United Kingdom authorities exercised their powers to disallow or refuse to approve a Bill passed by the General Assembly in order to protect its Imperial interests. All attempts to seek judicial intervention to prevent transmittal of a Bill to the Governor-General for signature have been unsuccessful for reasons relating to the separation of powers and comity between the different branches of government.

The reasons why a Governor-General should not now become involved in what are essentially political controversies have been fully canvassed in Chapter 10. There is, however, a tension between the Governor-General's duty to maintain political neutrality and act in accordance with ministerial advice

57 (23 July 1999) 355 GBPD HC 1545. See further on the UK experience, House of Commons Political and Constitutional Reform Committee "The impact of Queen's and Prince's Consent on the legislative process: Eleventh Report of Session 2013–14" (HC 784, 26 March 2014). Ministers tend not to advise the Queen to withhold consent, but simply do not seek consent in the first place.

to assent to a Bill and the fact that a Bill does not become law until that assent has been given. That perceived tension may, in an extreme case, be important in helping to maintain constitutional principles. The Governor-General might be faced with an extremely difficult decision. Before that point is reached, however, both the Clerk of the House and the Attorney-General would have also had important roles to play in the process of making sure that the Bill was in a form in which it would be proper to present it for assent. The Governor-General would not be acting alone. It should, however, be remembered also that, if there are serious worries about the possibility that legislation may be inconsistent with fundamental constitutional principle, there are other constitutional protections which could be put in place.

In the absence of evidence that the current parliamentary rule which requires the Sovereign's consent to the passing of Bills which affect the Sovereign's rights, powers and privileges serves a useful purpose, the rule should be abandoned.

CHAPTER 12

The Governor-General and the Administration of Justice

1
THE QUEEN AS THE FOUNT OF JUSTICE

The Sovereign is not only "in parliament"; she is also the "fount of justice". In this chapter we consider another remnant from a time of personal rule — this time in relation to the administration of justice. According to Blackstone writing in the 18th century, "the original power of judicature is lodged in society at large"[1] but for practical reasons this power has been entrusted to the Sovereign who appoints judges, erects courts, confers jurisdiction and lends his name to proceedings.[2] By the time Blackstone was writing, it had long been viewed as "impossible as well as improper, that [the Sovereign] should *personally* carry into execution this great and extensive trust".[3] Nevertheless, Blackstone considered that the courts of justice derived their power from the Crown (an emanation of the prerogative) and that the King "is supposed in contemplation of law to be always present".[4] Many of these ideas, which once served more functional purposes, are now primarily symbolic — though not entirely so.

1 George Tucker (ed) *Blackstone's Commentaries: Book II* (William Young Birch & Abraham Small, Philadelphia, 1803) at 266.

2 This is a partial acknowledgment of the fact that justice was originally local and communal.

3 Tucker (ed) *Blackstone's Commentaries: Book II*, above n 1, at 266. As early as 1328 the Statute of Northampton provided "that no royal command should disturb the course of law": see Peter Archer *The Queen's Courts* (2nd ed, Penguin Books, Harmondsworth (UK), 1963) at 27.

4 George Tucker (ed) *Blackstone's Commentaries: Book IV* (William Young Birch & Abraham Small, Philadelphia, 1803) at 24. Famously, Bentham took objection to Blackstone's notions of the Crown as serving such a central role in the Constitution. Blackstone is not always considered to have reflected the ideas of his own time, but rather much earlier ideas.

The Sovereign's power in relation to the administration of justice has now been largely superseded by statute. The early courts in New Zealand were established by authority of the Governor under his Letters of Commission but one of the first acts of the New Zealand Legislative Council constituted under authority conferred by the United Kingdom Parliament was to constitute the original Supreme Court of New Zealand — now the High Court. It is unlikely a court today could be established without some kind of statutory authority.[5] High Court Judges are still appointed by the Governor-General on behalf of the Sovereign but in the exercise of statutory rather than prerogative power and now following the advice of the Attorney-General. The judicial oath requires a judge to swear to "well and truly serve Her [or His] Majesty. . .".[6] But while the powers to remove judges remain in the Sovereign or Governor-General, such powers can only be exercised when statutory conditions have been met, and on advice.[7]

Some of the other indications of the Sovereign's role as fount of justice are more subtle, but no less fundamental. The reason that it is the Crown which prosecutes criminal offences is that (in Blackstone's words) "the King, in whom centres the majesty of the whole community, is supposed by the law to be the person injured by the infraction of the public rights belonging to that community".[8] Serious crimes came to be seen as affronts against the King and the King's peace, and from this derived the rationale for the criminal jurisdiction of the King's courts. Of course, some of these abstractions are not well understood or, indeed, still thought to be appropriate. There have been numerous calls to give the immediate victims of crime a more central role in criminal proceedings and sentencing.[9] Nevertheless, it is these common law understandings about the public nature of crime which remain central to the language and processes of contemporary criminal law.

There are other, still less obvious, ways in which the Crown features in the common law legal system. Centuries-old usages of the "Crown" terminology can be found in the judge-made common law. There is a tradition of referring to the Crown as representing the common good and the public in the way in which Blackstone understood it. This tradition portrays the Crown as the protector of a citizen's liberties and as a kind of moral exemplar. So, for example,

5 *Laws of New Zealand* Courts (online ed) at [3], fn 3.

6 Oaths and Declarations Act 1957, s 18.

7 Section 23 of the Constitution Act 1986 requires misbehaviour or incapacity before a High Court Judge can be removed and only on the address of the House of Representatives. Section 7 of the District Courts Act 1957 sets out the grounds for the removal of a District Court Judge.

8 George Sharswood *Commentaries on the Laws of England in Four Books by Sir William Blackstone: Book IV* (Childs & Peterson, Philadelphia, 1860) at 1.

9 See, for example, Victims' Rights Act 2002.

the ancient writ of *habeas corpus* allowed subjects incarcerated by officers of the Crown to challenge, in the King's courts, the legality of their detentions. The writ has its source in the royal prerogative; it flows from the King's mercy and grace. As White suggests:[10]

> The "liberty" of the "freeborn Englishmen" to challenge their incarcerations through habeas corpus was thus conferred directly by the king: he made his courts available to test the actions of his jailors out of a concern for the welfare of his subjects.

The writ contemplates the Crown as standing between the subject and his officials. In the 20th century, Sir William Wade described the modern law of judicial review which was developed out of the prerogative writs of certiorari, prohibition and mandamus in similar terms: "the King lends his prerogative to his subjects" in order to challenge the decisions of his officials.[11]

In a modern constitutional monarchy which aspires to some notion of the separation of powers, it is generally thought to be inappropriate for either the parliamentary or the executive branches of government to interfere with the administration of justice — and for the good reason that this would potentially undermine the rule of law. There are only two residuary powers in the executive to intervene in the administration of justice and significantly these both confer a discretion on the executive to grant mercy or clemency to an accused or offender. One is the Attorney-General's power of *nolle prosequi* (to decide not to prosecute), with which we are not concerned here. The other is the prerogative of mercy. In the next part of the chapter we will consider the nature of the prerogative of mercy. In particular, we discuss the powers vested in the Governor-General and the basis on which they are exercised, and also the efficacy and integrity of the system as a whole in its present form.

2
ORIGINS OF THE PREROGATIVE OF MERCY

The prerogative of mercy is a historical remnant from a time in which the Sovereign was regarded as central to the administration of justice. Blackstone's

10 G Edward White *Law in American History, Volume 1: From the Colonial Years Through the Civil War* (Oxford University Press, New York, 2012) at 135.

11 William Wade *Administrative Law* (2nd ed, Oxford University Press, Oxford, 1967) at 116.

explanation that the King is the person injured by "the infraction of public rights" led him to conclude:[12]

> And hence also arises another branch of the prerogative, that of *pardoning* offences; for it is reasonable that he only who is injured should have the power of forgiving.

Blackstone's notion that criminal offences are an injury against the King and that hence only he can pardon them again strikes an odd note today. But it does help us to think about the prerogative of mercy as something that exists apart from the ordinary judicial system.

The prerogative of mercy is independent of the judicial appeal structure.[13] It provides the last means of potential relief from punishment. Much of the case law has emphasised its role as a protection against the potential fallibility of the criminal justice system, as a "constitutional safeguard against mistakes",[14] and a "safety net".[15] It is not limited to that. It may also be used to recognise mitigating factors as well as the possible injustices of the law itself. As such, it is necessarily flexible and adaptable to a wide range of circumstances. Its adaptability is one of its most valuable characteristics and one which distinguishes it from ordinary court processes. There is, for example, no limit to the number of petitions a person can bring.

Alpheus Todd, writing in the late 19th century, was careful to distinguish the prerogative of mercy from judicial power: though a Governor (or Governor-General) may "remit a sentence, he does not technically reverse it, nor by his action in any way pronounce it wrong. . . . The act of pardoning a sentenced criminal is one of pure clemency: it is in no respect judicial."[16] The Judicial Committee of the Privy Council in *Freitas v Benny* seemed to agree, saying: "Mercy is not the subject of legal rights. It begins where rights end."[17]

There is a difficult tension involved in ensuring that the exercise of the prerogative is robust, fair and equitably applied (removing any "lingering thought that the prerogative of mercy is no more than an arbitrary monarchial [sic] right of grace and favour"[18]) and in retaining its extra-judicial and flexible character. In order to insulate such decisions from political considerations

12 Christian, Archibold and Chitty (eds) *Blackstone's Commentaries on the Laws of England: Volume 1* (Collins & Co, New York, 1827) at [269] (emphasis in original).

13 *Paul v Attorney-General* [2009] NZAR 405 (HC) found that the entitlement to invoke the royal prerogative is not a right of appeal protectable under s 25(h) of the Bill of Rights Act 1990.

14 *Burt v Governor-General* [1992] 3 NZLR 672 (CA) at 681.

15 At 682.

16 Alpheus Todd *Parliamentary Government in the British Colonies* (2nd ed, Longmans, London, 1894) at 348.

17 [1976] AC 239 at 247.

18 *Burt*, above n 14, at 681.

and in response to people's growing expectations about fairness, the process by which it is exercised has understandably become more legal and judicial. We ought not, however, to lose sight of the distinctly extra-judicial character of the prerogative of mercy.

For present purposes, we are focused on the question of how well the current system which allocates the power of pardon to the Governor-General insulates matters from politics and also achieves fair process.

The New Zealand practice

The terms of the delegation of the prerogative of mercy

From the early days of the British colonies, it had been the practice for the Sovereign to delegate to the colonial Governor the prerogative power to grant mercy. According to Roberts-Wray, the reasons for this included the importance of avoiding delay, difficulties in communication with London, and the significance of the unique individual circumstances of the offence and person concerned.[19] As with her other powers, in delegating the prerogative of mercy, the Sovereign retained the power to exercise it herself.[20] Todd considered that by the operation of the Royal Instructions and the colonial regulations "direct and exhaustive authority [was] conferred upon governors of British colonies holding commissions from the Crown to administer the royal prerogative of pardon to any criminal convicted in any court of justice in the colony".[21] He noted that while the United Kingdom Secretary of State *could* intervene on a general question such as the policy adopted by the Governor in exercising the authority, he was unlikely to do so.[22] The power of pardon at that time, then, was a matter for the *personal* discretion of the Governor.

Sir George Gipps, the Governor in Chief of New Zealand, acquired the prerogative of mercy through the 1837 Commission. That document contains the authority "to pardon all such offenders, and to remit all such offences, fines and forfeitures" where there was cause or where the Governor had judged any offender a fit object for mercy. The only exceptions were treason and murder, in which case the Governor had the power "upon extraordinary occasions" to grant reprieves until "our Royal pleasure may be known therein". In 1840 the authority to grant free and unconditional pardons and conditional pardons was also delegated.[23]

19 Kenneth Roberts-Wray *Commonwealth and Colonial Law* (Stevens & Sons, London, 1986) at 341.
20 At 341.
21 Todd, above n 16, at 345.
22 At 342.
23 New Zealand Charter 1840 (Delegated to Hobson).

Until 1892, the Royal Instructions and Letters Patent continued to emphasise the Governor's *personal* judgement in the exercise of the discretion to grant mercy. This reflected Colonial Office concerns that upon the introduction of responsible government the exercise of the prerogative might be too much influenced by political considerations.[24] Over time, however, procedures were developed by which to inform the Governor's exercise of the prerogative. From 1856, an application to the Governor for a pardon in a case involving the death penalty required him to obtain a report of the proceedings of the trial from the judge who presided and the opinion of that judge as to whether the conviction should stand.[25] The Governor could not remit any fine or forfeiture above the value of fifty pounds sterling without "signifying to Us the nature of the offence committed and the amount of the proposed remission, and receiving Our directions thereupon".[26]

The 1868 Instructions relating to capital cases further required a meeting of the Executive Council to which the judge would be summoned. The Governor was not to pardon or grant a reprieve to such an offender unless, on hearing the advice of the Executive Council, he still thought it expedient to do so — again explicitly recognising a place for his personal judgement, and presumably designed to mitigate the political pressure on him by combining the collective advice of Ministers with judicial advice.[27]

The 1892 Royal Instructions changed this practice. They required the Governor to obtain advice in relation to all proposed exercises of the prerogative of mercy. In relation to capital cases they specified that the Governor was to request the advice of the Executive Council, and in other cases, the advice of at least one of his Ministers. Only the effect of a pardon on Britain's Imperial interests remained a matter for the Governor's "own personal consideration".[28]

The current law and practice

The 1983 Letters Patent state in clause 11:

> And We do further authorise and empower Our Governor-General, in Our name and on Our behalf, to exercise the prerogative of mercy in Our Realm of New

24 John Lochiel Robson (ed) *New Zealand: The Development of its Laws and Constitution* (2nd ed, Stevens & Sons, London, 1967) at 11.

25 Royal Instructions to the Governor of New Zealand 1892, cl 23, reproduced in WD McIntyre and WJ Gardner *Speeches and Documents on New Zealand History* (Oxford University Press, Oxford, 1971) at 258.

26 Clause 25.

27 Royal Instructions to George Ferguson Bowen 14 November 1867, cl 14, reproduced in [1868] I AJHR A4 at 4–6.

28 Royal Instructions 1892, above n 25, cl 7.

> Zealand, except in any part thereof where, under any law now or hereafter in force, the prerogative of mercy may be exercised in Our name and on Our behalf by any other person or persons, to the exclusion of Our Governor-General; and for greater certainty but not so as to restrict the authority hereby conferred, Our Governor-General may:
>
> (a) grant, to any person concerned in the commission of any offence for which he may be tried in any court in New Zealand or in any other part of Our said Realm to which this clause applies or to any person convicted of any offence in any such court, a pardon, either free or subject to lawful conditions; or
>
> (b) grant, to any person, a respite, either indefinite or for a specified period, of the execution of any sentence passed on that person in any court in New Zealand or in any other part of Our said Realm to which this clause applies; or
>
> (c) remit, subject to such lawful conditions as he may think fit to impose, the whole or any part of any such sentence or of any penalty or forfeiture otherwise due to Us on account of any offence in respect of which a person has been convicted by any court in New Zealand or in any other part of Our said Realm to which this clause applies.

This formulation, based on the recommendations in the 1980 Report,[29] reflects the provisions in modern independence constitutions of Commonwealth monarchies. It explicitly allows the legislature to confer the power to exercise the prerogative of mercy on other officers or tribunals. Unlike earlier formulations, it does not specify from whom the Governor-General ought to seek advice or by what process, leaving those questions for the local decision-makers and constitutional convention.

The process

The Governor-General receives all requests for the exercise of the prerogative and refers them to the Minister of Justice for advice. The Minister asks officials for a report and recommendations. If the Ministry's recommendation is to refer the matter to the Court of Appeal, section 406 of the Crimes Act 1961 requires that recommendation to be referred to the Executive Council for consideration and decision. A recommendation to refer a matter to the Court of Appeal will come to the Executive Council with the Minister's recommendation, made on the Ministry's advice, and having also been considered by the Cabinet. The Governor-General is usually presiding and may ask questions or make a

29 Alison Quentin-Baxter *Review of the Letters Patent 1917 Constituting the Office of the Governor-General of New Zealand: Report* (Cabinet Office, Wellington, 1980).

comment, but the Executive Council will almost certainly approve it. The provision requiring the referral to be made by the Executive Council reflected the notion that the Governor-General might need to persuade Ministers to do the "right thing". In reality that degree of oversight never operated in New Zealand, but the requirement for the decision to be made by the Executive Council is nevertheless a mark of the decision's importance.

Under the section 406(1)(a) procedure, the matters identified in the reference effectively become the grounds of appeal. The Court of Appeal is empowered to hear and determine the issues surrounding the conviction or sentence as if it were a normal appeal. The ordinary appellate rules relating to admissibility and procedure apply. It has power to dismiss the appeal, quash the verdict, or both quash and order a retrial.[30] Unlike any ordinary appeal, however, an applicant may apply multiple times to the Governor-General for the exercise of the prerogative of mercy.[31]

The fundamental inquiry under section 406(1)(a) is, whether taken individually or collectively, the grounds of appeal demonstrate that there has been a miscarriage of justice requiring the conviction to be set aside.[32] The function of the Court of Appeal is to decide the case on its merits, but in doing so, in the overall interests of justice, it is required to apply established rules and principles.[33] In determining whether, in light of fresh evidence, there has been a miscarriage of justice, the Court considers whether, had the fresh evidence been available at the trial, the jury would reasonably have returned a different verdict.[34] This procedure effectively allows another judicial process once the appeal route has been exhausted.

Section 406(1)(b) allows the Court of Appeal to undertake a more free-ranging inquiry. The Governor-General in Council may request the opinion of the Court of Appeal on any point arising from the case prior to making a formal determination on the application. The Court's role is not to make a formal determination of the questions referred to it but merely to furnish an opinion.[35] It is also clear that the Court is free to conduct its *inquiry* in such a

30 See *R v Barr* [1973] 2 NZLR 95 (CA); *Collie v R* [1997] 3 NZLR 653 (CA).

31 *Burt*, above n 14. For an example of this see the case of Arthur Allan Thomas in *Re Royal Commission on Thomas Case* [1982] 1 NZLR 252 (CA).

32 *R v Ellis* [2000] 1 NZLR 513 (CA).

33 *Ellis*, above n 32. *Paul* found that the entitlement to invoke the royal prerogative is not a right of appeal protectable under s 25(h) of the Bill of Rights Act 1990; above n 13.

34 *R v Dougherty* [1996] 3 NZLR 257 (CA). See also *R v Zachan* CA304/94, 11 August 1995; *Collie*, above n 30; *R v Bain* (2003) 20 CRNZ 637 (CA).

35 Thomas Thorp "Opinion for the Secretary for Justice Re a Petition for the Exercise of the Royal Prerogative of Mercy by David Cullen Bain" (found at <www.justice.govt.nz>) at [36]; *R v Thomas* [1978] 2 NZLR 1 (PC).

manner and in accordance with such a procedure as it sees fit and is not obliged to conform to the rules governing criminal appeals.[36]

Section 406(1)(b) has received little judicial scrutiny. Prior to 2000, the only reference made under section 406(1)(b) was in the case of Arthur Allan Thomas.[37] In that case, two questions relating to Mr Thomas's conviction for murder were referred to the Court. Since then, by Order in Council on 18 December 2000, the Governor-General in Council has referred three points to the Court of Appeal under section 406(1)(b) in relation to the petition by David Bain.[38]

A decision under s 406(1)(a) is implemented by the Court as if it were a decision on an appeal, but any assistance by the Court given under s 406(1)(b) would go back to the Governor-General via the Ministry and then the Minister of Justice with the appropriate recommendation and the Governor-General would act on it accordingly.

Given that historically the prerogative of mercy was conferred on the Governor in the interests of speedy resolution and to insulate the issues from political interference, how well do the present New Zealand arrangements function? Questions have been raised in New Zealand about whether the system is sufficiently rigorous and transparent. Officials in the Ministry of Justice do not have sufficient resources to undertake an independent investigation which would bring new evidence to light. Nor does the process have the accessibility or transparency of other comparable systems. The modern practice in Scotland, England and Wales, and Northern Ireland, for example, has been to establish a Criminal Cases Review Commission to investigate and report on alleged cases of miscarriage of justice. There have been calls for a similar Commission to be established in New Zealand by Neville Trendle,[39] Sir Thomas Thorp[40] and Simon Mount.[41]

Despite New Zealand's comparable prison population with Scotland, the Scottish Criminal Cases Review Commission receives approximately 14 times more prerogative of mercy applications than the Governor-General (an average of 100 applications per year compared with seven to eight).[42] The Scottish Commission referred 127 of the 2,166 applications to the Court

36 *Thomas*, above n 35.
37 Thorp, above n 35, at [39].
38 See CO File 135/14/1.
39 Neville Trendle "The Prerogative of Mercy: A Review of New Zealand Practice" (Ministry of Justice, 2003). See also J Hammington "Royal Prerogative of Mercy: Practices and Procedures in the Ministry of Justice" (Ministry of Justice, 2003) at 35.
40 Thomas Thorp *Miscarriages of Justice* (Legal Research Foundation, Auckland, 2005).
41 Simon Mount "A Criminal Cases Review Commission for New Zealand" [2009] NZ L Rev 445.
42 The SCCRC received 2166 applications between 1 April 1999 and 31 March 2016, the Governor-General 160 applications between January 1995 and 31 December 2015.

of Session over a seven-year period compared to the 15 Governor-General in Council referrals to the Court of Appeal under section 406(1)(a) over a 10-year period. Thirteen of the 15 referrals in New Zealand were "successful". Seven resulted in retrials (though the outcomes of the retrials are not recorded), four convictions were quashed, one sentence was reduced, one stay of proceedings was ordered, and two referrals, both relating to Peter Ellis, were dismissed. This represents an 86 per cent success rate compared with 60 per cent in Scotland.

The high success rate of referrals in New Zealand could be because the Ministry of Justice effectively eliminates all but the most worthy cases for consideration, but it could also indicate that not enough applications are being referred. The New Zealand process is significantly more opaque than the Scottish one. There is limited public information and guidance about the criteria or procedures applied, there is no independent investigation,[43] and it is much slower in processing applications (the average completion time in New Zealand is 11.5 months compared with seven to eight months in Scotland).[44] The current practice (in the United Kingdom as well as New Zealand) also seems to suggest that the idea of clemency has been lost. Almost all of the cases which are referred are treated as if they are appeals in the ordinary legal process.

Powers of pardon have been less politically controversial than compensation payments to people who have been found to have suffered a miscarriage of justice. The questions of whether to make such payments, and their size, appear to be the subject of political judgements. The rejection of unpalatable legal advice from highly qualified persons has raised questions about the nature of the decision-making process. *Ex gratia* payments of this kind are not strictly part of the prerogative of mercy and we do not discuss them here. We would suggest, however, that they should be considered as part of a wider review.

There are issues to be addressed about how the processes surrounding the exercise of the prerogative of mercy could be improved in New Zealand. This is so regardless of whether and how New Zealand decides to reconsider its more fundamental constitutional arrangements. Like many other ancient prerogatives, the authority to exercise mercy is conferred by a range of constitutions — republican as well as monarchical. Looking into the future, the power to grant clemency is likely to remain a part of the New Zealand constitution in some form whatever the nature of the constitution itself.

43 Ministry of Justice "Royal Prerogatives of Mercy Procedures Guide" (October 2007) at 20. The Ministry may sometimes ask the police or outside counsel to carry out further investigations.

44 Note, however, that one New Zealand case took five years to resolve.

3
CONCLUSION

In this chapter we discussed the remnants of the Sovereign's power in relation to the administration of justice. We suggested that the substance of, and procedure by which the Governor-General exercises, the prerogative of mercy ought to be looked at again. In the next chapter we examine another important function which the Sovereign and Governor-General serve in New Zealand's constitution. That is the Sovereign's role as a party to the Treaty of Waitangi.

CHAPTER 13

The Crown as a Party to the Treaty of Waitangi

1
INTRODUCTION

The Queen is a central figure in both the Māori and the colonial stories of Māori–Pākehā relations. The historical sources demonstrate that even before the Treaty of Waitangi, different Māori rangatira (chiefs) sought to establish personal relationships with British monarchs. Mana was central to these dealings, as were ideas of reciprocity and honour. These ancestral meetings would be recalled by later generations. For their part, British representatives, in accordance with the usual British colonial practice, routinely invoked the monarch's[1] name as both a source of power and as a protector of indigenous Māori interests. And while as a matter of British and now New Zealand constitutional law the political aspects of that relationship have changed, the person of the Sovereign has continued to have a symbolic importance, representing as she does the historic promises made by and on behalf of her ancestors, and to play a role in statecraft.[2] Against changing politics and politicians the Sovereign has served as a personal link between the present and the colonial past, between present policies and the historic promises made. This chapter explores some of the constitutional aspects of those relationships.

We begin by briefly recapping who had the right to advise the Queen on Māori affairs according to British constitutional law. Next we attempt to assess

1 In contrast to the practice throughout the rest of the book we sometimes refer to the Sovereign as the monarch in this chapter to avoid as much as possible the controversial debate surrounding sovereignty and the Treaty of Waitangi texts.

2 Janet McLean "Crown Him With Many Crowns: The Crown and the Treaty of Waitangi" (2008) 6 NZJIPL 35–58 argues that the significance may run even deeper to the issue of constituent power.

the significance of the personal aspects of the relationship between certain Māori and successive monarchs so far as we are able to ascertain from the written record and practice in English and conscious that there is no single or pan-Māori version. We then suggest the ways that these historical understandings still play out in the Treaty settlement processes and other aspects of contemporary Māori–Pākehā relationships. Finally, we take a tentative look towards the future.

2
THE TRANSFER OF RESPONSIBILITY FOR "NATIVE AFFAIRS"

In Chapter 2 we discussed the process by which settler governments achieved independence from the United Kingdom. Promises of Māori self-government were not similarly realised. Māori did not achieve representation in the early General Assembly, the provision in section 71 of the New Zealand Constitution Act 1852 (UK) allowing for the designation of Māori self-governing districts was never implemented, and numerous proposals for Māori self-government under the aegis of the Crown were rejected. Instead, the struggles by Māori to continue to govern themselves became subjugated to settler aspirations.

We have already identified the question of who had the right to advise the Sovereign in respect of "native affairs" as a major source of tension between Governors, settler governments and Māori.[3] That history may even help to explain why Premiers and later Prime Ministers established and maintained a practice of keeping Governors and Governors-General at arm's length.[4]

From the outset, government actions in relation to Māori have been consistently performed in the name of the Sovereign or Crown: what *has* changed significantly over time has been the location of the Sovereign's advisers. Initially it was clear that the Sovereign acted on the advice of her responsible Ministers in Westminster: Crown policies in relation to Māori were in practice those of the Colonial Office and associated Ministers in London invoking the Queen's name and power. It is initially to London and the Colonial Office we should look to discover attitudes and policies which informed the English understanding of the Treaty of Waitangi and early colonial policies about land acquisition and native self-government. It was the Colonial Office which

3 See Chapter 2 Building the Modern Constitution, fn 29 ff, at 18–22; Chapter 7 The Office of Governor-General and Commander-in-Chief, after fn 32, at 129–130.
4 See Chapter 10 Guardian of the Constitution?, after fn 4, at 203–205.

issued Instructions to the first Governors of New Zealand and to whom they were answerable.

After the signing of the Treaty of Waitangi, the question of who should advise the Governor and Sovereign on "native" matters (as they were then called) almost immediately became the subject of prolonged controversy. A lack of "firmness" in native matters was among the reasons given for Governor Robert FitzRoy's (1843–45) recall by London (though in fact the Colonial Office policies were conflicted over this period and some of FitzRoy's difficulties were caused by the lack of funds from London). In his first term (1845–53), Sir George Grey warned the Colonial Office against the dangers of local representative institutions that did not include Māori and retained control of native and other matters in the office of Governor.[5] Even after the establishment of the General Assembly, Governor Thomas Gore Browne (with the approval of the Colonial Office) insisted on retaining control of Māori matters, and Donald McLean, the Native Secretary, answered directly to him, while he in turn answered to London. He wrote to Sewell: "as Govr I consider myself a Guardian and trustee for the Native Race and can never willingly delegate my power and responsibilities to a council the members of which are responsible neither to the Crown nor the Native Race, who are liable to constant change and always subject to pressure from their own constituents and the members of the Assembly".[6] In practice, however, the Assembly controlled the greater part of the funds allocated to Māori purposes. Supplementary funds from Britain were not forthcoming. This forced uneasy compromises in which final decisions rested in the Governor and financial limits with the Assembly.[7]

In July 1861, Browne was relieved by Sir George Grey, who took up a second term as Governor (1861–68). By then the Taranaki wars had begun and the Waikato wars were in contemplation. During this term Grey increasingly came into conflict with his generals, colonial politicians, Māori and the Colonial Office itself. Once again, there was a major point of disagreement about who should have the conduct of native affairs. While formally native affairs had now become the responsibility of the local representatives, local ministerial control had not yet been fully implemented. There were serious disagreements about the colonial government's policies of land confiscation and the detention of Māori prisoners, as well as about who should pay for

5 Grey was assisted in his imperial endeavour by William Martin J in *R v Symonds*: see Mark Hickford *Lords of the Land: Indigenous Property Rights and the Jurisprudence of Empire* (Oxford University Press, Oxford, 2011) at 119.

6 Cited in Gavin McLean *The Governors: New Zealand's Governors and Governors-General* (Otago University Press, Dunedin, 2006) at 57.

7 At 58.

the British troops.[8] Instructed by London to withdraw Imperial forces, Grey defied the Colonial Office with the collusion of Premier Edward Stafford.[9] Grey was promptly informed from London of the appointment of his successor, Sir George Bowen. Further Imperial assistance in fighting between the settlers and Māori was withdrawn and from then on the Assembly carried the full burden of its own defence, financially and politically, along with responsibility for native policy. From the time of Bowen's arrival, "the governor, so recently an executive officer, evolved into a ceremonial figure, retaining only a few narrowly defined prerogative powers".[10]

There was no single point at which all control over native affairs moved from the Imperial institutions to New Zealand. The United Kingdom Government's power to disallow or withhold assent to legislation of the General Assembly was exercised several times in relation to Māori matters: for example, the Waste Lands Act 1856, the Native Territorial Rights Act 1859 (which would have circumvented the Crown's right of pre-emption), the Indemnity Act 1866 (which would have given generous immunities for persons acting in suppression of "native insurrection"), the Native Council Bill 1860, and the Provincial Compulsory Land Taking Bill 1863.[11] The Governor also retained power to delay or "reserve" Bills for royal assent. The Colonial Office often used more "subtle methods of control" such as deferring submission of legislation to Her Majesty pending amendments as instructed.[12] Even as late as 1881, the British Colonial Office asked Governor Sir Arthur Gordon to investigate the Parihaka affair at the petition of Te Whiti.[13]

As we have explained, the Crown in right of New Zealand is now a separate political and legal entity. The United Kingdom Parliament has long since relinquished the power to legislate for New Zealand. The British Crown, advised by United Kingdom Ministers, no longer has any political, legal or financial interest or responsibility for matters relating to Māori and the Treaty. When governments now refer to the Crown in relation to the Treaty of Waitangi they mean to refer to the Crown in right of New Zealand. When Queen Elizabeth II speaks or acts in relation to Māori she is advised by her responsible New Zealand Ministers. In the discussions that follow, then, it is important to bear in mind on whose advice the Queen is acting even when she appears to be

8 See, for example, Grey's letter to Newcastle, reproduced in Gavin McLean, above n 6, at 67.

9 At 69.

10 At 71.

11 Hanna Wilberg "Facing Up to the Original Breach" [2007] NZ Law Review 527 at 535 and see further for controversial legislation relating to Māori, John E Martin "Refusal of Assent — A Hidden Element of Constitutional History in New Zealand" (2010) 41 VUWLR 51, 55, 58–67.

12 Wilberg, above n 11, at 536–537.

13 Matthew Palmer *The Treaty of Waitangi in New Zealand's Law and Constitution* (Victoria University Press, Wellington, 2008) at 245.

acting personally. Māori were never given the opportunity to consent to the change in who advised the Sovereign. Personal relationships with successive monarchs have served to maintain at least some continuity between past and present.

3
PERSONAL RELATIONSHIPS BETWEEN MĀORI AND MONARCHS

The Sovereign has served as an important symbol of Māori–Pākehā relationships. From the British side, the Colonial Office and successive Governors often referred to the Sovereign as the protector of aborigines and as having a special interest in and concern for the Māori people.

The preamble to the English version of the Treaty of Waitangi itself begins with the central relationship between Queen Victoria and the chiefs and states Her Majesty's intention to protect and secure chiefly independence:[14]

> Queen [Victoria] . . . regarding with Her Royal Favor the Native Chiefs and Tribes of New Zealand and anxious to protect their just Rights and Property and to secure to them the enjoyment of Peace and Good Order . . . .

The earlier 1835 Declaration of Independence written by James Busby and signed by 25 chiefs at Waitangi (during the reign of William IV in the United Kingdom) contained similar language:

> They also agree to send a copy of this Declaration to His Majesty, the King of England, to thank him for his acknowledgement of their flag; and in return for the friendship and protection they have shown, and are prepared to show, to such of his subjects as have settled in their country, or resorted to its shores for the purposes of trade, they entreat that he will continue to be the parent of their infant State, and that he will become its Protector from all attempts upon its independence.

References to the monarch as the legal source and symbol of British power and also as a protector with a special concern for Māori interests appear in all of the texts leading up to and including the Treaty of Waitangi. The idea of

14 The Māori text suggests that the Queen's main promises to Māori were to provide a government while securing tribal rangatiratanga (chiefly autonomy or authority over their own area) and Māori land ownership for as long as they wished to retain it.

this "special relationship" appeared to be reinforced by the frequently more sympathetic Māori policies of the early Governors as compared with those of the settler governments.

Prompted perhaps by these references and their own observations of the naval and military power of the British Crown, certain Māori, especially from the northern tribes, sought from the beginning to establish a personal relationship with the English monarchs. They wanted to be associated with the mana of the British monarchy and to establish relationships of trust. Gift-giving between monarchs and Māori leaders was important in establishing reciprocity and has continued to the present day.[15]

The Ngā Puhi chiefs Hongi and Waikato successfully met with George IV in 1820.[16] This meeting would later be recalled by Hongi's nephew Heke, as relationships with the British deteriorated. Heke wrote to Queen Victoria in July 1849 and called on her to honour her ancestor's wish that the substance of control should be left with Māori.[17] This idea that the personal honour of the Queen was at stake would be a constant theme of subsequent Māori petitions.

After the Treaty signing, there were numerous petitions and grievances addressed to the Queen and deputations to London to meet with her personally.[18] The Chiefs understandably sought to appeal to the highest authority. It would be a mistake, however, to assume that Māori simply misunderstood the nature of the monarch's personal involvement. Māori were sophisticated politicians. It is likely they were conscious of the different views on Māori policy held by the British authorities, the New Zealand Company, the settlers and later the local representative government and even at times the Governor. The presumption of the monarch's good intentions when asking her to intervene in the conduct of his or her officials has numerous historical precedents. Petitions to Charles I and George III were, after all, cast in a similar style. At least at the beginning the monarch could be treated as having honourable intentions — it was his officials who were bad. In this

15 King William IV, for example, gave Titore and Patuone of Hokianga each a suit of armour for placing a tapu on certain forests so that they would be available for defence purposes against the French: Claudia Orange *The Treaty of Waitangi* (2nd ed, Bridget Williams Books, Wellington, 2011) at 10. Chiefs of Rangiaowhia sent gifts of flour to Queen Victoria. The Colonial Office sent two family portraits of the royal family in exchange. These attracted much Māori interest: Vincent O'Malley *The Great War for New Zealand* (Bridget Williams Books, Wellington, 2016) at 53.

16 Orange, above n 15, at 10. One of the first (thwarted) deputations was that of Ruatara of the Bay of Islands who set out to visit George III in 1805. The ship master refused to pay him or let him ashore: James Belich *Making Peoples: A History of the New Zealanders from Polynesian Settlement to the End of the Nineteenth Century* (Penguin, Auckland, 2007) at 142.

17 Orange, above n 15, at 125.

18 In 1857 Matiaha Tiramorehu conveyed a petition to Queen Victoria in person on behalf of Ngāi Tahu: Graeme W Austin "Re-Treating Intellectual Property — The Wai 262 Proceeding and the Heuristics of International Property Law" (2003) 11(2) Cardozo J Int'l & Comp L 350 at 350.

way loyalty to the monarch could be manifested while the actions of officials could still be disputed. Crucially, honour on all sides was able to be preserved.

As relationships became strained to breaking point with the influx of settlers and pressure for land, petitions to the Queen became more frequent. There are a number of instances in which different chiefs sought to appeal to the Queen as the highest authority. In response to news of instructions from Earl Grey to register all Māori lands, Te Wherowhero, with four other prominent Waikato chiefs, presented Governor Grey with a letter for Queen Victoria. The letter expressed their concern about rumours that the Crown was to take all uncultivated lands and asked for confirmation from the Queen of the reassurances given by earlier Governors.[19] In 1865 and 1866, Wiremu Tamihana Tarapipi sent petitions to the Queen and the New Zealand Parliament in response to the 1865 land policies. The petitions observed that the Treaty of Waitangi preserved Māori mana and rangatiratanga (chiefly authority) and asked the Queen to appoint a commission of inquiry into the land confiscations.[20] In the 1870s the repudiation movement sent petitions to the General Assembly. These petitions are noteworthy in that they "professed loyalty to the Crown" and proposed petitioning the Queen to appoint an office to whom Māori representations could be made.[21]

In 1882 a deputation to the United Kingdom was led by Hirini Taiwhanga of Kaikohe[22] with the backing of northern chief Parore Te Awha. Although the Earl of Kimberley, Secretary of State for the Colonies, initially rebuffed the request for a visit, the petition was presented to the Colonial Office.[23] The basis of the petition was that the *sole* authority in relation to the Treaty was the Queen.[24] The petition stated:[25]

> These things [the disappearance of native reserves] and many of the laws which are being carried into effect are, according to Maori ideas, very unjust, creating disorder amongst us, giving heart pangs and sadness of spirit to your Maori children who are ever looking towards you, Most Gracious Queen; and it is averred by men of wisdom that these matters, which weigh so heavily upon us, are in opposition to the great and excellent principles of the Treaty of Waitangi.

19 Orange, above n 15, at 128.
20 At 180.
21 At 191.
22 At 206.
23 At 207.
24 At 206.
25 Waitangi Tribunal *Te Roroa Report 1992* (Wai 38, 1992) at [7.1].

In April 1884, the Māori King Tawhiao too set off for London. His petition requested the Queen to "confirm her words given in that treaty". The petition complained of the powerlessness of the Māori and made proposals for, among other things, a separate Māori parliament to control land matters, and a Queen's commissioner who would act as an "intermediary", a kind of all-purpose ombudsman, able to represent Māori interests.[26] The petition stated:[27]

> We, the Maori chiefs of New Zealand, have come to this distant land into your presence, on account of the great disaster which has overtaken your Maori race, which is beloved by the Queen and the Peoples of England.
>
> Accordingly we have now swum the ocean of Kiwa, which lies between us, and have reached England in safety, the source and fountain of authority, to the place where the Queen lives, that she may redress the ills of the Maori race inflicted on them by the government of New Zealand who have not directed their attention to right those wrongs up to the present time, and those wrongs are still being committed . . . because there was a tender regard displayed by the Queen to her Maori race, as shown in the Treaty of Waitangi, therefore it is well that those contracts and those ills should be brought before you for your consideration.

Although the new Secretary of State, Lord Derby, refused the requested audience with the Queen, he was prepared to meet with the delegation in person.[28] Derby was more sympathetic than Kimberley had been,[29] but he was forced to admit that Britain no longer had any right to interfere in New Zealand affairs.[30]

Orange records that, in 1913, the King movement funded another mission to England, to appeal to the Crown to rectify breaches of the Treaty. This time the petition was referred back to the New Zealand Government under the procedure that had, by then, become established.[31] On that occasion, however, the petitioners were accorded an audience with King George V and Queen Mary, but only on the condition that no grievances were to be aired. By this time Māori were represented in Parliament by active young leaders who accepted the authority of the elected government and saw the challenge

26 Orange, above n 15, at 212.
27 "Death of the Maori Queen Te Arikinui, Dame Te Atairangikaahu — Parliamentary Debates 22 August 2006" (August 2006) Maori L Rev 1 at 2.
28 Orange, above n 15, at 212.
29 Kimberley had told the deputation that he could not give them an official answer since the deputation had not gone through the official channels, namely the New Zealand Government.
30 Orange, above n 15, at 212.
31 See below, this chapter, under the subheading Waitangi Tribunal, at 268.

as making the government's power work well for the advancement of Māori. From then on, the question of how to implement the Treaty moved more into the New Zealand political domain. The Ratana Church, which had formed a political party in the early 1920s, mounted one last appeal to the King, seeking the appointment of a Royal Commission from England to investigate grievances, including the return of confiscated land. Once again, the petition was simply referred back to the New Zealand authorities.[32]

There is consistency in these petitions over time. The proposal for a Māori parliament and a Royal Commission to examine Treaty breaches had been made several times before (including by Wiremu Kingi to the Governor on the eve of the 1860s New Zealand wars as the British troops were preparing to attack).[33] Many of the petitions made references to the promises made by the monarch's ancestors both in the Treaty of Waitangi and earlier, and all of them proceed in the expectation that the monarch personally will keep her promises or those of her ancestors.

From our perspective, this record of Māori appeals to the Sovereign has greater significance than merely as a demonstration of the increasing inability to draw the United Kingdom Government into questions about the implementation of the Treaty of Waitangi. In the first place, although petitions to the Sovereign were referred back to the New Zealand Government, that government still had an obligation to address their substance. It may not have felt the weight of that obligation very heavily, except by reason of any adverse publicity the petition had attracted. But that publicity and its consequences are, after all, a significant aspect of what any subject probably hopes to achieve by exercising the right to petition the Sovereign — or her representative, the Governor-General. In the case of Māori petitioners, the petitions to the Sovereign helped to keep alive the Treaty of Waitangi as a statement of ongoing obligations. The petitions taken to London also sustained the Māori sense of a direct relationship with the Sovereign in person.[34] This idea was

32 Orange, above n 15, at 232.

33 At 206.

34 During the consultations that eventually led to Parliament's enactment of the Supreme Court Act 2003, abolishing the right of appeal from decisions of the New Zealand courts to the Judicial Committee of the Privy Council, and establishing a Supreme Court in its place, the question arose whether there was a special obligation to consult with Māori on the ground that the decisions of the Judicial Committee took the form of advice to Her Majesty's Privy Council. The then Solicitor General, John McGrath (now the Hon Sir John McGrath), advised that, like other interested groups in the community, Māori should be consulted about the proposed change, but the Judicial Committee was a court in all but name, and the question whether or not it should continue to have jurisdiction in New Zealand was not a matter affecting the Treaty relationship with Māori or any personal bond they might have with the Sovereign: M Richardson "The Privy Council and New Zealand" (1997) 46 Intl & Comp LQ 908 at 909, citing *Appeals to the Privy Council: Report of the Solicitor General to the Cabinet Strategy Committee on Issues of Termination and Court Structure* (Crown Law Office, Wellington, 1995) at 9.

encouraged by Governors and officials in London who reassured Māori of the monarch's concern for their fair treatment.

Of course there is no one single relationship between the Queen and Māori. Not all tribes sought personal relationships with or petitioned the Sovereign. Some tribes were never signatories to the Treaty of Waitangi; tribes fought on both sides of the wars;[35] some iwi strategically divided their loyalties between the British Crown and the Kīngitanga or King movement.[36] Only some iwi were involved in petitions. Despite these political variations, relationships between Māori and the Queen and Crown have been central in the grievance resolution and settlement processes to which we now turn.

4
THE HONOUR OF THE CROWN GIVEN LEGAL RECOGNITION

Waitangi Tribunal

Māori petitions to the Sovereign were met with the formulaic response (still used today) that "it is not a matter in which Her Majesty would interfere". Not only is such a response unhelpful, it does not reveal that the matter is routinely referred to her responsible Ministers. Redress for Māori from the local courts too had been largely unsatisfactory due to new judicial scepticism around the time of the wars about the legal force of Maori claims.[37]

For decades Māori had petitioned the House of Representatives, various Governors and the Sovereign for some kind of independent ombudsman to consider Māori grievances. Eventually, and in the context of the land marches, parliamentarians turned their minds to the Treaty once again. In 1972, Norman Kirk's Cabinet set out to deliver upon its electoral promise to "examine a practical means of legally acknowledging the principles set out in the Treaty of Waitangi". The Treaty of Waitangi Act was passed into law in 1975. It established the Waitangi Tribunal which would effectively become the independent ombudsman for which Māori had petitioned, and for so long.

35 Queen Victoria gave special recognition to Majors Te Keepa Te Rangihiwinui and Rapata Wahawaha for services to the colonial cause by gifts of swords of honour.

36 Hickford, above n 5, at 37.

37 We do not intend to discuss the issue of the domestic legal force of the Treaty of Waitangi here: it is ably discussed elsewhere. See, for example, Palmer, above n 13; David V Williams *A Simple Nullity? The Wi Parata Case in New Zealand Law and History* (Auckland University Press, Auckland, 2011).

The Treaty of Waitangi Act 1975 granted the Waitangi Tribunal the power to interpret the Treaty texts, to elaborate their principles and to hear grievances arising out of them. It was empowered to hear claims arising out of "enactments" (as defined in the Act) or out of a "policy or practice . . . adopted . . . or any act done or omitted . . . by or on behalf of the Crown".[38] In large part, the scope of the Tribunal's power is defined by reference to the Crown. The grant of jurisdiction to the Tribunal makes no distinction between actions of the Crown as advised by settler governments and actions advised by the United Kingdom Government.[39] The Tribunal is given authority to hear grievances and give authoritative interpretations but it has only limited power to grant redress. In relation to the majority of grievances it only has the power to *recommend* redress to the Crown. In practice, that has left the settlement of most grievances to negotiation between the claimants and Her Majesty's Ministers. Once again, the Crown has been given a central place in Māori–Pākehā relationships.

Together, the Waitangi Tribunal, the ordinary courts, and successive executive governments have developed principles to guide the settlement of Treaty grievances.[40] Most of these refer to the nature of the Crown–Māori relationship. The Crown cannot avoid its obligations under the Treaty by conferring authority on some other body, or by divesting assets to private parties. This last point is extremely significant. Many of the institutions which exercise public power (such as local government authorities) are not in fact part of the "Crown" (as it is strictly understood in English and New Zealand law) at all. Central government has had to put in place processes and structures to ensure that public authorities, which are not a part of the Crown, adhere to Treaty principles. An example of the legislature's attempt to comply with that principle can be found in section 4 of the Local Government Act 2002:

> In order to recognise and respect the Crown's responsibility to take appropriate account of the principles of the Treaty of Waitangi and to maintain and improve opportunities for Māori to contribute to local government decision-making

38 Section 6(1)(c) and (d) (conferring jurisdiction) says:

> Where any Maori claims that he or she, or any group of Maoris of which he or she is a member, is or is likely to be prejudicially affected —
>
> . . .
>
> (c) by any policy or practice (whether or not still in force) adopted by or on behalf of the Crown, or by any policy or practice proposed to be adopted by or on behalf of the Crown; or
> (d) by any act done or omitted at any time on or after 6 February 1840, or proposed to be done or omitted, by or on behalf of the Crown, —

39 At s 6(1)(c) and (d).

40 See further Palmer, above n 13, at 112–120, 125–129, 130–151.

processes, Parts 2 and 6 provide principles and requirements for local authorities that are intended to facilitate participation by Māori in local authority decision-making processes.

The courts

The Treaty-derived obligations that govern the Crown–Māori relationship have been considered, rearticulated and enforced by the New Zealand courts in successive judgments.[41] Much of that litigation has been triggered by government policies to divest state assets, the potential effect of which would be to remove the Waitangi Tribunal's jurisdiction and the possibility of Crown redress.

In his affidavit to the Court in the ground-breaking *New Zealand Maori Council*[42] case (the *Lands* case), Sir James Henare stated:[43]

> It's a very moot point whether the Maori people do love Governments in New Zealand because of what they have done in the past . . . The Maori people really do have no great love for governments but they do for the Crown.

The courts for the most part have emphasised processes and principles and focused on the Crown–Māori relationship rather than on the substance of the reparations and remedies. In doing so, they revived the idea of the honour of the Crown (a phrase commonly found in the colonial documents) and created procedural standards for Crown–Māori dealings. This idea of honour, also important in Canadian aboriginal law, builds on and modernises older ideas to be found in the common law tradition. That tradition:[44]

> distinguished between the Crown *per se*, which traditionally stood for what was just and reasonable, and the government of the day, which was susceptible to corruption and misconduct. Appealing to the "honour of the Crown" was an appeal,

41 The leading cases include *New Zealand Maori Council v Attorney-General* [1987] 1 NZLR 641 (HC); *New Zealand Maori Council v Attorney-General* [1994] 1 NZLR 513 (PC); *Te Runanga o Wharekauri Rekohu Inc v Attorney-General* [1993] 2 NZLR 301 (CA); *Ngai Tahu Maori Trust Board v Director-General of Conservation* [1995] 3 NZLR 553 (CA). These cases have been affirmed in numerous recent cases, including *New Zealand Maori Council* [2013] NZSC 6, [2013] 3 NZLR 31.

42 *New Zealand Maori Council v Attorney-General* [1987] 1 NZLR 641 (CA).

43 Andrew Stockley "Parliament, Crown and Treaty: Inextricably Linked?" (1996) 17 NZULR 193 at 213–214.

44 David M Arnot "The Honour of the Crown" (1996) 60(2) Sask L Rev 339 at 340. See also Brian Slattery "Aboriginal Rights and the Honour of the Crown" (2009) 29 SCLR (2d) 433; and Kirsty Gover and Mark McMillan "The Reasonable Settler Executive: The Honour of the Crown in New Zealand and Australia" (unpublished paper).

> not merely to the Sovereign as a person, but to a traditional bedrock of principles of fundamental justice that lay beyond persons and beyond politics.

The modern jurisprudence has created these obligations by operation of law. Changes to political practices have been equally if not more important. Parliament and the executive have changed some of their procedures to reflect their own understanding of what is required of the Treaty relationship.

The Deeds of Settlement

Deeds of Settlement, negotiated directly between Māori and the Crown's representatives, are the means by which substantive redress is agreed. It is the consistent practice in the Deeds of Settlement that it is "the Crown" who acknowledges past wrongdoing and apologises but it is the Ministers who are given obligations when *action* is required. In the context of the Deeds, the Crown appears to symbolise something distinct from the government of the day and represents the connection between past and present. It is the Crown which symbolises enduring relationships. The idea of the "Crown" in Treaty negotiations serves a number of subtle purposes. A common objection to remedying past wrongs is that present generations and governments are not at fault and therefore should not be held responsible for the actions of earlier generations. The Crown acknowledgement and apology means that the negotiating Minister does not have to take direct responsibility for the historic wrongs, it is the Crown which does so. The idea of the Crown at once depersonalises the fault (it is not the fault of the Ministers negotiating the settlements) but simultaneously locates the fault in a personification of the state.

The Deeds record the "acknowledgements" of past wrongdoing (always attributed to the Crown), the distress it has caused, and, separately, an apology by the Crown. It was Hon Douglas Graham's idea as Minister in Charge of Treaty of Waitangi Negotiations that apologies should be given in the Waikato-Tainui and Ngāi Tahu settlements and it is now the invariable practice.[45] Apologies sometimes appear in two different versions in the Deeds[46] — the more poetic of which is to be given orally and the other which will appear in the subsequent legislation. This is an example of a recent apology given

45 Maureen Hickey "Apologies in Treaty Settlements" in Nicola Wheen and Janine Hayward (eds) *Treaty of Waitangi Settlements* (Wellington, Bridget Williams Books, 2012) 79 at 81.

46 At 81.

orally to Ngai Tāmanuhiri by Minister for Treaty of Waitangi Negotiations Hon Christopher Finlayson:[47]

> The Crown unreservedly apologises to Ngai Tāmanuhiri and your ancestors and your descendants for the many failures to honour its obligations under the Treaty of Waitangi.
>
> The Crown seeks to restore its honour and reputation as a Treaty partner and atone for its past failures to uphold the Treaty of Waitangi with its apology and settlement. The Crown hopes to build a new relationship with Ngai Tāmanuhiri based on respect for the Treaty of Waitangi and its principles.

We will return to the Waikato-Tainui settlement and its apology in more detail presently.

There is no consistent practice about how the Crown is referred to in the Deeds of Settlement themselves. Each of the Waikato-Tainui Deeds of Settlement refers to the Crown party as Her Majesty the Queen in right of New Zealand. The Ngāi Tahu deed also names the Crown party as the Queen in right of New Zealand and recalls in a preamble Ngāi Tahu's earlier petition to Queen Victoria. More recent Deeds of Settlement usually refer to the "Crown" rather than "Her Majesty" or "Her Majesty represented by and on behalf of her New Zealand Ministers" as the Crown party. The differences in how the Crown party is referred to do not have any legal significance: this is because the Crown is defined in section 2(1) of the Public Finance Act 1989 to include the Sovereign, but the change from referring to the person of Her Majesty to the more impersonal Crown may reflect a different era and different Māori leadership and the less direct involvement of Ministers in more recent claims. Whoever is formally named as party, however, the importance of restoring honour to both parties, of healing relationships and creating "a new relationship" is pervasive. In a typical acknowledgement, the Ngāi Tahu Deed states: "The Crown recognises that it has failed to act towards Ngāi Tahu reasonably and with the utmost good faith in a manner consistent with the honour of the Crown."[48] The later Tūhoe Deed of Settlement states "there is no greater dishonour than a broken promise"[49] and that the Crown's apology will bring the "restoration of honour".[50]

47 At 80.
48 Ngāi Tahu Deed of Settlement, 21 November 1997, Section 2 at [4].
49 Deed of Settlement between Tūhoe and the Crown initialled 22 March 2013 and ratified by the people of Tūhoe 4 June 2013 at 5.11.
50 At 5.12.

Parliament

Parliament too has also recognised these ideas about the honour of the Crown in the process by which Deeds of Settlement are enacted into legislation. Deeds of Settlement negotiated directly between Māori and ministerial representatives are usually made conditional on the enactment of legislation. The Deeds of Settlement serve as "drafting instructions" to Parliamentary Counsel. Despite the orthodox view that Parliament is Sovereign and can make or unmake any law, a constitutional convention has emerged that Parliament will not alter the substance of any Deed of Settlement. Hon Douglas Graham helped to establish this practice. He argued that it followed from the Crown's obligation to deal fairly and in utmost good faith that the contract between the Crown and the Māori Treaty party should not be reopened by Parliament. The Parliamentary Select Committee confines its scrutiny to the issue of overlapping claims from different iwi and hapū rather than the fairness of the settlements themselves. Only technical changes to correct problems or mistakes are undertaken in the parliamentary process. Ordinary parliamentary practice has been altered to accommodate the special nature of these proceedings and the Crown's special role in them.

Two examples of redress

If the Crown has been central as a symbol of enduring relationships and honour, two examples demonstrate how much the personal connection with the Queen has been part of the settlement of grievances.

The Crown's apology to Waikato

Queen Elizabeth II herself played a part in the process of recording in an Act of Parliament[51] the Crown's apology to Waikato for the wrongs done to them.[52] The English text of the apology (in a slightly abbreviated form) records that the Crown:

> acknowledges that its representatives and advisers acted unjustly and in breach of the Treaty of Waitangi in its dealings with the Kiingitanga and Waikato in sending

51 Waikato Raupatu Claims Settlement Act 1995, s 5, Text in Maori and s 6, Text in English.

52 The apology was included in a Deed of Settlement signed on 22 May 1995 by the Crown and Waikato-Tainui.

its forces across the Mangataawhiri in July 1893 and in unfairly labelling Waikato as rebels;

expresses profound regret and apologises unreservedly for the loss of lives and the devastation of property and social life which resulted;

acknowledges that the subsequent confiscation of land and resources were wrongful, and have caused Waikato to the present time to suffer feelings in relation to their lost lands akin to those of orphans,[53] and have had a crippling impact on the welfare, economy and development of Waikato;

appreciates that, for these reasons, Waikato's two principles are "i riro whenua atu, me hoki whenua mai" (as land was taken, land should be returned) and "ko to moni hei utu mo te hara" (the money is the acknowledgment by the Crown of their crime): accordingly the Crown has agreed to return as much of the land it owns as is possible;

recognises that the lands confiscated in the Waikato have made a significant contribution to the wealth and development of New Zealand, while Waikato has been alienated from its lands and deprived of their benefit.

Accordingly, the Crown seeks on behalf of all New Zealanders to atone for these acknowledged injustices, so far as that is now possible, and, with the grievance of raupatu finally settled, to begin the process of healing and to enter a new age of cooperation with the Kiingitanga and with Waikato.

As part of the settlement, it had been agreed, with the Queen's consent, that, as she would be visiting New Zealand in November 1995, she herself would give the royal assent to the Bill for the Waikato Raupatu Claims Settlement Act. Her Ministers made it clear at the time that the apology was not a personal statement by the Queen but one made by her New Zealand Ministers. On 3 November 1995, the Queen signed the Bill for the Waikato Raupatu Claims Settlement Act 1995 in signification of her royal assent.[54] One of the two copies was signed and presented to Waikato-Tainui at Turangawaewae. Hon. Douglas Graham, Minister in Charge of Treaty of Waitangi Negotiations at the time, has noted the significance of the fact that the tribe now possesses a copy of the Act containing the apology that was signed by Queen Victoria's

53 For an explanation of the reason for including the comparison with the feelings of orphans in the apology see Alex Frame "Raupatu Settlement — Legal Finality and Political Reality" in Richard Boast and Richard S Hill (eds) *Raupatu: The Confiscation of Maori Land* (Victoria University Press, Wellington, 2009) 243 at 258.

54 As to the Queen's power to give the royal assent, see Chapter 11 The Governor-General in Parliament.

descendant. "Symbolically this is of the utmost importance, reaffirming as it does the links between Waikato and the Sovereign."[55]

Lance Sergeant Haane Manahi (Te Arawa, Ngāti Whakaue)

Some years after the final step in the Waikato settlement, the Queen reinforced, in quite a different way, the links between the Sovereign and a neighbouring Māori tribe, Te Arawa, which never signed the Treaty of Waitangi.[56] The story as it concerns the role of the Sovereign begins on 22 July 1943. On that date, Lance Sergeant Haane Manahi of the 28th (Māori) Battalion was awarded a Distinguished Conduct Medal (DCM) for his bravery and leadership in the battle for the taking of the Takrouna escarpment in Tunisia. Later, the battle was recognised as a decisive turning point in the North African Campaign.[57]

Originally, Manahi's superior officers and the whole chain of command had recommended him for the award of the Victoria Cross (VC). The recommendation was considered by senior military staff in London before being submitted to the King for the exercise of his royal prerogative of honour. At some point the typed letters "VC" in the recommending citation were crossed out, and were replaced with the handwritten letters "DCM". It is not clear when the "downgrade", as it was regarded, became widely known. When it did, there was speculation about the reasons.

As a result, Te Arawa, the tribe to which Manahi belonged, came to feel that it, as well as Manahi himself and the men under his command, had been let down. After Manahi died in 1986, a Haane Manahi VC Committee was established to press the New Zealand Government to seek the posthumous restoration of the original VC recommendation. When, by the year 2000, this initiative had failed to produce a positive result, the Te Arawa Maori Trust Board filed a claim with the Waitangi Tribunal.[58]

The Tribunal made a Preliminary Report on 16 December 2005.[59] It found that there was no definitive evidence as to who altered the recommendation from a VC to a DCM, or for what reason. At the hearing, the Crown had explained that, in recent times, various Governors-General had made inquiries of the Palace about the possibility of reopening the question of a Manahi VC

55 Douglas Graham *Trick or Treaty?* (Institute of Policy Studies, Victoria University of Wellington, Wellington, 1997) at 77, cited in Palmer, above n 13, at 247.

56 In telling the Manahi story, we have cited only the published sources, but everything in the public domain is consistent with the classified documents we have also perused.

57 "The Distinguished Conduct Medal" (22 July 1943) *Supplement to London Gazette* 3314.

58 The factual information in the first two paragraphs of this section is set out in the Preliminary Report of the Waitangi Tribunal, below n 59.

59 Waitangi Tribunal *The Preliminary Report on the Haane Manahi Victoria Cross Claim* (Wai 893, 2005).

award. It was clear that, after such a lapse of time, any question of a reconsideration was within the personal prerogative of the Queen. It was not a matter on which it would be appropriate for her responsible Ministers in either New Zealand or the United Kingdom to tender advice. The Queen's Private Secretary had, however, conveyed her view that it would not be right for her to depart, so many years afterwards, from her father's decision that, after 1949, no further bravery awards would be made in respect of actions performed during World War II.[60]

The Waitangi Tribunal explained what was in issue:[61]

> It was clear to us at the hearing that Lance-Sergeant Manahi, his reputation, and official recognition of his gallantry belonged to all of Te Arawa — and not just the tribe but to a generation of Māori and Pākehā who were called upon to make supreme sacrifices for their community, present in the returned servicemen and servicewomen who came to Tamatekapua[62] to support the claim. This coming together of two peoples in cooperation and mutual respect is, in our view, the heart of the Treaty.

The Tribunal considered it unlikely that the actions already taken by the Crown in right of New Zealand (which the Tribunal saw as including the Sovereign)[63] to pursue the reconsideration sought by Te Arawa fell short in a way that could be regarded as a breach of the principles of the Treaty. But it was also clear that the issue had not been adequately resolved. It suggested that the Crown and the Haane Manahi VC Committee should work together in preparing any future agreed submission to the Queen.[64]

On 19 December 2006, the Prime Minister, Helen Clark, announced that His Royal Highness, the Duke of York, would be visiting New Zealand in 2007, and would take part in a special ceremony to recognise the gallantry of Lance Sergeant Manahi. The government had worked with Te Arawa, the Haane Manahi VC Committee and Buckingham Palace on the form of a ceremony that would recognise Lance Sergeant's Manahi's deeds.[65]

At the ceremony in Rotorua on 17 March 2007, the Duke of York, representing Her Majesty the Queen, spoke at length of Lance Sergeant Manahi's exploits, quoting eyewitness accounts by others who had taken part in the

60 At 12.
61 At 13.
62 The famous whare at Te Papaiouru marae, Ohinemutu, where the claim was heard.
63 *Preliminary Report on the Haane Manahi Victoria Cross Claim*, above n 59, at 2.
64 At 17–18.
65 New Zealand Government Press Release "Duke of York to visit New Zealand" (19 December 2006) <www.scoop.co.nz/stories/PA0612/S00366.htm>.

battle and referring to the personal admiration of Her Majesty the Queen for Lance Sergeant Manahi's bravery. Then he continued:[66]

> Today on her behalf, I acknowledge your unswerving loyalty and lament the sacrifice of your young men over many wars. I celebrate with you the strength and courage of your warriors, and the victories to which they contributed.
>
> The 28th Māori Battalion, in which Haane Manahi served, epitomised the spirit of loyalty and courage that we are here to honour today. The Battalion's marching song includes the famous refrain "For God! For King! And for Country!" Today I am honoured to present, on behalf of Her Majesty the Queen, gifts to Te Arawa that reflect those words:
>
> For God: an embroidered altar frontal, destined for St Faith's Anglican Church, Ohinemutu.
>
> For King: a letter from Her Majesty the Queen, expressing her personal admiration for the bravery shown by Lance Sergeant Haane Manahi in the course of his service with the 28th Māori Battalion during the Second World War.
>
> For Country: a sword, to be held on permanent loan from the royal collection, as the Te Arawa Sword of Gallantry for Haane Manahi.

The idea that the Queen might present gifts to honour the valour of the Te Arawa soldier was inspired by the action of Queen Victoria who, in the last year of her life, crocheted eight scarves that were distributed among members of the English and Empire forces, including one New Zealander, who had fought bravely in the South African wars. At the iwi's request, the Te Arawa Sword presented by the Queen has been put on long-term display in the office of successive Chiefs of the Defence Force, as a symbol of Te Arawa's acknowledgement of the sovereignty of the Crown.[67]

Healing the wounds

In this section we have described quite fully two occasions when Queen Elizabeth II personally contributed in a special way to the healing of deeply felt hurts to leading Māori tribes. Other iwi, too, may well have their own stories. The two published accounts that we have retold here demonstrate clearly that the Queen has been willing to travel the extra mile. But the purpose

66 His Royal Highness the Duke of York, KG, KCVO "Speech Notes" in *Ceremony to Honour the Gallantry of Lance Sergeant Maanahi, Te Papaiouru Marae, Ohinemutu, Saturday, 17 March 2007*, a commemorative booklet presented to members of the 28th (Māori) Battalion at a reunion held in 2007, after the visit of the Duke of York, at 12.

67 Te Arawa did not sign the Treaty of Waitangi.

of recounting those stories is not simply to illustrate the importance of the relationship between the Queen and her Māori subjects. It is also to record the leadership given by many men and women, past and present, Māori and Pākehā, who have sought to bring closer together the people who make up the New Zealand nation, and thus to strengthen the nation itself. Those leaders include the Queens and Kings who have reigned over New Zealand, acting in their symbolic role as the Head of State.

What should happen next?

In this chapter we have suggested that the ideas about a personal Queen and an honourable Crown have played a large part in the settlement of Māori grievances under the Treaty of Waitangi.[68] Paul McHugh is of the same view:[69]

> [The] personalisation of the relationship between Crown and Maori has been a consistent theme of the Maori history of the constitution up into the present. The Pakeha tale of constitutional devolution and the growth of a parliamentary people has not been their narrative at all. The Sovereignty of the Crown does not transmute, for them, into the Sovereign of an elected parliament; the Crown and Maori remain distinct.

Not everyone, however, shares the view that this is altogether to the good. Hon Margaret Wilson, a former Minister for Treaty of Waitangi Negotiations, has suggested in a public discussion that the idea of the Crown has sometimes got in the way of Treaty settlements. The idea of the Crown and its honour may obscure the fact that Ministers of the Crown are answerable to Cabinet, Parliament and the electorate.

One line of thought is that moving from monarchy to a republic would leave the colonial past behind, along with historic grievances. We agree with Moana Jackson that:[70]

> . . . whether the government takes the form of a constitutional monarchy or a republic is . . . irrelevant. They are still bound by the terms of the agreement in 1840.

68 See further Janet McLean "Crown, Empire and Redressing the Historical Wrongs of Colonisation in New Zealand" [2015] NZ L Rev 187–212.

69 Andrew Sharp and Paul McHugh *Histories, Power and Loss: Uses of the Past — A New Zealand Commentary* (Bridget Williams Books, Wellington, 2001) at 192.

70 Moana Jackson, cited in A Tunks "Mana Tiriti" in Luke Trainor (ed) *Republicanism in New Zealand* (Dunmore Press, Palmerston North, 1996) 113 at 119.

A number of commentators have suggested that such a move would have to be premised on constitutional agreement of the role and status of the Treaty of Waitangi.

As Mason Durie said, in the context of removing appeals to the Judicial Committee of the Privy Council:[71]

> As with the Privy Council, the link with the Crown and the Sovereign has long-standing significance and offers some prospect of protection against unilateral action by government. Though symbolic only, it is a reminder that the Treaty was signed not with the settler government but with the British Crown, and is further evidence of a lack of complete trust in the government of New Zealand to act fairly and in a manner consistent towards the Treaty of Waitangi. However, many Māori also feel that the move towards a republic is inevitable and that it would present an opportunity to develop a written constitution within which the Treaty of Waitangi was entrenched and the position of Māori as tangata whenua enhanced.

Bruce Harris agrees that:[72]

> A decision to formalise Maori interests in constitutional law, or to leave the matter to ongoing dialogue, is a political prerequisite to addressing the issues in respect of the future of the monarchy and whether New Zealand becomes a republic . . .

Māori entered into a relationship with the imperial Crown and not with settler governments. The political and legal facts changed — and they did so without explicit Māori consent. Should the party who treats with Māori change again — that may need some significant degree of Māori consent. The requirement of special consent from the Māori people may make New Zealand different from many other parts of the Commonwealth if it were to consider a move to a republic.

71 Mason H Durie *Te Mana, Te Kāwanatanga: The Politics of Māori Self-Determination* (Oxford University Press, Auckland, 1998) at 234.

72 Bruce V Harris "The Constitutional Future of New Zealand" [2004] NZ Law Review 269 at 290.

CHAPTER 14

Exercising the Head of State Role

1
INTRODUCTION

In the 1980s, two concepts that had been part of the unwritten constitution were spelt out in the written law. The first was that the Sovereign in right of New Zealand is the Head of State.[1] The second was that the Governor-General is the Sovereign's representative in New Zealand.[2] When read together, the two statements support the perception that a present-day Governor-General "exercises the Head of State role".[3] The term "Head of State" originated in the foreign relations context. In the first part of this chapter we consider the Head of State role as that concept was originally understood in relation to the Governor-General's role in the conduct of New Zealand's international relations. In the second half we consider separately the Governor-General's evolving role in relation to the domestic life of the New Zealand nation — a "Head of State" role as it is more commonly understood in modern parlance.

2
INTERNATIONAL RELATIONS

Head of State at international law

The role of a Head of State has long been recognised in public international law. When the modern "law of nations" was still evolving, all of the European

1 Constitution Act 1986, s 2.
2 Letters Patent 1983; Constitution Act 1986, s 2.
3 <http://gg.govt.nz/>.

nations were monarchies. The monarch was viewed as representing the sovereignty of the state in every aspect of its interaction with other states, and therefore as its Sovereign.[4] When some states, such as France and the United States of America, became or were born as republics, headed by a "President" instead of a Sovereign, it was necessary to find a generic term which would include not only all Sovereigns but also all other heads of a state, whatever the name by which they were known in their own country. From that time on, all states, whatever the nature of their internal systems of government, have been seen, in international law, as having a "Head of State".[5]

Constitutionally, the conduct of foreign relations is essentially the responsibility of the executive branch. There are important questions about the extent to which the government should interact with Parliament before committing the country to treaty obligations or to participation in armed conflict, or even in peacekeeping, but those questions are outside the focus of this book. So also, in those contexts, is any involvement of the courts. We focus only on the things done by the Governor-General in the foreign relations field which can be seen as the exercise of the "Head of State" role.

In the foreign relations field, Heads of State act in person in maintaining diplomatic relations with other states. They issue credentials to their own state's Ambassadors or other Heads of Mission, and accept the credentials of the Ambassadors or other Heads of Mission issued by other Heads of State. They make Head of State visits to other countries, and receive visiting Heads of State. They may make treaties on their country's behalf with other Heads of State, but those are now rare. They used also to declare war and conclude peace, but, in the era of the United Nations, war, except in self-defence, is no longer a legitimate instrument with which to pursue the interests of the state.

Those are the four areas which are within the exclusive province of Heads of State by reason of their status in international law. Accordingly, in exercising the Head of State role in any of those contexts, the Governor-General represents the state of New Zealand and his or her official acts potentially engage New Zealand's international responsibility.[6] The Governor-General must therefore act in accordance with international law, and he or she will also enjoy its protection. Some of those official acts, such as the acceptance of the credentials of a foreign Ambassador, or the signing, on behalf of New Zealand, of a treaty with another state, may also have consequences, or may require further provision, in New Zealand's domestic law.

4 H Lauterpacht (ed) *Oppenheim's International Law* (8th ed, Longmans, London, 1955) [*Oppenheim*] at 346.

5 At 341.

6 Articles on Responsibility of States for Internationally Wrongful Acts, UN Doc A/56/10 (2001), art 4.

As we explained in Chapter 8,[7] the Sovereign has now authorised the Governor-General of New Zealand to do everything in the international relations field that she or her predecessors would once have done in person. The Governor-General exercises this aspect of the Head of State role only on the advice of the Prime Minster, or, in some cases, the Minister of Foreign Affairs. In this field, the Governor-General has no constitutional discretions. Nevertheless, the Head of State role is distinct from that of the elected government, and it requires good preparation and good judgement, as well as all the other qualities a Governor-General is expected to have, in order to carry it out successfully. We now describe each of the four areas in the foreign relations field in which international law accords an explicit role to a country's Head of State.

The accreditation of diplomats

Issuing the credentials of New Zealand diplomats

When the Sovereign issued the 1983 Letters Patent, she was still issuing in person the letters of credence, and subsequently of recall, of New Zealand Ambassadors, and receiving in London the credentials of foreign Ambassadors to New Zealand. These credentials are, in effect, messages from one Head of State to another, and are separate and distinct from the appointment of New Zealand Ambassadors or High Commissioners made by the Governor-General in the exercise of what now appears to be a wholly statutory power.

At the time of the making of the 1983 Letters Patent, it was made clear to the New Zealand authorities that, although the new instrument would continue to give the Governor-General the authority to issue letters of credence and recall, as well as exequaturs (official authorisations) to foreign Consuls, the Queen wished, for the time being, herself to continue issuing the credentials of New Zealand Ambassadors and receiving the credentials of foreign Ambassadors to New Zealand. Apparently she was worried that foreign Heads of State would wonder why they were receiving a letter of credence from a Governor-General instead of from the Sovereign, in her capacity as New Zealand's Head of State.

Heads of State still communicate formally with one another in the language devised in an earlier century to reflect the international law concept that all monarchs are equally sovereign. They are conceived of as being the members

7 See Chapter 8 The Governor-General in the Executive Branch, under the subheading The New Zealand solution, at 147–148.

of a single family. The Queen would have cast the letter of credence of a New Zealand Ambassador to another monarchy in the following terms:[8]

> Sir My Brother
>
> Being desirous of maintaining without interruption the relations of friendship and good understanding which happily exist between the two Crowns, I have selected My Trusty and Well-beloved XY to proceed to the Court of Your Majesty in the Character of My Ambassador Extraordinary and Plenipotentiary [of my Realm of New Zealand].
>
> . . .
>
> [Then follows a formal recommendation of XY]
>
> I request that you will give entire credence to all that XY shall have occasion to communicate to you in My name, more especially when he shall express to Your Majesty My cordial wishes for Your Happiness, and shall Assure You of the invariable attention and highest esteem with which I am,
>
> Sir My Brother
> Your Majesty's
> Good Sister
> Elizabeth R.

Obviously, no Governor-General could address a foreign Sovereign in those terms.

Eventually, the increasing scale of the international relations of the Queen's larger overseas realms made her continuing involvement unsustainable. Since 1977, the Governor-General of Canada had been signing the credentials of Canadian Ambassadors, although these were still issued in the Sovereign's name. In 2001, the Canadian Government took the view that the time had come to bring the letters of credence of Canadian Heads of Mission abroad fully into line with the role that the Governor-General was already exercising in the field of foreign affairs. Because the Sovereign could not visit a foreign state except as the Queen of the United Kingdom, the Governor-General alone was in a position to serve as Head of State in Canada's foreign relations, and to make state visits abroad on behalf of Canada.

The Prime Minister therefore wished the Governor-General to issue the credentials of Canadian Ambassadors in her own right. Similarly, the credentials of foreign Ambassadors to Canada should be addressed to the Governor-General

8 Neville Bland (ed) *Satow's Guide to Diplomatic Practice* (4th ed, Longmans, London, 1957) at 120.

of Canada, instead of to the Sovereign in right of Canada. Such a change needed only the Queen's agreement. She apparently expressed the wish that, if the existing practice was to change, it would be preferable for at least the larger realms to act in a coordinated way. Accordingly, the Governors-General of Canada, Australia and New Zealand now issue in their own right the credentials of their country's Heads of Mission to foreign states, and the credentials of the Heads of Mission of foreign states are addressed to them. So far as we are aware, that arrangement has been accepted without question by the foreign states concerned.

New Zealand now has diplomatic relations with some 90 foreign states and international organisations, and would itself have accredited an Ambassador to most, if not all, of them. That does not mean appointing 90 different Ambassadors. In these days of relatively easy communications, every Ambassador is likely to be accredited to a number of states. He or she will reside in one of the countries with which New Zealand has the closest relations, and from there will visit periodically each of the other countries to which he or she is accredited. Many other states, especially the smaller ones, follow the same practice. Even so, the formalities associated with the maintenance of New Zealand's diplomatic and consular relations is a significant aspect of the Governor-General's Head of State role.

Commonwealth High Commissioners

We have so far been discussing New Zealand's relations with "foreign" states. That is because the member states of the Commonwealth still regard their formal relations with one another as having a significantly different character. Originally, the concept that the United Kingdom and the self-governing members of the British Commonwealth were all within the sovereignty of an indivisible Crown meant that their relations with the United Kingdom, as well as with one another, were not seen as being governed by international law.

Even when that concept became untenable, they continued to be represented in one another's capitals, not by Ambassadors but by High Commissioners accredited at the Heads of Government level, by letters from Prime Minister to Prime Minister. A New Zealand High Commissioner to London had first been appointed in 1905. In 1949, when India became independent as a republic within the Commonwealth, it insisted that the High Commissioners of other Commonwealth countries should be accredited by Letters of Commission addressed by the Queen to the President of India. As other Commonwealth countries became republics, the same practice was followed.

The present-day New Zealand practice appears to be as follows. All New Zealand representatives to other Commonwealth countries, and all representatives of other Commonwealth countries in New Zealand, use the title "High Commissioner". In the diplomatic order of precedence, High Commissioners rank equally with Ambassadors. The credentials of a New Zealand High Commissioner to one of the Sovereign's other realms are signed by the Prime Minister, and are presented to the Prime Minister of the receiving realm. That is also the practice in respect of the High Commissioners to New Zealand of the other realms. Otherwise, the Governor-General, in the exercise of the Head of State role, issues the credentials of New Zealand High Commissioners to Commonwealth countries which are not realms, and receives the credentials of High Commissioners who represent such Commonwealth countries in New Zealand.[9]

Accepting the credentials of foreign and Commonwealth diplomats

At any one time, more than 120 Ambassadors and High Commissioners are likely to be accredited to New Zealand at the Head of State level. In each year, about 30 new appointees will present to the Governor-General, acting in the Head of State role, their letters of credence, along with the letter of recall of their predecessor. The presentation ceremony at Government House has a distinctive New Zealand character. It begins with a pōwhiri, the traditional Māori challenge, and is followed by the inspection of a military guard of honour. Newly arrived High Commissioners who have already presented their credentials to the Prime Minister will be invited to attend the next such credentials ceremony, be formally introduced to the Governor-General, and join in the ensuing lunch which the Governor-General hosts.

Once Heads of Mission have presented their credentials to the Governor-General, they are entitled to enter on the duties of the office. They also become entitled to the privileges and immunities accorded to them by international law. Since the Bill of Rights of 1689, however, the Sovereign has had no power to waive the law of the land by an exercise of the royal prerogative. In 1708, after the Russian Ambassador to the United Kingdom had suffered civil arrest for debt, the United Kingdom Parliament had urgently to pass an Act according foreign diplomats immunity from suit in the courts of the United Kingdom and its colonies, as required by international law.[10]

9 See <http://gg.govt.nz/content/credentials-ceremonies>.
10 Diplomatic Privileges Act 1708 (UK) 7 Ann c 12.

In 1957, the New Zealand Parliament confirmed that what had become known as "the Act of Anne" was in force as part of the law of New Zealand.[11] The 1957 Act, and with it the Act of Anne, was replaced in 1964 by a new Act[12] giving effect to the 1961 Vienna Convention on Diplomatic Relations, to which New Zealand is a party.[13] It is important to add that, although foreign and Commonwealth diplomats have immunity from suit, unless their governments choose to waive it, the executive retains the right to require the immediate recall of anyone with diplomatic immunity who fails to obey the law of the land.

Treaty-making

An executive responsibility

As in the case of diplomatic relations with other states, the executive branch of government has the constitutional authority to enter into treaties with another state or states, but the exercise of that authority is subject to special safeguards. Any formal step towards becoming a party to a treaty or terminating a treaty obligation must have the approval of the Cabinet. The treaty must also be presented to the House of Representatives, along with a national interest analysis in the required form, for scrutiny and report by a parliamentary select committee.

Treaties now made at Head of Government level

In the ordinary course, a present-day Governor-General has nothing to do with the treaty-making process. Modern treaties are almost always made at the Head of Government level, rather than that of Head of State. That, however, was not always the case. Originally, the European monarchs had themselves negotiated and signed treaties directly with one another. Later, they gave to a "plenipotentiary" what became known as "full powers" to make and sign a treaty in the Sovereign's name. That was the basis on which Hobson's Instructions from Queen Victoria had authorised him to negotiate and sign in her name what became the Treaty of Waitangi.

When, for the first time, the Dominions themselves became parties to an international treaty — the Treaty of Versailles which put an end to World War I and established the League of Nations — King George V was listed as a party to the Heads of State treaty. Then followed a list of the members of the

11 Diplomatic Immunities and Privileges Act 1957, s 3.
12 Diplomatic Privileges and Immunities Act 1964 (UK).
13 Vienna Convention on Diplomatic Relations 500 UNTS 95 (signed 18 April 1961, entered into force 24 April 1964). The treaty entered into force for New Zealand on 23 October 1970.

Commonwealth which would be signatories to the treaty: the United Kingdom, Canada, Australia, New Zealand, South Africa and India, preceded by the word "for . . .". The plenipotentiary of each signed the treaty on behalf of his country.[14]

After that, the Commonwealth countries taking part in the negotiation of treaties at the Head of Government level were listed by name in alphabetical order along with the other states parties. The 1926 Imperial Conference clarified the relationship between the Sovereign and each of the Dominions, but without accepting the notion of a divisible Crown. Satow records that, after 1926, during the negotiation of what were, by implication, Heads of State treaties, there were in some instances:[15]

> difficulties with individual Dominions, notably at the Rome Copyright Conference of 1928.[16] As a result, the tendency during recent years has been to avoid the Heads of State form of treaty entirely in the case of multilateral treaties and to adopt the governmental form instead.

There is a clear implication that the "difficulties" arose from the unwillingness of the Dominions to be listed as signatories in a way that suggested a continuing subordination to the United Kingdom. Then, and for some time to come, the United Kingdom authorities strove as stubbornly as King Canute to hold back the tide of what was clearly becoming a divisible Crown.

Although few, if any, multilateral treaties of general application were concluded at the Heads of State level after 1928, Lauterpacht later recorded that:[17]

> [w]hile it was customary in the past to obtain from the Crown in London full powers for Dominion representatives with regard to treaties of a formal kind, the constitutional conventions of the British Commonwealth of Nations have altered as a result of the achievement of full international status by its members, and it is now customary for the Governor-General to confer the necessary authority.

Clearly, Lauterpacht was speaking about Heads of State treaties, few as there still were.

14 Versailles Peace Treaty 225 Parry 188; 2 Bevans 235; 13 AJIL Supp 151,385 (1919).

15 *Satow's Guide to Diplomatic Practice*, above n 8, at 728.

16 International Convention for the Protection of Literary and Artistic works 1850 UNTS 828 (revised at Rome on 2 June 1928). In all probability, the New Zealand Government would have asked that the Full Powers issued by the Sovereign to the Head of the United Kingdom delegate to the conference should empower him also to represent New Zealand. New Zealand did not ratify the Convention but acceded to it on 4 December 1947.

17 *Oppenheim*, above n 4, at 486.

New Zealand treaty practice

The New Zealand Consolidated Treaty List published in 1996 does not distinguish between Heads of State and Heads of Government treaties, and there is no easy way of ascertaining whether any treaties signed by New Zealand after 1926 were in the first-mentioned category. We have not ourselves come across any reference to the issue of full powers by a New Zealand Governor-General. The members of the European Union have, however, concluded certain treaties at the Heads of State level with developing states within the Commonwealth, among others. In each case the Governor-General of the realm concerned issued the necessary full powers.

Accordingly, in the unlikely event of New Zealand ever wishing to take part in the negotiation and signature of a treaty at the Heads of State level, the Governor-General would have both the authority of the Sovereign, and also her concurrence, in issuing to the leader of the New Zealand delegation to the negotiating conference the necessary full powers.

We turn now to a more likely event — the Governor-General's visit to a foreign state in the exercise of the Head of State role.

Visits to other countries at the Head of State level

Under this heading we look first at the international law implications of a visit to a foreign state at the Head of State level. Then we look at New Zealand practice, especially as it has developed since 2001.

The international law implications

(a) Visiting monarchs

Oppenheim explains that, in international law, a monarch represented the sovereignty of his or her state. Special consideration was therefore due to a monarch when visiting another state, in peacetime and with the consent of the host state's government. The monarch's home state has the right to expect that, while in the host state, the monarch will be accorded certain ceremonial honours. Because the person of the monarch is sacrosanct, the home state also has the right to insist that the personal safety and dignity of the monarch be granted special protection, and an unrestricted ability to communicate with his or her home government. The home state would also expect that any offence against the visiting monarch would be severely punished. At the same time, the visiting monarch must be accorded protection and exemption in the host state from every kind of criminal and civil jurisdiction.[18]

That prescription has the ring of a bygone age, but the underlying principles remain valid. If the Sovereign in right of New Zealand were able to visit a foreign state in her capacity as New Zealand's Head of State, she would be accorded the required dignities, facilities and protection. As we have shown, however, it is impracticable for the Sovereign to represent in a foreign state any realm other than the United Kingdom. It may seem obvious that, if the Sovereign cannot represent New Zealand in a foreign state, then the Governor-General ought to be able to do so. It was some time, however, before it became generally accepted that it was appropriate for a Commonwealth Governor-General to make such a visit and to receive the consideration due to the Head of State in international law.

(b) Visiting Presidents

Oppenheim explains that although the President of a republic represents the state in the totality of its international relations, he or she is a citizen of that state, not its Sovereign. Consequently, the position of a President at home and abroad cannot be compared with that of a monarch, and:[19]

> International Law does not empower [a President's] home State to claim for him the same, *but only similar*, consideration as that due to a monarch. . . . [A] president of a republic is usually addressed in letters from monarchs as "my friend" [instead of "my brother"]. His home state can certainly claim for him such honours as are due to its dignity, but not such honours as must be granted to a Sovereign monarch.

States therefore differ in the extent to which they accord to a visiting President the dignities and immunities due to a visiting Sovereign.[20] That seems likely to remain the case today.

(c) Status of visiting Governors-General

The immediate relevance of the status of a visiting President as compared with a visiting Sovereign is where do visiting Governors-General fit in? Colonial Governors and Governors-General were usually authorised to make visits to neighbouring British colonies, but any other absence from the colony to which they had been appointed required the Sovereign's formal approval. After 1926,

18 *Oppenheim*, above n 4, at 348.
19 At 355 (emphasis added).
20 At 354–356.

that approval would need to be given on the advice of the Prime Minister of the realm concerned. Even so, such a visit appears not to have been contemplated until long after the end of World War II.

Once again, Canada led the way. While some foreign states are not familiar with the office and status of a "Governor-General", it seems that well-chosen and well-prepared-for visits at the Head of State level by a Commonwealth Governor-General are acceptable and successful. The governments of Australia and New Zealand eventually followed the precedent set by Canada. Our understanding is that the three governments now maintain a united front in insisting that, if their Governor-General makes a visit to a foreign state in the exercise of the Head of State role, they must be accorded all due consideration in accordance with international law. If they receive an assurance on that point, it seems that they are usually willing to leave the details of what constitutes "due consideration" to the government of the host state.

The New Zealand practice

(a) Overseas visits for various purposes

New Zealand Governors-General have long made overseas visits for a variety of purposes. They have an audience with the Sovereign after their appointments have been announced and before taking office. All Governors-General also visit the other parts of the Realm of New Zealand at least once in their term. There are also particular occasions on which the Prime Minister and the government may ask the Governor-General to represent New Zealand overseas. In the period since resident New Zealand citizens began to be appointed as Governor-General in the early 1970s, they have regularly represented New Zealand at particular overseas events. These include the celebration of happy events in the lives of other nations or of their leaders, the deaths of those leaders, the commemoration of wars or battles, the honouring of those killed on active service, and visits to members of the New Zealand Defence Force deployed abroad. The Prime Minister decides who will represent New Zealand on such occasions — the Governor-General, the Prime Minister or another Minister, or occasionally both.

While visits for some of these purposes have their own constitutional implications, they do not, generally speaking, involve the Governor-General in what is specifically an exercise of the Head of State role.

(b) Country visits at the Head of State level

As we have shown, however, the Governor-General also makes visits to other countries at the Head of State level. By that we mean that the Governor-General makes the visit in his or her capacity as the representative of the Sovereign in right of New Zealand. He or she must therefore be received at the level appropriate to the Sovereign herself, if she were able to represent New Zealand as an independent member of the international community.

Accordingly, New Zealand has its distinctive values and aspirations and ways of doing things, but it is also committed to behaving as a good international citizen, with the desire for positive working relations with other countries, in its region and in the wider world. Although a state visit takes place at the highest level of the states concerned, their focus is on the bilateral relationship as it affects the interaction of the two peoples.

Sir Michael Hardie Boys made the first state visit of a New Zealand Governor-General, to China in 2000, at the invitation of the President. Dame Silvia Cartwright made over 15 state visits during her time in office. Sir Anand Satyanand made 19 separate trips to 17 different countries and Sir Jerry Mateparae undertook 25 overseas trips to 27 different countries. Such visits are now firmly established as a significant feature of the Governor-General's Head of State role. All proposed Governor-General travel is noted by Cabinet before the visit takes place, and all Governors-General provide a report of their trip that is noted by Cabinet.

The constitutional implications

It is outside the ambit of this book to discuss the international relations considerations which a New Zealand government is likely to take into account in deciding to agree, or to propose, that the Governor-General should make a state visit to another country in the exercise of the Head of State role. As early as 2001, however, the government established guidelines which also took into account the constitutional implications of such a visit. The guidelines have since been revised and supplemented in the light of experience. We draw on that source in summarising the main constitutional principles.

The Governor-General undertakes official international travel at the invitation of the Prime Minister. It is usual for the Prime Minister to put before the Cabinet any proposals that the Governor-General make a particular visit overseas. Unless the government of the host state has invited the Governor-General to visit as its guest, the New Zealand Government meets the costs incurred. The proposal put to the Cabinet therefore includes an estimate of the costs likely to be involved.[21] The government therefore has the constitutional

21 See Chapter 7 The Office of Governor-General and Commander-in-Chief, under the subheading The Governor-General's salary and expenses, at 126–127.

responsibility for the decision that the Governor-General should make a particular visit.

The nature of a country visit by the Governor-General will be largely symbolic and focused on raising New Zealand's profile in the country concerned. The visit will therefore be appropriate to the role of a politically neutral, non-executive Head of State. The Governor-General will not normally undertake visits, or carry out tasks during visits, that would more appropriately be undertaken by the Prime Minister or another Minister. It would not be appropriate to involve the Governor-General if highly political issues were likely to arise. The Ministry of Foreign Affairs and Trade remains the government's principal adviser on the foreign relations implications of any proposal for the Governor-General to make a Head of State visit to another country. Once a particular visit has been approved by the Cabinet, the Ministry of Foreign Affairs and Trade supports the Governor-General in carrying it out.

In particular, the Governor-General may need support if the Head of State of the host country has executive responsibilities, and also in meetings with its Prime Minister or other Ministers. The New Zealand constitution does not permit the Governor-General to make any commitments on behalf of the government or on behalf of New Zealand as an international person. Although the Sovereign has delegated to the Governor-General the exercise of the executive authority of New Zealand vested in her, the Governor-General has a constitutional duty to act only on the advice of the Prime Minister or another responsible Minister.

A visiting Governor-General has, however, by prior arrangement, occasionally signed for New Zealand a bilateral treaty that has already been negotiated with the host state. We understand that, in such a case, the Governor-General is seen as having the necessary authority at international law, without any need for the Minister of Foreign Affairs to issue full powers.[22] That view accords with the constitutional authority of the Governor-General, but it would still be necessary to have the prior approval of the Cabinet and to observe all other aspects of New Zealand's treaty-making process.[23]

Governors-General also play a key part in receiving and interacting with the Heads of State of other countries who make a state visit to New Zealand. It is, however, the recognition that the Governor-General makes visits to other states at the Head of State level which has added a new dimension to the office. Such visits are a valuable tool in strengthening New Zealand's relations with

22 See Vienna Convention on the Law of Treaties 1155 UNTS 331 (entered into force 27 January 1980), art 7.

23 See above, this chapter, under the subheading An executive responsibility, at 286.

other states. They filled a gap that had existed from the time it became clear that the Sovereign is unable to speak internationally for any of her realms other than the United Kingdom. Such visits can be made only by a Head of State or a person exercising that role. While not a substitute for conventional diplomacy, they are a hugely visible demonstration of engagement at the highest level by both the state visiting and, more especially, the visited state.

Declarations of war

Traditionally made by the Head of State

In earlier times, Heads of State were also seen in international law as having the authority to declare that their country was at war with another state. The existence of a state of war has many consequences in international law. It may also be the trigger for emergency legislation in domestic law providing, for example, for the internment of enemy aliens.

In 1914, King George V, acting on the advice of the Privy Council, declared war on Germany, once the United Kingdom Government's ultimatum had been ignored. The declaration bound the whole of the Empire, including New Zealand. As reported in the *Evening Post* on 5 August 1914 under the headline "WAR DECLARED", the King had sent a message to Lord Liverpool, the Governor of New Zealand, received that day. Lord Liverpool read the message aloud to the large crowd gathered in the parliamentary grounds, along with the Speakers of the two Houses of Parliament, Members of Parliament and the judges of what was then the Supreme Court:[24]

> I desire to express to my people of the Overseas Dominions with what appreciation and pride I have received the messages from their respective Governments during the last few days. These spontaneous assurances of their fullest support recall to me the generous self-sacrificing help given by them in the past to the Mother Country. I shall be strengthened in the discharge of the great responsibilities which rest upon me by the confident belief that in this time of trial my Empire will stand united . . .

The Governor also read his own reply to His Majesty the King:[25]

> New Zealand desires me to acknowledge Your Majesty's gracious message, and to say that come good or ill she, in company with the dominions and other

24 The Supreme Court is now the High Court of New Zealand.
25 "War Declared" *The Evening Post* (New Zealand, 5 August 1914) at 8.

> dependencies of the Crown, is prepared to make any sacrifice to maintain her heritage and her birthright . . .

The Governor's reply and any earlier messages to the King would of course have been sent on the government's advice but, as soon as the King had declared war on Germany, New Zealand had been committed.

New Zealand declares war

In 1939, war with Hitler's Germany came to be seen as inevitable. By then, the King's declaration of war on the advice of the United Kingdom Government no longer bound the Dominions. The New Zealand Government, then led by Michael Joseph Savage, was determined that if the King declared war on behalf of the United Kingdom Government, New Zealand would immediately make its own declaration of war. Gerald Hensley gives a circumstantial account of the tense days after 24 August 1939 when Germany entered into a pact with the Soviet Union. By that time, Savage was gravely ill. Peter Fraser became New Zealand's wartime leader. The government cabled its support of Britain's decision to stand by its guarantee to Poland. On 1 September, Fraser described the situation to Parliament. Hitler's attack on Poland became known in New Zealand late that night. It was then a matter of waiting until the United Kingdom ultimatum expired. That was calculated to be 9.30 pm New Zealand time on the night of Sunday 3 September. Ministers, heads of department and service chiefs gathered around the radio in the Prime Minister's Department in the Parliament Building. But static made the British Prime Minister Neville Chamberlain's broadcast hard to understand. When it had finished, no one was quite sure what he had said.

When the Cabinet learnt of the British Admiralty's notification to the fleet that war had broken out, it approved the draft declaration of war with little or no discussion. The official war message did not come through until just before midnight. It was still thought necessary to observe the tradition going back to Charles I that the Crown does not enter the Parliament Building while Parliament is in session. In the early hours of the morning, the Ministers and their advisers walked across the road to the Government Building where the Governor-General, Lord Galway, was waiting to make an Order in Council approving the following Proclamation:[26]

26 Gerald Hensley *Beyond the Battlefield: New Zealand and its Allies 1939–45* (Penguin, London, 2009) at 17–21.

> His Excellency the Governor-General has it in command from His Majesty the King to declare that a state or war exists between His Majesty and the Government of the German Reich, and that such a state of war has existed from 9.30 pm, New Zealand standard time, on the third day of September, 1939.[27]

On 4 September 1939, the government sent the following telegram to the British Secretary of State for Dominion Affairs:[28]

> His Majesty's Government in New Zealand desire immediately to associate themselves with His Majesty's Government in the United Kingdom in honouring their pledged word. They entirely concur with the action taken, which they regard as inevitably forced upon the British Commonwealth if the cause of justice, freedom and democracy is to endure in this world. The existence of a state of war with Germany has accordingly been proclaimed in New Zealand, and His Majesty's Government in New Zealand would be grateful if His Majesty's Government in the United Kingdom would take any steps that may be necessary to indicate to the German Government that His Majesty's Government in New Zealand associate themselves in this manner with the action taken by His Majesty's Government in the United Kingdom. The New Zealand Government wish to offer the British Government the fullest assurance of all possible support.

Hensley records that the American Embassy in Berlin delivered the New Zealand Government's statement to the German authorities.[29]

On the facts, the King did not expressly authorise, let alone command, the Governor-General of New Zealand to declare war on Germany. In the post-war period one or two commentators suggested that the declaration of war was therefore outside the authority conferred on the Governor-General by the 1917 Letters Patent. That conclusion is inconsistent with the view that the "things belonging to the office of Governor-General" expanded with the expanding constitutional authority of the New Zealand Government as recognised by the conventions of the Commonwealth.

In early September 1939, the members of the Cabinet and their advisers must have been aware that it was for the Sovereign to take the momentous step of declaring war on another state. The assertion that the Governor-General was acting at the command of the King was, in effect, a declaration that the

27 Telegram to the Secretary of State for Dominion Affairs 4 September 1939, associating HM Government in New Zealand with the British declaration, reproduced in WD McIntyre and WJ Gardner *Speeches and Documents on New Zealand History* (Oxford University Press, London, 1971) at 283.

28 At 283.

29 Above n 26, at 21.

Governor-General was acting in the exercise of the Head of State role. It is almost certainly the first occasion on which a New Zealand Governor-General had done so. The King did not need to give his express authority. It was enough that, in the circumstances, he should be willing for the Governor-General to act on his behalf. The New Zealand Government's long night-time wait to ensure that the King had already declared the United Kingdom to be at war with Germany gave an assurance on that point.

New Zealand also declared war on the other European states that were under the control of Nazi Germany and joined in the war against the Allies. On 8 December 1941, a day after Pearl Harbor, New Zealand declared war on Japan. Peace, when it eventually came with the countries with which New Zealand had been at war, was made by a series of treaties with the Allied powers, including New Zealand. The peace treaties did not involve the King or the New Zealand Governor-General, but were made and signed at the Head of Government level.

Declarations of war incompatible with the UN Charter

Since the end of World War II, in the era of the United Nations, no state has declared war on any other state. All members of the United Nations must refrain in their international relations from the threat or use of force against the territorial integrity or political independence of any other state, or in any other manner inconsistent with the purposes of the United Nations.[30]

Armed conflicts do still occur. They are sometimes given a name which includes the word "war", but the states concerned no longer initiate them or join them by making a formal declaration of war at the Head of State level. Their consequences, in international law and in the domestic law of any of the states concerned, are outside the scope of this book.

An evaluation of the Head of State role in international relations

It can be seen from this description that the Head of State role as explicitly recognised in international law is significant, but relatively small in the scheme of things. It comprises the remnants of all that was once done by Sovereigns, and subsequently by the heads of states that were not monarchies, thus giving

30 Charter of the United Nations, art 2(5).

rise to the concept of a "Head of State". It would have been unthinkable not to include them in explaining the concept that the Governor-General of New Zealand exercises the Head of State role.

It seems likely, however, that in New Zealand the Governor-General will increasingly be seen as exercising the "Head of State role" understood in a broader sense. In the last few years, the Governor-General has begun to be described as exercising the Head of State role when carrying out some or all of the other functions of the office.

3
THE "HEAD OF STATE ROLE" AT HOME

Although it is nearly a hundred years since the formal acknowledgement that the Governor-General is no longer instructed by or answerable to the Sovereign in right of the United Kingdom, the only formal statement of the Governor-General's modern role is that he or she is the Sovereign's representative in New Zealand.[31] That idea can be understood well enough in the context of the right to exercise powers or perform functions vested in the Sovereign in right of New Zealand, but it says nothing about the leadership the Governor-General is now seen as giving in his or her own right to all the people of New Zealand. Except on formal occasions like investitures, discussed below, it is no longer necessary, and would not be credible, for a Governor-General to emphasise the representative nature of his or her role.[32] The Sovereign or members of her family have long interacted directly with the people of New Zealand. The Governor-General is seen as having a role in his or her own right.

That seems to be the reason why, today, the concept that the Governor-General exercises the "Head of State role" tends to be used in domestic contexts as well as in the field of foreign relations, where the concept of a "Head of State" originated.[33] As, however, the constitutional role of a Head of State differs from country to country, depending on the terms of its constitution, the label alone is not illuminating unless it is spelt out. In part 4 of this chapter we give our view of how the office of Governor-General is now understood, not only in the constitution itself, but also in the eyes of those who live under it.

31 Letters Patent 1983, cl 1.

32 Note, however, that, in one part of the Realm of New Zealand, the self-governing state of the Cook Islands, the Sovereign is separately represented by the "Queen's Representative" who has no other title and must therefore use it in the constitutional as well as the international relations spheres.

33 See generally Chapter 12 The Governor-General and the Administration of Justice.

The practice of appointing New Zealand citizens who have maintained a close connection with the country as Governor-General has reinforced the impression that the office itself exists in its own right. Certainly, Governors-General who are New Zealanders see themselves differently from their predecessors. Sir Denis Blundell, who was appointed in 1972, was the trailblazer. At his pre-appointment audience with the Queen, he explained that he did not think it would be appropriate for him, on ceremonial occasions, to wear the traditional white silk stockings, knee breeches and plumed hat. His instinctive inclination foreshadowed a more general change of style. Government House no longer tried to maintain a formality, and still less a borrowed grandeur, faintly echoing Buckingham Palace. Governors-General, however, remain committed to maintaining the dignity of the office, but in a manner appropriate to their New Zealand setting.

The objective is to find ways of making the office meaningful to a wide range of New Zealanders. To that end, Governors-General now use modern strategic planning tools. A recent Governor-General's website included a summary of his strategy for his five-year term. We do not intend to make a close examination of the techniques which a present-day Governor-General would use in seeking to interact with their fellow citizens. Our interest is in the constitutional implications of this relatively recent activism, along with the maintenance of some older, more reactive ways of connecting with sections of the wider community.

We look at how the Governor-General's personal programme is shaped. In particular, we discuss the Governor-General's involvement with individuals and groups, especially in those cases where traditional practices have been maintained, alongside the modern initiatives.

The Governor-General's programme

A personal responsibility

As the representative of the Sovereign, a Governor-General has always been free to make personal decisions about the use of the available time. A sense of duty, and of what is called for by the nature of the office, is usually the only guide, at least in the case of activities within New Zealand. In Chapter 7 we explained that there is now a separate appropriation to meet the costs of the Governor-General in carrying out his or her programme within the country.[34] The details of the programme need to be planned as far in advance as possible,

34 See Chapter 7 The Office of Governor-General and Commander-in-Chief, under the subheading The Governor-General's salary and expenses, at 126–127.

but it is normally for the Governor-General to determine its details, consistently with the other duties of the office. On rare occasions, however, the Prime Minister and government may take a policy decision bearing on some aspect of the Governor-General's activities. The Governor-General will have a constitutional duty to comply.

Sir Michael Hardie Boys relates in his memoirs how the Prime Minister Helen Clark informed him, during one of their rare meetings, that the Crown should not be represented at Waitangi on 6 February 2001. He initially took her to mean that the government would not attend but that his own attendance was a matter for him to decide. The Clerk of the Executive Council, Marie Shroff, soon clarified that he "was not to go either".[35] He wrote to the Prime Minister "expressing [his] strong disagreement with an action [he] believed could only damage relations further".[36] But at the point at which he had clarified that the government had decided that he should not attend, he understood that he was obliged to comply with government policy. The Prime Minister subsequently made a series of public statements that Cabinet had made a decision that no one would represent the Crown at Waitangi on that occasion. Statements such as that making it clear that the Government had decided against any representation of the Crown that year are to be seen as required by constitutional convention, to protect the Governor-General's political neutrality.

The Prime Minister's stance on that occasion was a rare departure from the established practice. In undertaking activities within the community, the Governor-General normally acts on his or her own responsibility. Neither the Prime Minister nor any other Minister is responsible to Parliament for anything the Governor-General does or says. If, however, the Governor-General were clearly to overstep the bounds of constitutional propriety, the Prime Minister could be expected publicly to disassociate the government from what was said or done. We have not, however, come across any examples of such a disclaimer. Later in this chapter we discuss the rather more difficult question of what a modern Governor-General ought to be free to say publicly about a matter of general interest or concern.[37]

Different but parallel roles

Essentially, the politically neutral Governor-General's interaction with the people of New Zealand runs in parallel with that of the Prime Minister as the

35 Michael Hardie Boys *The Boy From Evans Bay: The Memoirs of Sir Michael Hardie Boys* (Evans Bay Press, Wellington, 2016) at 281.

36 At 281.

37 See below, under the subheading The Governor-General's public statements, at 307–308.

political leader of the government. Although they occasionally appear in public together, they take some care to remain within their respective spheres, never competing for the limelight. If situations arise that either could appropriately respond to — for example, an event involving a member of the royal family — there is careful consultation about which of them will, on that occasion, take the necessary action, in private or in public, on behalf of New Zealand. On a notable occasion, such as the coronation of a Sovereign who has newly acceded to the throne, both of them will attend.

4 INTERACTING WITH CERTAIN INDIVIDUALS AND GROUPS

The connecting thread

We now look at the way in which the Governor-General, in the performance of the duties of the office, may interact in a personal way with some individual New Zealanders or members of a group which has some constitutional or other special connection with the Governor-General. The individuals and groups we discuss are the recipients of New Zealand royal honours or awards, members of the New Zealand Defence Force, and not-for-profit organisations of which the Governor-General, his or her spouse, or both, are Patrons. In each case it is important to explain the limits of the Governor-General's involvement as well as the things to which it extends.

The Governor-General's powers in respect of royal honours and awards

We have explained the nature of the New Zealand Royal Honours system in Chapter 5.[38] When the Queen has signified her acceptance of the Prime Minister's recommendation that she should grant a particular honour or make a particular award within the New Zealand Royal Honours system to a named recipient, Government House writes to each of them on behalf of the Governor-General to inform them of the proffered award, ask whether they wish to accept it, and if so, whether they would like to receive the honour or

38 See Chapter 5 The Sovereign in Right of New Zealand: A Personal Touch, under the subheading The fount of honour, at 83.

award at one of the investiture ceremonies which the Governor-General holds twice in each year, at Government House in both Wellington and Auckland. At the ceremony, the citation for the honour or award to each recipient is read out, and the Governor-General invests each recipient with the insignia of their honour.

Generally speaking, while certain powers have been delegated to the Governor-General (such as the informal approval of honours lists), the Sovereign acts in person, both in instituting particular awards, and in granting formal approval of an award to a particular person. In some areas, such as in relation to the New Zealand Defence Force, the Governor-General now has delegated authority to make regulations, and can give formal approval of certain awards.[39] That is a relatively recent innovation, and was not always the case, as was sharply brought home to an early Governor, Sir George Bowen, who overstepped his authority.

On 10 March 1869, on the advice of the Executive Council, he made an Order in Council instituting an award for bravery in action during the New Zealand wars by a member of the Militia, Volunteer forces or Armed Constabulary. The award later became known as the "New Zealand Cross". At the time, the members of those forces were not eligible for a bravery award constituted by the Queen. Bowen bestowed the award on four European and one Māori member of the forces concerned. On receiving this news, the Secretary of State for the Colonies wrote a despatch to the Governor, chiding him "in no uncertain terms" for exceeding his authority, and pointing out that the actions he had taken required the "personal sanction of the Queen". In the circumstances, however, the Queen in Council had ratified the Order.[40] Long ago as the incident was, the Governor-General still has limited authority to establish a new honour or award within the New Zealand Royal Honours system.

The Governor-General acts as the Queen's representative in investing recipients with the insignia or other signification of the honours or awards that she herself has personally approved, on the Prime Minister's recommendation. The honours and awards within the New Zealand Royal Honours system were constituted and are awarded by the Sovereign herself, acting on the advice of the Prime Minister of New Zealand.

39 For example, the New Zealand Gallantry Medal and the New Zealand Bravery Medal.
40 PE Abbott and JMA Tamplin *British Gallantry Awards* (2nd ed, Guinness World Records Ltd, 1981) at 231.

The New Zealand Defence Force

The personal role of the Governor-General

In Chapter 7 we explained in some detail the potentially misleading nature of the long-standing provision, still included in the Defence Act 1990, that the Governor-General, as the Commander-in-Chief, has "such duties and obligations relating to any armed forces raised and maintained . . . [in New Zealand] as pertain to the office of Commander-in-Chief".[41] We remain of the opinion that the office of Commander-in-Chief gives the Governor-General no duties or obligations which he or she does not already have as Governor-General. It was not appropriate in that context to discuss more generally the Governor-General's role in respect of the armed forces.

Accordingly, we now provide an overview of the Governor-General's statutory powers in respect of the armed forces and how they are exercised in practice, so far as that is relevant to the thrust of this book. Then we look at the ways in which the Governor-General maintains a personal involvement with members of the New Zealand Defence Force, and draw some conclusions about their constitutional significance.

The power to raise armed forces

The first substantive section of the Defence Act 1990 provides that:[42]

> The Governor-General may, from time to time, in the name and on behalf of the Sovereign, continue to raise and maintain armed forces, either in New Zealand or elsewhere.

Then follows a list of the purposes for which armed forces may be raised. Read together, those purposes appear to cover every contingency in which the armed forces might need to be deployed, but it is expressly provided that they do not have a limiting effect.[43] The 1689 Bill of Rights has expressly forbidden the raising or maintaining of a standing army in a time of peace without the consent of Parliament.[44] For a long time that consent was given by an annual

41 See Chapter 7 The Office of Governor-General and Commander-in-Chief, under the subheading The title "Commander-in-Chief", at 129–137.

42 Defence Act 1990, s 5. The present-day implications of Parliament's authority to raise and maintain armed forces "elsewhere" are unclear.

43 Section 6(2).

44 The maintenance of the Royal Navy in a time of peace was not seen as posing a threat to the Sovereign's subjects or to Parliament.

Act, in New Zealand as well as in the United Kingdom, but since the time of the Cold War there has in both countries been permanent statutory provision for the maintenance of all three branches of the armed forces. Despite the fact that the statutory powers are vested in the Governor-General, acting on behalf of the Sovereign, neither of them is personally involved in the raising and maintenance of New Zealand's armed forces.

The deployment of the armed forces

In contrast, the power to deploy the armed forces, at home or abroad, is to be found solely in the royal prerogative as part of New Zealand law.[45] That is also the case in the United Kingdom. It has been said in a leading English case that "[t]he Crown has, and this is not disputed, the right as head of the State to decide in peace and war the disposition of its armed forces . . .".[46] As a power vested in the Sovereign, its exercise is an element of the executive authority of New Zealand, which is exercisable, through the Governor-General, by Ministers of the Crown, usually acting collectively within the Cabinet, but responsible to Parliament for the decisions they make.

Again, however, the Governor-General plays no part in the decision-making or its implementation. That has been the position in New Zealand since 1870. Sir Michael Hardie Boys[47] mentioned in a public lecture that he had not been consulted or informed in advance about the decision to send troops to East Timor or to disband the Air Strike Force.[48] There is, of course, considerable public interest in how decisions should be made about controversial deployments of the armed forces to overseas war zones, but that question is outside the ambit of this book.

A culture of loyalty to the Sovereign and the Governor-General

In the public lecture just mentioned, Hardie Boys went on to say:[49]

> On the other hand, the Services themselves place considerable store by the role of Commander-in-Chief, and are anxious to have him or her present on every important occasion, as well as visiting ship or camp or base as often as possible.

45 Sections 5 and 5(1) of the Defence Act 1990 do not affect any other power vested in the Governor-General.
46 Lord Hodgson in *Chandler v DPP* [1964] AC 763 (HL) at 800.
47 Governor-General from 1996 to 2001.
48 Michael Hardie Boys "Nodding Automaton?" (2001–2002) 8 Canterbury Law Review 425 at 434.
49 At 434.

That continuing interest reflects a long-standing culture of loyalty to the Sovereign and the Governor-General deliberately perpetuated in the Defence Act itself.

The Governor-General has a statutory power to appoint officers to the service of the armed forces.[50] Officers of the armed forces are true "servants of the Crown" who hold office during pleasure.[51] The Governor-General also has statutory powers in respect of their promotion and their release or discharge or the variation of their Terms of Appointment.[52] The Governor-General may delegate all of those powers to the Chief of Defence Force, but there is one power which the Governor-General cannot delegate. He or she is empowered:[53]

> in the name and on behalf of the Sovereign, [to] issue commissions under the Seal of New Zealand to officers of the Armed Forces.

We understand that there has been a long-standing tradition that the commissions of officers of the armed forces in the United Kingdom should be signed in person by the King or the Queen. It is said that when Queen Victoria came to the throne after a regency, the young Queen was faced with a backlog of unsigned commissions which it took her years to clear. Officers of the New Zealand armed forces receive a commission signed by the Governor-General and Commander-in-Chief on behalf of the Queen, and bearing the Seal of New Zealand, reserved for use only by the Queen in right of New Zealand or the Governor-General. The involvement of the Governor-General in person is seen as an important element in building the code of loyalty and service to the nation on which the efficacy of the armed forces depends.

The Defence Act provides also for the appointment, enlistment or engagement of "other persons" — better known by the old term "other ranks" — to serve in the Navy, the Army or the Air Force.[54] All members of the three services must take an oath of allegiance.[55] In its prescribed form the oath reads as follows:[56]

> I, [*name*], solemnly promise and swear that I will be faithful and bear true allegiance to our Sovereign Lady the Queen, her heirs and successors, and that I will faithfully serve in the New Zealand Naval Forces/the New Zealand Army/the Royal

50 Defence Act 1990, s 13. The term "officer" is defined in s 2(1).
51 *Deynzer v Campbell* [1950] NZLR 780, 811 (CA).
52 Defence Act 1990, s 32(1).
53 Section 32(1)(b).
54 Section 33.
55 See Chapter 7 The Office of Governor-General and Commander-in-Chief, around fn 62, at 134–135.
56 The current oath is prescribed by Defence Regulations 1990, cl 3.

> New Zealand Air Force . . . , and that I will loyally observe and obey all orders of Her Majesty, her heirs and successors, and of the officers set over me, until I shall be lawfully discharged. So help me God.

The oath of allegiance binds the person subscribing to it until discharged from the service.[57]

In a recent Canadian case, an Army captain sought relief from being obliged to participate in "outward displays of loyalty to an unelected monarch of foreign origin".[58] On appeal, the Court determined that loyalty and allegiance to the Queen and specific demonstrations of loyalty were specifically provided for and reflected the constitutional and legislative position. The requirement existed in order "to foster respect and loyalty, to enhance good order and discipline within the ranks and to maintain the effectiveness of the hierarchical command structure".[59] The Court had no doubt as to the necessity and value of these practices, and the captain's claims to a breach of his freedom of expression and religion failed. The Canadian understanding of the rationale for such practices appears to be equally well-accepted in New Zealand.

The Governor-General's symbolic significance for the Defence Force

The legal framework supporting the New Zealand Defence Force and the ethos it is intended to promote go a long way in explaining the interest in the involvement of the Governor-General on formal occasions and through the making of less formal visits. The New Zealand nation owes much to its armed forces, in times of peace as well as war. But as we have shown in Chapter 7, the enthusiasm for the office of "Commander-in-Chief" in particular can have its dangers. These need to be guarded against by repealing the provision of the Defence Act which perpetuates the false impression that, as Commander-in-Chief, the Governor-General has unspecified powers, duties and obligations.[60]

Vice-regal patronage

The former Governor-General, Sir Jerry Mateparae, was the Patron of about 150 New Zealand not-for-profit organisations. His wife, Lady Janine

57 Defence Act 1990, s 35.
58 *Aralt Mac Giolla Chainnigh v Attorney-General of Canada* [2008] FC 69.
59 At [35].
60 See Chapter 7 The Office of Governor-General and Commander-in-Chief, under the subheading The title "Commander-in-Chief", at 129-137.

Mateparae, was the Patron of about 14, and the two of them jointly were the Patrons of another 10 or so.[61] This way of recognising worthy institutions is modelled on the patronage accorded to similar bodies by the Sovereign, and other members of the royal family. Royal patronage originated in the United Kingdom some three centuries ago.

Vice-regal patronage in New Zealand is a reflection of the United Kingdom practice, but does not extend to the endorsement of commercial products. It is personal to the Governor-General concerned, and comes to an end on his or her recall, normally on the expiration of an agreed term. Organisations which wish to maintain their vice-regal patronage or to seek it for the first time must make a request to the incoming Governor-General, once he or she has entered on the duties of the office. Organisations are advised that the patronage is only for the term of office of the incumbent Governor-General, and that its renewal by a subsequent Governor-General cannot be guaranteed.

That limited duration provides an opportunity not only to consider the current standing of the organisation concerned but also for Governors-General and their spouses to consider whether there are particular issues or activities they wish to emphasise during their term of office. That said, most Governors-General are the Patrons of a wide range of organisations. Sir Jerry's list included organisations in the fields of health, heritage, the arts; bodies having an interest in particular regions or ethnic communities, in New Zealand or worldwide; and in music, education, sport, youth and families, servicemen and servicewomen, the merchant navy, horticulture and agriculture, business, ballet, literature, and animal welfare; professional groups, charitable bodies, and search and rescue and lifesaving organisations, to mention a representative range. In the context of the Governor-General's interaction with the people of New Zealand, patronage can be seen as giving the Governor-General what is potentially a meaningful connection with many sections of the community in all parts of the country.

More general interaction with the public

No formal prescription

Apart from the acknowledgement of the fact that the Governor-General is the representative in New Zealand of the Sovereign, the way in which he or she should interact with the people of New Zealand is not formally prescribed,

61 "Vice-Regal Patronage" <http://gg.govt.nz/the-governor-general-patronage>.

any more than it is in the case of the Sovereign herself. Over time, both have changed, in their perceptions of their roles, and in their respective styles. That process of change seems likely to continue.

The Governor-General's programme

In more recent years, New Zealand Governors-General have taken greater initiative rather than primarily responding to the invitations and opportunities that presented themselves. They now take a much more proactive approach, identifying their broad objectives and planning ways of achieving them. Their personal programme is likely to be focused on New Zealand and New Zealanders, while taking account of their obligations to the government and their wider representative role, in New Zealand and overseas.

Individual Governors-General who have spoken publicly about their time in office or written a published account of it usually express the pleasure it gave them to meet with people in their own settings, learn of their difficulties and their achievements, and generally obtain a better understanding of their ways of life. In the process they no doubt themselves gave pleasure and encouragement. The interaction is an important aspect of nation-building, and for that reason goes to the heart of the office. There is, however, an aspect of nation-building which has not yet been fully acknowledged as a legitimate or even as an essential aspect of a Governor-General's role.

The Governor-General's public statements

A Governor-General's duty to remain above politics has always been seen as precluding any public comment on the policies of the government, or, for that matter, those of any political party. Traditionally, that convention allows the Governor-General to speak publicly to, or on behalf of, the nation on ceremonial occasions and in relation to important events in national life. What he or she says on those rare occasions is likely to be perceptive, sometimes memorable, and always uncontroversial because it remains well away from the political sphere.

Occasionally, however, Governors-General have responded to what appears to be the increasing expectation of the public that they will give non-political leadership on important issues of the day, especially in fields in which they have previously shown a capacity for leadership. Inevitably, the press is quick to point out that the matter is one on which the government, or possibly an Opposition party, has a particular view, implying if not asserting that the

Governor-General has gone further than was constitutionally proper. Taken literally, the notion that the Governor-General is precluded from mentioning such a matter publicly would amount to a gag. There are signs, however, that the politicians themselves are developing a greater robustness about what a Governor-General should be free to contribute to the public discussion of important issues.

On 14 August 2002 at the Prime Minister's press conference, there were questions concerning the Opposition parties' concerns about the Governor-General's comments on the role of prisons in a recent public speech. Prime Minister Helen Clark said:[62]

> The challenge is to what extent in the future we want the person who carries out the nominal Head of State duties to be able to have an opinion. Clearly it is desirable for the Governor-General to be able to be seen as a unifying, rather than a polarising, figure. . . . I think there is a role for a thoughtful person who dispassionately sets out the issues which she [Dame Silvia Cartwright] did. . . . I think we need to consider how the role of the Governor-General might evolve further. . . . [Y]ou will not get intelligent and able people to serve in these positions if they are told that they cannot make a considered speech of substance on something they've spent their professional lives dedicated to. . . . I think what . . . is evolving [is] a unifying [role] above politics . . . but able to make a reasoned contribution to public discourse.

A national leadership role?

More recently, one commentator has envisaged the possibility of the Governor-General and the Prime Minister each making broadcast speeches to the nation on a Waitangi Day aimed more specifically as a celebration of New Zealand's national day. The speeches, however, would be different in kind:[63]

> The Governor-General's speech should be at breakfast time on national television and radio. It should be an anticipated event in much the same way as the Queen's Christmas message used to be. But we should give him real words to say. We should give him words of wisdom and inspiration and hope. Words that tell us who we are and what we can become and why we should celebrate this day; words that send us into the Waitangi Day morning feeling proud to be New Zealanders.

62 Extracts from transcript of Prime Minister's press conference, TVNZ National News, 14 August 2002.

63 Buddy Mikaere ("writer, historian and environmental consultant") "Waitangi Day: How can we reclaim the day?" *Weekend Herald* (New Zealand, 4 February 2012) at A4 <http://www.nzherald.co.nz/nz/news/article.cfm?c_id=1&objectid=10783253>.

> Waitangi Day should also be the day the Prime Minister gives his State of the Nation address — the day he tells it to us straight. Why do politicians always find that hard to do? Why can't the Prime Minister just say: "look guys, this is how I see the past year: this is what we need to do to make things better; this is the resource we have available to do it with; and this is how we are going to do it. Furthermore, throughout the year I am going to give you regular updates against these same points. Happy Waitangi Day!"

The author then suggested further ways of making Waitangi Day truly a national day.

The scenario just described is simply one person's vision of future possibilities, but it casts the Governor-General in a national leadership role, helping to inspire and unify the nation in a non-political way, and followed later by a Prime Minister who provides the nation with a political assessment of how the government can best meet the challenges it faces. The Governor-General has already established a regular practice of broadcasting a New Year's message on the internet. Many New Zealanders would, we think, be attracted by such a public manifestation of the Head of State role, as well as that of the Head of Government. The more visible exercise of the Governor-General's Head of State role in a domestic setting would be a logical development of the already accepted practice of appointing New Zealand citizens to the office of Governor-General, and choosing men and women who have already shown that they have the necessary experience and leadership capacity to carry it out effectively. Such a change of practice, along with the acceptance of our proposed clarifications of the conventions governing the exercise of the Governor-General's power to appoint or change a Prime Ministers,[64] would establish definitively the modern role of the Governor-General in New Zealand's constitutional monarchy.

5
THE MONARCHICAL CONSTITUTION AND THE POSSIBILITY OF CHANGE

It is fitting that we should end our account of the working of the monarchical constitution with a chapter about aspects of the Governor-General's modern role. There is now a tendency to refer to the Governor-General, not as being

64 See Chapter 9 Finding and Changing a Prime Minister, under the subheading The New Zealand principles, at 198-200.

the representative of the Sovereign, but as exercising the Head of State role, and not only in the context of international law and relations where the term "Head of State" originated. The more general use of the term may reflect a change of perception about the nature of New Zealand itself. The Sovereign in right of New Zealand has been wholehearted in performing her distinct role as the Queen of New Zealand, but, for some New Zealanders, that is no longer as meaningful as it once was. Some people would like the non-political leader of their country to be a New Zealand citizen whom they could look to as one of their own. Instead of remaining a constitutional monarchy, they would like New Zealand to become a republic.

In the Afterword of this book, we respond to that perception of the future. In doing so we do not advocate change, but we do not oppose it. We are willing to think about what such a change would involve, and how it could be achieved.

AFTERWORD

Thinking About a Republican Constitution

1
THE PARAMETERS OF CONSTITUTIONAL CHANGE

This book has discussed the working of New Zealand's current constitutional monarchy. At various points we have foreshadowed the possibility that New Zealanders may one day seriously consider whether to turn their country into a republic. In this afterword we think about what that would involve and suggest the kinds of questions that would need to be addressed.

In respect of both form and substance, the remaking of the constitution could range as widely as people wish. Three forms of republicanism have been mooted: "full" republicanism, which would involve an elected President and a completely new constitutional structure; a constitution which does not provide for a Head of State at all; and "soft" republicanism, which contemplates that the constitution would basically stay the same but that the Sovereign and Governor-General's roles would be transferred to a non-partisan Head of State appointed by the Prime Minister or by the House of Representatives.[1]

For reasons both principled and pragmatic, we focus our comments on the third option. As far as we can gauge, the current appetite for a republic seems to be driven not so much by a desire for broader constitutional change, but rather by a sense of New Zealand identity which is no longer focused on an inherited King or Queen or a shared British heritage.[2] We as authors have

1 <http://www.stuff.co.nz/nelson-mail/opinion/editorial/9916651/Editorial-A-post-royal-NZ-brings-hard-calls>.

2 The wide-ranging proposals by Margaret Mutu and Moana Jackson for a more tikanga-based constitutional structure deserve serious consideration which we are unable to give them here: *He Whakaaro Here Whakaumu Mō Aotearoa: The Report of Matike Mai Aotearoa — The Independent Working Group on Constitutional Transformation* (January 2016).

a strong preference for constitutions based on the parliamentary system of government as being a more stable basis for democratic government than those based on a presidential system with a stricter separation of powers.[3] And as a practical matter, soft republicanism seems to have the greatest level of current political and public support and thus to be the most politically viable.[4]

While soft republicanism is frequently presented as the "simple" option, in fact as a matter of law, quite a lot of other things would need to change. Removing the Sovereign from the constitution would also remove its present conceptual core. Instead, the parliamentary system of government could become the new organising principle. At the practical level, however, such changes could be made in a way that would enable the constitution to go on functioning little differently from the way it functions now.

In thinking about a republican constitution, we have not made a systematic inquiry into the parliamentary constitutions of other republics, inside or outside the Commonwealth. That would have taken us well beyond the limits of what is an afterword in a book about the constitutional monarchy. In some contexts, however, we make a brief comparison with the republican constitution of another country of which we happen to have some knowledge. Our general approach is to identify the issues that will need to be considered. Often, we raise questions without supplying the answers. We do not provide a blueprint for a republican constitution as a whole.

Things which New Zealand cannot change

The other parts of the Realm of New Zealand

The advocates of a move to a republic usually make it clear that they are thinking only about the future of New Zealand itself. They accept that the peoples of the other inhabited parts of the Realm of New Zealand must be free to remain within the territorial sovereignty of the King or the Queen, unless its own people should decide otherwise. In principle, that approach is sound. The fact is that New Zealand does not have the legal power to make any change to the constitutions of the self-governing states of the Cook Islands and of Niue. And no New Zealand Act of Parliament applies to either Tokelau or the Ross Dependency unless that Act or some other statute so provides.[5]

3 Fred W Riggs "The Survival of Presidentialism in America: Para-constitutional Practices" (1988) 9 International Political Science Review 247.

4 See New Zealand Republic Inc at <http://www.republic.org.nz/> and Dean Knight's "minimalist republic" discussed in D Knight "Republic can be a simple matter" *The Dominion Post* (New Zealand, 2 February 2011).

5 Interpretation Act 1999, s 29.

A republican New Zealand would almost certainly retain its existing territorial jurisdiction in respect of the Ross Dependency which has no permanent inhabitants, but is the subject of some of New Zealand's obligations under the Antarctic Treaty which are implemented in New Zealand law.[6] For the purposes of this discussion, we assume that, at least for the time being, the peoples of the Cook Islands, Niue and Tokelau would wish to maintain their existing allegiance to the Sovereign. Their constitutions, however, reflect the fact that each is now part of the Realm of New Zealand.

The New Zealand Government should therefore keep their governments fully informed about official interest in a move to a republic, and should assist them in maintaining their own relationships with the Sovereign, if that is their wish. In addition, the shared common allegiance to the Sovereign in right of New Zealand has always been regarded as reflecting common values. If that bond were to be lost, the New Zealand citizenship they share could take its place.

Having outlined our general approach, we now discuss the key issues.

What the statute law provides for now

The Constitution Act 1986 does not attempt to spell out all the implications of the constitutional monarchy. It simply records its central features, the first of which reads as follows:[7]

> The Sovereign in right of New Zealand is the Head of State of New Zealand . . .

It is logical to suppose that, if someone else were to become the Head of State of New Zealand, that person would, in effect, step into the shoes of the Sovereign, and would have the authority to exercise the former Sovereign's constitutional role. While the appointment of someone else as New Zealand's Head of State would signify that the role of the Sovereign in right of New Zealand had come to an end, it would not, in our opinion, have the effect of transferring to the new Head of State all the former Sovereign's constitutional functions and powers.

As we explained in Chapter 14, the only *powers* and *authorities* of the Sovereign as the Head of State are those which public international law assigns to a Sovereign or other Head of State.[8] A reference to the Sovereign's role as

6 The Antarctic Treaty 402 UNTS 71 (signed 1 December 1959, entered into force 23 June 1961).
7 Constitution Act 1986, s 2(1).
8 See generally Chapter 14 Exercising the Head of State Role.

"Head of State" by itself does not capture the other constitutional aspects of her role.[9] "Head of State" and "Sovereign" are not interchangeable terms. Another provision of the 1986 Constitution Act has the effect of "transferring all the functions, duties, powers, authorities, rights, privileges, and dignities belonging to the Crown" to another person,[10] but that provision applies on the death of the Sovereign, and transfers all the attributes of the Sovereign to the next person in the line of succession to the throne. It gives New Zealand a new Sovereign in place of the old. It is not a good model for the selective reassignment of the former Sovereign's rights, powers and authorities to the appropriate organ of a republican state.

A better way, in our view, of giving New Zealand a republican constitution would be to identify the aspects of the monarchical constitution that will need to be replaced, and then to look at how they could best be provided for in the new setting. On that basis, we now consider how the Sovereign's role as the King or Queen in right of New Zealand could be brought to an end, and the gaps that step would leave in the constitution as a whole.

2
ENDING THE SOVEREIGN'S ROLE

The decision-making process

An overview

Long before an Act bringing the monarchy to an end was made and passed by Parliament, and became law, a carefully thought-out process would have been put in place, enabling the people of New Zealand to play a full part in the decision-making. It is likely, given past processes for major constitutional change, that individual citizens would be given an early opportunity in a referendum to express their views about the desirability or otherwise of making their country a republic. Most people would probably see a decision to proceed as needing to have the support of more than a bare majority of the voters. In view of the fact the Sovereign is, in name, a party to the Treaty of Waitangi, the views of Māori voters, in particular, would need to be canvassed as part of the constitutional process.[11]

9 See Chapter 4 The Sovereign in Right of New Zealand: The Institutional Role.
10 Constitution Act 1986, s 5.
11 See the discussion in Chapter 13 The Crown as a Party to the Treaty of Waitangi, under the subheading What should happen next?, at 278–279.

Obviously, the Members of Parliament would have a major role in the decision-making process. By then, some of them may have been elected on the basis of their support for, or opposition to, the idea that the country should become a republic. It would, however, be wrong for such important decisions to be made solely on a party political basis. In making a modern democratic constitution the objective must be to consult, and, if possible, gain support from all sections of the community. The decision-makers would need to take account of special interests as well as the advice of the experts.

We think that all referendums until the final one should be indicative. To put it simply, nothing should change until everything changes, and if everything changes, there would be no going back to the monarchy. For that reason, it would be desirable to consider whether, in the final referendum count, a majority of voters on both the general and the Māori rolls should be required. The objective must be to make a constitution that even those who would have preferred a different constitution will be willing to live under, once it is in place.

Keeping the Sovereign informed

From the moment that a government in office decides to take any initiative on the republican question, or even to respond to an initiative of others, the Prime Minister will have the duty of keeping the Sovereign informed. As we have explained in Chapter 5, the Prime Minister would communicate personally with the Sovereign through the Private Secretary.[12] While the Clerk of the Executive Council, as the responsible official, might maintain the flow of information, the Prime Minister in person would need to inform the Sovereign of the key developments so directly affecting the monarchy. That said, the news of a possible New Zealand move to a republican form of government would not come as any surprise.

Queen Elizabeth II, on what was almost certainly her final visit to New Zealand, indicated her wish to speak publicly about "the republic question". Her speech would have been drafted in New Zealand and approved by the Prime Minister. Her message was veiled, but its import was clear:[13]

> . . . I have admired your increasing energy and confidence. I know that this process of evolution will continue as you, the people of New Zealand, map out your path for the future in your own time and in your own way.

12 See Chapter 5 The Sovereign in Right of New Zealand: A Personal Touch, under the subheading The Sovereign and the Prime Minister, at 75–76.

13 "State dinner in Wellington, New Zealand, 25 February 2002" <www.royal.uk/state-dinner-wellington-new-zealand-25-february-2002>.

The Queen's successors to the throne can be expected to accept just as graciously any constitutional change that the people of New Zealand wish to make.

Ending the monarchy by an Act of the New Zealand Parliament

A short operative provision in an Act of the New Zealand Parliament is all that would be required to bring monarchy to an end. In referring to the Sovereign, it would be appropriate, for the last time, to use the royal style and titles in respect of New Zealand which the reigning Sovereign would have formally assumed on coming to the throne. The operative provision would, however, need to do more than simply depose the reigning King or Queen. Otherwise, the member of the royal family next in the line of succession would then become the King or Queen in right of New Zealand. Parliament would need to use words which would clearly manifest its intention to bring to an end the office of "Sovereign in right of New Zealand".

In a recital to the Act itself or in a separate Address to the Sovereign adopted by the House, it would be appropriate to express the appreciation of the House and of the people of New Zealand for the faithful service of the reigning Sovereign and of his or her predecessors in the period since 1840. Once passed by Parliament, an Act of Parliament ending the Sovereign's role as King or Queen in right of New Zealand would need the assent of the Sovereign or a Governor-General who is the Sovereign's representative. Once again, the governing principle is well established. The Sovereign "must sign her own death warrant if the two Houses unanimously send it up to her".[14] Almost certainly, the task would fall to Commissioners appointed by the Governor-General.

The Act would have become law when it had received the royal assent, but the operative clause making New Zealand a republic would likely not come into force until an appointed future date and time (either fixed or to be fixed and after any stated conditions had been met). At the appointed moment, the reigning King or Queen of the United Kingdom would cease to be the Sovereign in right of New Zealand. No future British Sovereign would assume that office. New Zealand would become a republic with a new or revised constitution already approved in advance.

14 Walter Bagehot *The English Constitution* (Fontana ed, Collins, London, 1963) at 98 (originally published 1867). See also Chapter 11 The Governor-General in Parliament.

3
DESIGNING THE REPUBLICAN CONSTITUTION

Some guiding principles

Those preparing for the possible ending of the Sovereign's role will also need to consider the effect which that would have on New Zealand law generally, including the common law. The governing principle is that, except so far as it would become spent because there was no longer a Sovereign, or would otherwise be inconsistent with the republican constitution, the existing law would remain in force. That principle would apply to the legal powers, rights or duties which originated as aspects of the royal prerogative but have been recognised by the courts as being part of the common law. So far as they are to be seen as conferring rights or imposing duties on the Sovereign in right of New Zealand, the Governor-General or the Crown, and are still required, at least for the time being, they would need to be revested in the appropriate person or body.[15] Most if not all of the armoury of the Crown, including quite a lot of statute law, would be affected in that way.

In considering the design of a republican constitution providing for a parliamentary system of government we discuss two key questions. The first is who should replace the Sovereign as the Head of State?[16] The second is where should the executive authority of New Zealand be vested? One option is to vest the executive authority in the Cabinet. The other is to vest it in the Head of State. Those two questions are interrelated, but although they are often conflated for the purposes of analysis, they need to be kept distinct. In working through the issues, we move back and forth between them.

Providing for the office of Head of State

The international law role

States like New Zealand with a parliamentary system of government have several options. Some of the small Pacific states have provided that the Prime Minister or other head of the government will also be the Head of State. Usually, however, republican states with a parliamentary system of government prefer to constitute a separate office of Head of State.

15 The prerogative of honour, being personal to the Sovereign, would cease to exist unless a new system was established by law and the continued recognition of earlier awards was provided for.

16 Most states have a Head of State who is a person, but in Switzerland the Federal Council is the Head of State.

In modern international law the responsibilities of the necessary office of Head of State are essentially ceremonial. From time to time, the Head of State is likely, in that capacity, to make a formal visit to another state. Such visits play an important part in foreign relations. Even so, the duties involved leave time for other activities. Most states with parliamentary governments usually give the Head of State some responsibilities not only for international relations but also in the functioning of the constitution itself.

A constitutional role?

There is a question whether, in addition to having functions and responsibilities in the field of international relations, the Head of State of a New Zealand republic should also have some constitutional responsibilities. In considering what those responsibilities might be, we concentrate on two issues: the revesting of the executive authority and the choice of a Prime Minister. Should the Head of State have a role in respect of either of those matters, and if so, what kind of role should be considered in respect of each?

The need to revest the executive authority

Essentially, the executive authority of New Zealand is the authority — and the duty — to govern the country, presently vested in the Sovereign in right of New Zealand. We discussed its nature in Chapter 8. If New Zealand no longer has a Sovereign, the executive authority now vested in the Sovereign will also disappear. In making a republican constitution the people of New Zealand must grant it anew, and vest it elsewhere. That is what the "Founding Fathers" saw the people of the United States of America as doing in giving themselves their independence constitution. The people of New Zealand would have to do the same, even if their constitutional change is peaceful and made with the consent of the Sovereign in the New Zealand Parliament.

The right and duty to exercise the executive authority of New Zealand, now delegated to Ministers through the Governor-General, enables them to exercise or otherwise benefit from the prerogative powers and privileges which are part of New Zealand law. It also authorises them to exercise all statutory powers vested in the Crown.[17] The executive authority is not in itself a power. If powers are needed, they must be sought in the law books. There may well

17 See Chapter 3 Constitutional Monarchy: Key Concepts, under the subheading The Queen and Crown as a corporation, at 40–42.

be a good case for doing away with some prerogative powers and privileges and codifying others in legislation,[18] but that is a matter of law reform, not of constitutional design.

The revesting of the executive authority involves more than the exercise of legal powers. The things done in the exercise of the executive authority include the introduction in Parliament of proposed legislation including revenue-gathering proposals, proposals for the expenditure of public money, and the duty to account for all money spent. The executive authority also includes the provision of all government services, the conduct of foreign affairs and trade arrangements, the maintenance of public order and the defence of the state.

The executive branch in a republic: the options

The perception of the executive authority of New Zealand provided for in a republican constitution, as having been newly constituted and reassigned by the people themselves, instead of being an attribute of the Sovereign, would colour its interpretation. Lawyers may instinctively look to the old precedents, so it would be important to signal that the revesting of the executive authority by the republican constitution is a new beginning, and all that follows will need to be understood in that light.

We consider that there are two options, each of which is worthy of serious consideration. The first is vesting of the executive authority of New Zealand in the Cabinet. The second is vesting the executive authority in the Head of State on the basis that he or she may exercise it directly or through Ministers and officials. We now look more closely at each of these options.

Vesting the executive authority of New Zealand in those who exercise it

In making a republican constitution, deciding to vest the executive authority in those who will actually exercise it would have a certain logical appeal. In a republican constitution with a parliamentary system of government, most aspects of executive authority will be exercised by or on the advice of the members of the Cabinet. They will function collegially, under the leadership of the Prime Minister, and will be individually and collectively responsible to Parliament for the consequences of their actions or inaction

18 Geoffrey Palmer and Andrew Butler *A Constitution for Aotearoa New Zealand* (Victoria University Press, Wellington, 2016) Constitution of Aotearoa New Zealand, cl 13 and at 85–86.

in the particular circumstance. As well as having authority, they would also have responsibility.

An example from a republican constitution

The constitution of the Republic of the Marshall Islands vests the executive authority of the Republic in the Cabinet in this way:[19]

> **The executive authority vested in the Cabinet**
> 1. The executive authority of the Republic shall be vested in the Cabinet whose members are responsible to Parliament.
> 2. Except as otherwise provided by law, the Cabinet may exercise elements of the executive authority directly, or through its individual members, and through other government officials responsible to the Cabinet; but neither the provisions of any such law, nor any delegation of elements of the Cabinet's executive authority shall have the effect of limiting the responsibility of the Cabinet and of each of its members to the Parliament for the direction and implementation of executive policies.

In that example the names of offices and institutions of government in the local language have been rendered in English. The President is, in effect, both the Head of State and the Prime Minister, but that concentration of power is offset by the fact that there is also a representative Council of Chiefs which has a constitutional right of access to the Cabinet, to discuss any matter of concern, and may also request the Parliament to reconsider any Bill.[20]

In making a republican constitution for New Zealand, it would be possible to vest the executive authority of the country in the Cabinet, in the manner just illustrated. That is essentially the model put forward by Sir Geoffrey Palmer and Andrew Butler,[21] although they suggest vesting the "executive power"[22] of the "State"[23] in the "Government".[24] Their draft constitution does not

19 Constitution of the Republic of the Marshall Islands, art V, ss 1(1) and (2). The constitution came into force on 1 May 1979. Before they became independent, the Marshall Islands had been a Trust Territory administered by the United States. Because of the difficulties of other Micronesian territories in reaching agreement between the executive and the legislature, each seperately elected, the elected Convention decided to adopt a parliamentary system of government. Alison Quentin-Baxter was Legal Counsel to the Constitutional Convention. Professor Laurence Tribe of Harvard University provided advice particularly on the aspects of the constitution based on the model of the United States Constitution, such as the Bill of Rights.
20 Article III, ss 2 and 3.
21 Palmer and Butler, above n 19, at 34–77.
22 Palmer and Butler, above n 19, Constitution of Aotearoa New Zealand, cl 16(2).
23 Clause 2.
24 Clause 16(3).

establish a very clear connection between those entities and the "Cabinet",[25] although the central role of the Cabinet is acknowledged in the commentary.[26] We are broadly agreed that, in a parliamentary constitution, the Cabinet would remain the effective decision-making body. In our view, that would remain the case, whether the executive authority is vested in the Cabinet or elsewhere in the executive branch. Careful consideration should therefore be given to the option of vesting in the Cabinet the executive authority of a republican New Zealand. That might well be the preferred option if the republican constitution of New Zealand were being written on a clean slate.[27] That, however, is not the case.

A number of the New Zealanders interested in a move to a republican constitution have assumed that the Head of State of a republican New Zealand would have a role very like that which the Governor-General exercises now.[28] That role is more complex than most people suppose, and that makes it the more necessary to look closely at the constitutional role that a New Zealand Head of State might have. In the next section, we explore our second option: vesting the executive authority of a New Zealand republic in the Head of State.

Vesting the executive authority of New Zealand in the Head of State

At present the Governor-General is authorised by the Sovereign to exercise the executive authority of New Zealand, directly or through Ministers and officials.[29] If there were no longer a Sovereign, it would be a small step to *vest* the executive authority of New Zealand in the Head of State, but to provide that, with a few specific exceptions, Ministers would continue to exercise the executive authority, directly, or through their officials.

That was the course taken by one of the Sovereign's smaller former territories, now the Republic of Mauritius. The relevant provisions of its constitution take the following form:[30]

> **The executive authority of Mauritius vested in the Head of State**
>
> 1. The executive authority of Mauritius is vested in the Head of State [known as the President].

25 Clause 24.
26 At 118–123.
27 As was the case in the former Trust Territory of the Marshall Islands.
28 See Knight, above n 4, and see also 3.4(b) of the Draft Constitution for the 21st Century <http://www.mcguinnessinstitute.org/wp-content/uploads/2016/08/20120906-EmpowerNZ-Draft-Constitution-for-the-21st-Century-Web.pdf>.
29 See Chapter 8 The Governor-General in the Executive Branch.
30 In order to facilitate a comparison, we have again used the New Zealand terminology, while bracketing the actual name.

> 2. Except as otherwise provided in this constitution, that executive authority may be exercised by the Head of State either directly or through officers subordinate to the Head of State.
> 3. Nothing in this section shall preclude persons or authorities, other than the President, from exercising such functions as may be conferred upon them by any law.[31]

The constitution also contains a clear statement that the Cabinet is to advise the President in the exercise of the country's executive authority, and is responsible to the legislature (called "the Assembly") for the advice so tendered.[32] The President is required to act on that advice, unless the constitution requires him to act on the advice of any other person or authority or in his own deliberate judgement.[33] The structure is modelled on that of the 1968 monarchical independence constitution of Mauritius which had incorporated the applicable constitutional conventions in the form of constitutional rules.

The people of Mauritius can be seen as having vested the country's executive authority in the President because, in a country committed to maintaining the well-being of all ethnic communities, they saw the President as able to provide an element of balance in the exercise of governmental power.[34] To that end, the republican constitution takes the further step of empowering the President to require the reconsideration of both any advice tendered to the President by the Cabinet and also of any Bill passed by Parliament and submitted for the President's assent. Occasionally, the dynamics of the political situation produce a Parliament in which there are no Opposition members, so it is important that the President would be able to put forward an alternative view.[35] That is not likely to happen in New Zealand. If the executive authority of New Zealand were to be vested in the Head of State, we do not suggest that it should give the Head of State any powers going beyond those the Governor-General has now. In Chapter 10 we reached the conclusion that the Governor-General should not now be seen as having the authority to override or publicly question a decision made by the government. Presumably, that would also be the case

31 Constitution of the Republic of Mauritius, art 58. The constitution came into force in 1992.
32 Article 61.
33 Article 64.
34 At the time of its colonisation by France, Mauritius had no indigenous inhabitants. In 1815 it became a British sugar colony. It now has a mixed population made up mainly of the large Hindu and smaller Muslim communities, together with a small Creole community, originating from Africa, as well as smaller numbers of Chinese and Franco-Mauritians. See Alison Quentin-Baxter "Ethnic accommodation in Malaysia, Mauritius and South Africa" in Brij V Lal and Tomasi R Vakatora (eds) *Fiji and the World* (School of Social and Economic Development, The University of the South Pacific, Suva, 1997) 137 at 137 and 139.
35 Constitution of Mauritius, art 46.

in a republic. Otherwise, the government and its supporters would almost certainly see the Head of State as breaching the duty to maintain political neutrality. By definition, the maintenance of that same neutrality would be incumbent on a non-executive Head of State.

We think that serious consideration should be given to vesting the executive authority in such a Head of State. The *exercise* of that authority would, however, continue to be delegated to the Prime Minister and the other Ministers, and the Cabinet would still be the executive's power house. The authority to govern of the Head of State would, however, be real, not notional. If there were ever to be a situation in which the elected government was unable to act, the Head of State would have the authority to do so.

Such a contingency is most unlikely, but the latent authority of the Head of State would have an effect on the perception of the office. As we explain below, that perception will be important. The choice between vesting the executive authority of New Zealand in the Cabinet and vesting it in the Head of State is, of course, a matter on which the voice of the people themselves will need to be heard.

The constitutional role of the Head of State

It seems to be widely accepted that a Head of State would have a similar place in the life of the nation to that of the Governor-General now, but perhaps enhanced by no longer being under the shadow of the distant Sovereign. Palmer and Butler outline their own vision of the Head of State in a republic:[36]

> The most important function of the Head of State we [propose] will be to act as a symbol of the State; to signify its unity, its legitimacy and its values. Symbols are important, . . . [they] can help to provide a sense of national unity and purpose. They can nourish a sense of belief about the ideals of the nation and give people a sense of aspiration, even destiny. . . . [I]n our view the time has come to move on by not only deepening and thickening our constitutional arrangements but also by allowing our own symbols, such as a home-grown Head of State, space to develop.

That vision is attractive, but we think the Head of State would be set an impossible task if he or she were required to be a symbol without a role.

In Chapter 14 we explained that the Governor-General's present interaction with the people of New Zealand is still in a process of development. In Chapters

36 Palmer and Butler, above n 19, at 91–92.

8 to 10 we discussed both the theoretical and the practical aspects of the Governor-General's role in the executive branch of government. The truth is that, ever since Governors and Governors-General ceased to govern, there has been an element of uncertainty and ambiguity about their constitutional role, not only in New Zealand but in other realms as well. Despite the best efforts of individual Governors-General to carve out a role for themselves, the Governor-General's modern role has never been formally articulated in positive terms.

It would be desirable not to perpetuate that vacuum. We therefore put forward for consideration a statement of principle about the constitutional role the Head of State might have.

1. The Head of State holds a non-political office in the executive branch of government.
2. In representing New Zealand internationally, and in interacting with the people of New Zealand, the Head of State acts consistently with the policies of the government, and must act in accordance with any advice tendered by the Prime Minister.
3. The Head of State has the other functions and powers expressly or impliedly conferred by the republican constitution or any other law.
4. Subject to principles 1, 2 and 3, the Head of State shares with the Prime Minister and the other Ministers a responsibility for promoting the well-being of all the people of New Zealand, and carries out that responsibility in the exercise of his or her judgement, but must always act in a non-political way. That last-mentioned duty does not prevent the Head of State from publicly expressing a personal view about a matter of public interest or concern, as long as that view is not inconsistent with any formally announced policy of the government.

The express recognition that the Head of State is a part of the executive branch of government would make that branch a little less monolithic than it would be otherwise. It would also help to provide a basis for making other decisions about the reconstitution of the executive branch.

Governing principles for choosing a Head of State

With the role and responsibilities described above, the Head of State clearly needs to remain non-political. That need is generally seen as ruling out the popular election of the Head of State. Ireland appears to be the one republic with a parliamentary system of government and a politically neutral Head of State (called the President) elected by popular vote. Our understanding, however, is that a candidate needs the nominal support of a main political party in order to bring their candidature to the attention of the people, but, apparently, that is not seen as politicising the election.

In contrast, it seems that politicians in Australia could not see how a Head of State could be popularly elected without the active participation of the various political parties in a way which would turn the election of the Head of State into a party-based contest. It was clear that, as well as creating a risk that the electoral base of the Head of State might be different from that of the government,[37] a nationwide election of the Head of State would itself politicise the office. In the run-up to the 1999 referendum on the question of whether Australia should become a republic, both main parties resisted the public demand that the Head of State should be democratically elected. There were also uncertainties about the powers the Head of State would have. It came as no surprise that the referendum resulted in a "No" vote on the question of whether Australia should become a republic in all the states and territories except the Australian Capital Territory.[38]

In New Zealand, with its different political background, it seems to be generally accepted that the Members of Parliament, acting non-politically, should choose or endorse the choice of a Head of State. Palmer and Butler propose that the Head of State should be "appointed to office . . . by the House of Representatives on a free vote . . .".[39] The proposal for a "Draft Constitution for the 21st Century" suggests that the Head of State should be chosen by a 75 per cent majority in Parliament.[40] Neither proposal seems yet to deal with nominations to the office. Who may make them, and must there be only one, or could there be more? The constitution of the Republic of Mauritius provides for the President and Vice-President each to be elected by the Parliament (called the Assembly). The Prime Minister makes a single nomination to each office, which is then voted on without debate.[41] These and other questions will need to be considered.

The guiding principle is the need to choose the Head of State in a way that does not politicise the office, or appear to do so. The method of choosing a Head of State should be commensurate with the responsibilities of the office.

37 At 149–150.

38 As already mentioned, we have left to others any scholarly comparative law research into the republican constitutions of other states in a similar position to New Zealand.

39 Palmer and Butler, above n 19, Constitution of Aotearoa New Zealand, cl 9(2). See also at 101–102.

40 <http://www.mcguinnessinstitute.org/wp-content/uploads/2016/08/20120906-EmpowerNZ-Draft-Constitution-for-the-21st-Century-Web.pdf> at 3.4.

41 Constitution of the Republic of Mauritius, art 28.

We have discussed above the general nature of the office of Head of State and also looked at two possibilities: the vesting of the executive authority in the Head of State or in the Cabinet. Whichever the choice, it will also be necessary to look at the specific responsibilities and powers which might be vested in the Head of State.

The Head of State's specific duties, rights and powers

The applicable principles

The specific duties, rights and powers that a republican constitution might give to the Head of State could include most if not all of the specific powers now exercisable by the Governor-General, acting on the advice of the Prime Minister or another Minister. But, instead of remaining exercisable as part of the executive authority, wherever that is vested, they could be vested by the republican constitution itself in the holder of the office of Head of State, in his or her own right.

The powers in question are prerogative powers now vested in the Sovereign but which the Governor-General is expressly authorised to exercise. They are the power to *constitute*, and to *make appointments* to, an office in the service of the Crown, and the power to exercise what is at present known as "the prerogative of mercy". Both powers will continue to be needed in some form. A republican constitution could confer those powers in an appropriate form on the Head of State.

In the exercise of the power to constitute offices and make appointments to them, the Governor-General currently *constitutes* the offices of Prime Minister and the other Ministers. The Executive Council is at present constituted by the Sovereign,[42] and the Cabinet has always remained an informal meeting of Ministers. The republican constitution could and probably should itself constitute all of those offices and institutions, and provide expressly for the making of appointments to them, as well as granting to the holders of those offices or the institutions themselves any necessary functions and powers. Below we discuss the way in which the Prime Minister of a republican New Zealand could be chosen, and, in particular, the part which a Head of State could play. First, however, we look at the opportunity the making of a republican constitution would provide for the clarification of an important principle, the duty of the Head of State to act on ministerial advice.

42 Letters Patent 1983, cl 7.

The duty to act on advice

If, in the republican constitution, or indeed the ordinary law, of a country which has a parliamentary system of government, a non-executive Head of State is to have any legal powers, there will be a need to make it clear whether the Head of State must exercise those powers on ministerial advice. The answer is usually "Yes", but there may be exceptions to the general rule. The constitution of the Republic of Mauritius contains the following provision:[43]

> In the exercise of his functions under this Constitution or any other law, the Head of State [called the President] shall act in accordance with the advice of the Cabinet or of a Minister acting under the general authority of the Cabinet except in cases where he is required by this Constitution to act in accordance with the advice of, or after consultation with, any person or authority other than the Cabinet or in his own deliberate judgement.

There would already have been a corresponding provision in their earlier monarchical constitution.

If included in a republican constitution for New Zealand, a similar provision[44] would take much of the mystery out of the principle that, in general, a non-executive Head of State acts on the advice of Ministers. While it is true that a Head of State who is required to exercise a power on the advice of a Minister is not personally exercising power,[45] there would be powerful symbolism in the fact that a power has been conferred in the name of the Head of State. Whether or not the republican constitution confers powers on the Head of State, the statute law is likely to continue to do so.

If a Head of State were authorised to exercise a power "in his or her own deliberate judgement", it would still be possible to establish the criteria on which the decision should be made. There have always been criteria. In Chapters 9 and 10 we demonstrated that, in respect of the monarchical constitution, those criteria can be codified and authoritatively recorded. It is true, however, that a judgement must still be made. In recent times, people seem to have become fearful of relying on someone else's judgement, and look for fixed rules. But, like the law itself, a constitution may sometimes need to rely on principles, rather than rules, in order to serve human needs.

43 Constitution of the Republic of Mauritius, art 64(1), Exercise of President's Functions.

44 In the case of New Zealand, the provision would need to take account of the fact that the statute law sometimes requires the Governor-General to act on the advice of a person or body other than a Minister.

45 Palmer and Butler, above n 19, at 89.

On that note, we turn to an area of the republican constitution in which we think there is a need for the application of principle and judgement by all the constitutional actors. That is in finding or changing a Prime Minister, if that should become necessary.

Choosing a Prime Minister

Should a republican constitution provide for the Head of State to continue to oversee the process of finding and choosing a Prime Minister? In the constitutional monarchy, the responsibility of finding a Prime Minister is nominally that of the Governor-General, but the leaders of the political parties and the other Members of Parliament have the main responsibility.[46]

Even so, the Governor-General does not just make the formal appointment after the identity of the new Prime Minister is known. He or she has the overarching responsibility of ensuring that it is possible to appoint a Prime Minister who is able to form a government which will have the support of a majority in the House of Representatives on issues of confidence. The need for the government to have and to retain that support goes to the heart of the parliamentary system of government. That principle would be just as fundamental to the functioning of a republican constitution.

People should think about whether it would be appropriate for a republican constitution to give the Head of State the same responsibility for finding and changing a Prime Minister as the Governor-General has now.[47] If we were drafting a provision for a New Zealand republican constitution providing that the Head of State appoints a Prime Minister, we would want to stay close to the statement of principle we have already set out in Chapter 9. A republican constitution could provide as follows:[48]

> The Head of State must appoint as Prime Minister a Member of Parliament who, in the light of the distribution of seats among the political parties and the public statements of the political leaders, is, in his or her judgement, able to form a government which has the support of a majority of the members of the House of Representatives on issues of confidence.

In contrast, Sir Geoffrey Palmer and Andrew Butler propose that the Prime Minister of a republican New Zealand should be "elected by a majority of the

46 See Chapter 9 Finding and Changing a Prime Minister.
47 See, for example, Constitution of the Republic of Mauritius, art 49(3).
48 See Chapter 9 Finding and Changing a Prime Minister, under the subheading The New Zealand principles, Principle 1, at 198.

voting members of the House of Representatives from among its members".[49] They make that proposal because the constitution they have drafted would abolish the Sovereign's prerogative power to appoint a Prime Minister. They also see it as:

> . . . important that the Constitution should state the fundamental rules of the system and they not be left completely to constitutional convention and the Cabinet Manual.[50]

We have already shown, however, that it is a relatively straightforward matter for a constitution to grant the Head of State a *constitutional* power to determine which member of the Parliament ought to be appointed as the Prime Minister, and the basis upon which the Head of State should make that determination.[51]

It is noteworthy that in the Australian states and territories in which a similar provision to that which Palmer and Butler propose is in place, it has not replaced the constitutional duty of the Sovereign or the Governor, after a government's defeat at a general election, to find a Premier who is able to form a government.

There should be a provision requiring there to be a further search for a government within the existing Parliament after a defeat in an early confidence vote to ensure that there is not another general election unless it is very clear that no viable government can be found. Certainly, the political actors will respond to the incentives provided by any constitution, but a totally mechanised constitution is not necessarily the answer.

We would ourselves prefer the Head of State to appoint the Prime Minister of a republic on the same basis as the Governor-General appoints a Prime Minister now, but with an acknowledgement of that responsibility in the constitution itself. There seems to be widespread support for a non-political Head of State who has a significant leadership role alongside the Prime Minister who is the leader of the government. In our view, that would be difficult to achieve unless the constitution itself assigns to the Head of State some significant responsibilities consistent with its apolitical nature. Only then would the Head of State be able to take his or her place alongside the Prime Minister as an essential element of the executive branch of government.

49 Palmer and Butler, above n 19, Constitution of Aotearoa New Zealand, cl 18(3).
50 At 131.
51 See the Republican Constitution of Mauritius.

Parliament

Whichever option is pursued, in providing for the executive branch of government, the Parliament of New Zealand would have to be reconstituted without the Sovereign. It presently consists of the Sovereign in right of New Zealand and the House of Representatives.[52] In our view, the historical concept that the Sovereign is part of the Parliaments of her realms should not be reflected in a republican constitution. The House of Representatives alone should become the Parliament of a republican New Zealand. That would, however, require new provision about how and when a Bill passed by Parliament would become law.

If the Prime Minister were to become, also, the new Head of State, then it would be desirable for the Speaker or the Clerk of the House to have a constitutional role in signing Bills into law. If the new Head of State were outside of Parliament, which seems much more likely, it would be necessary to consider whether the holder of that office, acting on the advice of the Prime Minister, would signify that a Bill has been duly passed by Parliament and has therefore become law. If that course were chosen, it would be desirable for the Head of State to share that task with the Speaker and/or the Clerk of the House and the Attorney-General.

If it were thought that further constitutional safeguards were required, it would be possible to investigate the South African and Mauritius models which give the Head of State the power to send a Bill back to the House to reconsider the constitutionality of a measure.[53] Such a course, however, may endanger the political neutrality of the Head of State. In any event, given that constitutional change to a republic is likely to be part of a wider constitutional settlement, the possibility of conferring powers on the judges to judicially review legislation for compliance with guaranteed rights and other constitutional principles is likely also to be considered and may be a preferred solution.

The existing law

A move to a republican constitution would leave the existing law in force, so far as it is still compatible with any new constitution or other laws made for that purpose, but some of that existing law would become "spent", to use the technical term. In other words, it would cease to have any effect because the office-holders whom it empowers will have ceased to exist. For that reason,

52 Constitution Act 1986, s 14(1).
53 Constitution of the Republic of South Africa, s 84(2)(c).

the republican constitution would normally amend or repeal the existing law so far as is necessary to make it consistent with the republican constitution. For the avoidance of doubt, however, it would be usual for the republican constitution to confirm that, except so far as it is inconsistent with the republican constitution, the existing law remains in force, but with the necessary adaptations.

We now consider some of the more important consequential changes that would need to be made to other aspects of New Zealand law and practice if the country were to become a republic, and the Sovereign, including the Crown in all its manifestations, were to disappear.

4
CONSEQUENTIAL CHANGES

In this part, we identify consequential changes, not only to what can be identified as part of "the constitution", but also to other aspects of New Zealand law and practice. So far as they would still be required, the present rights and obligations of "the Sovereign", however described, and of "the Crown" would have to be provided for in some other way. The meanings of each term in their present contexts are so varied that there is limited scope for simply substituting some other general term. Some matters, including the important question of the Crown's successor as a party to the Treaty of Waitangi, would need to be looked at in the contexts in which they would arise.

In the present constitution and law, certain rights, powers and duties are vested in a legal entity with a name which evokes the monarchy — the "Sovereign", "Queen", "Crown", "Governor-General", "Governor-General in Council", or a "Crown entity". In one or other of those names, the executive branch of government has many legal rights, privileges and powers. The origin of some was the royal prerogative, but they should not be thought of as in some way personal to the Sovereign, or forever coloured by their origin. They have survived because Parliament has not yet codified them so far as they are still required. In the meantime, they operate in the same way as the unwritten common law. Their content must be ascertained from the case law.

The vast majority of the laws reflecting the executive authority of the Sovereign, through which the country is governed, are part of the statute law. Parliament has conferred a vast range of rights, powers and also duties on one or other of the organs mentioned above. For ease of reference, we refer to them collectively as the attributes of the Crown. If a particular attribute of the Crown is recognised by New Zealand law, it no longer matters whether it is a prerogative of the Crown or an attribute conferred by Parliament. For example, the Governor-General has a prerogative power to appoint a Prime Minister but a statutory power to dissolve Parliament. Nothing now turns on that distinction.

In a republic, any name signifying the monarchy would become unusable. The republican constitution would need to constitute a new entity with a different name. For the moment, we refer to it as the republican legal entity. The transitional provisions of the republican constitution would need to transfer the attributes of the Crown to the republican legal entity. Immediately, they would become the attributes of the republic. From then on they would be no different in kind from the attributes which the legislature of the republic may later give the republican legal entity, or its courts may find it to have.

The new legal entity of the republic would be an organ of the executive branch of government. It would need to be given a suitable name of its own. The rights and obligations concerned could be vested in "New Zealand" as a legal person, or in the "state".

At this early stage, however, it is the conceptual framework which is important. Preferably, in the constitutional context, "the state" or "New Zealand" epithet should be reserved for the abstract, permanent and non-elected elements of the constitution as a whole. It would bring some conceptual clarification lacking in the monarchical constitution and the underlying law if, instead of resorting to a multifaceted concept such as the Crown or a monolithic concept such as the state, the constitution-makers (including the judges) deliberately attempted where possible to use standardised terminology distinguishing between the abstract permanent aspects of the executive branch ("New Zealand", "the nation") and the elected government of the day.

In general, the provision made in the republican constitution for the exercise of the executive authority of New Zealand will determine the allocation of responsibility within the executive branch, but, as we have suggested in part 3, the powers to appoint a Prime Minister or to dissolve Parliament would need to be specifically provided for. Whether the executive authority is vested in the Cabinet or in the Head of State, the Cabinet would continue to have the controlling authority to govern.

There are, however, some contexts in which, in the present constitutional monarchy, "the Crown" can be seen as being the Sovereign herself, now usually acting through the Governor-General. That possibility introduces a non-partisan human involvement into what would otherwise be the ordinary exercise of executive authority by the executive government. The recognition of that need, at times, for an impartial human presence may strengthen the case for vesting the executive authority of New Zealand in the Head of State.

In contrast, there may be other contexts in which it may be appropriate to eliminate any existing personifications altogether. In relation to land tenure, it would be possible to borrow some of the innovative approaches which have been taken in relation to Treaty of Waitangi settlements: the Treaty of Waitangi could become the basis and source of fee simple title instead of the Queen in right of New Zealand.

It may sometimes be appropriate to invoke the concept of "the nation" or "the people" as a substitute for the Crown — in relation to bringing criminal proceedings, for example. In part 3 we made the point that the constitution of a New Zealand republic must be seen as an act of the people, rather than of Parliament alone. The expression "Treaty peoples" may be an appropriate description of the nation itself, evoking as it does the distinctive history and identity of Aotearoa/New Zealand.

The Treaty of Waitangi in a republic

The single biggest political controversy is likely to concern the successor to the commitments, obligations and liabilities of the Crown under the Treaty of Waitangi or in respect of a breach thereof. In law, the Government of New Zealand has already succeeded to those obligations and liabilities, but, unless the Crown as a party to that solemn compact were to be succeeded by a specified person or body provided for in the constitution, many of the current legal and political nuances, and the central idea of a relationship between peoples, may be put at risk. A creative approach which continues to capture the sense of an ongoing relationship between peoples within a single nation is likely to be required. Again, it may be that a politically neutral Head of State, especially one in whom the executive authority of New Zealand has been vested, could be given a special role in maintaining the Treaty relationship. It would also be a good idea to make provision in the constitution for the special role of the Waitangi Tribunal so that it could continue to act in the historical place of the Sovereign or the Governor, as the intermediary between the tangata whenua and "settler" governments of the present day, and as an institution to which Māori can bring petitions. The Waitangi Tribunal has proved itself to be a much more effective vehicle for addressing Māori petition in the modern era than the Queen or the Governor-General.

Another consequential issue is that New Zealanders would no longer owe allegiance to the Sovereign in right of New Zealand. It would be necessary to consider whether the concept of allegiance still has a place in a republican constitution, and, if so, the person or concept to which allegiance would be owed. "New Zealand", "the Constitution" and "the laws of New Zealand" might be possibilities and could perhaps be combined. The question will be especially important for those who are now required by law to make an oath of allegiance to the Sovereign, including Members of Parliament, judges, military personnel and some other officials. The sensibilities of those who have already made an oath or affirmation of allegiance to the Sovereign would need to be considered. In addition, the law of treason would need to be revised.

These and other matters of terminology and the reallocation of powers and functions would require careful, nuanced and case-by-case consideration.

5
CONCLUSION

A New Zealand republic?

In this afterword, we have described the main processes and policy choices that would need to be worked through if the people of New Zealand were seriously to consider making their country a republic. We have made comparisons with the present constitution on the assumption that the changes of practice recommended in earlier chapters will be put in place, but if that is not the case, they would still be needed — perhaps more than ever. In moving to a republic, much of the present constitution could well remain in its present form. Even so, we think that a republican constitution would need to be written down and made accessible to the public. People need to know what is in their constitution — but that can be only a starting point in understanding how it works.

In thinking about a republican constitution, we have not gone beyond the changes that would be essential. All other constitutional changes which might be possible or even desirable are outside the scope of this book. Although surprisingly few changes to the existing constitution would be required, they would need to be carefully thought out. Any changeover would need to be seamless. On the first day of the republic, the constitution must work as well as it did on the last day of the monarchy. The decision-making process would need to be carefully considered.

We have not discussed the process of making a republican constitution in any detail. Key decisions would need to be voted on in a series of referendums. The public would also need to be involved in an appropriate way in the formulation of the republican constitution itself. Feelings may run high, but the outcome would be less likely to be divisive if the republican constitution itself is generally acceptable. Then, all New Zealanders would be able to live under it, some, perhaps, with regrets for what has been lost, but all of them with reason to be confident that the republican constitution itself will work well.

Valediction

We have now come to the end of our story about the working of New Zealand's present-day constitutional monarchy, and the possibility that a republic may someday take its place. We have looked back at the past, assessed the present, and peered into the future. The structure of the constitution and its governing principles can and should be written down in an authoritative way. It should then be made available to the public. But the constitution cannot be fully understood simply by reading its words. A constitution is a living organism because it needs people to make it work. Ever since New Zealand became a British colony in 1840, the constitutional actors of the day have been trying to make the constitution work in a way that would satisfy the sometimes conflicting aspirations of those who were able to assert influence or power. The constitution was still working in that way as we were writing this book, and it was changing in the process. Sometimes, it was hard to keep up.

We have seen our task as that of identifying the way in which the changing perceptions and expectations of those with an interest to pursue brought about changes in the constitutional roles of the Sovereign, the Governor or Governor-General and the Crown. The changes themselves and the main reasons for making them can usually be identified. It has been harder to evaluate the way in which the constitutional monarchy is now working for the people of New Zealand. That is the insight we have been trying to capture. The story must speak for itself.

BIBLIOGRAPHY

Books and Articles

Abbott, PE and Tamplin, JMA *British Gallantry Awards* (2nd ed, Guinness World Records Ltd, 1981).

Aikman, CC and Robson, JL "Introduction" in John Lochiel Robson (ed) *New Zealand: The Development of its Laws and Constitution* (2nd ed, Stevens & Sons, London, 1967) 1.

Angelo, Tony "The Letters Patent" [2007] NZLJ 5.

Archer, Peter *The Queen's Courts* (2nd ed, Penguin Books, Harmondsworth [UK], 1963).

Arnot, David M "The Honour of the Crown" (1996) 60(2) Sask L Rev 339.

Austin, Graeme W "Re-Treating Intellectual Property — The Wai 262 Proceeding and the Heuristics of International Property Law" (2003) 11(2) Cardozo J Int'l & Comp L 350.

Bagehot, Walter *The English Constitution* (Fontana ed, Collins, London, 1963) (originally published 1867).

Belich, James *Making Peoples: A History of the New Zealanders from Polynesian Settlement to the End of the Nineteenth Century* (Penguin, Auckland, 2007).

Bland, Neville (ed) *Satow's Guide to Diplomatic Practice* (4th ed, Longmans, London, 1957).

Bogdanor, Vernon *The Monarchy and the Constitution* (Oxford University Press, Oxford, 1997).

Brazier, Rodney "Legislating about the Monarchy" (2007) 66(1) CLJ 86.

Buick, Thomas Lindsay *The French at Akaroa: An Adventure in Colonisation* (New Zealand Book Depot, Wellington, 1928).

Christian, Archibold and Chitty (eds) *Blackstone's Commentaries on the Laws of England: Volume 1* (Collins & Co, New York, 1827).

Crommelin, Michael "Governor-General and the Republic: Powers of the Head of State" (2015) 38 MULR 1118.

de Bracton, H *Bracton on the Laws and Customs of England: Volume 2* (translated by Samuel E Thorne, William S Hein & Co, Buffalo [NY], 1997).

de Smith, SA "The Royal Style and Titles" (1953) 2(2) Int & Comp LQ 263.

Documents on Canadian External Relations: Volume 3: 1919–1925 (Department of External Affairs, Ottawa, 1970).

Durie, Mason H *Te Mana, Te Kāwanatanga: The Politics of Māori Self-Determination* (Oxford University Press, Auckland, 1998).

Evans, Gareth (ed) *Labor and the Constitution 1972–1975: Essays and Commentaries on the Constitutional Controversies of the Whitlam Years in Australian Government* (Heinemann, Richmond [Vic], 1977).

Fieldhouse, DK "Autochthonous Elements in the Evolution of Dominion Status: The Case of New Zealand" (1962) 1(2) Journal of Commonwealth Political Studies 85.

Fletcher, Ruth "The Governor as Commander-in-Chief" (1943) 2 Historical Studies Australia and New Zealand 209.

Frame, Alex "Lawyers and the Making of Constitutions: Making Constitutions in the South Pacific: Architects and Excavators" in D Carter and M Palmer (eds) *Roles and Perspectives in the Law: Essays in Honour of Sir Ivor Richardson* (Victoria University Press, Wellington, 2002) 277.

—— "Raupatu Settlement — Legal Finality and Political Reality" in Richard Boast and Richard S Hill (eds) *Raupatu: The Confiscation of Maori Land* (Victoria University Press, Wellington, 2009) 243.

Graham, Douglas *Trick or Treaty?* (Institute of Policy Studies, Victoria University of Wellington, Wellington, 1997).

Halsbury's Laws of England (4th ed, reissue, 1998) vol 8(2) Introduction: Basic Principles of the Constitution of the United Kingdom.

—— (4th ed, reissue, 1998) vol 12(1) Crown and Royal Family.

Hardie Boys, Sir Michael "Governing under MMP: the Constitutional and Policy Challenges" (Institute of Policy Studies Seminar, Wellington, 1998).

—— "Nodding Automaton?" (2001–2008) 8 Canterbury Law Review 425.
—— *The Boy From Evans Bay: The Memoirs of Sir Michael Hardie Boys* (Evans Bay Press, Wellington, 2016).
Harris, Bruce V "The Law-Making Power of the New Zealand General Assembly: Time to Think About Change" (1984) 5 Otago Law Review 565.
—— "The Constitutional Future of New Zealand" [2004] NZ Law Review 269.
Harris, C (ed) *House of Representatives Practice* (5th ed, Department of the House of Representatives, Canberra, 2005).
Hennessy, Peter *The Prime Minister: The Office and its Holders Since 1945* (Allen Lane, London, 2000).
Hensley, Gerald *Final Approaches: A Memoir* (Auckland University Press, Auckland, 2006).
—— *Beyond the Battlefield: New Zealand and its Allies 1939–45* (Penguin, London, 2009).
Hickey, Maureen "Apologies in Treaty Settlements" in Nicola Wheen and Janine Hayward (eds) *Treaty of Waitangi Settlements* (Wellington, Bridget Williams Books, 2012) 79.
Hickford, Mark *Lords of the Land: Indigenous Property Rights and the Jurisprudence of Empire* (Oxford University Press, Oxford, 2011).
Hocking, Jenny *The Dismissal Dossier: Everything you were never meant to know about November 1975* (Melbourne University Press, Carlton (Vic), 2015).
Holmes, Brenton *Tracking the push for an Australian republic* (Parliamentary Library, 2013), available at <http://parlinfo.aph.gov.au/parlInfo/download/library/prspub/2394055/upload_binary/2394055.pdf;fileType=application/pdf>.
Howard, John "Response to Paul Keating's 'An Australian Republic: The Way Forward'" (House of Representatives, 8 June 1995), available at <http://australianpolitics.com/1995/06/08/howard-response-to-republic-proposal.html>.
Jennings, Ivor *Cabinet Government* (3rd ed, Cambridge University Press, Cambridge, 1959).
—— *The Law and the Constitution* (5th ed, University of London Press, London, 1959).
Jones, GW "The Office of Prime Minister" in Herbert Van Thal (ed) *The Prime Ministers (Vol 1): Sir Robert Walpole to Sir Robert Peel* (Allen & Unwin, London, 1974) 11.
Joseph, Philip A "Commentary on Alison Quentin-Baxter 'Implications for the Governor-General'" in *The Constitutional Implications of MMP* (Dunmore Press, Wellington, 1998) 96.
—— *Constitutional and Administrative Law in New Zealand* (4th ed, Thomson Reuters, Wellington, 2014).
Keating, PJ "An Australian Republic: The Way Forward" (House of Representative, 7 June 1995), available at <http://australianpolitics.com/1995/06/07/an-australian-republic-the-way-forward.html>.
Kumarasingham, Harshan *Onward with Executive Power: Lessons from New Zealand 1947–57* (Institute of Policy Studies, Victoria University of Wellington, Wellington, 2010).
Lal, Brij V and Tomasi R Vakatora (eds) *Fiji and the World* (School of Social and Economic Development, The University of the South Pacific, Suva, 1997).
Lauterpacht, H (ed) *Oppenheim's International Law* (8th ed, Longmans, London, 1955).
Laws of New Zealand Courts (online ed).
Laws of New Zealand Defence: Warfare (Reissue 1) (online ed).
Leigh, Ian "By Law Established? The Crown, Constitutional Reform and the Church of England" [2004] Public Law 266.
Little, William *The Shorter Oxford Dictionary on Historical Principles* (3rd ed, Clarendon Press, 1944).
Loughlin, Martin "The State, the Crown and the Law" in Maurice Sunkin and Sebastian Payne (eds) *The Nature of the Crown: A Legal and Political Analysis* (Oxford University Press, New York, 1999) 33.
McGee, David G *Parliamentary Practice in New Zealand* (3rd ed, Dunmore Publishing, Wellington, 2005).
McIntyre, WD and WJ Gardner *Speeches and Documents on New Zealand History* (Oxford University Press, Oxford, 1971).
McKay, William (ed) *Erskine May's Treatise on the Law, Privileges, Proceedings and Usage of Parliament* (23rd ed, LexisNexis UK, London, 2004).
McLay, Jim "1984 and All That" (2012) 10 NZJPIL 267.

McLean, Gavin *The Governors: New Zealand's Governors and Governors-General* (Otago University Press, Dunedin, 2006).

McLean, Janet "Crown Him With Many Crowns: The Crown and the Treaty of Waitangi" (2008) 6 NZJIPL 35.

—— *Searching for the State in British Legal Thought* (Cambridge University Press, New York, 2012).

—— 'Crown, Empire and Redressing the Historical Wrongs of Colonisation in New Zealand' [2015] NZ L Rev 187.

Marshall, Geoffrey and Graeme C Moodie *Some problems of the Constitution* (Hutchison, London, 1959).

Martin, John E "Refusal of Assent — A Hidden Element of Constitutional History in New Zealand" (2010) 41 VUWLR 51.

Milne, RS *Political Parties in New Zealand* (Oxford University Press, London, 1966).

Mount, Simon "A Criminal Cases Review Commission for New Zealand" [2009] NZ L Rev 445.

O'Malley, Vincent *The Great War for New Zealand* (Bridget Williams Books, Wellington, 2016).

Orange, Claudia *The Treaty of Waitangi* (Allen & Unwin, Wellington, 1987).

—— "The Maori People and the British Crown (1769–1840)" in Keith Sinclair (ed) *The Oxford Illustrated History of New Zealand* (2nd ed, Oxford University Press, Auckland, 1996).

—— *The Treaty of Waitangi* (2nd ed, Bridget Williams Books, Wellington, 2011).

Palmer, Geoffrey "The Cabinet, the Prime Minister and the Constitution" (2006) 4 NZJPIL 1.

Palmer, Geoffrey and Andrew Butler *A Constitution for Aotearoa New Zealand* (Victoria University Press, Wellington, 2016).

Palmer, Matthew *The Treaty of Waitangi in New Zealand's Law and Constitution* (Victoria University Press, Wellington, 2008).

Pugh, Ralph B *The Crown Estate: An Historical Essay* (HM Stationery Office, London, 1960).

Quentin-Baxter, RQ "The Governor-General's constitutional discretions: An essay towards redefinition" (1980) 10 VUWLR 289.

Richardson, M "The Privy Council and New Zealand" (1997) 46 Intl & Comp LQ 908.

Riggs, Fred W "The Survival of Presidentialism in America: Para-constitutional Practices" (1988) 9 International Political Science Review 247.

Roberts-Wray, Kenneth *Commonwealth and Colonial Law* (Stevens & Sons, London, 1966).

Robson, John Lochiel *New Zealand: The Development of its Laws and Constitution* (Stevens & Sons, London, 1954).

—— *New Zealand: The Development of its Laws and Constitution* (2nd ed, Stevens & Sons, 1967).

Salmond, John William *Jurisprudence* (6th ed, Stevens & Haynes, London, 1920).

Saunders, Cheryl *The Constitution of Australia: A Conceptual Analysis* (Hart Publishing, Oxford, 2011).

Scott, Kenneth John *The New Zealand Constitution* (Clarendon Press, Oxford, 1962).

Sharp, Andrew and Paul McHugh *Histories, Power and Loss: Uses of the Past — A New Zealand Commentary* (Bridget Williams Books, Wellington, 2001).

Sharswood, George *Commentaries on the Laws of England in Four Books by Sir William Blackstone: Book IV* (Childs & Peterson, Philadelphia, 1860).

Sinclair, Keith *Walter Nash* (Auckland University Press, Auckland, 1976).

Slattery, Brian "Aboriginal Rights and the Honour of the Crown" (2009) 29 SCLR (2d) 433.

Sossin, Lorne and Peter H Russell (eds) *Parliamentary Democracy in Crisis* (University of Toronto Press, Toronto, 2009).

Spender, J and C Asquith *Life of Herbert Henry Asquith: Volume 2* (Hutchinson, London, 1932).

Stephens, Mamari "To Work Out Their Own Salvation: Māori Constitutionalism and the Quest for Welfare" (2015) 46 VUWLR 907.

Swinfen, DB *Imperial Control of Colonial Legislation 1813–1865: A Study of British Policy towards Colonial Legislative Powers* (Clarendon Press, Oxford, 1970).

The Encyclopaedia Britannica: Volume VIII (11th ed, Cambridge University Press, Cambridge, 1910).

The Royal Commonwealth Society *An Uncommon Association — A Wealth of Potential: Final Report of the Commonwealth Conversation* (March 2010) <www.thecommonwealthassociation.org>.

Tiernan, Anne *Caretaker Conventions in Australasia: Minding the Shop for Government* (ANU E-Press (Centre for Governance and Public Policy), 2007), available at <http://epress.anu.edu.au/anzsog/caretaker/pdf_instructions.html>.

Todd, Alpheus *Parliamentary Government in the British Colonies* (2nd ed, Longmans, London, 1894).

Townend, Andrew "The Strange Death of the Realm of New Zealand: The Implications of a New Zealand Republic for the Cook Islands and Niue" (2003) 34 VUWLR 571.

Tucker, George (ed) *Blackstone's Commentaries* (5 vols, William Young Birch & Abraham Small, Philadelphia, 1803) *Book II* and *Book IV*.

Twomey, Anne "The Refusal or Deferral of Royal Assent" (Sydney Law School, Legal Studies Research Paper No 07/58, August 2007).

—— "Changing the Rules of Succession to the Throne" (Sydney Law School, Legal Studies Research Paper No 11/71, October 2011) <http://ssrn.com/abstract=1943287>.

—— "Two approaches to the application of succession to the throne in the realms" (unpublished paper, 2012).

Wade, ECS and G Godfrey Phillips *Constitutional and Administrative Law* (9th ed, Longman, London, 1977).

Wade, William *Administrative Law* (2nd ed, Oxford University Press, Oxford, 1967).

Ward, Alan *A Show of Justice: Racial "Amalgamation" in Nineteenth Century New Zealand* (Auckland University Press, Auckland, 1973).

Watts, Peter and FMB Reynolds (eds) *Bowstead and Reynolds on Agency* (20th ed, Sweet & Maxwell, London, 2014).

Wheeler, Graham John "Royal Assent in the British Constitution" (2016) 132 LQR 495.

White, G Edward *Law in American History, Volume 1: From the Colonial Years Through the Civil War* (Oxford University Press, New York, 2012).

Wicks, Elizabeth *The Evolution of a Constitution: Eight Key Moments in British Constitutional History* (Hart Publishing, Oxford, 2006).

Wilberg, Hanna "Facing Up to the Original Breach" [2007] NZ Law Review 527.

Williams, David V *A Simple Nullity? The Wi Parata case in New Zealand Law and History* (Auckland University Press, Auckland, 2011).

Zines, Leslie *The High Court and the Constitution* (5th ed, Federation Press, Annandale [NSW], 2008).

PhD Theses

Fletcher, Ned "A Praiseworthy Device for Amusing and Pacifying Savages? What the Framers Meant by the English text of the Treaty of Waitangi" (PhD Thesis, University of Auckland, 2014).

Speeches and Lectures

"A speech by the Queen on her 21st Birthday 1947" <www.royal.uk/21st-birthday-speech-21-april-1947>.

Hardie Boys, Rt Hon Sir Michael "Continuity and Change" (Harkness Henry Lecture, 31 July 1997).

Kitteridge, Rebecca "The Cabinet Manual: Evolution with Time" (paper presented at the 8th Annual Public Law Forum, March 2006), available at <www.dpmc.govt.nz/sites/all/files/reports/the-cabinet-manual-evolution-with-time.pdf>.

"The Queen's Diamond Jubilee message" <www.royal.uk/queens-diamond-jubilee-message>.

Prerogative Instruments (in date order)

Letters Patent issued by Queen Victoria on 16 November 1840 entitled "Charter for erecting the Colony of New Zealand, and for creating and establishing a Legislative Council and an Executive Council" published in *The Ordinances of New Zealand passed in the first ten years of the General Legislative Council, AD 1841 to AD 1848*, the Colonial Government, Wellington, 1850, 3. That instrument is reproduced in part in WD McIntyre and WJ Gardner (eds) *Speeches and Documents on New Zealand History* (Oxford University Press, Oxford, 1971) at 54–56.

Royal Instructions to George Ferguson Bowen 14 November 1867, cl 14, reproduced in [1868] I AJHR A4.

Letters Patent Constituting the Office of the Governor and Commander-in-Chief of the Dominion of New Zealand and accompanying Royal Instructions [1908] I AJHR A2.
Letters Patent Constituting the Office of the Governor-General and Commander-in-Chief of the Dominion of New Zealand 1917, as amended by Letters Patent dated 18 December 1918, *New Zealand Gazette*, 24 April 1919, 1213.
Instructions passed under the Royal Sign Manual and Signet to the Governor-General and Commander-in-Chief of the Dominion of New Zealand dated 11 May 1917, *New Zealand Gazette*, 24 April 1919, 1213.
Royal Instructions 1917, *New Zealand Gazette*, 24 April 1919, 1213.
Letters Patent Constituting the Office of the Governor-General of New Zealand 1983, reprinted with amendments as at 22 August 2006 (SR 1983/225).

Official Documents and Reports

"British Nationality Bill: Summary of Main Provisions" (Cmd 7326, 1948).
Cabinet Office *Cabinet Manual 2008* (Department of the Prime Minister and Cabinet, Wellington, New Zealand, April 2008).
Conference on the Operation of Dominion Legislation and Merchant Shipping Legislation 1929 [1930] I AJHR A6.
Constitution Advisory Panel *New Zealand's Constitution: A Report on a Convention* (Ministry of Justice, Wellington, 2013).
Constitutional Reform: First and Second Reports released by the Minister of Justice, the Hon. Geoffrey Palmer (Department of Justice, Wellington, 1986).
Craig, GM (ed) *An Abridgement of Report on the Affairs of British North America by Lord Durham* (McGill-Queen's University Press, Quebec, 2007).
"Death of His Majesty — Public Observance of Mourning" *New Zealand Gazette Extraordinary* No 8 (7 February 1952) 159.
Department of Justice *Constitutional Reform: Reports of an Officials Committee* (Wellington, New Zealand, 1986).
Hammington, J "Royal Prerogative of Mercy: Practices and Procedures in the Ministry of Justice" (Ministry of Justice, 2003).
House of Commons Political and Constitutional Reform Committee "The Impact of Queen's and Prince's Consent on the legislative process: Eleventh Report of Session 2013–2014 (HC 784, 26 March 2014).
Law Commission *Final Report on Emergencies* (NZLC R22, 1991).
—— *Tenure and Estates in Land* (PP20, 1992).
—— *Review of the Civil List Act — the Governor-General* (NZLC R112, 2009).
—— *The Crown in Court: A Review of the Crown Proceedings Act and National Security Information in Proceedings* (NZLC R135, 2015).
McIntyre, WD and WJ Gardner (eds) *Speeches and Documents on New Zealand* (Oxford University Press, Oxford, 1971).
Ministry of Justice "Royal Prerogatives of Mercy Procedures Guide" (October 2007).
Palmer, M., "Legal Analysis of New Zealand Defence Legislation" in DK Hunn *Review of Accountabilities and Structural Arrangements between the Ministry of Defence and the New Zealand Defence Force: Annex F* (30 September 2002) <www.defence.govt.nz/reports-publications/hunn-review/annexes/annex-f.html>.
"Proclamation notifying the Demise of the Crown" *New Zealand Gazette Extraordinary* No 9 (7 February 1952) 161.
"Proclamation of Accession of Her Majesty Queen Elizabeth II" *New Zealand Gazette Extraordinary* No 12 (11 February 1952) 197.
Quentin-Baxter, Alison *Review of the Letters Patent 1917 Constituting the Office of the Governor-General of New Zealand: Report* (Cabinet Office, Wellington, 1980).
"Report of the 1911 Colonial Conference" (Cmd 5745, 1911).
"Report of the Imperial War Conference 1917" (Cmd 8566, 1917).
"Report of the Inter-Imperial Relations Committee of the Imperial Conference of 1926" (Cmd 2768, 1926) (also reproduced at [1927] I AJHR A6).

"Report of the Conference on the Operation of Dominion Legislation and Merchant Shipping legislation 1929" (Cmd 3479, 1929).
"Report of the Imperial Conference 1930" (Cmd 3717, 1930).
"Second Supplement to The London Gazette Extraordinary of Wednesday, 6th February, 1952" (8 February 1952) 39463 *The London Gazette* 837.
"Supplement to the London Gazette Extraordinary of Wednesday, 6th February, 1952" (7 February 1952) 39458 *The London Gazette* 757.
"The London Gazette Extraordinary of Wednesday, 6 February 1952" (6 February 1952) 39457 *The London Gazette* 755.
"The Queen's Coronation Oath" <http://www.royal.uk/coronation-oath-2-june-1953>.
Thorp, Thomas *Miscarriages of Justice* (Legal Research Foundation, Auckland, 2005).
—— "Opinion for the Secretary for Justice Re a Petition for the Exercise of the Royal Prerogative of Mercy by David Cullen Bain" (found at <www.justice.govt.nz>).
Trendle, Neville "The Prerogative of Mercy: A Review of New Zealand Practice" (Ministry of Justice, 2003).
Waitangi Tribunal *Te Roroa Report 1992* (Wai 38, 1992).
—— *The Preliminary Report on the Haane Manahi Victoria Cross Claim* (Wai 893, 2005).
White QC, Douglas and Graham Ansell "Review of the Performance of the Defence Force in Relation to Expected Standards of Behaviour, and in Particular the Leaking and Inappropriate Use of Information by Defence Force Personnel" (20 December 2001) </www.ssc.govt.nz/defence-force-report-dec-02>.

Official Correspondence

AD McIntosh to Sidney Holland, 2 December 1949, AAFD 816/1A 10/1, Archives New Zealand/Te Whare Toku o Aotearoa, Head Office, Wellington.
"Commission of Colonel Thomas Gore Browne CB as Governor of New Zealand" [1856] I AJHR B5.
"Commission of His Excellency Sir G Grey KCB, Together with the Royal Instructions Accompanying the Same" [1862] I AJHR A1.
Despatch No 32 from Sir George Grey to the Rt Hon Earl Grey (30 August 1841).
Despatch from Earl Grey Secretary of State for the Colonies, to RH Wynyard, Officer Administering the Government (8 December 1854).
Despatch from the Duke of Newcastle to Governor Sir George Grey (26 May 1862).
Despatch from the Duke of Newcastle to Governor Sir George Grey (28 February 1863).
Despatch from the Right Hon Duke of Buckingham to Sir George Grey dated 18 June 1867 [1867] I AJHR A1.
"Despatches from the Secretary of State to the Governor of New Zealand" [1878] AJHR A02.
"Despatch from the Secretary of State for the Colonies, Enclosing Copy of Order in Council and Proclamation by His Majesty the King Declaring that the Colony of New Zealand Shall be Called and Known by the Title of the 'Dominion of New Zealand'" [1907] I AJHR A2a.
Despatch number 178 dated 9 August 1923, preserved in the Archives of the Governor-General (reference G.484/3).
"Instructions to Colonel Thomas Gore Browne, CB, Governor of New Zealand" [1856] I AJHR B5.
Letter from Mr T Dorset to Earl Grey (27 August 1849).
Letter from PG Millen, Secretary of the Cabinet, to the Rt Hon Sir Philip Moore, Private Secretary to the Queen (17 November 1982).
Letter from Rt Hon Sir Philip Moore, Private Secretary to the Queen, to Patrick G Millen, Secretary of the Cabinet (2 December 1982).
Letter from Rt Hon Sir Philip Moore, Private Secretary to the Queen, to Patrick G Millen, Secretary of the Cabinet (8 March 1983).
Letter from the Queen's Private Secretary to the Private Secretary to the Prime Minister (4 June 1991).
Letter from Alison Quentin-Baxter to Rebecca Kitteridge (Clerk of the New Zealand Executive Council) (16 April 2012).
Minute of Herman Merivale CO 209/135.

Legislation

United Kingdom legislation with application to New Zealand

Act of Settlement 1700 (UK) 12 and 13 Will III c 12.
Bill of Rights 1689 (UK) 1 Will & Mar Sess 2 c 2.
Colonial Laws Validity Act 1865 (UK) 28 & 29 Vict c 63.
Constitution Act 1852 (UK) 15 & 16 Vict c 72.
His Majesty's Declaration of Abdication Act 1936 (UK) 1 Edw VIII and 1 Geo VI c 3.
New Zealand Constitution (Amendment) Act 1947 (UK) 11 Geo VI c 4.
New Zealand Constitution Act 1846 (UK) 9 & 10 Vict c 103.
Ross Dependency Boundaries and Government Order 1923 No 974 — Order in Council providing for the Government of the Ross Dependency (SR & O and SI Rev 1948, Vol XVI, 865; *Gazette* 1923, Vol II, at 2211).
Statute of Westminster 1931 (UK) 22 Geo 5 c 4.
Western Samoa Order 1920, made by His Majesty with the advice of His Privy Council on 11 March 1920.

New Zealand statutes

Acts and Regulations Publications Act 1989.
Antarctica Act 1960.
British Nationality and New Zealand Citizenship Act 1948.
Canterbury Earthquake Recovery Act 2010.
Citizenship Act 1977.
Colonial Defence Force Act 1862.
Constitution Act 1986.
Cook Islands Constitution Act 1964.
Crimes Act 1961.
Defence Act 1886.
Defence Act 1909.
Defence Act 1990.
Demise of the Crown Act 1908.
Diplomatic Immunities and Privileges Act 1957.
Electoral Act 1979.
Electoral Act 1993.
Foreign Affairs Act 1988.
Governor-General Act 2010.
Imperial Laws Application Act 1988.
Income Tax Act 2007.
Interpretation Act 1999.
Militia Act 1865.
Militia Act 1870.
Niue Constitution Act 1974.
Oaths and Declarations Act 1957.
Official Information Act 1982.
Public Finance Act 1989.
Royal Powers Act 1953.
Royal Succession Act 2013.
Royal Titles Act 1974.
Samoa Act 1921.
Samoa Amendment Act 1947.
Seal of New Zealand Act 1977.
State Sector Act 1988.
The New Zealand Constitution Amendment (Request and Consent) Act 1947.
Tokelau Act 1948.
Treaty of Waitangi Act 1975.
Victims' Rights Act 2002.

Volunteer Act 1881.
Volunteer Force Act 1865.
Waikato Raupatu Claims Settlement Act 1995.
Western Samoa Act 1961.

Subordinate legislation
Cook Islands Constitution Act Commencement Order 1965 SR 1965/128.
Governor-General (Allowance) Order (No 2) 2011 SR 2011/251.
Niue Constitution Act Commencement Order 1974 SR 1974/286.
Royal Succession Act Commencement Order 2015.
The Seal of New Zealand Proclamation SR 1977/29.

Other United Kingdom statutes
British North America Act 1867 (UK) 30 & 31 Vict c 3.
Canada Act 1982 (UK) 30 Eliz II c 11.
Commonwealth of Australia Constitution Act 1900 (UK) 63 & 64 Vict c 12.
Constitution Act 1867 (UK) 30 & 31 Vict c 3.
Diplomatic Privileges Act 1708 (UK) 7 Ann c 12.
Diplomatic Privileges and Immunities Act 1964 (UK).
New South Wales Continuance Act 1840 (UK) 3 & 4 Vict c 62.
Regency Act 1937 (UK) 1 Edw VII & Geo VI c 16.
Regency Act 1943 (UK) 6 & 7 Geo VI c 42.
Regency Act 1953 (UK) 2 Eliz II c 1.
Royal Titles Act 1953 (UK) 1 & 2 Eliz II c 9.
Succession to the Crown Act 2013 (UK).
Union with Scotland (Amendment) Act (UK) 1707 6 Ann c 40.

Other United Kingdom subordinate legislation
Union Islands (No 1) Order 1925.
Union Islands (No 2) Order 1925.

Australian statutes
Constitution Fixed Term Parliaments Amendment Act 1993 (NSW).
Royal Style and Titles Act 1973 (Cth).
Succession to the Crown Act 2015 (Cth).
The Statute of Westminster Adoption Act 1947 (Cth).

Canadian statutes
Succession to the Throne Act Canada 2013 c 20.

Constitutions

Constitution of the Republic of Mauritius.
Constitution of the Republic of South Africa.

International Instruments

Antarctic Treaty 402 UNTS 71.
Articles on Responsibility of States for Internationally Wrongful Acts, UN Doc A/56/10 (2001).
Charter of the United Nations, 24 October 1945, 1 UNTS XVI Joint Centenary Declaration of the Principles of the Relationship between New Zealand and the Cook Islands, Rarotonga, 11 June 2001 Vienna Convention on Diplomatic Relations 500 UNTS 95.

Cases

Adams v Naylor [1946] AC 543 (HL).
Angove's Pty Co Ltd v Bailey [2016] UKSC 47, [2016] 1 WLR 3179.
Aralt Mac Giolla Chainnigh v Attorney-General of Canada [2008] FC 69.
Attorney-General for New South Wales v Trethowen [1932] AC 533 JC.
Baldwin v Pascoe (1889) 7 NZLR 759.
Bradley v Attorney-General [1988] 2 NZLR 454 (HC).
Bradley v The Governor-General and Commander-in-Chief HC Auckland M1864/89, 28 February 1991.
Burt v Governor-General [1992] 3 NZLR 672 (CA).
Chandler v DPP [1964] AC 763 (HL).
Collie v R [1997] 3 NZLR 653 (CA).
Deynzer v Campbell [1950] NZLR 780.
Gregory v Bishop of Waiapu [1975] 1 NZLR 705.
Kassongo Tunda v The Minister of Citizenship and Immigration [2001] FCA 151.
Morrell v Workers Savings and Loan Bank [2007] UKPC 3.
New Zealand Maori Council [2013] NZSC 6, [2013] 3 NZLR 31.
New Zealand Maori Council v Attorney-General [1987] 1 NZLR 641 (CA).
New Zealand Maori Council v Attorney-General [1987] 1 NZLR 641 (HC).
New Zealand Maori Council v Attorney-General [1994] 1 NZLR 513 (PC).
Ngai Tahu Maori Trust Board v Director-General of Conservation [1995] 3 NZLR 553 (CA).
Paul v Attorney-General [2009] NZAR 405 (HC).
R v Bain (2003) 20 CRNZ 637 (CA).
R v Barr [1973] 2 NZLR 95 (CA).
R v Dougherty [1996] 3 NZLR 257 (CA).
R v Ellis [2000] 1 NZLR 513 (CA).
R v Secretary of State for Foreign and Commonwealth Affairs [1982] QB 892.
R v Thomas [1978] 2 NZLR 1 (PC).
R v Zachan CA304/94, 11 August 1995.
Re Royal Commission on Thomas Case [1982] 1 NZLR 252 (CA).
Smith v Attorney General HC Wellington CP 950/89, 11 June 1990.
Taylor v Attorney-General [2016] 3 NZLR 111 (CA).
Taylor v NZ Poultry Board [1984] 1 NZLR 394 (CA).
Te Runanga o Wharekauri Rekohu Inc v Attorney-General [1993] 2 NZLR 301 (CA).
Tesky v Attorney-General 2014 ONCA 612.
Viscount Canterbury v Attorney-General (1843) 41 ER 648.
Westco Lagan Ltd v Attorney-General [2001] 1 NZLR 40 (HC).

INDEX